MW00653775

On God's action per temperament 143 ff

"affectionate curiosity" 223
on diverse approaches   231-232

# I WANT
# TO SEE
# GOD

# I WANT
# TO SEE
# GOD

P. Marie-Eugéne, O.C.D.

## A Practical Synthesis of Carmelite Spirituality

### Volume I

Translated by
Sister M. Verda Clare, C.S.C.

**Christian Classics**™
A Division of
RCL · Resources for Christian Living™
*Allen, Texas*

NIHIL OBSTAT
Rev. Albert Schlitzer, C.S.C., S.T.D.,
University of Notre Dame

IMPRIMATUR
John F. Noll, D.D.,
Bishop of Fort Wayne, Indiana

Send all inquiries to:
CHRISTIAN CLASSICS™
A division of RCL • Resources for Christian Living™
200 East Bethany Drive
Allen, Texas 75002-3804

Toll Free  800–888–3065
Fax  800–688–8356

Printed in the United States of America

ISBN 0–87061–223–9

# A Word on how
# this book came to be

What one can expect to find in this book, *I Want to See God*, and in another that will follow it under the title, *I Am a Daughter of the Church*, will be made clear by a word on the way they came to be.

About fifteen years ago a group, in which were several professors from secondary schools and universities, came to our monastery solitude to ask for the science of Carmelite prayer. Hesitations, objections, even refusal, disclosed our embarrassment in the face of so simple a request. Delicate persuasions became increasingly pressing; there was nothing to do but yield.

A generous offer of hospitality, later rewarded by a divine call to complete dedication, made it possible to organize a course on prayer in the large town nearby. The conferences, seven or eight a year, drew a choice gathering. These were followed by a half-hour of prayer which in turn gave way to private conversations and a general exchange of views.

Contact with the members of the group soon made it evident that it was less a matter of satisfying legitimate intellectual curiosity on a subject of current importance, than of throwing light on a spiritual experience that was becoming conscious of itself and urging souls to enter more profoundly into the life of God. Vigorous and brilliant as some of these minds were, this interior experience aroused in them little concern about the speculative problems of dogma or of spiritual theology that were being discussed in the reviews—a fact that may at first seem surprising—but rather, it created a marked taste for a practical teaching, for the simple but authentic testimony of a doctrine as it was being lived.

These manifest desires for an enlightened interior life led us back to the teaching of the great masters of the reformed Carmel just as they gave it, illumined by a sublime personal experience of God and a marvelous psychological penetration of souls, based on a theological doctrine that conceals its powerful structure within simple and at times symbolic formulas; and the whole, orientated to the spiritual ascent of souls that it guides to the summit of perfection. Clearly, this teaching, simple and absolute, direct and delightful, responded to the needs of these souls and to the exigencies of modern minds, impregnated perhaps with a certain skepticism in the realm of ideas, yet ready to accept a lived testimony and to bow before affirmations when they are guaranteed by a practical effectiveness.

One thing appeared certain: the need and the time were at hand for a presentation in its integrity of the testimony and the doctrine of the masters who were the Reformers of Carmel. The one doing this should take every care to avoid imprisoning it in a system or putting it at the service of a thesis. He should be as unobtrusive as possible in order to let the masters themselves speak, gathering their teachings exclusively, clarifying them by parallel passages, and arranging them in a synthesis which would still be theirs. His special function would be to express them in a form adapted to the needs of our time.

Among those masters a guide had to be chosen. The members of the group declared some preference for Saint John of the Cross. I, to whom the task was delegated, have chosen Saint Teresa. I did this, first because she is the Mother of the reformed Carmel; but especially because she alone, in her last treatise, her masterpiece, the *Interior Castle,* gives the complete progression in the ascent of a soul. I thought that her descriptive style, her concrete language, would place us in the living and practical atmosphere in which we wanted to stay; the division of the soul's journey into stages or mansions, besides providing a plan for the work, would create the setting and the perspective in which each thing would find its place and its value. It would be easy to insert the helpful teaching that Saint John of the Cross imparts to the soul in places of special danger, and to let the light that his principles project towards the

Infinite, shine over it all. Moreover, the division into mansions would allow us better to appreciate the astonishing rapidity of the spiritual ascent of Saint Therese of the Child Jesus and the sublime simplicity of her little way.

These conferences, having been offered to widely different groups before being written in their present form, gave me occasion to note that the thirst for God is not the exclusive right of a cultured few; that God is very happily arousing it in many souls today; and that to have received this gift is enough to enable one to grasp the language of the masters who have traced out for us the steep slopes that lead to the Source of living waters.

Before handing over these pages to a larger public, may I thank those who obliged me to write them, and so effectively helped in the task. To analyze for them the teaching of the Saints of Carmel was for me an invaluable grace. To do it in their company added to that benefit a deep supernatural joy, that of breathing in abundantly the delightful perfume that rises from fields made fruitful by the blessing of God.

P. Marie-Eugène de l'E.-J., O.C.D.

1894-1967
(Henri Grialou)
1920 Recovered writings
of St. John of the Cross

St Teresa of Avila    1515-1582
St John of the Cross  1542-1591
St Therese Lisieux    1873-1897

# Translator's Note

Anyone who reads this book will know why I think that the privilege of translating it was a distinct spiritual favor. In addition to the personal joy found in it, I am happy to make accessible to others the teachings here given on the interior life of prayer, so carefully explained by one who has lived and directed many along this way marked out by the masters of Carmel. *I Want to See God* should find numerous souls ready for its message, as does its French original, *Je veux voir Dieu.*

For the right to make this translation into English, I must thank the R. P. Marie-Eugène de l'E.-J., first Definitor in the General Council of Discalced Carmelites, Rome. For permission and encouragement to do so, I am more grateful than I could well express to Mother M. Rose Elizabeth, C.S.C., Superior General of our Congregation, and to Mother Kathryn Marie, C.S.C., Mother Provincial of the Midwest. The work of it has been lightened by the continued interest in its completion always shown by our religious superior at Saint Mary's College, Sister Mary Agnes, C.S.C., and our president of the College, Sister M. Madeleva, C.S.C.

As chapters of the translation were finished, I sent them to Father Marie-Eugène. Father had another member of the General Council of Discalced Carmelites, Father Michael, Definitor for the English members of the Order, read them. Father Michael was most painstaking and generous with his suggestions, by which I profited greatly in the revising process. There are some sentences that I rewrote entirely, in accord with Father Michael's better light on them. Both translation and translator have benefited by his good critical sense.

In presenting a synthesis of Teresian spirituality, Father Marie-Eugène has drawn frequently on the writings of the saints themselves who were masters of it. It seemed best, then, to use already accepted translations of those writings. I am indebted to several publishers for their kind permission to quote from them:

To Sheed and Ward, for the *Complete Works of Saint Teresa,* 3 Vols., translated and edited by Allison Peers, from the critical edition of P. Silverio de Santa Teresa, C.D.; also for the *Collected Letters of Saint Thérèse of Lisieux,* translated by F. J. Sheed. To Burns and Oates, for the *Works of St. John of the Cross,* 3 Vols., translated and edited by Allison Peers from the critical edition of P. Silverio de Santa Teresa, C.D.; and *Soeur Thérèse of Lisieux,* the *Little Flower of Jesus,* an *Autobiography,* edited by T. N. Taylor. To Newman Press, for the *Letters of Teresa of Avila,* 2 Vols., translated and edited by Allison Peers from the critical edition of P. Silverio de Santa Teresa, C.D. To Herder, for *Christian Perfection and Contemplation,* by the Reverend Reginald Garrigou-Lagrange, O.P., translated by Sister M. Timothea Doyle, O.P. To Benziger Brothers, for the *Summa Theologica* of Saint Thomas Aquinas, 3 Vols., translated by the Fathers of the English Dominican Province. To Saint Anthony's Guild, for the Confraternity edition of the *New Testament.* Quotations from the *Old Testament* are from the Douay-Rheims version.

An expression of gratitude is assuredly due in tribute to the late Allison Peers for his years of devoted labor in making the works of Saint John of the Cross and Saint Teresa available in English, and for his willingness to let me borrow from them.

Several other persons aided in furthering this translation: Reverend Louis Putz, C.S.C., by his sustained interest in its publication, and Reverend Albert Schlitzer, C.S.C., by a complete reading of the manuscript—both of the University of Notre Dame; Sister Alice Eileen and Sister Mary Immaculate, of Saint Mary's College faculty, and Miss Elizabeth Higgins, of Saint Mary's School of Sacred Theology, by their help in preparing the manuscript. Miss Anne Pavlina, a sophomore at the college, typed much of the final copy with nice precision.

If I kept the manuscript longer, I might perfect it more, in such ways as supplying a more pointed reference for passages from several French books which the author mentions without giving full bibliographical data; that of Saint Epiphane and Sainte Angèle de Foligno, for example. But these seemed too minor in relation to the whole either to trouble Father Marie-Eugène to search for page and publisher or to delay publication till I could secure copies myself, if possible.

As to the translation, I have made prayerful effort to convey Father Marie-Eugène's message exactly, while using the liberty he allowed me of rephrasing according to our idiom. To say that it is a message from one who has a rare and rich experience of the spiritual life of souls is wholly unnecessary for anyone who reads it. I am happy to leave it now in the hands of our Blessed Mother, who will see that it goes wherever her divine Son wills.

Sister M. Verda Clare, C.S.C.

Saint Mary's College
Notre Dame, Indiana
Feast of the Purification
February 2, 1953

# Contents

## PERSPECTIVES

# MYSTICAL LIFE AND CONTEMPLATION

# Perspectives

*St. Theresa's magnum opus demonstrates both natural ability and the aid of grace. It's composition — done with ease and without error — so demonstrates.*

# CHAPTER I
# The Book of the Mansions

Before entering into the study of Teresian spirituality, let us acquaint ourselves with the guide that we have chosen: the *Book of the Mansions* or the *Interior Castle* of Saint Teresa of Avila. We might ask:

A. *Under what circumstances was this treatise composed?*

B. *What are its method and its divisions?*

C. *What is its value?*

The answer to these questions will show us at the outset the singular originality of our guide and the confidence it merits.

## A. Historical circumstances

Saint Teresa wrote the *Interior Castle* or *Book of the Mansions* in 1577. The Saint was then sixty-two. According to her, she was "old and worn out, but not in desires." [1] From her work we can judge that she was in full possession of her graces and her genius. Fifteen years earlier, she had founded the first convent of the reformed Carmelites, Saint Joseph's in Avila. And ten years before, following the visit of P. Rubeo, the superior general of the Carmelites, she had begun to extend her Reform among both friars and nuns. In these ten years (1567–77), how much work there had been, and suffering! And what graces!

For four years, Teresa worked with success at her twofold foundations. Then, in 1571, the Father Visitor took her away

---

[1] Cf. Letter to P. Gracián, May 14, 1578: "I am very old and tired now, though I still have good desires." Quotations from the letters are taken from the *Letters of Teresa of Jesus*, translated by Allison Peers from the critical edition of P. Silverio de Santa Teresa, C.D., Westminster, Maryland: Newman Press, 2 vols., 1950. This reference is to Vol. II, p. 567.

from her consoling labors to send her as prioress to the Convent of the Incarnation at Avila, where she had lived for twenty-eight years and from which she had set out to begin her Reform. The religious there wanted none of this prioress who was being imposed upon them; and Teresa, for her part, would gladly have let this cross pass her by. Our Lord required her to submit. She went as assigned, triumphed over stormy opposition, and succeeded in re-establishing regularity while winning all hearts. God rewarded her for her sacrifice by granting her the grace of spiritual marriage.

Freed of her charge in 1574, the Saint continued with her foundations, which went on multiplying during the next two years (1575–76). But in Andalusia, where she had first seen P. Gracián, the first superior of the Carmelite Reform, ("To me, he is perfect," she writes, and surpasses for our needs "all that we could ever have thought of asking from God." [2]) there began the most painful difficulties that her heart as a daughter of Carmel was to know.

The affectionate trust in her that P. Rubeo had always shown had been one of her surest comforts. But now, reports went to the Father General as to the extension of the Reform beyond the limits fixed by him, and the uneasiness that this was creating among the nonreformed. In fact, the disturbed lukewarmness of some, the ardent fervor of others, the zeal of the king and of the nuncio for reform, the conflicts of power between the superiors of the Order and the visitors named by the nuncio at the suggestion of the king, had given rise to a most confused situation. A general chapter of the Order was held at Piacenza, in Italy. The nonreformed Spanish Carmelites presented their grievances against the Teresian Reform. Their quiet complaisance was troubled by this fervor; their lukewarmness hurt to the point of irritation. The chapter declared that the reformed groups must be treated as rebels; that the reformer, Teresa of

[2] Cf. Letter to M. Inés de Jesús, prioress of Medina; from Beas, May 12, 1575; *Letters*, I, 174.

Jesus, must stop her foundations and remain in one convent of her choice. Visitors were named to see that these decisions were carried out.

In Andalusia, Teresa first learned in an indirect way of the sentence denouncing her. Actually, she was protected by the orders of the visitor who had received full powers from the nuncio. She was of a mind to submit, however, to the order which came from the general chapter—very happy to be able to live in quiet, she says, but unable to help feeling hurt at being treated as a very disobedient person.[3] She chose the convent in Toledo for her retirement. When winter was over she would go there; and there she would be in July 1576.

The storm rumbled on. What was to become of the Teresian Reform? True, the Nuncio Ormaneto was protecting it; and so the visitors named by the chapter did not dare to act. But Ormaneto died, June 18, 1577. His successor arrived, already biased against the work of the foundress and disposed to destroy it. The Calced friars could act boldly: in December 1577, they took into custody Saint John of the Cross. In 1577 and 1578, the Carmelite Reform went through hours of agony from which no one could suffer like Teresa. Yet, the tempest gave leisure to the reformer, and God profited by it to put the writer to work.

It was, in fact, at the time that the menace was mounting, that Saint Teresa received the order to write. P. Gracián had previously asked her to finish her spiritual works. The Saint had made objections: Had she not already written several versions of her *Life* (the last one, complete, in 1565) in which she stated and explained the graces that she had received; the *Way of Perfection* (1562 and 1569–70) in which she gave most useful counsels to her daughters; the book of *Exclamations of the Soul to God* (1566–69); and was she not still engaged in writing the treatise on the *Visitation of Convents*

---

[3] Cf. Letter to P. Juan Bautista Rubeo, general of the Order of Carmel, Rome; from Seville, February 1576; *Letters*, I, 220.

(1576), besides some chapters for the *Book of the Foundations?* What more had she to say?

This time the order came from her confessor at Toledo, Dr.
Velasquez.[4] The Saint was too obedient to refuse, but she had
too much simplicity to conceal difficulties. And so, she was later
to say in the Prologue:

> Few tasks which I have been commanded to undertake by obedience
> have been so difficult as this present one of writing about matters re-
> lating to prayer: for one reason, because I do not feel that the Lord
> has given me either the spirituality or the desire for it; for another,
> because for the last three months I have been suffering from such
> noises and weakness in the head that I find it troublesome to write
> even about necessary business. . . .
> I really think I have little to say that I have not already said in other
> books which I have been commanded to write; indeed, I am afraid
> that I shall do little but repeat myself, for I write as mechanically as
> birds taught to speak, which, knowing nothing but what is taught them
> and what they hear, repeat the same things again and again.[5]

That spiritual poverty had in its keeping immense riches;[6]
obedience would bring them to light.

Teresa began to pray, to ask our Lord for an indication as to
what she was to do. The vision of a just soul, with which she
was favored on the Feast of the Holy Trinity, June 2, 1577,
was the divine response which gave her the subject of her
writing.[7] Saint Teresa went to work at once and continued till

[4] Dr. Velasquez, confessor of the Saint at Toledo, was canon of Toledo;
later, he was bishop of Osma.

[5] Prologue, *Interior Castle.* This quotation is taken from the English translation of the *Complete Works of Saint Teresa of Jesus,* made by Allison
Peers from the critical edition of P. Silverio de Santa Teresa, C.D., London:
Sheed and Ward, 3 vols., 1946. Hereafter, the name of the translator, the
number of the volume and of the page, will be given for any quotation from
these volumes. This quotation is from Vol. II, p. 199.

[6] Spiritual poverty seems to be an effect of the domination of a soul by
the Holy Spirit (Cf. *infra,* pp. 351-6: Experience of the gifts).

[7] The Dominican Diego de Yepes deposed at the process of canonization:
"This holy Mother had been desirous of obtaining some insight into the
beauty of a soul in grace. Just at that time she was commanded to write a
treatise on prayer, about which she knew a great deal from experience. On
the eve of the festival of the Most Holy Trinity she was thinking what subject she should choose for this treatise, when God, Who disposes all things
in due form and order, granted this desire of hers, and gave her a sub-

the end of July. An important affair [8] called her then to Avila. There she found new troubles among the Carmelites of the Incarnation who, in spite of her and especially in spite of the opposition of the superiors, wanted to re-elect her as prioress; and for that, they were undergoing a violent persecution.[9] About the middle of October the Saint was free, however, to resume the composition of her work at the fourth chapter of the Fifth Mansions.[10] She finished it November 29, 1577.[11]

The *Interior Castle* was written, then, in the space of six months (June 2–November 29), and in three months of actual work, since it was interrupted. We must remember, too, that

---

ject. He showed her a most beautiful crystal globe, made in the shape of a castle, and containing seven mansions, in the seventh and innermost of which was the King of Glory, in the greatest splendour, illumining and beautifying them all. The nearer one got to the centre, the stronger was the light; outside the palace limits everything was foul, dark and infested with toads, vipers and other venomous creatures.

"While she was wondering at this beauty, which by God's grace can dwell in the human soul, the light suddenly vanished. Although the King of Glory did not leave the mansions, the crystal globe was plunged into darkness, became as black as coal and emitted an insufferable odour, and the venomous creatures outside the palace boundaries were permitted to enter the castle." This report is given in a letter from Fray Diego to Fray Luis de León, quoted in the Introduction to the *Interior Castle*, Peers, II, 187.

[8] She wanted to have Saint Joseph's Convent placed under the jurisdiction of the Order; since its foundation it had been under the bishop of Avila.

[9] On this subject the Saint writes from Avila at the end of October 1577 to M. María de San José, prioress at Seville:

"The provincial of the Calced friars came about two weeks ago, on the order of Tostado, to preside over the elections. He threatened with censures and excommunication any religious who would give me their vote. In spite of that, fifty-five of them, far from being intimidated, acted as if nothing had been said and voted for me. At each vote that was given me, he excommunicated the nun who handed it to him and heaped maledictions upon her; then he crumpled the papers, hit them with his fist, and burned them. And so those religious have been excommunicated for two weeks. He has forbidden them to hear Mass or go to the choir, even when the divine office is not being recited. . . . As for me, I willingly pardon those who voted for me, provided they leave me in peace."

[10] "Almost five months have passed since I began this book, and, as my head is not in a fit state for me to read it through again, it must all be very confused and I may possibly say a few things twice over" (V Mansions, iv; Peers, II, 264).

[11] "The writing of this was finished in the convent of Saint Joseph of Avila, in the year one thousand five hundred and seventy seven, on the vigil of Saint Andrew" (VII Mansions, iv; Peers, II, 351).

the Saint could find time to write only in the morning and at night; calls to the parlor, correspondence, and the work she was obliged to do, occupying as they did the moments that the religious exercises left free during the day.

## B. Composition and division of the work

While I was beseeching Our Lord today that He would speak through me, since I find nothing to say and had no idea how to begin to carry out the obligation laid upon me by obedience, a thought occurred to me which I will now set down, in order to have some foundation on which to build. I began to think of the soul as if it were a castle made of a single diamond or of a very clear crystal, in which there are many rooms, just as in Heaven there are many mansions.[12]

Such is the discreet statement the Saint makes at the beginning of the *Interior Castle*. Better informed by her confidences to Diego de Yepes, we know that she had had a vision of a soul in the state of sanctity.

The just soul appeared to her like a most beautiful globe of crystal or a very clear diamond, all lustrous with brilliant lights radiating out from a great fire, God Himself, which was in the center. The Saint noticed, too, that the globe was more luminous, the nearer to the center. The differences in the intensity of the light formed distinct regions that could easily be marked by a series of circles concentric with the innermost part of the globe. These separate zones, the more resplendent with light in proportion as they were more interior, constituted distinct "mansions," each one of them containing, moreover, many others.[13]

Such is the plan of the vision; we could trace it in a geometric figure. But what would that dead symbol amount to in comparison with the beautifying splendor of light that shone out from it for the Saint, and with all the spiritual riches that she discovered in it? A moment before, she had not known what to say nor how to begin; now she goes immediately to the

[12] I Mansions, i; Peers, II, 201.
[13] VII Mansions, iv; 351.

task. First she will describe the castle "which is nothing else than a paradise where Our Lord, as He says, takes His delight." [14]

In the light of this vision, Teresa penetrates into one mansion after the other; she describes, narrates, advises, as a mistress familiar with the domain. She writes rapidly, with ease, without erasures, not even taking time to read things over.[15] Comparisons, images, precise terms, crowd quickly under her pen to express what she sees and what she wants to make clear. She distinguishes seven mansions; hence her treatise will have seven parts, each of them divided into several chapters.

When the Saint reached the innermost Mansion, however, where the light is more dazzling, she stopped to ask the particular help that she needed.[16] How could she, without a special grace from God, penetrate into the darkness of the mystery, discover there the delicate and sweet operations of the Holy Spirit; and how speak of them with exactitude and precision? God answered her prayer. She relived the states that she was to describe; she was immediately favored with the graces of which she wanted to emphasize the effects. And so her daughters—whom affection sometimes renders indiscreet—saw her as she was writing, her face radiant or in ecstasy.[17]

The holy mother was to dwell longer, then, on those mansions where the extraordinary signs of God's action in souls are more abundant. The Sixth Mansions would include eleven chapters, while two or three or four at the most sufficed for the

---

[14] I Mansions, i; Peers, II, 201.

[15] "God help me in this task which I have embarked upon. I had quite forgotten what I was writing about, for business matters and ill-health forced me to postpone continuing it until a more suitable time, and, as I have a poor memory, it will be very much confused, for I cannot read it through again" (IV Mansion, ii; Peers, II, 236).

[16] IV Mansions, i; Peers, II, 230; V Mansions, i; Peers, II, 247; VII Mansions, i; Peers, II, 329.

[17] "At the time when our holy Mother was writing the book of the *Mansions* at Toledo," deposed M. María del Nacimiento, "I often saw her as she wrote, which was generally after Communion. She was radiant and wrote with great rapidity, and as a rule she was so absorbed in her work that even if we made a noise she would never stop, or so much as say that we were disturbing her" (Introduction, *Interior Castle;* Peers, II, 196).

others. Should we reproach her for this, she would be astonished. Had she not been asked to write what she knew and
what she had experienced? Her treatise contains, it is true, a
most exalted doctrine; but it was precisely her intention to
throw light on those extraordinary exepriences of which few
had hitherto written. She was not ignorant of the fact—and
she has noted it [18]—that such favors are not essential to progress in the spiritual life and are distinct from it. They are met
with on the direct road, the short cut leading straight to the
summits; but one can climb by other, more winding ways.
Hence her spiritual doctrine is independent of extraordinary
graces and could be separated from them.[19] But does it not
seem right to enlighten the souls that God does lead by such
roads, which are often dangerous? Moreover, these favors,
which at first seem frightening, become for one who studies
them without any preoccupation with personal analysis, luminous signs that mark the stages on the way to union; signs that
reveal that marvelous activity of God in His saints; symbols
that help to explain the nature of that hidden action.[20]

The Saint interrupts her narration with many digressions,
vindicating herself with charming grace. While she is describing a mansion, an apt recollection or a comparison comes to
her mind, and a more thorough analysis of it seems to her
necessary. She lets herself follow it. Being neither a theologian
nor a philosopher, she does not see how this new development

[18] V Mansions, iii; Peers, II, 260.

[19] In comparing, in the course of the present study, the doctrine of Saint
Teresa with that of Saint John of the Cross and Saint Therese of the Child
Jesus, we hope to be able to show that no extraordinary grace (under the
form described by Saint Teresa) is indispensable to spiritual progress; and
that, on the other hand, the psychological descriptions very happily state
precisely the teaching of Saint John of the Cross.

[20] We do not mean that extraordinary graces are only signs and symbols—
in fact they bear in themselves a particular efficacy—but that the sensible
phenomenon which characterizes them symbolizes and explains habitually
the interior grace that accompanies them: for example, ecstasy shows the
domination of God over the whole being, the senses included; spiritual
marriage, with the signs and words that accompany it, tells us of constant
and definitive union, etc. . . .

is bound to what preceded and thinks it an *hors d'oeuvre*. She excuses herself, then, but without serious intent. And how could we hold her to account, when we find on more profound scrutiny that the digression is only an apparent one; it gives us in fact the most important point of the doctrine, the most precise psychological trait, the clearest explanation of the problem treated.

Her work finished, Teresa writes to her daughters:

> Although when I began to write what I have set down here it was with great reluctance, as I said at the beginning, I am very glad I did so now that it is finished, and I think my labour has been well spent, though I confess it has cost me very little. And considering how strictly you are cloistered, my sisters, how few opportunities you have of recreation and how insufficient in number are your houses, I think it will be a great consolation for you, in some of your convents, to take your delight in this Interior Castle, for you can enter it and walk about in it at any time without asking leave from your superiors.[21]

The Saint is happy. Obviously she loves to move about in this "castle" of her soul, the palace and domain of her Master; seeing everywhere the handiwork of His merciful love; lingeringly contemplating the rare and most precious of His gifts; thanking Him for it all. Her joy is greater still in being able to introduce us into this mysterious and reserved domain, making us admire its riches, that we may desire them; showing us the ways that give access even to the most secret mansions, that we may follow her in.

## C. Value of the work

The joy of the Saint has another motive: she is pleased with the perfection of her work and lets this be seen. She writes, in fact, to P. Gaspar de Salazar, S.J.[22] that if he could come now, he would find another jewel much more valuable than the other one (the book of her *Life*). She tells him that this jewel (the *Book of the Mansions*) is enriched with enamels more delicate

---

[21] *Interior Castle,* Epilogue; Peers, II, 350.
[22] Cf. Letter to P. Salazar, S.J., Dec. 7, 1577; *Letters,* I, 500.

than the first, and the workmanship is more perfect; for the goldsmith, when he made the other, did not know as much as now. Besides, the gold of this jewel is of more excellent quality, though the precious stones in it are less in evidence.

Literary critics and spiritual writers have all subscribed to this judgment. The *Interior Castle* or the *Book of the Mansions* is *par excellence* the jewel of Saint Teresa; it is her masterpiece. The "workmanship is more perfect," because the born writer that Teresa is has been brought to perfection in the delicate art of analyzing and explaining God's action in the soul. Her spiritual vocabulary has become more rich. Her supple pen obeys her thought better. She can let it run: it will always be faithful, correct, delightful with life and verve. Formerly "the goldsmith did not know as much as now."

Actually, the spiritual knowledge and experience of the Saint had been considerably enriched and deepened since the time of her writing the book of her *Life*.[23] She had met many souls who gave her their confidences and whom she directed in the spiritual way: souls of her daughters in her convents, persons in the world for whom she was an oracle, religious who testified to great trust in her. She had seen them commit themselves to the ways of perfection, walk with courage, follow the path after her in spite of the tempests, or stop here or there before some obstacle, especially in those dark thickets of the fourth Mansions that many reach but few go beyond.

The holy mother knew the pitfalls of the way and the weakness of souls. She had sought the advice of numerous theologians, and the best. The privilege of meeting them and consulting them was, in her opinion, one of the great graces of her life. The science of those masters of the university had calmed many doubts and cast light on many problems. For three years Saint John of the Cross was her confessor at the Convent of

---

[23] The Saint wrote in the First Mansions of the *Interior Castle:* "And although the Lord has thrown some light upon many matters of which I have written, I do not think I have understood some of them, especially the most difficult, as well as I do now" (I Mansions, ii; Peers, II, 207).

the Incarnation, to which he came at her request. They compared their experiences and put their spiritual goods in common. Teresa gave from her grace as mother of souls; John of the Cross used his authority as father and communicated his knowledge as mystical doctor. Their conversations sometimes ended in ecstasy; and it was after a Holy Communion received from the hands of John of the Cross that Teresa was raised to spiritual marriage (November 18, 1572).

This grace marks the complete transformation of the soul in God. As the Saint herself explains it in the Seventh Mansions,[24] she is then enjoying in an habitual mode, by intellectual vision, the presence of the Holy Trinity in the center of her soul. No longer in a transitory and fleeting way, but constantly, her gaze can penetrate the light of the mystery of God and there gather new riches. She is seated at the banquet of Wisdom, who communicates to her the innumerable goods that flow from this source—the light of truth that puts each thing in its place in the perspective of the Infinite and thus determines its value, together with charity that overflows in ardent zeal.

The science of Teresa has thus become more profound and more vast, more elevated and more simple. From the summits that she has reached, she discerns better the rights of God and the duties of the creature, the demands of the absolute and the weakness of man; she can look at the road traversed, measure its stages, appreciate the difficulties and compassionate the suffering of souls who are struggling up the slopes. She can describe with precision, advise with authority, stoop down with love. Through spiritual marriage she has become a mother of souls, sharing with others the fruitfulness of her own soul.

It was at the Convent of the Incarnation, before the founding of Saint Joseph's in Avila, that Saint Teresa had her heart transpierced by the dart of a seraph.[25] It is of relatively small importance for us to know whether the wound was really

---

[24] VII Mansions i; Peers, II, 331.
[25] *Life,* xxix; Peers, I, 192.

physical;[26] but it is certain that the Saint received at that time the primacy of the spirit that God gives to heads of family, as well as other spiritual gifts, wealth and glories and grandeurs, in proportion to the extent of her spiritual posterity.[27] This is what we call her grace of spiritual maternity.

Among other privileges, this charismatic grace ensures its recipient the power to impart the teaching necessary for the development of the spirit that is to be transmitted. We could not doubt that such a grace was particularly active in the composition of the *Interior Castle* and—taking into its service the resources of the talent of Saint Teresa, the lights of her experience, and the riches of her soul—contributed generously to that luminous synthesis which completes the Teresian doctrine.

It might be said, perhaps, that for the production of a human work we are introducing these supernatural elements in an entirely gratuitous and useless way. Certainly it is difficult to distinguish the natural and the supernatural in a work where they are so closely united. From just an objective appraisal of the *Interior Castle,* however, we do not see how, without special supernatural assistance, the author could have written in so short a time, at first stroke, without erasure, a work remarkable for its perfect order and for the finesse of its psychological analyses, as well as for the sureness of its doctrine and the precision of its terms; and this, in very elevated subjects never before treated in so complete a manner. Moreover, the work is remarkable for the spirit that animates its pages and the fruitfulness of its teaching for all centuries and among all peoples.

[26] Cf. P. Gabriel de Sainte Marie Madeleine, "Les blessures d'amour mystique," *Etudes Carmélitaines,* 7:208-42, 1936.

[27] Cf. Saint John of the Cross, the *Living Flame of Love,* stanza ii. For quotations from Saint John of the Cross, I am using the English translation made by Allison Peers from the critical edition of P. Silverio de Santa Teresa, C.D., London: Burns Oates, 3 vols., 1943. Hereafter, any quotation from these volumes will be indicated with the name of the translator, the number of the volume and of the page. This reference is found in Vol. III, p. 45.

Beyond a doubt, the genius of Saint Teresa was illumined and elevated by an abundant mystical light when she wrote the *Interior Castle*. It was under the influence of her double grace as spouse of Christ and mother of souls that she gave to Christian literature one of its masterpieces among the treatises on spirituality—the most elevated, the best ordered, and the most complete, in our opinion, that it possesses.

# CHAPTER II

# "I Want to See God"

*—and to see Him we must die.*

Teresa was only a child when she went off towards the country of the Moors, taking her brother Rodrigo, in the hope that there they would have their heads cut off.[1] The two fugitives were overtaken by an uncle who brought them back home. To the anxious parents, asking why they ran away, Teresa, the younger of the two children but the head of the expedition, answered: "I went because I want to see God, and to see Him we must die." Already, this reply of the child foreshadows the life-long quest, the happy torment of her soul.[2] Teresa wants to see God, and to find Him she is willing to set out for the heroic and the unknown.

Since she could find no one who would put her "to death for God's sake," she would seek the vision of Him by other ways. First, she would be a hermit. She used to build "little hermitages," she tells us, "in an orchard which we had at home.

---

[1] *Life*, i; Peers, I, 11. For this episode, cf. also: *Histoire de Sainte Thérèse* by Les Carmélites de Caen d'après Les Bollandistes, Lethielleux, Paris; ch. i.

[2] We can compare this word of Teresa, at the age of seven, with the question that the young Thomas of Aquino never tired of putting to the monks of Monte Cassino: "What is God?"

The souls of these two children tended towards God, but a difference in their desires indicates the difference in their ways nevertheless convergent:

Thomas Aquinas wants to know what God is, and his life will be consumed in study under the lights of faith and of reason; he will be the prince of dogmatic theology.

Teresa wants to "see" God, to possess Him with all her powers of apprehension, even should this be in obscurity, in order to be united with Him; she will be the mistress of the interior ways that lead to the transforming union.

We would make heaps of small stones, but they at once fell down again." [3]

Failures do not discourage her, however; they turn her to surer trails. This time she sets out for the Carmel of the Incarnation, again accompanied in her quest by a brother; now it is Antonio whom she has persuaded to be a Dominican. In the religious life, even while she is as yet a novice, God reveals His presence to Teresa in fleeting graces of union. These meetings serve but to quicken her desires:

Having won such great favors, the soul is so anxious to have complete fruition of their Giver that its life becomes sheer, though delectable torture.[4]

The delightful torment increases. It indicates to the Saint the direction in which she must seek her Master, "the place where He lies hid." She writes:

Remember how Saint Augustine tells us about his seeking God in many places and eventually finding Him within himself. Do you suppose it is of little importance that a soul which is often distracted should come to understand this truth and to find that, in order to speak to its Eternal Father and to take its delight in Him, it has no need to go to Heaven. . . . We need no wings to go in search of Him but have only to find a place where we can be alone and look upon Him present within us.[5]

It is towards the depths of her own soul that Teresa will now turn to see God. The whole of Teresian spirituality is in this movement towards God present in the soul, seeking to be united perfectly with Him.

Let us consider each of its essential elements:

A. The presence of God in the soul. This is its fundamental truth.

B. The progressive interiorization of the soul. This expresses its movement.

C. Profound union with God. This is its end.

[3] *Life, ibid.*
[4] V Mansions, vi; Peers, II, 297.
[5] *Way of Perfection*, xxviii; Peers, II, 114.

## A. God is present in the soul

In her initial vision of the *Interior Castle,* Saint Teresa observed God's presence in the soul and regarded it as of first importance: God is in the center, in the seventh Mansions. He is the great reality of the castle; He is its whole adornment. He is the life of the soul. He is the spring that irrigates it and "without which it would wither and be barren." [6] He is the sun that shines upon it, whose warming rays enable it to produce the fruit of good works. The soul cannot be withdrawn from His influence without losing its splendor, its beauty, and its fruitfulness, for

any good thing we do has its source, not in ourselves but rather in that spring where this tree, which is the soul, is planted, and in that sun which sheds its radiance on our works.[7]

Besides, the soul is made for God. It is nothing else than the "paradise" of God.[8]

The presence of God in the castle is not a symbol, a creation of the imagination. It is a reality. God truly dwells there; of this, Saint Teresa is certain. But this interior certitude in regard to her own mystical experiences never sufficed for her.[9] There was all the more reason, then, why it could not content her now when there was question of the truth of God's indwelling in the soul, a truth which was to be the basis of her whole spiritual teaching. She needs the assurance of the teachings of faith and the conclusions of theology.

Teresa consults at length. Let us hear the account she gives of her search for advice, before giving its results; we shall see the importance she attaches to it:

There was one thing of which at first I was ignorant; I did not know that God was in all things, and, when He seemed to me to be so very present, I thought it impossible. I could not cease believing that He

[6] I Mansions, ii; Peers, II, 206.
[7] *Ibid.;* 207.
[8] *Ibid.,* i; 201.
[9] V Mansions, i; 250.

was there, for it seemed almost certain that I had been conscious of His very presence. Unlearned persons would tell me that He was there only by grace; and so I continued to be greatly distressed. From this doubt I was freed by a very learned man of the Order of the glorious Saint Dominic (Fr. Baron, O.P.): he told me that He was indeed present.[10]

We shall try to rediscover the teaching of the learned Dominican and even to complete it with the aid of more searching studies made in the same Thomist tradition.

God is present in the just soul according to two modes that complete one another and that we call, "active presence of immensity" and "objective presence."

## I. ACTIVE PRESENCE OF IMMENSITY

Pure spirits, not having bodies that localize them in space, are said to be where they are acting. Our guardian angel for example is near us, although he has no body, because he helps us by acting on our senses and our intellectual powers in the manner of spirits. Thus the activity of a spirit extends to different places in a radius proportionate to its power.

God, the infinite Being, has created all things; He must, moreover, by a continual act sustain His creature in order to maintain it in existence. Should God cease for a single instant from that conserving action which is called continued creation, the creature would fall into nothingness. God has created and sustains all things by the power of His Word. "In Him all things are," says the apostle.[11] God is present everywhere, then, by His active power. This presence of power which carries with it the real presence is designated under the generic term of "presence of immensity."

Universal and active in all creation, the presence of immensity produces diverse effects and different degrees of participation in being and in the perfection of God. In the inani-

[10] *Life*, xviii; Peers, I, 110 f.
[11] Col. 1:17.

mate creatures it imprints a simple similitude of God which
is only a vestige: "He passed in haste," Saint John of the Cross
will say in the *Spiritual Canticle*.[12] Man it seals with a true
likeness of God. It is the breath of God that animates the slime
shaped by His hands. Grace, a participation in the divine
nature, is also a work, and the highest, wrought by the presence
of immensity. The different quality of the effects produced,
from the merest vestige of God to the participation in His
nature, does not change the mode of the presence of immensity
which remains the same under its diverse manifestations and
is more or less eloquent of divine power.[13]

God is then present substantially in the soul of the just, to
whom He gives both natural being and the supernatural life
of grace. He sustains us, but not as a mother sustains and
carries her child in her arms; He penetrates us and envelops us.
There is not a molecule of our being where He is not; there
is no movement of our members nor of our faculties that He
has not animated. He is around us and even in those regions
more intimate and more profound than our soul itself. God is
the soul of our soul, the life of our life, the great reality in
which we are, as it were, immersed; He penetrates all that we
have and all that we are by His active presence and His vivifying power: "In Him we live and move and have our being." [14]

Was it not this presence of God by grace, of which the semi-
savants spoke to Saint Teresa, and which did not suffice to explain what she had experienced in her graces of mystical union?
We are tempted to think so. But whatever be the case, it does
not in fact explain our relations with our interior God; we must
have recourse to another mode of presence that we shall call
"objective presence."

[12] Cf. st. v; Peers, II, 48.
[13] The different modes of the presence of God in creatures are not created by the diversity of the gifts of God, but by the diversity of His relations with creatures.
[14] Acts 17:28.

## 2. OBJECTIVE PRESENCE

Grace produced in the soul, as we have seen, by the presence of immensity, is a participation in the divine nature, which draws it into the cycle of the life of the Trinity as a child of God. This grace establishes, then, between the soul and God new relations, distinct from the presence of immensity itself.

By His immensity God is present in the soul sustaining and enriching it, but leaves it to itself with its gifts.* He establishes between the soul and Himself the relations of Creator to the creature. But grace diffused into the soul by the presence of immensity, gives it power in its turn to act under God's gifts, to return to Him, to know Him directly as He knows Himself, to love Him as He loves Himself, to embrace Him as a father. It establishes between the soul and God reciprocal relations of friendship, and filial bonds.

Thus by the presence of immensity God fills the soul but resides there as a stranger. To the soul enriched by grace and bringing it into action, however, God gives Himself as a friend and father. By the presence of immensity God reveals His presence and His nature by His works. To the soul that has become His child by grace, God opens up His intimate life, His life in a Trinity, and has the soul enter to share in it like a true child. To these new relations created by grace there corresponds a new mode of divine presence that we shall call "objective presence"; because in this, God is embraced directly as the object of our knowing and our love.[15]

Far from excluding one another, objective presence and presence of immensity complete each other in the just soul. In this soul God resides as in His temple of election here below, be-

[15] "As the essence of natural things corresponds to our natural intelligence; and to the angelic intellect, its spiritual essence corresponds; so to the intellectuality of grace, a participation in God, there corresponds directly the divine essence, hence Pure Act, hence the divine Being, offering Himself to be grasped intellectually by it, such as He is in Himself" (John of St. Thomas, quoted by P. Gardeil in *Structure de l'âme et l'expérience mystique,* Vol. I, Part II, conclusion).

* which alone would be a sort of Deism

cause "His delights are to be with the children of men." Engendering it to supernatural life by the gift of His grace, He communicates His life to it as a father does to his child, and with His life He gives a share in His secrets and His treasures. And the soul, having become a child of God by participation in the divine Life, can in turn receive its God as a father, and love Him with a filial love.

Concerning the mystery of this substantial indwelling of God in the soul, of the activity of love that He unfolds there, the filial relations between the soul and God, Holy Scripture speaks to us with a precision and charm that allow us to see its intimacy: "Do you not know," writes Saint Paul to the Corinthians, "that you are the temples of God and that the Spirit of God dwells in you? Charity is poured out in our hearts by the Holy Spirit that is given to us."[16] And Saint John keeps for us this word among others, of our Lord's discourse after the Last Supper: "If any one love me, . . . my Father will love him, and we will come to him and will make our abode with him." [17]

---

[16] I Cor. 3:16. The presence of God in the soul and the work of sanctification, although common to the three Persons, are especially attributed by appropriation to the Holy Spirit. The Holy Spirit is, in fact, Love in the bosom of the Trinity; the gift of God made to the soul through love. The works of sanctification that proceed from love belong then especially to Him.

[17] John 14:23. A comparison can be established between the presence of the Holy Trinity in the soul and the Eucharistic Presence in the communicant.

| Eucharistic Presence | Holy Trinity |
| --- | --- |
| Jesus: humanity and divinity united by the hypostatic union in the Person of the Word. | Three divine Persons. |
| Presence localized by the accidents of the bread and wine. | Penetrates the whole being and each part. |
| Disappears with the accidents of the bread and wine. | As permanent as grace. |
| Gives Jesus Christ, unique Mediator, diffusing divine Life by His immolation. | Gives life, movement, being, and grace. |

### 3. LOCALIZATION OF THE OBJECTIVE PRESENCE IN THE CENTER OF THE SOUL

In the opening vision of the *Interior Castle,* the presence of God is localized in the most profound part of the soul, in "the centre, the room or palace occupied by the King." [18] Certainly, there is no doubt that God is in all the parts of the human composite. Is the localization, then, of the presence of God a pure fiction of the imagination, created to justify and illustrate the movement of the soul towards God? There is good reason not to think so, for Saint Teresa has habituated us to a more objective symbolism.

Let us remark first that this localization of the presence of God expresses the spiritual experience of Saint Teresa and of the majority of the mystics who have had experimental knowledge of God's loftiest action in the soul—and consequently of His presence in the innermost parts of the soul, parts that seem more interior than the soul itself, and that it can reach to, only with its finest point. Thus, already in the prayer of quiet, Saint Teresa declares that:

this water begins to overflow all the Mansions and faculties, until it reaches the body. It is for that reason that I said it has its source in God. . . . I do not think that this happiness has its source in the heart at all. It arises in a much more interior part, like something of which the springs are very deep; I think this must be the centre of the soul, as I have since realized and as I will explain hereafter.[19]

In the mystical union of the fifth Mansions, according to the Saint, it pleases

---

By bestowing grace, permits better to attain to the Holy Trinity; thus, develops the objective presence.

Cannot be obtained without at least the desire to receive the Body of Christ. Does not give grace except by the mediation of Christ.

By uniting ourselves to Jesus Christ, we take our place as son in the Holy Trinity. We are in Christ, and Christ is in God.

[18] I Mansions, ii; Peers, II, 207.
[19] IV Mansions, ii; 237.

His Majesty to put us right into the centre of our soul,[20] [where He] is in such close contact and union with the essence of the soul that the devil will not dare to approach, nor can he even understand this secret thing . . . so secret that God will not even entrust our thoughts with it.[21]

When it [the soul] returns to itself, it cannot possibly doubt that God has been in it and it has been in God.[22]

And the Saint adds this precision:

> Later on you will see how it is His Majesty's will that the soul should have fruition of Him in its very centre, but you will be able to realize that in the last Mansion much better than here.[23]

This experience, so clearly mystical, invites an inquiry. We shall thus discover that, far from resting on an illusion, the experience on the contrary admirably illustrates the truth that although God acts in the whole of our being as the author of the natural order, He can infuse His grace only into the most spiritual part of our soul, which is alone capable of receiving this participation of the divine nature.[24] It is in the essence of the soul, to which grace is added as an entitative quality, and in the roots of the faculties in which are engrafted the theological virtues, that God communicates Himself directly to the soul, and that contact is made with Him. It is, then, in these profound regions, at the center of the castle, that the soul will properly experience the active presence of God the sanctifier; it is towards these regions that it will go to find Him and to be united perfectly with Him.

We may conclude that although God is truly present in all of our being, which He sustains as the soul of our soul and the life of our life, nevertheless His presence as host and

---

[20] V Mansions, i; Peers, II, 252.

[21] Ibid.; 249.

[22] Ibid.; 251.

[23] Ibid.; 252.

[24] Grace and the infused virtues which permit us to accomplish the operations of knowledge and love of the life of the Trinity, are engrafted in the soul and the faculties whose activity they use. The soul and the faculties can receive efficaciously this divine engrafting only if they already possess the natural power of knowing and of loving.

x relating to material existence

friend is very happily localized in the depths of the soul; for
it is in the most profoundly spiritual part of the soul that He
diffuses directly His divine life, and through it He exercises
all His spiritual activity in a man's whole being.

## B. The spiritual life is a progressive interiorization

Once God is discovered to be in the depth of the soul, all its
desire will be directed to Him there. In order to see Him and
to find Him, the soul must be orientated and move towards its
own depths. The spiritual life will be *par excellence* an interior life; the movement towards God will be a progressive interiorization leading to the meeting with Him, the embrace
and union in darkness, while awaiting the vision of heaven.
Each stage in the interiorization will be a "mansion" that will
mark, in fact, a progress in union. Such is the conception of
the spiritual life that accords with the vision of the castle. Let
us lay aside the image, and consider the underlying reality and
the lessons to be drawn from it.

God, who dwells in the innermost mansion, is Love. Love is
ever tending to give itself. It could not cease from communicating its goodness without ceasing to be itself; *bonum diffusivum
sui.* Essentially dynamic and dynamogenic, it carries along in
its train all that belongs to it, and it seeks conquest so that it
may give itself more fully to the conquered. In the seventh
Mansions, God is a sun that constantly sends forth its rays, a
furnace ever glowing, a fountain unceasingly in flow. His love
is always active in the soul in which He dwells. This soul is
the tillage-field of God; "you are God's tillage." [25] God is its
workman, its vine-dresser; "My Father is a vine-dresser." [26]
Artisan of our sanctification, He brings it about by the diffusion
of grace which He gives according to our merits, or simply to
satisfy the need of His mercy: "the charity of God is poured
forth in our hearts by the Holy Spirit who has been given to

[25] I Cor. 3:9.
[26] John 13:1.

us." [27] He wants to rule over us; and grace is His instrument for peaceful conquest and sweet domination.

The grace that is poured out into the soul is of the same nature as God: life, love, good communicative of itself as He is, conquering like Him. There are two differences, however: love, in God, engenders and gives; supernatural charity in the soul is engendered and rises towards its source. The first is paternal, the second is filial.[28] Moreover, the love that is God is eternal and unchangeable. Grace, on the contrary, although already unifying even in its lowest degree such as it is received at baptism, is like a seed in so far as it is capable of various degrees of development until it reaches full flowering in glory. The kingdom of God, our Lord tells us, is like a grain of mustard seed, which is the smallest of seeds and becomes the largest of herbs; [29] or better still, as concerns the grace in our soul: the kingdom of God is like the leaven that a woman put in three measures of flour and it transformed all the dough.[30]

Invading and filial, grace will accomplish its work of transformation and conquest. Engrafted on human nature, with its living organism of infused virtues and gifts of the Holy Spirit, grace espouses perfectly with the forms of the human complex, lays hold on all its powers and all its activities. Invading, it penetrates and dominates progressively the human faculties, freeing them from their egoistic and unruly tendencies. Filial, it brings the faculties thus conquered in its train as it returns to God dwelling within, the Father of light and of mercy, and offers them to Him, henceforth purified and faithful, submissive to His lights and to His action.

[27] Rom. 5:5.
[28] "Now you have not received a spirit of bondage so as to be again in fear, but you have received a spirit of adoption as sons, by virtue of which we cry, 'Abba! Father!' The Spirit himself gives testimony to our spirit that we are sons of God. . . . We ourselves also who have the first-fruits of the Spirit—we ourselves groan within ourselves, waiting for the adoption as sons" (Rom. 8:15, 16, 23).
[29] Matt. 8:31.
[30] Matt. 8:33.

It may be useful to point out here that in the conquering action of grace, God seems at first to leave much to the initiative and activity of the soul. Later He affirms His mastery—sometimes even by revealing His presence—reserves the initiative to Himself, and imposes on the soul an attitude of submission and willing abandonment until, transformed by charity into a true child of God, it obeys only the Spirit of God living in it: *"For whoever are led by the Spirit of God, they are the sons of God."* [31]

Thus the reign of God is established in the soul; the transforming union is effected by the invading of grace which progressively conquers, transforms, and subjects the soul to God within. By freeing itself of the exterior exigencies of the senses and its own egoistic tendencies, by obeying lights and motions that are more and more spiritual and interior, the soul deepens within until it belongs completely to Him who resides in its finest point. Such is the spiritual life and its movement.

The advance of the soul through the diverse mansions as described by Saint Teresa, in order to be united with God in the seventh where He resides, is more than a symbol; it is a very precise one and rich in meaning.

## C. Transforming union: the end of Teresian spirituality

Divine union, the term of the spiritual life, differs according to souls. Its degrees are almost indefinite in number, from that of the infant that dies immediately after baptism on up to the ineffable union of the Blessed Virgin with her God, on the day of her blessed Assumption. Saint Teresa aspires to a very high degree of union, one whose characteristics she accurately describes. We shall study it more completely in due course; but here we must pause to consider the goal of Carmelite spirituality.

Certain mystical favors (an intellectual vision of the Holy Trinity and a vision of Christ giving her a nail, sign of her

[31] Rom. 8:14.

spiritual marriage) brought into relief for Teresa those summits of the spiritual life which consist essentially in a complete
union of the soul with God through a transformation that
makes it like to Him; hence, the name of "transforming union"
or union by the likeness of love. She writes:

> We might say that union is as if the ends of two wax candles were
> joined so that the light they give is one; the wicks and the wax and
> the light are all one; yet afterwards the one candle can be perfectly
> well separated from the other and the candles become two again, or
> the wick may be withdrawn from the wax.[32]
> And in her *Relations* she says: It seems to me that like a sponge all
> penetrated and saturated with water, my soul was filled with the
> divinity, and that it was truly enjoying, in some way, the presence of
> the Three Persons and had possessed them with it.[33]

This union takes place in the substance of the soul, but cannot be seen there in itself. Only the light of glory, the *lumen
gloriae* which will permit us to see God, will also disclose to us
grace, which is of the same nature.[34] But though not visible
in itself, it can be seen in the good dispositions and virtuous
acts that result from it. The will, laid hold of by charity, abdi-
cates its own desires in order to make its own, through love,
the will of God—and that, with sweet perfection and docility.
"I only will what He wills; it is what He does that I love!"
writes Saint Therese of the Child Jesus.[35] "Perfection consists
in doing His will." [36] Saint Teresa says of this:

> So extreme is her longing for the will of God to be done in her that
> whatever His Majesty does she considers it to be for the best: if He wills
> that she should suffer, well and good; if not, she does not worry her-
> self to death as she did before.[37]

[32] VII Mansions, ii; Peers, II, 335.
[33] XI *Relations*, June, 1571.
[34] I John 3:2.
[35] *Autobiography*, Epilogue, 204. Quotations from the *Autobiography* are
taken from the translation of *L'Histoire d'une âme*, edited by T. N. Taylor,
copyright 1912, Burns Oates, London.
[36] Letter to Céline, July 6, 1893. From *Collected Letters of Saint Thérèse
of Lisieux*, translated by F. J. Sheed, copyright 1949, Sheed and Ward, Inc.,
New York; p. 189.
[37] VII Mansions, iii; Peers, II, 339.

And further: Do you know when people really become spiritual? It is when they become the slaves of God and are branded with His sign, which is the sign of the Cross, in token that they have given Him their freedom. Then He can sell them as slaves to the whole world, as He Himself was sold.[38]

The desire of glorifying God completes this submission.

These souls have now an equally strong desire to serve Him, and to sing His praise, and to help some soul if they can. So what they desire now is not merely not to die but to live for a great many years and to suffer the severest trials, if by so doing they can become the means whereby the Lord is praised, even in the smallest thing.[39]

The intelligence is drawn towards the center of the soul by a consuming fire that shines out through a veil of obscurity:

For the soul clearly understands, by certain secret aspirations, that it is endowed with life by God . . . that there is someone in the interior of the soul who . . . gives life to this life, and that there is a sun whence this great light proceeds, which is transmitted to the faculties in the interior part of the soul.[40]

The seemingly constant experience of God's presence within can take various forms. Saint Teresa notes it as a vision of the Holy Trinity, more or less clear at different times.[41] For Saint John of the Cross, the soul is always aware of the Word, its Spouse, reposing within, and "when these awakenings take place, it seems to the soul that the Beloved is now awakening in its bosom, where aforetime He was, as it were, sleeping." [42] As to Saint Therese of the Child Jesus, she has a constant experience of the divine mercy that penetrates and surrounds her.[43]

---

[38] *Ibid.*, iv; Peers, II, 346.
[39] *Ibid.*, iii; Peers, II, 340.
[40] *Ibid.*, ii; Peers, II, 336.
[41] *Ibid.*, i; Peers, II, 332.
[42] *Living Flame*, st. iv.; Peers, III, 214.
[43] *Autobiography*, viii. These experiences which seem to bear on different divine Persons, are in reality the same. Saint John of the Cross, who experiences especially the presence of the Word, the Spouse, when explaining his experience points out the special action of each of the three divine Persons. Likewise, Saint Therese of the Child Jesus, who seems to experience only the purifying action of the Spirit of Love, addresses herself to Jesus her "divine Eagle" when revealing the riches of her filial grace, and asks Him to carry her away into the bosom of the Trinity, into the fire of love.

Like Saint Teresa, then, Saint John of the Cross and Saint Therese of the Child Jesus discover within themselves the Holy Trinity.

From the interior fire there comes a diffuse light which gives to the intelligence a marvelous penetration into the depths of God and of men, and enlightens it so well in its judgments that they seem made under the light of eternity.

The transforming union extends its influence too over the sense powers and even radiates out to the body:

"When Our Lord brings the soul into this Mansion of His . . . it seems, on entering, to be subject to none of the usual movements of the faculties and the imagination, which injure it and take away its peace." [44]

These latter powers of the soul, however, are flighty and remain so; yet the soul is established firmly in its center and cannot be disturbed in its depths by the natural agitation of the faculties.

The body itself is sanctified by the radiation of grace; it is by virtue of this that it is honored in the case of the saints, and that God Himself sometimes glorifies it even here below.

This complete transformation satisfied the desires of Teresa, those ardent desires that are expressed in her "I want to see God" and that betray the thirst of all the powers of her soul to take hold of God in order perfectly to be united with Him.

If a special grace had not made her experience the dynamism of grace in its filial upward movement towards God, reason and faith would have sufficed to make her value such a union, realized at so elevated a degree.

This union, in fact, answers to the dearest desires of God Himself. God-Love needs to give Himself and finds His joy in this, a joy according to the measure of His giving. The infinite beatitude of God has its source in the perfect gift of Himself that He makes in engendering the Word and in spirating the Holy Ghost. In all creation, God can give nothing more perfect than grace, a created participation in His nature. Hence there is no joy for God superior to that which He finds in the diffusion of His grace.

[44] VII Mansions, ii; Peers, II, 337.

What, then, will be God's joy when He finds a soul that leaves Him entirely free, and in which He can pour out His love in the measure of His desire! The confidences made by our Lord to certain saints indicate this joy of God. "There is more joy in heaven over the conversion of a sinner than for the ninety-nine just who persevere," for the conversion of a sinner gives God occasion to pour out a larger measure of grace. And when a soul, called to receive great graces, disappoints the divine expectation, the misfortune is greater than the loss of a multitude of ordinary souls.[45]

It was to bring about this union of man with God that the Word became incarnate. Before His Passion, Christ makes explicit the intentions of His sacrifice. These intentions are the union of the apostles and of all those who will believe their word, with Him; and through Him, with the Father. His priestly prayer defines the measure, the quality, and the extension of this union: *That all may be one, even as thou, Father, in me and I in thee. . . .* Thus the end of the Incarnation and of the Redemption is revealed to us. The blood that is going to flow is the blood of the new alliance between God and the people, those who have been chosen, who will be sanctified and consummated in unity.

This unity, imposed by God on man as his supernatural end, has its value already here below. The effective power of the soul in the supernatural world is according to the measure of its unitive charity. A Saint Teresa, who has arrived at spiritual marriage, normally obtains much more from God by one sigh of the soul than do many imperfect souls by long prayers.

[45] Saint John of the Cross is speaking of those little nothings that stop the delicate unctions of the Holy Spirit, and says: ". . . this harm that has been done should be a matter for greater sorrow and regret than the perturbation and ruin of many souls of a more ordinary nature which have not attained to a state of such supreme fineness and delicacy. It is as though a portrait of supreme and delicate beauty were touched by a coarse hand, and were daubed with coarse, crude colors. This would be a greater and more striking and pitiful shame than if many more ordinary faces were besmeared in this way" (*Living Flame*, st. iii; Peers, III, 182).

III 42 (Kavanaugh 689) speaking of incompetent sp. direction

The happiness of heaven is regulated also by this union. From the ocean of the divinity, says Saint John of the Cross, each one draws out with the vase that he brings to it. It is the degree of unitive charity that determines the capacity of that vase, and hence the power for vision and the measure of beatific joy.

It was towards that vision of God, begun here below in living faith and realized perfectly in Heaven, that the aspirations of Teresa were drawn when she said: "I want to see God." This desire of drawing from the infinite ocean as directly as possible, with all the powers of her being, and thus uniting herself perfectly with it, lifted up her soul, gave to her spirituality its force and its dynamism, its direction and its end. Teresa of Avila calls around her and leads on, souls who are thirsty for God and who accept the condition of giving themselves completely to Him in order to be transformed by His love and do His will. This primacy of God, which is expressed by a constant seeking for perfect union with Him, dominates the Teresian spirituality and constitutes one of its essential qualities.

# CHAPTER III

# Knowledge of Self

> *Self-knowledge with regard to sin is
> the bread which must be eaten with
> food of every kind, however dainty it
> may be . . .*[1]

In the crystal globe that represents the just soul, God is,
for Saint Teresa, the great reality, the lover who from the inmost Mansions attracts irresistibly its mind and heart. Nevertheless, God must not, she thinks, cause the soul that serves
Him as a temple, to be completely forgotten. It is of the highest
importance for the soul to know itself. She asserts:

> Would it not be a sign of great ignorance, my daughters, if a person
> were asked who he was, and could not say, and had no idea who his
> father or his mother was, or from what country he came? Though
> that is great stupidity, our own is incomparably greater if we make no
> attempt to discover what we are, and only know that we are living
> in these bodies.[2]

Here, the realistic good sense of Saint Teresa is speaking. She
must reflect before acting; she wants to know all the facts; she
needs every light there is to guide her on her journey towards
God: "this matter of self-knowledge must never be neglected." [3]

How, in fact, could we prudently organize and lead our interior life without knowing the interior compass within which
it is to unfold? Without this knowledge we would be doomed,
if not to complete failure, at least to great sufferings. Thus the
Saint cries out:

[1] *Life,* xiii; Peers, I, 80.
[2] I Mansions, i; Peers, II, 201-2.
[3] *Life,* xiii; Peers, I, 80.

33

O Lord, do Thou remember how much we have to suffer on this road through lack of knowledge! The worst of it is that, as we do not realize we need to know more when we think about Thee, we cannot ask those who know; indeed we have not even any idea what there is for us to ask them. So we suffer terrible trials because we do not understand ourselves; and we worry over what is not bad at all, but good, and think it very wrong. Hence proceed the afflictions of many people who practise prayer, and their complaints of interior trials—especially if they are unlearned people—so that they become melancholy, and their health declines, and they even abandon prayer altogether.[4]

We could not so effectually advance towards God without knowing the structure of the soul, its possibilities, its deficiencies, the laws that regulate its activities. Again, it is the knowledge of what we are and of what we are worth that will permit us to take before God the attitude of truth that He requires:

I was wondering once why Our Lord so dearly loved this virtue of humility; and all of a sudden without, I believe, my having previously thought of it—the following reason came into my mind: that it is because God is Sovereign Truth and to be humble is to walk in truth, for it is absolutely true to say that we have no good thing in ourselves, but only misery and nothingness; and anyone who fails to understand this is walking in falsehood. He who best understands it is most pleasing to Sovereign Truth because he is walking in truth.[5]

This knowledge of self which makes truth triumph in one's attitudes and actions is indispensable at all times, at the beginning as well as in all the degrees of the spiritual life:

However high a state the soul may have attained, self-knowledge is incumbent upon it, and this it will never be able to neglect even should it so desire.[6]

And so it must be the object of our daily thought:

However sublime your contemplation may be, take care both to begin and to end every period of prayer with self-examination.[7]

The Saint sums up her teaching by this affirmation, clear and striking as a maxim:

[4] IV Mansions, i; Peers, II, 233-4.
[5] VI Mansions, x; 323.
[6] I Mansions, ii; 208.
[7] *Way of Perfection*, xxxix; Peers, II, 171.

And self-knowledge with regard to sin is the bread which must be eaten with food of every kind, however dainty it may be, on this road of prayer: without this bread we could not eat our food at all.[8]

Knowledge of oneself in the light of God will assure to the spiritual life its equilibrium, will make it human at the same time as sublime, practical as well as very elevated.

## A. Object of the knowledge of self

All that we have quoted shows us that Teresa wants to know herself only in order to attain to God more surely. It is almost exclusively in the light of God that she is going to ask for the necessary bread of self-knowledge. God must be at the same time the end and the beginning of the knowledge of self.

This characteristic, of a high practical importance, will be properly stressed in a moment. It was necessary to point it out here in order to show precisely under what particular aspect that twofold knowledge of self, which Saint Teresa demands from her disciple, is going to be developed: a certain *psychological* knowledge of the soul, and a knowledge that we can call *spiritual,* which bears on the value of the soul before God.

### 1. PSYCHOLOGICAL KNOWLEDGE

In an Introduction to the works of Saint Teresa, M. Emery, restorer of Saint Sulpice after the French Revolution, declared that Saint Teresa had advanced the science of psychology more than any philosopher. In her treatises, in fact, descriptions with precise nuances of the interior world of the soul and of the life that goes on there are abundant. The Saint opens up to us her rich nature which vibrates to the impressions of the exterior world, and still more to the potent shocks as well as the delicate unctions of grace. The regions of the soul, which to us are habitually obscure, are all luminous to her. She writes:

It is very important, sisters, that we should not think of the soul as of something dark. It must seem dark to most of us, as we cannot

8 *Life,* xiii; Peers, I, 80.

see it, for we forget that there is not only a light that we can see, but also an interior light, and so we think that within our soul there is some kind of darkness.[9]

Without doubt, this light is that of God Himself who enlightens the depths of the soul and, acting on the different powers, produces in them effects just as the rays of the sun, playing through the branches of a tree, enrich them with variegated tonalities.

Thanks to her fine spiritual sense and her marvelous power of analysis, Saint Teresa penetrates into this interior world, picks up all its vibrations, distinguishes the activity and the reactions of each one of the faculties, dissects in a manner the soul itself to its very depths. From her works, one could draw out a treatise on psychology, interesting and alive as a demonstration lesson. We shall limit ourselves to pointing out those psychological truths that seem the most important for the spiritual life.

1. The first is the distinction of the faculties. We "fail to realize that there is an interior world close at hand," [10] writes the Saint. All is not so simple as the simplicity of our soul _faculties_ would seem to require. This world is complex and moving. Forces are stirred up there in opposite directions. The violence and diversity of these movements under the action of God were for Saint Teresa a cause of anguish. An explanation on the distinction of the faculties, each of which has its own activity, was enlightening for her:

_thought vs understanding_

I have sometimes been terribly oppressed by this turmoil of thoughts and it is only just four years ago that I came to understand by experience that thought (or, to put it more clearly, imagination) is not the same thing as understanding. I asked a learned man about this and he said I was right, which gave me no small satisfaction. For as the understanding is one of the faculties of the soul, I found it very hard to see why it was sometimes so timid; whereas thoughts, as a rule, fly so fast that only God can restrain them.[11]

[9] VII Mansions, i; Peers, II, 330.
[10] IV Mansions, i; 234.
[11] _Ibid.;_ 233.

2. The action of God in her soul permitted Saint Teresa to distinguish in it two regions: an *exterior* region, ordinarily the more disturbed, in which are the imagination which creates ~regions~ and produces images, and the understanding which reasons and discourses (these two faculties are volatile and could not remain for a long time enchained, even by a powerful action of God); a region *more interior* and more peaceful where are the intelligence properly so-called, the will, and the essence of the soul, which are nearer to the sources of grace, more docile also to its control, and remain more easily submissive to it in spite of exterior agitations.

This distinction between the exterior and the interior, between sense and spirit, that we find over again with different terminologies in all the mystical writers,[12] will permit her to give a precise teaching on the interior attitude to be kept in contemplation when the depth of the soul is taken hold of by God, while the understanding and especially the imagination are agitated:

> It exasperated me to see the faculties of the soul, as I thought, occupied with God and recollected in Him, and the thought, on the other hand, confused and excited. . . .
> Just as we cannot stop the movement of the heavens, revolving as they do with such speed, so we cannot restrain our thought. And then we send all the faculties of the soul after it, thinking we are lost, and have misused the time that we are spending in the presence of God. Yet the soul may perhaps be wholly united with Him in the Mansions very near His presence, while thought remains in the outskirts of the castle, suffering the assaults of a thousand wild and venomous creatures. . . .
> As I write this, the noises in my head are so loud that I am beginning to wonder what is going on in it. . . . My head sounds just as if it were full of brimming rivers, and then as if all the water in those rivers came suddenly rushing downward; and a host of little birds seem to be whistling, not in the ears, but in the upper part of the head, where the higher part of the soul is said to be. . . .

[12] Saint John of the Cross describes a very high experience of this distinction between the higher spiritual part and the lower sensitive part, in the *Dark Night*. Bk. II, xxiv. ~Kavanaugh   p. 455~

All this physical turmoil is no hindrance either to my prayer or to
what I am saying now, but the tranquility and love in my soul are
quite unaffected, and so are its desires and clearness of mind.[13]

From this experience the Saint draws the conclusion that "it
is not good for us to be disturbed by our thoughts or to worry
about them in the slightest." [13]

3. The flight of the spirit brings Saint Teresa to face another psychological problem, less important than the preceding, but more difficult; and the mere statement of it reveals the
penetration of her thought. The problem is this: Is there a distinction between the soul and the spirit, between the essence
of the soul and the intellectual power?

Certain philosophies answer her that they are the same thing.
And yet, in the flight of the spirit she is aware at the same time
that "the soul really seems to have left the body," and that the
soul has not left it since the person "is not dead."[14] How explain this phenomenon? She wishes she had the science to do
so. Lacking this, she will clarify the problem by a comparison:

Anyone who has experience of this, and possesses more ability than
I, will perhaps know how to express it. . . . I have often thought that
if the sun can remain in the heavens and yet its rays are so strong that
without its moving thence they can none the less reach us here, it
must be possible for the soul and the spirit, which are as much the
same thing as are the sun and its rays, to remain where they are, and
yet, through the power of the heat that comes to them from the true
Sun of Justice, for some higher part of them to rise above itself.[15]

## 2. SPIRITUAL KNOWLEDGE

A few psychological notions are necessary for the spiritual
person in order to avoid sufferings and difficulties; it is much
more important, however, to possess that knowledge that we
have called "spiritual" which reveals to the soul what it is before God, the supernatural riches with which it is adorned,
the evil tendencies that hinder its movement towards God.

[13] IV Mansions, i; Peers, II, 233-4.
[14] VI Mansions, v; 295.
[15] Ibid.; 296; Cf. also, Life, xviii; Peers, I, 109.

If psychological knowledge is useful for perfection, spiritual knowledge is a very part of it, for it feeds humility and involves it. And so it is of the latter that Saint Teresa says that it is the bread with which one must eat all the other foods, however delicate they may be.

Divine action, by the diverse effects it produces in the soul, has revealed the organization of the interior world. It is only under the light of God that we can now explore the triple domain of the spiritual knowledge of self.

### a. *What we are before God*

God is the friend of order and of truth, says Saint Teresa. Order and truth require that our relations with God be based on what He is and what we are.

God is the infinite Being, our Creator. We are finite beings, His creatures who depend in everything on Him. Between God and us: the abyss of infinitude that separates the Infinite from the finite, the eternal self-subsistent Being from the creature brought into existence in time. The intimacy to which God calls us does not fill up that abyss. Now and always God will be God; and man, even divinized by grace, will still remain a finite creature.

Reason gives us a glimmering light on the abyss of the Infinite; faith enlightens us more fully. The gifts of the Holy Ghost give a certain experience of it. By looking into that abyss, the soul learns obscurely what it itself is in the perspective of the Infinite. "Do you know, my daughter, who you are and who I am?" our Lord asked Saint Catherine of Siena. "You are she who is not; I am He who is." [16]

Saint Teresa calls royal those souls who, in the flash of illumination or a swift embrace of divine love, have had some glimpse of the abyss of the Infinite divine. She wishes that kings might have such knowledge, in order that they might

[16] *Dialogue* x.

better learn the value of human things and discover their duty in the perspective of the Infinite.

No creature has ever looked into that abyss as did Christ, whose gaze, illumined even here below by intuitive vision, penetrated into it most marvelously; yet His human gaze, it too, lost itself in the infinite immensity of the Divinity which dwelt within Him. This sight plunged Him into depths of adoration never attained by another: "Learn of me for I am meek and humble of heart," He said under the overwhelming sweetness of the unction that penetrated Him. No one could be humble before God as Christ was, nor even as the Virgin Mary, because no one can measure as they did the abyss of the infinite that separates man from his Creator.

But Jesus and Mary were of a perfect purity. We are sinners. We have used our liberty to refuse to obey Him on whom we depend absolutely every instant of our existence. The creature who deserves to be called "nothing" before the infinite Being, braves God by disregarding His rights; and that bravado would appear ridiculous if God had not left him the privilege of disturbing the realization of the designs of Providence. Sin, which is an act of ingratitude, a crime of high treason, is also a disorder in creation.

Sin disappears under the divine pardon. To have sinned remains a fact that shows the perversity of our nature.

This science of the divine transcendence, in which there is revealed the nothingness of the creature and the true face of sin, is the science *par excellence* of the contemplative. What has he contemplated, if he does not know God? And if he does not know his own nothingness, then he has not found God. For he who has truly touched God, has experienced in his being the extreme littleness and the profound misery of our human nature.

Thus the double knowledge of the all of God and the nothingness of man is fundamental for the spiritual life, develops

with it, and, according to Saint Angela of Foligno, in its eminent degree constitutes perfection.[17] It creates in the soul a
profound humility that nothing can disturb; it places the soul
in an attitude of truth which attracts all the gifts of God.

In reading the writings of Saint Teresa, one has the impression that she was constantly looking into this double abyss of
the all and the nothing. Through multiple contacts with God,
she knew Him experimentally until, having arrived at spiritual
marriage, she beheld Him in almost constant intellectual vision.
It is in this twofold light too that she acquires that profound
respect for God, the touching fear of a humble subject for His
Majesty, and that horror of sin, which are so happily allied to
the ardors and flights of her daring love as daughter and
spouse. This science of the Infinite, expressed sometimes in
powerful terms, inspires all her attitudes, reveals itself in her
judgments and her counsels, and causes the sweet perfume of
simple and profound humility, free and delightful, which is one
of her most captivating charms, to rise constantly from her soul.

### b. *Supernatural riches*

Self-knowledge must not reveal to us only one aspect of the
truth, even one so fundamental as that of the nothingness of
the creature before the infinitude of God. It must assure in us
the triumph of all truth, even if it bring to light disconcerting
contrasts. These contrasts do, in fact, exist in man.

A creature, so insignificant before God and so often in revolt,
the soul is nevertheless made to the image of God and capable
of carrying on the divine operations of knowledge and of love;
and it is called to be perfect as its heavenly Father is perfect.
Saint Teresa demands that these truths, which constitute the
grandeur of the soul, be not diminished in any way. She says:

---

[17] "To know oneself! to know God! that is the perfection of man. . . .
Here, all immensity, all perfection and the absolute good; there: nothing;
to know that, is the end of man. . . . To be eternally bent over the double
abyss, that is my secret!" (*Sainte Angèle de Foligno*. French translation by
Hello, ch. lviii).

1248-1309 Franciscan Tertiary
"Mistress of Theologians"

In speaking of the soul, we must always think of it as spacious, ample and lofty; and this can be done without the least exaggeration, for the soul's capacity is much greater than we can realize.[18]

And so in order to give an "idea of the good qualities" [19] of the sublime dignity and beauty of the soul which is "the palace occupied by the King," [20] the Saint does not hesitate to use the most brilliant comparison. The soul is "a castle made of a single diamond or of a very clear crystal." [21] God makes of it a crystal, dazzling with light, a "castle, so beautiful and resplendent, this Orient pearl, this tree of life planted in the living waters of life—namely, in God." [22] As for me, she adds, "I can find nothing with which to compare the great beauty of a soul and its great capacity." [23]

The Christian ought to know his dignity. He ought not be ignorant, either, of the value of the many special graces he has received.

Saint Teresa never minimizes spiritual favors, nor progress that is made, even when they still leave room for numerous faults as in the third Mansions. Speaking of the soul that enjoys the prayer of quiet, she says, "It is very important that the soul which arrives thus far should recognize the great dignity of its state and the greatness of the favours which the Lord has granted it." [24] She does not leave it in ignorance of the sublime hopes contained in the graces received:

If God gives a soul such pledges, it is a sign that He has great things in store for it. It will be its own fault if it does not make great progress.[25]

A soul to which such favors have been given must hold itself in high esteem. True humility triumphs in the truth; so

[18] I Mansions, ii; Peers, II, 208.
[19] Ibid, i; 202.
[20] Ibid., ii; 207.
[21] Ibid., i; 201.
[22] Ibid., ii; 205.
[23] Ibid., i; 201.
[24] Life, xv; Peers, I, 89.
[25] Way of Perfection, xxxi; Peers, II, 133.

much the worse for "the timid, half-learned men," writes the Saint, "whose shortcomings have cost me very dear." [26] Truth frees us from danger, and from wondering "if the devil was transfigured into an angel of light." [27] It moves us to gratitude towards God and urges us to be faithful to graces received.

### c. Evil tendencies

Along with the supernatural riches in the interior castle illumined by the presence of God, Saint Teresa discovers "so many bad things—snakes, vipers, and venomous creatures," [28] "so venomous and so active and it is so dangerous for us to be among them that it will be a miracle if we escape stumbling over them and falling." [29] The reptiles represent the forces of evil settled in the soul, the bad tendencies consequent upon original sin. These are formidable powers that we cannot disregard; and so they constitute one of the most important objects of the knowledge of self.

Created in the state of justice and holiness, our first parents had received not only the supernatural gifts of grace, but also preternatural gifts (mastery over their passions, preservation from sickness and death) which ensured the rectitude and harmony of the powers and faculties of human nature. Deprived of these gifts by original sin, human nature remained intact but was wounded by this privation. Thenceforth, the dual, divergent forces of body and spirit war, one against the other. While awaiting the death that is going to separate them, each one claims its proper satisfactions. Man discovers in himself concupiscence, the disordinate strivings of the senses; and pride of mind and of the will, or the lusting of these two powers for self-independence. A profound disorder is embedded in human nature.

Adam and Eve transmitted to their posterity human nature

[26] V Mansions, i; Peers, II, 250.
[27] Ibid.; 249.
[28] I Mansions, ii; 210.
[29] II Mansions, i; 214.

such as their sin left it; hence, deprived of the superior gifts
that completed it. This privation, with the disordered tendencies that it lets loose, is called original sin. These tendencies
will take particular shape in each person according to the education received, the environment frequented, the sins committed, and habits contracted. Thus shaped, they will in turn be
strongly rooted in the physical order by the forces and laws of
heredity. In each soul, consequently, among the tendencies that
accompany original sin, there are dominant ones that seem to
win over the energies of the soul to their own profit. Their demands can be extreme. Even when less violent, they are still
such formidable powers that it is impossible for the soul not to be
carried along to numerous falls.[30]

These tendencies exercise a sort of peaceful reign over the
soul in the first Mansions. Combatted in the second, they become irritated and make one suffer. The victory over their external manifestation, obtained in the third Mansions, leaves
them still with strength interiorly. They draw sustenance now
from less apparent sources to reappear once more on the spiritual plane when the divine light falls upon them there.

Saint John of the Cross points out certain effects of these
evil tendencies, especially the privative one of eliminating God
and God's action wherever they prevail:

For it is the same thing if a bird be held by a slender cord or by a
stout one; since, even if it be slender, the bird will be as well held as
though it were stout, for so long as it breaks it not and flies not
away.[31]

Whatever may be the voluntary inordinacy and the smallness
of its object, it will hinder union between the soul and God.
Saint John also tells us in detail how these unruly desires

*unruly desires* (margin)

[30] There are some of these tendencies fixed in us by heredity, that seem
to have several centuries of existence. They seem to resist all assaults, and,
even when mortified in all their external manifestations, they raise up tidal
floods at times that seem to carry away everything.
[31] *Ascent*, Bk. I, xi; Peers, I, 53.

Kavanaugh p. 143

"cause torment, fatigue, weariness, blindness, and weakness in the soul." [32]

The whole of spiritual asceticism is motivated by these inclinations. In order to see the necessity of this asceticism, and guide it efficaciously, the spiritual man must know his evil tendencies, especially his dominant ones.

The knowledge of self will have no domain more complex, more changing, more difficult to explore, more painful and at the same time more useful to know, than these disordered appetites, the "venomous reptiles, so dangerous, and so disturbing" that each man bears in himself, that have made the saints groan and that, ceaselessly recalling to us our misery, urge us to incessant combat.

## B. How to acquire knowledge of self?

The answer to this question should be apparent from what has just been said: It is the action of God in her soul that reveals to Saint Teresa the structure of the interior world; it is the light of God that discovers to her what she is, the value of the supernatural riches and the harmfulness of evil inclinations. The conclusion is clear: it is in the light of God that the soul learns to know itself. This important point of the spiritual doctrine of Saint Teresa deserves to be emphasized.

Are not contemplatives often reproached with being self-centered, of speaking constantly of themselves, of self-complacently displaying their graces, their sentiments, and of seeing the world only through the veil of their own interior lights and visions?

And in fact, is there not a great danger for the contemplative who must seek God in the depths of his soul, of finding frequently only himself or at least of perceiving, in the silent obscurity that surrounds the life of God within, only the emotions of sensibility and the confused agitation of the faculties, amplified by the silence?

[32] *Ibid.;* 58.

These reproaches and these dangers place in singular relief
the counsels of Saint Teresa, who asks the soul not to seek to
know itself by analyzing itself directly, but to search itself
under the light of God. This is, besides, the best way to know
oneself well:

> As I see it, we shall never succeed in knowing ourselves unless we
> seek to know God: let us think of His greatness and then come back
> to our own baseness; by looking at His purity we shall see our foul-
> ness; by meditation upon His humility, we shall see how far we are
> from being humble.
> There are two advantages in this. First, it is clear that anything
> white looks very much whiter against something black, just as the black
> looks blacker against the white. It is the same with the divine per-
> fections; they show forth much higher in contrast to our baseness.
> Secondly, if we turn from self towards God, our understanding and
> our will become nobler and readier to embrace all that is good: if we
> never rise above the slough of our own miseries we do ourselves a
> great disservice.[33]

This advice is addressed to souls who are in the first Mansions and who must make use of considerations and reflections
in order to know themselves. Later, in the higher Mansions,
each time that the divine light reveals the grandeur of God,
it will reveal at the same time the littleness and the misery of
the creature. The knowledge of self thus acquired is more considerable and more profound:

> When the Spirit of God is at work, there is no need to go about
> looking for ways of inducing humility and confusion; for the Lord
> Himself reveals these to us in a very different manner from any
> which we can find by means of our puny reflections, which are noth-
> ing by comparison with a true humility proceeding from the light
> given us in this way by the Lord. This produces a confusion which
> quite overwhelms us . . . the greater are the favors we receive from
> Him, the better we learn it.[34]

The knowledge of self is precious; "it is the bread which
must be eaten with food of every kind," and yet, adds the
Saint, "it must be taken in moderate proportions. When a
soul finds itself exhausted and realizes clearly that it has no

[33] I Mansions, ii; Peers, II, 209.
[34] *Life,* xv; Peers, I, 95.

goodness of its own . . . what need is there for it to waste its time on learning to know itself? It will be wiser to go on to other matters which the Lord sets before it." [35] The Saint has pity on the lot of a person whom her director "kept in bondage for eight years; he would not allow her to aim at anything but self-knowledge." [36]

Hence, no examens uselessly prolonged; no repeated returns on self, which would nourish the natural tendencies of the soul, such as melancholy, and would permit the devil to suggest under color of humility all sorts of paralyzing thoughts, for thus:

> We get a distorted idea of our own nature, and, if we never stop thinking about ourselves, I am not surprised if we experience these fears and others which are still worse. It is for this reason, daughters, that I say we must set our eyes upon Christ our Good, from whom we shall learn true humility. . . . Our understanding, as I have said, will then be ennobled, and self-knowledge will not make us timorous and fearful.[37]

The action of the devil in the knowledge of self is notable enough for the Saint to point it out several times:

> Beware also, daughters, of certain kinds of humility which the devil inculcates in us and which make us very uneasy about the gravity of our past sins. There are many ways in which he is accustomed to depress us. . . .
> Everything such a person does appears to her to be dangerous, and all the service she renders, however good it may be, seems to her fruitless. She loses confidence and sits with her hands in her lap because she thinks she can do nothing well and that what is good in others is wrong in herself.[38]

*[margin note: false humility]*

How distinguish the light of God from the false light of the devil, and the forms of self-knowledge that proceed from

[35] *Ibid.,* xiii; 80.
[36] *Ibid.*
[37] I Mansions, ii; Peers, II, 209.
[38] *Way of Perfection,* xxxix; Peers, II, 169.

it? Saint Teresa will tell us, for in these important but delicate and often subtle questions, precisions are very useful:

> Humility, however deep it be, neither disquiets nor troubles nor disturbs the soul; it is accompanied by peace, joy and tranquility. Although, on realizing how wicked we are, we can see clearly that we deserve to be in hell, and are distressed by our sinfulness, and rightly think that everyone should hate us, yet, if our humility is true, this distress is accompanied by an interior peace and joy of which we should not like to be deprived. Far from disturbing or depressing the soul, it enlarges it and makes it fit to serve God better. The other kind of distress only disturbs and upsets the mind and troubles the soul, so grievous is it. I think the devil is anxious for us to believe that we are humble, and, if he can, to lead us to distrust God.[39]

Here we are far, almost at the opposite pole, from sterile self-absorption with its cortege of vague reveries, of subtle analyses, of sometimes anguishing introspection and vain displays of self, often ridiculous and always proud.

Saint Teresa wants to know herself only to serve God better and to attain to Him who is the friend of order and of truth. Acquired under the light of God, this self-knowledge develops with the knowledge of God. It is united with humility and, whether it explores the structure of the soul, or reveals to man his smallness before the infinitude of divine grandeurs, or his sinful misery, it aspires only to make light reign and to make truth triumph. When self-knowledge arouses in a soul sorrowful contrition at the same time as ardent love, profound adoration and the most elevated aspirations, the feeling of its own powerlessness along with most generous resolutions, one can declare it authentic: it bears the divine mark of its origin, which is peace, spiritual balance, freedom, and fecundity.

[39] *Way of Perfection*, xxxix; Peers, II, 169-70.

*Mental prayer, simply defined*
*Comparison to other teachers of prayer*
*The imperceptability of supernatural converse*
*Four ways of "watering the garden"*

# CHAPTER IV

# Mental Prayer

*The door of entry into this castle*
*is prayer and meditation.*

*Prayer is holding converse*

To know God, to know oneself in the light of God: such is the twofold knowledge that constitutes the foundation of the spiritual life, regulates its movement, indicates its progress, assures its perfection.

By what means is the soul going to bring itself to its own depths, to be united with God who dwells there? In the first pages of the *Interior Castle,* Saint Teresa gives the answer:

Now let us return to our beautiful and delightful castle and see how we can enter it. . . . As far as I can understand, the door of entry into this castle is prayer and meditation.[1]

The quotation suggests at once the essential role of prayer in Teresian spirituality. We shall state precisely this role; then explain the definition and the classifications that Saint Teresa gives of prayer.

## A. Role of prayer in Teresian spirituality

"The door of entry into this Castle    is prayer." Teresa is writing in the first place for her daughters who are living under the Carmelite rule of Saint Albert.* This rule, that codifies the usages of the hermits of Mount Carmel, contains one precept around which all the others gravitate: "Meditate upon the law of the Lord, night and day."

It is simple, clear, and absolute. Such was the life of the

[1] I Mansions, i; Peers, II, 203.

* The shortest of all rules for the consecrated life, composed entirely of Scripture

1206

hermits of Carmel. They had come to the holy mountain to live according to the spirit of the great prophet Elias, whose entire soul was expressed in his battle cry: *"Vivit Dominus in cujus conspectu sto!* The Lord is living in whose sight I stand."  [2]

This battle cry, inscribed in the emblem of Carmel, crystalizes the essential characteristics of the Carmelite ideal. The presence of God is the haven to which the soul must return whenever its several tasks are done. This is what the prophets of the desert did, as also the hermits on Mount Carmel. Saint Teresa claims descent from those solitaries, and wants to revive their form of life in all its ancient fervor.

All of us who wear this sacred habit of Carmel are called to prayer and contemplation—because that was the first principle of our Order and because we are descended from the line of those holy Fathers of ours from Mount Carmel who sought this treasure, this precious pearl of which we speak, in such great solitude and with such contempt for the world.[3]

A spiritual daughter of these hermits, Saint Teresa like them hungers and thirsts for God. She too lays claim to the silence and the solitude of the desert. Not being able to go there, she will create a desert in the midst of the cities by founding the reformed convent of Saint Joseph of Avila. In it, life will be hermitical, thanks to a strict enclosure, grills, veils, a small number of religious, and solitude in one's cell. This is the triumph of her genius as an organizer, which excels in working out a great thought by means of a multitude of details.

In solitary silence, souls can and must revive the primitive ideal of continual prayer. The Saint recalls this fact to them on all occasions. From the time of their entrance into religious life, they are to habituate themselves to live constantly in the company of the good Master who has called them. And they have not come for any other purpose. In order to perfect this habit, more or less time will be necessary according to the facility that grace will give them. Whatever may be the diffi-

[2] III Kings 17:1.
[3] V Mansions, i; Peers, II, 247.

culties, they must work at it until they have succeeded. Without this habitual intimacy with Jesus, the hermitical setting would make no sense and would have lost its soul. It would offer only ennui or, worse still, a refuge for misanthropy and idleness.

When Saint Teresa, having found her apostolic vocation, decides to open other convents on the model of Saint Joseph of Avila, she is guided by the desire to bring together generous souls who want to pray "for those who are defenders of the Church, and for the preachers and learned men who defend her." And she adds:

> Help me to entreat this of the Lord, who has brought you together here for that very purpose. This is your vocation; this must be your business; these must be your desires; these your tears; these your petitions.[4]

The mission of the Teresian Reform is to pray for the Church, to maintain within it a high level of prayer, and to teach other souls the ways of prayer.

For Carmelite souls, then, prayer is not only a means of perfection, an exercise of the spiritual life; it is the essential occupation that must fill the day, that must form the woof of the spiritual life. It is the way of perfection that Saint Teresa is going to mark out and describe by summing up in a treatise the counsels that she gave her daughters. It is, moreover, the way of perfection that she herself followed. Her personal spiritual life was so closely bound up with her prayer that the one followed the vicissitudes of the other, and their history is blended. She advanced as long as she was faithful to prayer, and the periods of least fervor were marked by a relaxation in that exercise. The book of her *Life* gives accurate testimony to this and remains the best illustration of her teaching.

It might be asked if these historical circumstances that explain the Teresian teaching do not make of it the doctrine of a school. The necessity for mental prayer, the role that is at-

---

[4] *Way of Perfection*, i; Peers, II, 3-4.

tributed to it, do these not correspond to a particular form of life, to a Carmelite concept of perfection revolving around mental prayer as others seem to rest on liturgical prayer or works of charity? In answer, there is no doubt that the teaching of Saint Teresa is addressed to all Christians; or rather, to all interior souls. Does the Church not seem to recognize this by proclaiming the Saint, *Mater spiritualium?*

Saint Teresa asserts in fact that mental prayer is as necessary as vocal prayer from which it cannot be separated.

I want you to understand that, if you are to recite the Paternoster well, one thing is needful: you must not leave the side of the Master Who has taught it you.
You will say *at once* that this is meditation, and that you are not capable of it, and do not even wish to practice it, but are content with vocal prayer. . . . You are right to say that what we have described is mental prayer; but I assure you that I cannot distinguish it from vocal prayer faithfully recited with a realization of Who it is that we are addressing. Further, we are under the obligation of trying to pray attentively." [5]

Better still, mental prayer is identified with every vital movement of grace in our soul. This grace is filial; its essential movement is to rise towards God. When the soul no longer can, nor knows how to make this gesture which constitutes prayer properly so-called, it is because grace is dead, or very near to dying. Writes Saint Teresa:

A short time ago I was told by a very learned man that souls without prayer are like people whose bodies or limbs are paralyzed: they possess feet and hands but they cannot control them. In the same way, there are souls so infirm and so accustomed to busying themselves with outside affairs that nothing can be done for them, and it seems as though they are incapable of entering within themselves at all. [6]

With this said, we can enumerate some of the benefits that mental prayer procures for the soul. It fortifies convictions and sustains generous resolutions to work and to suffer. [7] It is a

[5] *Way of Perfection,* xxiv; Peers, II, 103.
[6] I Mansions, i; Peers, II, 203.
[7] Cf. *Foundations,* v; Peers, III, 19.

source of light and fulfills with regard to charity the same role
as the intellect with regard to the will; it precedes it, orientates
it, and enlightens it at each step. When one has become contemplative, prayer transforms the soul from glory to glory, according to the word of the apostle, into the very image of God.[8]
Thus Saint Teresa can conclude:

> If, then, prayer is so good, and so necessary, for those who do not
> serve God, but offend Him, and if no one can possibly discover any
> harm that prayer can do him which would not be much greater if he
> did not practice it, why should those who serve and desire to serve
> God give it up? Really I cannot see any reason. . . .[9]

From these diverse considerations we can note:

1. For Saint Teresa, mental prayer—the door of the castle
and the way of perfection—is less a particular exercise than
the very practice of the spiritual life, being one with it, regulat-
ing and encompassing all the other elements (mortifications,
readings, works of charity). Asceticism will be guided by
mental prayer and will have for its aim, to purify the gaze of
faith and to destroy whatever is an obstacle to more profound
intimacy with God. Study will furnish food for mental prayer
and will search out the best spiritual ways. Works of mercy
will be the fruit of the overflowing of contemplation.

2. The way of prayer is not a way of perfection exclusively
for Carmelites. It opens out luminous and practical, before all
souls who aspire to penetrate into the depths of the divine
intimacy, even if they are giving themselves to works of the
apostolate. Saint Teresa, a master in the spiritual science of
prayer, is not only the mother of the reformed Carmel, but of
all interior souls: *Mater spiritualium.*

We can attribute to mental prayer this preponderant role in
the spiritual life and impose it on all souls desirous of divine
intimacy, only on condition of extending the limits, a little too
narrow, in which certain definitions seem to enclose it. Let

[8] II Cor. 3:17-8.
[9] *Life,* viii; Peers, I, 52.

us leave this care to Saint Teresa, who is going to tell us what she means by "mental prayer."

## B. What is mental prayer?

In the book of her *Life* Saint Teresa says:

Mental prayer, in my view, is nothing but friendly intercourse, and frequent solitary converse, with Him Who we know loves us.[10]

This is a well-known definition, and rightly so, because with a simplicity astonishingly precise she places in relief the constitutive elements of mental prayer. It will suffice for us to explain the terms.

"Mental prayer is only a friendly intercourse with God," says the Saint. It is then a contact with God, an actualization of the supernatural union that grace establishes between God and our souls; or again, an exchange between two loves: that which God has for us, that which we have for Him.

God is Love, He created us out of love. He redeemed us out of love, and has destined us to a very close union with Him. God-Love is present in our soul by a supernatural presence, personal and objective. There His love is in constant activity, a fire forever giving its warmth, a sun never ceasing to diffuse its light, a fountain always springing up into life everlasting.

In order to meet with this Love that is God, we have sanctifying grace, of the same nature as God and consequently love like Him. This grace, which makes us His children, is an aptitude for union, for friendly exchange or intercourse with God, for reciprocal penetration. God-Love, always active, calls to us and awaits our response. But He is immutable: it is our love which must go to Him. The turning of our love towards God, His persistent love for us, the meeting of our love with God-Love, the affectionate exchange that is immediately established: that is what mental prayer is according to Saint Teresa. Thus mental prayer supposes supernatural love, hence sanctifying grace. It requires that love be active. But the activity of super-

[10] *Life,* viii; Peers, I, 50.

natural love suffices; for, as Saint Teresa insists, mental prayer *is only* a friendly intercourse with God.

Nevertheless this love does not operate in the purely supernatural domain alone; it expresses itself in the most varied forms of human activity. Through the mediation of the will, in which it resides, supernatural love takes into its service all the natural powers and all the faculties, and it uses them as it finds them in each one of us. Mental prayer becomes thus an exchange of friendship between the living being such as we are and the living God who dwells in us.

If we consider, then, the natural activities brought into play, this exchange of friendship—already differentiated by the different modes of the divine action in each soul—will find a new and astonishing variety in the diversity of temperaments, the differences of age and development, and even in the multiplicity of the actual dispositions of the souls who are praying.

According to temperaments, the intercourse of friendship will assume an intellectual form, or an affective, or even sensitive one. The child will put its love for Jesus in a kiss, a smile sent to the tabernacle, a caress for the Infant Jesus, an expression of sadness before the crucifix. The youth will sing his love for Christ and will encourage its growth by using expressions and images that strike his imagination and his senses, while waiting until his intellect can provide strong thoughts to form a more spiritual and more nourishing prayer.

Mental prayer will espouse even the changing nature of our dispositions. Sorrow, joy, numerous preoccupations, sickness and fatigue which make all activity impossible, or at least the activity of one faculty or another, will diversify this exchange which must always remain sincere and living in order to fulfil its definition of friendly intercourse.

Under these various forms and throughout all these vicissitudes, the exchange will remain essentially the same. Supple and active, the love that animates it will make use of means and obstacles by turn, of ardor and aridity, of intellect or imagination, external senses or pure faith, in order to assure nourishment for its life and new modes for its expression. According to temperaments, and even at different hours, it will be sad or joyful, moved or insensible, silent or expansive, active or inert. It will take the form of vocal prayer or peaceful recollection, meditation or simple regard, affective prayer or painful dryness. It will experience elevation of spirit or the grip of anguish, sublime enthusiasm in the light or sweet abasement in profound humility. Among the manifold modes and prayers, the best will be the one that will best unite the soul to God and will assure it the best food for its development and its action; for after all:

> Love for God does not consist in shedding tears, in enjoying those consolations and that tenderness which for the most part we desire and in which we find comfort, but in serving Him with righteousness, fortitude of soul and humility.[11]

Independent of any external forms set up in advance, Teresian prayer knows no other law than the free expression of two loves that meet and give themselves to each other. Does this freedom place the Teresian teaching in opposition to that of other great masters of the spiritual life? Some might think so.

The masters of the Ignatian school state in fact that it is by an activity of the imagination and of the senses that the soul must go to meet God, and that vivid impressions give rise to firm resolutions. The masters of Saint Sulpice ask that we make use of considerations in order to arrive at that communion with Christ which is true prayer, and which must have as its fruit the efficacious co-operation of the soul with Him. The first address themselves to the generality of persons of piety; the second are concerned with priests and seminarians. Both want to guide their disciples to friendship with God and determine for them the method of prayer that is best adapted to their moral and spiritual temper. Likewise, modern masters of the spiritual life, adapting themselves to the needs of the spirit of our time,

[11] *Life,* xi; Peers, I, 68.

invite us simply to stop before some attitude of Jesus, or a
word rich in meaning, in order to find a direct and living
contact with Christ.

Of these modes of prayer transformed into methods suited
to various categories of souls, Saint Teresa does not speak in
her definition. Her silence is not one of depreciation, any more
than it is lack of knowledge. Its purpose is to put in relief the
constitutive and essential elements of mental prayer.[12] "Mental
prayer is only a friendly intercourse," she says. Her definition
(which includes the humble recitation of memorized formulas
as well as the ecstasies which penetrate the divine secrets), because it is universal, is for that reason only the more illuminating and practical. It is that of a master of spiritual life, who
is speaking not just for one category of souls but for the universal Church.

This definition finally, so wide and at the same time so exact,
takes care to respect the sovereign liberty of God and that of

*uses and dangers of methods*

[12] Saint Teresa took counsel with the Fathers of the Society of Jesus almost from the time of their installation at Avila (1555). She had Father
Balthazar Alvarez, S.J., as director for six years. She certainly knew, then,
the Exercises of Saint Ignatius and the method of prayer propagated by the
Society. Avid for all that concerned prayer, she very probably also knew the
method of a certain Abbot of Montserrat, which was widely spread in Spain.

Methods can be very useful, especially at the beginning of the spiritual
life, for, adapted to the temperament of each one, they sustain and judici-
ously guide the efforts of souls. They are beneficial only on the condition
that one knows how to abandon the multiple and ordered acts that they
prescribe when one has arrived at the end, namely, intimacy with God.

Sometimes, unfortunately, these methods are badly understood. One considers the work of the faculties that they require, much more than the
friendly intercourse to which they are to lead. One confounds the mode of
prayer with prayer itself. To make a prayer, they think, is to construct an
imaginary framework, to feel, to hear, to see, to have strong impressions, or
again, to formulate considerations or to have before the eyes some truth to
contemplate. They devote all their efforts to work out the mode that has
been imposed or chosen; they deprive themselves of the liberty of soul
necessary for the life of love. The accessory has become the essential to the
point that they forget that prayer is an exchange, and they are no longer
even thinking of God, to whom they ought to speak. The soul is enclosed
in a particular mode of prayer, or rather is making vain efforts to restrain
itself there; and, not succeeding or not finding any grace in such a hard
effort that remains sterile, it gives up discouraged, with the conviction that
it is not made for a life of mental prayer.

the soul in their relations, a care over and over again evinced by Saint Teresa. Such liberty seems to her necessary for the growth of the soul and its perfect submission to the action of God. And so she defends it against all tyranny, should this come from methods that are too rigorous [13] or from direction that would suppress it. If one finds in a soul signs of the action of God, namely, humility and progress in virtue, one must not disturb it in its modes of prayer; it has a right to its liberty, and all have a duty to respect this.

"Intimate exchange of friendship and *frequent solitary converse with God .    ."* the exchange is essentially intimate, for love has need of intimacy.

Contact with God is established in the depths of the soul, in those regions where God dwells and where supernatural love is poured out in us. In the measure that this love is strong and active, the friendly exchanges with Him will be frequent and intimate.

Mental prayer is also a personal prayer. Even in the form of public prayer, or when it is the prayer of a group in unison, it remains a solitary converse with God in each individual soul because of the soul's intimate contact with Him. And this silent personal converse of the soul with its inner Guest is the inspiration, the soul of the combined exterior expression.

"Friendly intercourse *with God Who we know loves us"* concludes the Saint. These so simple words conceal a grave problem: that of the nature of the love that unites us to God and of the laws that regulate it. The first terms of the definition "intimate exchange of friendship with God" call up the thought or memory of the affectionate intimacy that unites us to persons. We dream of a like intimacy with God. Is it possible?

The friendly intercourse with God in prayer and the affec-

---

[13] In the *Way of Perfection* Saint Teresa herself will give a method which is the prayer of recollection. This method is not bound to any precise form of activity of the faculties and only stresses the preoccupation of leading the soul to God through Christ Jesus.

tionate relations with a human friend are both inspired by love, but the two loves are not in the same order. The first is supernatural; the second is natural. We see the friend that we love, we appreciate his good qualities by experience, we feel his affection for us and ours for him. This affection, even very pure, develops on the natural plane and affects our human faculties. On the other hand, I do not see God to whom prayer unites me. He is pure Spirit, infinite Being, beyond the grasp of my human faculties. No one has seen Him. It is His only Son, who is in His bosom, who has spoken to us of Him.

The supernatural love that unites me to God is of the same nature as God; hence, as far removed from any apprehension by my natural powers as is God Himself. The friendly commerce of mental prayer develops between supernatural realities which are outside the domain of the merely human faculties. Faith alone reveals them to us with certitude, but without dispelling the mystery that surrounds them. It is, then, thanks to the certitude of faith, yet through the obscurity that it leaves, that we can have this commerce of friendship with God who, according to Saint Teresa, "we know loves us." That God loves us is certain; that we have contact with Him by faith is a certain truth; but supernatural penetration in God can be effected without leaving us any light, any feeling, any experience whatever of the riches that we have drawn from it.

Nevertheless, the commerce of friendship with God by faith enriches us surely. God is Love, communicating Himself eternally. Just as one cannot plunge his bare hands into water without getting them wet, or into a fire without burning them, likewise one cannot have contact with God by faith without receiving from His infinite riches. The poor sick woman who tried to reach Jesus through the dense crowd, in the streets of Capharnaum, said within herself, "If I can touch but the hem of His garment, I shall be cured." She finally succeeds and, with a touch that thrills her Master, she draws from Him the healing cure.[14] Every contact with God by faith is likewise efficacious. Independently of the particular graces that it might ask and obtain, it takes from God an increase of supernatural life, a deepening of charity. Love seeks in mental prayer a sustenance, a development, and the perfect union that will satisfy all its desires.

Speaking of mental prayer, Saint Therese of the Child Jesus writes:

With me prayer is an uplifting of the heart; a glance towards heaven; a cry of gratitude and love, uttered equally in sorrow and in joy. In a word, it is something noble, supernatural, which expands my soul and unites it to God. Sometimes when I am in such a state of spiritual dryness that not a single good thought occurs to me, I say very slowly the 'Our Father' or the 'Hail Mary,' and these prayers suffice to take me out of myself, and wonderfully refresh me.[15]

One could not better describe this loving converse, at once so simple and profound, so living a thing and so supernatural, which tells of the soul's love for God, and in telling it, enkindles it further.

## C. Degrees of prayer

Mental prayer which, for Saint Teresa, is the essential exercise of the spiritual life, must normally develop with it until it reaches perfection. A classification according to degree of perfection must then be possible and appears to be necessary; yet, how evaluate the perfection of prayer? On what bases establish this classification? Saint Teresa remains faithful to her definition in which she underlined friendly commerce with God as the essential element of mental prayer. It is on this quality of friendship, that is, on the quality of supernatural love and its effects in virtue and in union,[16] that she is going to judge the perfection of prayer itself.

[14] Mark 5:25-34.
[15] *Autobiography*, x, 163.
[16] In the *Interior Castle*, Saint Teresa no longer distinguishes as a special degree of prayer this third water, or sleep of the powers. Probably, although very strongly impressed at first by the effects of this prayer—of sensible in-

In the book of her *Life* she gave a well known classification of the degrees of prayer, illustrated by the gracious comparison of the four ways of watering a garden: *[watering of the Garden]*

It seems to me that the garden can be watered in four ways: by taking the water from a well, which costs us great labour; or by a water-wheel and buckets, when the water is drawn by a windlass (I have sometimes drawn it in this way: it is less laborious than the other and gives more water); or by a stream or a brook, which waters the ground much better, for it saturates it more thoroughly and there is less need to water it often, so that the gardener's labour is much less; or by heavy rain, when the Lord waters it with no labour of ours, a way incomparably better than any of those which have been described.

"And now I come to my point, which is the application of these four methods of watering by which the garden is to be kept fertile, for if it has no water it will be ruined. It has seemed possible to me in this way to explain something about the four degrees of prayer to which the Lord, of His goodness, has occasionally brought my soul.[17]

### The Saint explains her comparison:

. . . Beginners in prayer, we may say, are those who draw up the water out of the well: this, as I have said, is a very laborious proceeding, for it will fatigue them to keep their senses recollected, which is a great labour because they have been accustomed to a life of distraction. . . . Then they have to endeavor to meditate upon the life of Christ and this fatigues their minds. . . . This is what is meant by beginning to draw up water from the well—and God grant there may be water in it.[18] *labor*

By using a device of windlass and buckets the gardener draws more water with less labour and is able to take some rest instead of being continually at work. It is this method, applied to the prayer called the Prayer of Quiet, that I now wish to describe. . . . This state is a recollecting of the faculties within the soul, so that its fruition of that contentment may be of greater delight. But the faculties are not lost, nor do they sleep. The will alone is occupied, in such a way that, without knowing how, it becomes captive. It allows itself to be im- *Quiet*

---

tensity notably greater than prayer of simple quiet—she realized later, in a more precise and complete vision of all the degrees of prayer, that the sleep of the powers was only an overflowing into the senses of the divine taste of quiet; and, being an imperfect union, it would be attached to the prayer of quiet.

[17] *Life*, xi; Peers, I, 65.
[18] *Ibid.;* 66.

prisoned by God, as one who well knows itself to be the captive of Him Whom it loves. . . .[19]

Let us now go on to speak of the third water . . . that is, of running water proceeding from a river or a spring. The Lord is now pleased to help the gardener, so that He may almost be said to be the gardener Himself, for it is He Who does everything. This state is a sleep of the faculties, which are neither wholly lost nor yet can understand how they work.[20]

When the fourth water falls from heaven, the soul feels itself in the midst of the most profound and sweet delights, in an almost complete swoon. This water produces at times complete union, or even a flight of the spirit in which "the Lord gathers up the soul . . . and raises it up till it is right out of itself (I have heard that it is in this way that the clouds or the sun gather up the vapour)." [21]

At the time that Saint Teresa was writing the book of her *Life,* she had not yet come to the spiritual marriage. The classification of the prayers that she gives in the *Interior Castle,* when she is enjoying the plentitude of her grace and her experience, is richer and more precise in nuances, more detailed and more complete.

Since prayer is a friendly intercourse with God—and consequently the fruit of the double activity of the love of God for the soul, and of the supernatural love of the soul for God— Saint Teresa distinguishes two phases in the development of this double activity. In the first phase, God testifies to His love by a general help or ordinary grace given to the soul; it is the soul itself that keeps the initiative and the principal share of activity in prayer. In the second phase, God, intervening in the prayer by a more and more potent special help, progressively asserts His mastery over the soul and reduces it little by little to passivity.

The first phase, which corresponds to the first way of watering the garden by laboriously drawing water from the well,

[19] *Life,* xiv; Peers, I, 83.
[20] *Ibid.,* xvi; 96.
[21] *Ibid.,* xx; 119.

includes the first three Mansions of the *Interior Castle.* The second phase, which corresponds to the three other ways of watering the garden, includes the four other, more interior Mansions. The prayer of quiet (second water) and the sleep of the powers (third water), imperfect contemplative prayers, are in the fourth Mansions. The fourth way of watering the garden, which admits of a whole range of the prayer of union increasingly perfect, is studied with great care and a marvelous wealth of detail in the fifth, sixth, seventh Mansions.

From a consideration of the classification given in the *Life,* one might have thought that progress in prayer was in proportion to the intensity of the sensible effects and the diminution of the effort of the soul. A study of the *Interior Castle* reveals clearly that Saint Teresa considered only the quality of love and the excellence of the effects produced. She declares a form of prayer higher when it produces a greater degree of love, and when that love exercises greater influence over human activity, which it must master and render docile to God who dwells in the soul.[22] Prayer then will be perfect when the soul, transformed by love, has all its energies strong and supple, altogether attuned to the delicate touches of the Spirit of God.

[22] "The prayer that is the best made and the most pleasing to God is always the one that leaves after it the best effects. I am not speaking of great desires, for, although desires are a good thing, they are not always such as our self-love presents them to us. I call 'good effects' those that are made manifest in works, so that the soul lets the desire that it has for the glory of God be known by its attention to work only for Him."

# CHAPTER V
# The Good Jesus

*This method should be the beginning,
the middle and the end of prayer for
all of us.*[1]

Saint Teresa has a way of her own for establishing the friendly converse with the Master, which is mental prayer.

The first things must be examination of conscience, confession of sin and the signing of yourself with the Cross. Then, daughter, as you are alone, you must look for a companion—and who could be a better Companion than the very Master who taught you the prayer that you are about to say? Imagine that this Lord Himself is at your side, and, believe me, you should stay with so good a Friend for as long as you can before you leave Him.[2]

Being recollected and purified in humility, the soul that would find God, must go to Christ Jesus.

Here is a point of Saint Teresa's teaching which because of its importance must be regarded as one of the fundamental notes of her spiritual doctrine. After explaining it, we shall give a theological justification for it so as to stress its value.

## A. Christ Jesus in the Teresian prayer [3]

To begin prayer with Jesus is not sufficient; we must continue it in His company. Saint Teresa writes:

Believe me, you should stay with so good a Friend for as long as you can before you leave Him. If you become accustomed to having

[1] *Life*, xiii; Peers, I, 79.
[2] *Way of Perfection*, xvi; Peers, II, 106.
[3] Saint Teresa had given her doctrine on this point in many places in the book of her *Life* (Ch. xii, xxii) and in the *Way of Perfection* (xxxviii) speaking of prayer. Having arrived at spiritual marriage she sees better its high importance. And so she returns to it in the *Interior Castle* (VI Mansions, vii) with more precision and more assurance.

64

Him at your side, as if He sees that you love Him to be there and are always trying to please Him, you will never be able, as we put it, to send Him away.[4]

In order to keep Him company, one need not seek for great thoughts nor be bound to beautiful formulas. It is enough to speak to Him simply:

If you are happy, look upon your risen Lord. If you are suffering trials, or are sad, look upon Him on His way to the Garden. Love to speak to Him, not using forms of prayer, but words issuing from the compassion of your heart.[5]

Carried away by her love, the Saint converses familiarly in our presence with Jesus and thus, in a delightful and practical way, illustrates her teaching:

Art Thou so needy, my Lord and my God, that Thou wilt accept poor companionship like mine? Do I read in Thy face that Thou hast found comfort, even in me? How can it be possible, Lord, that the angels are leaving Thee alone and that Thy Father is not comforting Thee? If Thou, Lord, art willing to suffer all this for me, what am I suffering for Thee? What have I to complain of? [6]

This method is good not for just a few souls or proper for only certain states of the spiritual life; it is excellent for all, affirms Saint Teresa:

This method of bringing Christ into our lives is helpful at all stages; it is a most certain means of making progress in the earliest stage, of quickly reaching the second degree of prayer, and, in the final stages, of keeping ourselves safe from the dangers into which the devil may lead us.[7]

And she adds:

This method should be the beginning, the middle and the end of prayer for all of us: it is a most excellent and safe road until the Lord leads us to other methods, which are supernatural.[8]

[4] *Way of Perfection*, xxvi; Peers, II, 106.
[5] *Ibid.;* 107-8.
[6] *Ibid.;* 108.
[7] *Life*, xii; Peers, I, 71.
[8] *Ibid.*, xiii; 79.

Saint Teresa does not, then simply counsel this method of prayer; <u>she declares it to be obligatory:</u> everyone must make his prayer with Christ until God raises the soul higher. This affirmation under the pen of Saint Teresa—habitually so liberal, so understanding of the diverse needs of souls, so careful to respect their liberty and the will of God for them—takes on singular force and almost astonishes us. She herself heard protests and objections, as she says:

> This is a thing of which I have written at length elsewhere. . . . I have been contradicted about it and told that I do not understand it.[9]

She is not disturbed by this, but her anxiety to enlighten souls in so important a matter makes her summon up difficulties and objections in order to answer them to the point.

First of all, there are minds that cannot represent to themselves our Lord: how, then, will they be able to place themselves near Him and speak to Him? The Saint finds the answer in her personal experience; she was never able herself to use her imagination for prayer, but this did not hinder her from practising what she teaches. Let us listen to the explanations that state her method:

> I could not use my imagination, as other people do, who can make pictures to themselves and so become recollected. Of Christ as Man I could only think: however much I read about His beauty and however often I looked at pictures of Him, I could never form any picture of Him myself. I was like a person who is blind, or in the dark: he may be talking to someone, and know that he is with him, because he is quite sure he is there—I mean, <u>he understands and believes he is there</u>—but he cannot see him. Thus it was with me when I thought of Our Lord.[10]

Others have a mind that cannot stay fixed and could not produce long reasonings in order to converse with the Master. Addressing herself to these, the Saint writes:

> I am not asking you now to think of Him, or to form numerous conceptions of Him, or to make subtle meditations with your under-

[9] VI Mansions, vii; Peers, II, 304.
[10] *Life,* ix; Peers, I, 55.

standing. I am asking you only to look at Him. For who can prevent you from turning the eyes of your soul (just for a moment, if you can do no more) upon this Lord? [11]

This gaze of faith is always possible. The Saint testifies to it from her own experience, and insists:

Form this habit. I know quite well that you are capable of it—for many years I endured this trial of being unable to concentrate on one subject, and a very sore trial it is.[12]

In short, little matter the way in which one has contact with our Lord; representations of the imagination, meditations of the understanding, simple regard of the intelligence or of faith; all ways are good, and it is always possible to use one or the other. The contact established, one must converse with Him:

If words do not fail you when you talk to people *on earth*, why should they do so when you talk to God. Do not imagine that they will—I shall certainly not believe that they have done so if you once form the habit.[13]

But here now is a graver difficulty. It is presented by "learned and spiritual men who know what they are saying." [14] These are contemplatives who are speaking to other contemplatives who have passed the first stages of the spiritual life. They say: since the contemplative has learned to go beyond corporeal things and to find God directly, who penetrates us and surrounds us, why oblige him to return to the humanity of our Lord, an excellent intermediary for beginners, but one that would only retard those who have already found the way of the spirit. "When we have got over the first stages," they say, "we shall do better to occupy ourselves with matters concerning the Godhead and to flee from corporeal things. . . ." [15]

That the humanity of Christ is to be reckoned among the corporeal things from which one must withdraw, is evident—according to them—from the words of our Lord Himself to

[11] *Way of Perfection,* xxvi; Peers, II, 107.
[12] *Ibid.,* xxvi; 106.
[13] *Ibid.;* 109.
[14] *Life,* xxii; Peers, I, 137.
[15] VI Mansions, vii; Peers, II, 304.

His apostles: "It is expedient for you that I depart"; [16] and
from the experience of the apostles who in fact, after the
Ascension, discovered better the divinity of Christ, which until
then had been veiled from them by His humanity. These specious arguments made a strong impression on Saint Teresa.
She herself had had the experience of being carried beyond all
sensible forms in passive recollection. Desirous of returning
often to those higher regions and living in them, she had
sought out and read with avidity the treatises which, like the
*Third Spiritual Alphabet* of Francisco de Osuna, taught the
art of preparing for such supernatural experiences and using
them. The Saint wanted to put to profit the advice of men who
seemed so learned and so virtuous.

> I would take less pleasure than previously in thinking of Our Lord
> Jesus Christ and would go about in that state of absorption, expect-
> ing to receive spiritual consolation.[17]

But she very soon saw clearly that she "was going wrong," [18]
and this transient error left her with sharp regrets:

> Never once do I recall this opinion that I held without a feeling
> of pain: I believe I was committing an act of high treason.      Is it
> possible, my Lord, that for so much as an hour I could have enter-
> tained the thought that Thou couldst hinder my greatest good? [19]

She would have been glad not to have to contradict such
serious authors; yet, truth has its rights, especially when it
bears on the good of souls. And so, she discusses vigorously
the dangerous assertions of those masters and proves her doctrine; namely, that in all the states of the spiritual life one must
return to the humanity of our Lord and never withdraw from
it as long as grace does not lead us elsewhere. In this she
could invoke the authority of Christ:

[16] John 16:7.
[17] VI Mansions, vii; Peers, II, 309.
[18] *Ibid.*
[19] *Life,* xxii; Peers, I, 137-8.

For the Lord Himself says that He is the Way; the Lord also says that He is light and that no one can come to the Father save by Him; and: he that seeth Me seeth my Father! [20]

These words of our Lord are clear and absolute. There is no state in which they do not retain their value.

As to the contention based on: "It is expedient for you that I depart," Saint Teresa says she cannot allow it as an argument:

I cannot, however, allow that as an argument. He did not say this to His most sacred Mother, because she was firm in faith and knew that He was God and Man; and, although she loved Him more than they, her love was so perfect that His being on earth was actually a help to her. The Apostles could not at that time have been as firm in the faith as they were later and as we have reason to be now.[21]

In other words, the humanity veils the divinity only for those who, like the apostles before the Ascension, are timid in faith. For those, on the contrary, who believe firmly in the divinity, following the example of the Blessed Virgin, the sacred humanity brings a help to that faith.

After this terse and precise refutation, we come to the arguments of the Saint in support of her teaching. They are dictated by experience and sane reasoning. First of all, to place one's faculties in a state of aridity when God has not taken them captive, is to lose one's time. In fact, "to remain in that state of aridity, hoping for fire to come down from Heaven to burn up this sacrifice of itself which it is making to God as did our father Elias," [22] is to await a miracle that the Lord will perform when it pleases Him, and when the soul is fittingly prepared. The hope is sterile; Saint Teresa has tried it:

As it was impossible always to be having consolations, my thoughts would keep passing from one subject to another, until my soul, I think, got like a bird flying round and round in search of a resting-

---

[20] VI Mansions, vii; Peers, 305. For the biblical quotations, cf. John 14:6; 8:12; 14:6; 14:9.
[21] *Ibid.;* 308-9.
[22] *Ibid.;* 306.

place and losing a great deal of time, without advancing in the virtues
or making progress in prayer.[23]

The Saint states that thus she made progress neither in virtue nor in prayer. To what can the sterility of this method be
attributed? Certainly one of the reasons "is that the soul is
somewhat lacking in humility and that what it has, is so completely disguised and hidden as not to be noticed." [24] There is
"a desire on the soul's part to rise before the Lord raises it," [25]
a desire that makes it despise the favor of being allowed "to
stand with Saint John, at the foot of the Cross." [26] This subtle
pride which "seems to be of no importance, does a great deal
of harm to those who wish to make progress in contemplation," [27] for the divine Mercy pours out His gratuitous gifts
as a rule only on the humble. In all pride there is at least a
grain of stupidity, and this sort does not escape the general
law. In fact, the Word became incarnate in order to save us,
but also to put Himself within our reach, to adapt His teaching to the duality of our nature which is made up of body and
spirit. Jesus dwelt among us, embodied in this nature. Yet here
is a soul that wants to seek God only in the spiritual regions
and by means purely spiritual. The realistic good sense of Saint
Teresa protests with energy:

> We are not angels and we have bodies. To want to become angels
> while we are still on earth . . . is ridiculous. As a rule, our thoughts
> must have something to lean upon, though sometimes the soul may go
> out from itself and very often may be so full of God that it will need
> no created thing to assist it in recollection. But this is not very usual:
> when we are busy, or suffering persecutions or trials, when we cannot
> get as much quiet as we should like, and at seasons of aridity, we
> have a very good friend in Christ." [28]

Excepting the soul that has arrived at the seventh Mansions,
who "very rarely, or never, needs to engage in this activity,"

[23] *Ibid.*; 309.
[24] *Life*, xxii; Peers, I, 138.
[25] *Ibid.*; 140.
[26] *Ibid.*; 138.
[27] *Ibid.*; 140.
[28] *Ibid.*

and who "in a wonderful way never ceases to walk with Christ," all must return to the sacred humanity of our Lord. Such is the law:

> We need to cultivate, and think upon, and seek the companionship of those [the Saints] who, though living on earth like ourselves, have accomplished such great deeds for God: the last thing we should do is to withdraw of set purpose from our greatest help and blessing, which is the most sacred Humanity of Our Lord Jeus Christ.[29]

But to return constantly to our Lord, is this not to condemn oneself never to go beyond mental prayer and practically to renounce contemplation? Not at all, for in order to prepare for contemplation, this is the best means, and a continuing one:

> His Majesty wants us to realize our wickedness, which makes us unworthy of their being wrought (miracles), and to do everything we possibly can to come to our own aid. And I believe myself that, however sublime our prayer may be, we shall have to do this until we die.[30]

We can progress in prayer only by using the mediation of Christ. This mediation is more especially necessary after the contemplative graces of the fourth Mansions. If the soul does not then go back to Christ, it will not find liberty of spirit and will make no progress.

> I believe myself that this is the reason why many souls, after succeeding in experiencing the Prayer of Union, do not make further progress and achieve a very great spiritual freedom.[31]

The error they make, we can guess, is to abandon Jesus Christ. The souls that are victims of this error may perhaps be able to remain in these Mansions, but they will certainly not enter into the higher Mansions (VI and VII):

> At any rate, I can assure them that they will not enter these last two mansions: for if they lose their Guide, the good Jesus, they will be unable to find their way; they will do well if they are able to remain securely in the other Mansions.[32]

[29] VI Mansions, vii; Peers, II, 304.
[30] *Ibid.;* 306.
[31] *Life,* xxii; Peers, I, 138.
[32] VI Mansions, vii; Peers, II, 305.

The firm assurance with which this warning is sounded shows the importance of the matter and the reason for the care that Teresa gave to it. Elsewhere, she comes to this charitable conclusion:

> I cannot believe that people can really do this; it must be that they do not understand themselves and thus do harm to themselves and to others.[33]

We might wonder if these reflections, which set forth the most sane and well balanced realism, convince all the contemplatives ("a great many have spoken to me about this" [34])? No, not completely. Some still present objections that the Saint does not want to neglect. They claim, and they are authentically spiritual, that "they can no longer meditate upon the mysteries of the Passion and the life of Christ, as they could before." [35] This inability does exist, Saint Teresa grants,[36] but it is not complete. Such souls cannot make a meditation, that is, "prolonged reasoning with the understanding," [37] yet:

> A man will not be right to say that he cannot dwell upon these mysteries, for he often has them in his mind, especially when they are being celebrated by the Catholic Church. . . . But these mysteries will not be apprehended by the understanding: the soul will understand them in a more perfect way. First, the understanding will picture them to itself, and then they will be impressed upon the memory, so that the mere sight of the Lord on His knees, in the Garden . . . will suffice us, not merely for an hour, but for many days. . . . This, I think, is why the soul cannot reason properly about the Passion. . . . But if it does not already meditate in this way, it will be well advised to attempt to do so; for I know that the most sublime kind of prayer will be no obstacle to it.[38]

If any soul "told me that she experienced consolations continuously (I mean so continuously that she could never medi-

[33] VI Mansions, vii; Peers, II, 305
[34] *Ibid.*
[35] *Ibid.*
[36] *Ibid.;* 307.
[37] *Ibid.*
[38] *Ibid.*

tate in the way I have described)," adds the Saint, "I should consider it suspicious," [39]—and we remember the unhealthy states that she describes in the Fourth Mansions.[40]

The statements of the Saint are, then, very clear: the contemplative who, at certain times, is carried away by grace beyond the humanity of Christ, will be able and will have to return to these mysteries, each time that this is possible—not to meditate upon them, for this might be harmful, but to consider them with a simple regard and be aroused by them. It has seemed advisable to state explicitly this important doctrine which is no longer disputed in our day but remains the object of different practical interpretations.

Some have said that the teachings of Saint John of the Cross differ notably from those of Saint Teresa, the mystical doctor insisting much more on detachment from all created things. But this is to forget that he begins with a soul already entering on contemplative prayer, and he therefore has to express with vigor the necessity of detachment from creatures. The place that he gives to Christ is shown us by the chapter in the *Ascent of Mount Carmel,* entitled: "Wherein is solved a question, namely, why it is not lawful, under the law of grace, to ask anything of God by supernatural means, as it was under the ancient law"; [41] and by accounts of his life, which depict him passing long hours before the tabernacle and before the image of Jesus on the cross. John of the Cross, like Teresa, drank from the living waters of the mysteries of Christ and led his disciples to them.[42]

The doctrine of the two Reformers of Carmel finds a gracious illustration too in Saint Therese of the Child Jesus. Tired of learned treatises and useless efforts, the little Saint of Lisieux looks for a simple key to arrive at perfection, a rapid

[39] *Ibid.;* 308.
[40] Cf. IV Mansions, iii.
[41] *Ascent,* Bk. II, xxii; Peers, I, 172. ✓ A "hinge" chapter
[42] Cf. the excellent article on this subject by the R. P. Elisée, *Etudes Carmélitaines,* April, 1934.

means for climbing the mountain of love. She dreams of a lift, an elevator as in the apartments for the rich. The answer is given her: "Thine Arms, then, O Jesus, are the lift which must raise me up even unto Heaven." [43] She takes her place in this lift, by trust and *abandon*. She meditates first on the Infant Jesus in His crib. Then, on the Holy Face whose sorrowful mystery had been revealed to her. Thereafter, she walks in the light issuing from that veiled countenance. The Holy Face is "the star that enlightens" her steps, her unique devotion. And this elevator lifts her quickly to the summit of the mountain, as she had hoped and longed for.

The marvelous success of Saint Therese of the Child Jesus is a precious confirmation of this point of spiritual doctrine. The dogmatic truth that supports it can alone, however, show all its importance and state it perfectly.

## B. Theological justification

In the earthly paradise, our first parents, endowed as they were with the supernatural gift of grace, talked familiarly with God and attained to Him without an intermediary. Their sin separated them from God and left between divinity and humanity an impassable abyss.

God then put into effect a new plan to replace the one that sin rendered ineffectual. In this new plan, the Incarnate Word is the universal and unique Mediator. God, who had created everything by His Word, decrees that all will be restored by the Word Incarnate. A mediator because of the union in Him of the divine nature with our human nature separated by sin, Jesus Christ is constituted Mediator by the divine mandate that is entrusted to Him. According to the word of Scripture, He has been made "a Priest forever according to the order of Melchisedech." [44]

During the course of His public life, our Lord revealed and

---

[43] *Autobiography,* ix, 136.
[44] Ps. 109; Heb. 7:17.

explained progressively His mediation: "I am the way, the truth, and the life," [45] He says. This language is more clear to us than it was to the Jews, who heard it with surprise.

Jesus, the Son of God, begotten eternally as the Word of the Father and engendered in time as the Word Incarnate, bears within Himself the uncreated Light which is God, and all the light that God wants to manifest to the world; [46] the life that is in the bosom of the Trinity, and the life that God wants to infuse in souls.[47] In Him are all the treasures of wisdom and of grace, and it is from His plenitude that we receive them. By the merits of His Passion, He acquired the right to diffuse them and render us worthy to receive them. By him alone the divine light and grace can descend here below; by Him alone we have access to the throne of the Father of light and mercy. Universal and unique Mediator, bringing about our redemption, our sanctification, He can say: I am the way. . . . I am the door of the celestial sheepfold; he who does not go in by the door is a thief.[48]

In order that the outpouring of the divine life might be more abundant, Christ wanted our contact with His humanity, which is the physical instrument for this, to be as intimate as possible. He placed Himself under the appearances of bread and wine, and thus gives us for food His living and immolated humanity. By it all the floods of the divine life penetrate into our soul and are poured out into it according to the measure of our capacity: "I am the bread of life. . . . He who eats my flesh and drinks my blood has life everlasting. Unless you eat the flesh of the Son of man and drink His blood you shall not have life in you." [49] The words are clear: one can have life only by communion with Jesus Christ. The other sacraments themselves have efficacy only by their relation to the Holy

[45] John 14:6.
[46] John 1:9.
[47] John 1:16.
[48] John 10:7-13.
[49] John 6:48-55.

Eucharist; such as baptism, which has efficacy only by the vow of the baptized to receive the Eucharist.[50]

Holy Communion transforms. But it is not the heavenly food which is transformed into the one who eats it; Jesus Christ gives Himself, He comes as a conquerer to transform us into His light and His charity. Here, we have come to the mystery of the union of Christ with souls and with His whole Church. After the Last Supper, Jesus let this mystery be glimpsed by His apostles who communicated for the first time and were ordained priests: "I am the vine, you are the branches. . . . If anyone does not abide in me, he shall be cast outside as the branch and wither; and they shall gather them up and cast them into the fire. . . . Without me you can do nothing." [51] All our supernatural life is linked to our union with Jesus Christ. Separated from Him we are nothing; we have neither value nor existence in the supernatural order. And so in His priestly prayer before the Passion, Christ made only one request for His apostles and for those who will believe in their word: that they may be one with Him as He and His Father are one,[52] in order that they may see His glory.[53] Christ exacted this as the price of His sacrifice. This unity is the end of the Incarnation and the Redemption. It is vital for our souls and for the Church.

The apostle Saint Paul teaches the same doctrine more explicitly in a marvelous synthesis. He proclaims himself the herald of the great mystery which is the great mystery of Christ, of the eternal plan of the divine mercy of God who, after the Fall, restoring all things by His Incarnate Word, gave Him the primacy in all things. God brought together in Him all that sin had separated. He united us all in Christ in order that by Him and in Him we might have purification,

---

[50] "Even the first grace is not given to a person unless he receives this Sacrament (the Eucharist in desire and in value: the Eucharist is in fact the end of all the Sacraments) Catechism of the Council of Trent, on the Sacrament of the Holy Eucharist, n. 50.

[51] John 15:5-6.

[52] John 17:21.

[53] John 17:24.

salvation, and sanctity, and that with Him we might form a single body which is the whole Christ of the Church, *In Christo Jesu*. Such is the master idea of the teaching of Saint Paul. It is the essence of Christianity.

The Church is Christ diffused in His members. The Church extends Christ by furnishing Him additional humanities in which He displays the riches of His grace, and by which He continues His priestly mission here below. Divine grace, which cannot come to us except through Christ, binds us to Christ and makes us truly His. Thus, we belong to Christ, and Christ is God's.

The nature of grace reveals to us another aspect of our dependence on Christ and our unity with Him. Grace is in fact filial; that is an essential note. We have received a spirit of adoption by virtue of which we cry, "Abba! Father!" [54] In the bosom of the Holy Trinity we are sons or we are not. Now, the Father has only one Son; and that is His Word. The eternal rhythm of life in the bosom of the Holy Trinity is immutable: God the Father, by the knowledge He has of Himself, engenders the Word who expresses it; the Father and the Son, by a common spiration of love, produce the Holy Spirit. Neither centuries nor eternity will change anything of this movement. How is it possible for us to enter into it and participate in it as our supernatural vocation requires? Not otherwise than by the favor of an adoption and a bond such that it can create a certain unity with one of the divine Persons. The Word became incarnate, took on a human nature that He brought, a happy captive, to the bosom of that glory that the Word had, before the world existed.[55] By this holy humanity of Christ, the Word lays hold on and draws after Him all men who let themselves be taken captive by His grace. The whole Christ extended and complete is placed, by His unity with the Word, under the eternally fruitful paternity of the Father of

[54] Rom. 8:15.
[55] Cf. John 17:5.

light and of mercy; and with Him breathes forth the Love that
is the Holy Spirit who, as Spirit of the Father and the Son,
becomes in consequence the Spirit of the Church and ours.

Such is the plan of God that envelops us, and the design
that He wants to realize in us and by us. We shall belong to
Christ, or we shall not have supernatural life; we shall be sons
with the Word Incarnate in the bosom of the Holy Trinity, or
we shall be excluded from the kingdom of heaven. These
truths must not just furnish food for our contemplation. Since
they lie at the root of the whole divine work of the Redemption and the organization of the Church, they must direct the
cooperation that this divine work demands of us. These truths,
high as they are, are among the most practical for the spiritual
life and for the apostolate. Consequently, the philosopher must
not expect to find divine intimacy at the term of his intellectual
speculations, however high they be. Should it happen that by a
leap or a swoon of his spirit, he succeeded in touching on pure
intellectuality; and should he return, his mind heavy with profound intuitions, he ought not to believe that he touched God
if he did not pass through faith in Christ Jesus. Loving intimacy with God cannot be attained by the way of pure intellectuality. The contemplative, too, will not arrive at the perfection
of his loving contemplation uniquely by burying himself in the
obscurity of the night. In order to find their place in the Holy
Trinity, both the one and the other will have to go to Christ
and humbly solicit the all-powerful but necessary mediation of
Him who is the way, the door of the sheepfold, and the good
Shepherd. Shepherd or Wise Man, one can attain to God here
below only by kneeling before the crib of Bethlehem and
adoring Him hidden under the weakness of a Babe.

Let souls who aspire to intimate communing with God,
seek no other way than Christ. To meditate on Christ, to imitate
Him in His actions, His thoughts, His sentiments and desires,
to follow Him from Bethlehem to Calvary, is the surest way
and the shortest. To put on Christ and to make Him live in

oneself is the highest perfection. United to Jesus and fixed in Him, we are at the term of our ascent and already in our place for eternity.

Any doctrine or any way that would withdraw from Christ or would not lead to Him would be a false doctrine or a suspect way. To have established the practical consequences of this truth in the spiritual domain, constitutes one of Saint Teresa's titles to glory, one of those that justify her authority as master of the spiritual life.[56]

She is at an equal distance from the timid souls who fear to leave the active ways of prayer in due season, and from those souls who through subtle pride dream only of emptying themselves of sensible things that they may enter the dark night of the soul. Taking into account at the same time the laws of God's action in souls and the weakness of human nature, the spiritual nature of God and the plan of His loving mercy, this great spiritual mother teaches us to become "rooted" in Christ who is the "way and truth and life," as well as not to resist the prompting of grace when it wants to carry us off into the obscure depths of Wisdom.

We shall find this teaching again, detailed and precise, in the different mansions. In going through the first three, the soul will have to keep its eyes fixed untiringly on the good Jesus. The Wisdom of the Word will be manifest, obscure or delightful, in the fourth and fifth Mansions. In the complete stripping and poverty of the sixth Mansions, the soul will share in the sorrowful mysteries of Christ, while waiting until it participates in the triumph of His life within it, in the transforming union of the seventh Mansions.

[56] The teaching of Saint Teresa had nowhere, it seems, a more profound influence on spirituality than in France where it was rapidly spread by the translation of her writings, from the beginning of the XVII century, and by numerous monasteries of Carmelites. The French mystical school of the XVII century, whose leaders were devotees of Carmel, owes it its Christocentric character.

# CHAPTER VI
# Teresian Asceticism

*To see God we must die.*

"To see God we must die," we have heard Teresa the child explaining to her parents on her return from the ineffective expedition to the country of the Moors. Only death, in truth, can open the gaze of our soul to the vision of the Infinite. It is by a dying, too, but more slowly, effected by continual mortification, that one enters even here below into the divine intimacy. Teresa takes cognizance of this; she writes:

The least that anyone who is beginning to serve the Lord truly can offer Him is his life.[1]

The primacy that she gives to prayer in her spirituality does not make her forget the importance of asceticism: "Prayer cannot be accompanied by self-indulgence."[2]

The soul that is exposed to the divine light must surely discover better the requirements of the divine purity. In order to arrive at perfect union with God, it must submit itself to an energetic and absolute asceticism. And in order for this asceticism to be efficacious at the same time as proportionate to human strength, it will have to be adapted to that strength and progressive.

Absolute, adapted, and progressive: these are the three characteristics of Teresian asceticism that we are going to examine.

## A. Absolute asceticism

A breath of warrior energy animates the writings of Teresa. She is the daughter of a noble family and a native of Avila

[1] *Way of Perfection,* xii; Peers, II, 49.
[2] *Ibid.,* iv; 16.

which, during a memorable siege, was defended by the heroism of its women. In this spirit she tells us that the Convent of Saint Joseph of Avila is "a little castle inhabited by good Christians," [3] protected by the strong wall of poverty and humility.[4] Here the battles are only spiritual ones, but they are "very painful and need more courage than do many others in the world." [5]

The standard-bearer is not a combatant, yet none the less he is exposed to great danger, and, inwardly, must suffer more than anyone, for he cannot defend himself, as he is carrying the standard, which he must not allow to leave his hands, even if he is cut to pieces. Just so contemplatives have to bear aloft the standard of humility and must suffer all the blows which are aimed at them without striking any themselves. Their duty is to suffer as Christ did, to raise the Cross on high, not to allow it to leave their hands.[6]

In many places in her writings, but especially in the first twenty chapters of the *Way of Perfection,* Saint Teresa explains in detail the virtues to be practised and the sufferings to be borne. These are the virtues of poverty, charity, humility, detachment from one's family and from one's self; and all, with that absolute character that is truly the note of Teresian asceticism. Let us listen to the Saint:

Keep your eyes fixed upon your Spouse. . . . If you should do as I say and yet die of hunger, then happy are the nuns of Saint Joseph's.[7]
Unless we resolve to put up with death and ill-health once and for all, we shall never accomplish anything. Try not to fear these and commit yourselves wholly to God, come what may. What does it matter if we die? [8]

She wants her daughter to be virile and to know how to bear without complaining those minor ailments from which women suffer, which "come and go." [9] "When the ailment is

[3] *Ibid.,* iii; 10.
[4] *Ibid.,* ii; 8.
[5] *Life,* xi; Peers, I, 67.
[6] *Way of Perfection,* xviii; Peers, II, 74.
[7] *Ibid.,* ii; 5.
[8] *Ibid.,* xii; 48.
[9] *Ibid.;* 47.

serious," she says, "it proclaims itself; that is quite another
kind of moaning, which draws attention to itself immediately." [10]

Generosity is necessary from the very beginning of the spiritual life:

> As I say, it is most important—all-important, indeed—that they
> should begin well by making an earnest and most determined resolve
> not to halt until they reach their goal, whatever may come, whatever
> may happen to them, however hard they may have to labour, who-
> ever may complain of them, whether they reach their goal or die on
> the road or have no heart to confront the trials they meet, whether
> the very world dissolves before them.[11]

Many never manage to finish their course because they did
not "embrace the Cross from the beginning." [12]

In the *Interior Castle* the Saint sums up in few words:

> All that the beginner in prayer has to do—and you must not for-
> get this, for it is very important—is to labour and be resolute and
> prepare himself with all possible diligence to bring his will into con-
> formity with the will of God. . . . You may be quite sure that this
> comprises the very greatest perfection which can be attained on the
> spiritual road.[13]

The entire asceticism has for its aim the complete gift of
the will and of oneself:

> The aim of all my advice to you in this book is that we should sur-
> render ourselves wholly to the Creator, place our will in His hands and
> detach ourselves from the creatures.[14]

Saint Teresa does not condemn to hell, however, those who
bring a lesser generosity to the spiritual journey. If God has
already granted them some supernatural favor, He "does not
take away all that He has given from those who live in purity
of conscience." [15] Nevertheless, they do not go beyond the

[10] *Way of Perfection*, xii; Peers, II, 46.
[11] *Ibid.*, xxi; 89.
[12] *Life*, xi; Peers, I, 69.
[13] II Mansions, i; Peers, II, 216.
[14] *Way of Perfection*, xxxii; Peers, II, 137.
[15] *Ibid.*, xxxi; 133.

stage of mental prayer. Contemplation makes absolute demands, concerning which the Saint expresses herself, somewhat irked:

If you have no wish either to hear about them or to practise them, continue your mental prayer all your life.[16]

As for herself, she wants to address only those whose desire is set on the summits, who long to drink at the fountain of living waters. It is so they may prepare for this grace, that she asks of them the absolute gift of their will.[17] Only these can be the disciples of Saint Teresa and bring to reality the definition that she gives of the spiritual man:

Do you know when people really become spiritual? It is when they become the slaves of God and are branded with His sign, which is the sign of the Cross, in token that they have given Him their freedom. Then He can sell them as slaves to the whole world, as He Himself was sold.[18]

Saint John of the Cross sets forth the same ideal as Saint Teresa. He posits the same requirements, with more incisive formulas and, on certain points, more precise. At the beginning of his treatise, the *Ascent of Mount Carmel,* he puts a chart which indicates the possible ways a soul may go. Three ways are open to the beginner: at the right and the left, two wide and winding avenues. The first, which is the way of the soul that is led astray, follows the search for the goods of earth: liberty, honors, knowledge, comfort; the second, called the way of the imperfect, leads towards the goods of heaven: glory, sanctity, joy, wisdom. But because it seeks them, the soul finds them less abundantly, and it does not scale the mountain of perfection. In the middle of the chart and going straight to the summit there is a narrow path on which the Saint has written four times over: "Nothing, nothing, nothing,

[16] *Ibid.,* xvi; 64.
[17] *Life,* xi; Peers, I, 63. Also, *Way of Perfection,* xxxii; Peers, II, 134.
[18] VII Mansions, iv; Peers, II, 346.

nothing." This path leads to the fullness of the gifts of God, to the banquet of divine Wisdom.

The design is suggestive. Sairɨ John of the Cross comments on it by the doctrine of the *Ascent:*

> Strive always to choose, not that which is easiest, but that which is most difficult . . .
> Not that which gives most pleasure, but rather that which gives least;
> Not that which is restful, but that which is wearisome;
> Not that which is a desire for anything, but that which is a desire for nothing;
> Strive not to go about seeking the best of temporal things, but the worst.
> Strive thus to desire to enter into complete detachment and emptiness and poverty, with respect to that which is in the world, for Christ's sake.[19]

This detachment, remarks the Saint, applies to spiritual goods as well as to goods of this world. He definitely states his advice in the spiritual sense:

> In order to arrive at having pleasure in everything,
> Desire to have pleasure in nothing.
> In order to arrive at possessing everything,
> Desire to possess nothing.
> In order to arrive at being everything,
> Desire to be nothing.
> In order to arrive at knowing everything,
> Desire to know nothing.[20]

There is no use multiplying quotations. It is clear that the slopes of Carmel are steep and that there are no winding paths to climb them to the top; no plateaus where one can rest; just an occasional level where one may stop a moment, not to consider the road traversed, but to contemplate the height whence comes the light and towards which one must mount, straight up, helping oneself with the only support permitted and useful for that ascent: the staff that is the cross.

The poor Convent of Saint Joseph of Avila, the tumble-

[19] *Ascent,* Bk. I, xiii; Peers, I, 61.
[20] *Ibid.;* 62-3.

down hovel of Duruelo that John of the Cross decorated with crosses and death's heads to bring tears of devotion, the life that was led there, these offer to our view the living realization of absolute asceticism. This spirituality makes no parade of its austere strength. Neither does it hide it, however, for it wants to attract only the strong. Teresa stresses this to her daughters:

> What I earnestly beg of you is that anyone who knows she will be unable to follow our customs will say so: there are other convents in which the Lord is also well served.[21]

> I should not like you to be that [effeminate], or even to appear to be that, in any way, my daughters; I want you to be strong men.[22]

Are these the exaggerations, as some will say, of valiant souls who want to make a law of heroism and thus isolate themselves a little proudly from the crowd? To judge of this, let us consult the Gospels:

"Unless you do penance, you will all likewise perish!" our Lord tells us. That is already a very austere law. Jesus states explicitly the quality of the effort that He exacts: "The kingdom of heaven has been enduring violent assault, and the violent have been seizing it by force." [23] All the disciples of Christ must, then, exercise violence; for one cannot, in fact, without doing violence to oneself, fulfil the formal precept of the Master: "If anyone wishes to come after me, let him deny himself, and take up his cross, and follow me." [24]

There is no other way of ascent to God than the way of Calvary, rugged and bloody as the ascent of Carmel. To the disciples of Emmaus, still scandalized by the terrible drama of Calvary, Jesus says: "Did not the Christ have to suffer these things before entering into his glory?" [25] He proclaims to them a law: the one that He imposed on Himself, the one that they will have to follow. He had announced it:

---

[21] *Way of Perfection*, viii; Peers, II, 38.
[22] *Ibid.*, vii; 35.
[23] Matt. 11:12.
[24] Matt. 16:24.
[25] Luke 24:26.

The disciple is not above his Master. The world hated me and it will hate you. They will persecute you as they have persecuted me . . . I am sending you forth as sheep among wolves.[26]

The law of suffering is a law of life. Jesus Christ remains among us under the eucharistic species in a state of immolation, the bread and the wine separate on the altar. It is in this state that He bestows the grace of divine union in the Church. This grace is life and death, like the immolated Christ who pours it out from His open wounds. It gives us the superabundant life of the Christ who does not die, and it announces through us His Passion, His suffering, the necessity of participating in His sacrifice, of completing what is lacking to His Passion for the application of His merits to our souls. It will be developed in us only through suffering united to Christ, and will come to perfect fruition in the joy of the beatific vision only when, by death, it will join us with Christ immolated and resurrected from the dead.

On Calvary, Christ alone was immolated; on the altar, He offers Himself each day with the whole Church which participates in His sacrifice; and He calls for the sacrifice of all His members. Jesus crucified is the perfect type of regenerated humanity, the ideal and model according to which God forms souls. The Holy Mass is celebrated in our presence every day. Everywhere, the Church lifts up the image of Christ on the Cross. And yet, these awe-ful realities, this constant Presence, do not succeed in dissipating the mirages of temporal happiness and the hopes of earthly triumphs, which we relentlessly bind up with the realization of our desires for Christian perfection.

We try to forget that Christ announced no other victory than that of the Cross on Calvary: no other revenge on His enemies than that of the day when He will come on the clouds of heaven with His Cross, to judge the living and the dead. On that day, those only will triumph with Him, who will have

[26] Matt. 10.

passed through great tribulation and been purified in the **Blood** of the Lamb.[27]

The masters of Carmel understood and accepted these profound truths, painful but practical. They owed it to the souls grouped around them, eager for an integral Christianity, to proclaim the hard, but fruitful law of the cross, and to put them on guard against false prophets.

If someone comes to you, preaching an easy doctrine, even if he were an angel and worked miracles to support it, do not believe him. Put your trust in austere penance and detachment from all things.[28]

United to Christ crucified, by a participation in His divine life and His passion, they merited the power to communicate in His sentiments, to take on His attitudes in the face of suffering and death. Did He not say: "But I have a baptism to be baptized with; and how distressed I am until it is accom-

---

[27] One may not affirm, however, that only suffering is sanctifying and meritorious here below. "Sweetnesses enslave," Saint Therese of the Child Jesus insists.

Overflowing delights are purifying, as are painful wounds. The degree of charity carries more weight for the merit of an act than does the suffering of which it is the occasion.

The crucified Christ who was lifted up on Calvary as the exemplary type of regenerated humanity, was the most sorrowful of men by reason of the torments that He bore; and at the same time, the happiest by the Beatific Vision that He continued to enjoy and by the triumph that His suffering secured.

And so the saint who puts on Christ, knows here below the most sublime and pure joys as well as the most painful interior and exterior sufferings.

On her death bed, Saint Therese of the Child Jesus said: "You see this little glass? One would suppose that it contained a most delicious draught, whereas, in reality, it is more bitter than anything else I take. It is the image of my life. . . . The chalice is full to overflowing! I could never believe that it was possible to suffer so intensely." Almost immediately she added, not to rectify the preceding statements but to avoid misunderstanding: "I am at peace. . . . I do not regret having surrendered myself to Love." (*Autobiography*, Epilogue, 203, 210).

But, as suffering is a door necessary for entrance to supreme happiness, and since our appetite for happiness tends constantly to diminish the divine exigencies and to reconcile humanism and Christianity, we understand the insistence of the spiritual masters on the necessity of the Cross, and the equivalence they establish between sacrifice and perfection.

[28] John of the Cross, Maxim 124. *Do not find this in Kavanaugh*

plished!" [29] With all the ardor of His soul as Saviour, Jesus moved on to the magnificent realization of Calvary. The saints of Carmel, too, in the hours when their soul is on fire with love, sigh for the suffering that likens them to their Master, that saves souls; and for death which will give them the beatific vision and free them for fruitful missions:

"To suffer or to die!" Saint Teresa cries.
"To suffer and be despised!" begs Saint John of the Cross.
"Suffering has been my Heaven here below," declares Saint Therese of the Child Jesus.

And yet, they were human beings like us: "Elias was a man like ourselves, subject to infirmities." [30] They suffered painfully; sometimes, with sadness, without courage, weakly. But throughout all, even when the ardors had gone from them, their generosity was at the height of their teaching.

We could not efface anything from that teaching without touching the Christian perfection that it guarantees, without diminishing the beauty, the power, and the fecundity of the spirituality of Carmel of which it is a part.

## B. Adapted asceticism

"The spirituality of giants! Spirituality for exceptional beings of the stature of Saint Teresa and Saint John of the Cross!" some will say after hearing the sublime cries that rise from those burning souls.

"A spirituality which, because it is sublime, is no longer human," others will add. "Fortunately there are masters of the spiritual life that are more comprehensible, such as Saint Francis de Sales, for instance, or even Saint Therese of the Child Jesus—she, too, of the Carmelite family—who know how to take into account human weakness and the needs of our time." This is a specious objection, often heard; but a closer scrutiny of it will permit us to bring out the vital suppleness of

[29] Luke 12:50.
[30] James 5:17.

adaptation, in the absolute asceticism of the masters of Carmel.

Let us first note that it would do a great injury to the spirit- *Ans.* uality of Saint Francis de Sales or Saint Therese of the Child Jesus, to declare that these two are not armed with an absolute asceticism. We might as well assert that they are not Christian. The violence that they impose is perhaps hidden, but it is necessarily there, since only the violent bear away the kingdom of God. In fact, we know the violence that the gentle Saint Francis de Sales did to himself in order to conquer a fiery temperament, the heroism he required of Saint Jane de Chantal especially at the moment when she had to leave her home and walk over the body of her son, to found the Order of the Visitation. We are still better enlightened as to Saint Therese of the Child Jesus, who held it as a principle that one must accept everything in the spiritual life,[31] and must go to the end of her strength without complaining; and of whom her sister Celine, her faithful companion, used to say that the virtue of fortitude was her characteristic virtue.

The gentleness of Saint Francis de Sales, then, as well as the smile of Saint Therese of the Child Jesus, screen virtues practised to a heroic degree. Both, like Teresa of Jesus and John of the Cross, are pilgrims of the absolute. Notable differences, however, mark their forms of sanctity and their teaching. It is necessary to recognize this, and more useful still to explain it.

Mortification can have a double end: the destruction of sin in us and the redemption of souls. For the moment, only the first end concerns us since we are speaking of asceticism. For this asceticism to be effective, it must be adapted to temperament in order to attain to the dominant tendency that is to be destroyed. Now we know that these tendencies, differing in individuals, are nevertheless found with a certain constancy in men of the same epoch, and the same class of society. We are, for instance, acquainted with the Spaniard of the sixteenth century, the Frenchman of the seventeenth century; we could tell

[31] "I chose everything!" (*Autobiography,* i).

their qualities and their faults, displayed as they are in the
political, the literary and social works of their time.

The masters of the spiritual life, saints ordinarily, with
which the Holy Spirit provides the Church in every age, are at
the same time minds enlightened on the exigencies of God,
and penetrating psychologists. They know the principles of the
spiritual life and draw precise counsels from them, adapted to
the needs of the souls that they are to direct. Their teaching
finds in its faithfulness to traditional principles and its adaptation to the needs of the time doctrinal security, originality, and
efficacy.

Saint John of the Cross and Saint Teresa are doctors of the
universal Church.* Their mystical science is for all times. They
belong, however, to a certain period and nation; they are
Spaniards of the sixteenth century and are among the most
qualified representatives of that brilliant classical century of
Spain. They spoke with their rich Spanish genius, and for the
audience that was before them; and hence, they took into account the needs of the listeners, in giving practical commentaries on their doctrine.

We know the Spanish temperament of the sixteenth century.
It has a profound faith and piety like its King Philip II, who
lives like a religious and is very much preoccupied by the reform of the various Orders, wanting at any price to preserve
his subjects from the Protestant error which is raging in Europe.
He supports the zeal of the Inquisition which, without pity and
without respect of person, puts into its prisons the unknown
stranger, the renowned professor, or even the archbishop im-
prudent in his speech. The faith is protected; sin will not be
in the intellect which faith subjects. Sin will be in the senses
and the sense powers. The Spaniard of the sixteenth century
is overflowing with life and ardor. Having finished his battle

---

* This title is commonly given to Saint Teresa although it is not stated in
the official documents of the church. Popes Gregory XV and Urban VII considered her writings to be equal in value to those of a doctor of the Church.
—Translator's note.

with the Moors in the peninsula, he now goes everywhere that there is fighting, or rather he carries war everywhere, into the Netherlands, to Italy, to America. His senses are stimulated in his piety as in his wars. Illuminism threatens them.

Then all the masters of the spiritual life go into combat against those ardors of the senses, to calm them by the most violent physical mortification. Saint Teresa and Saint John of the Cross excel in this; and yet, they are on this point among the moderate.[32] Their doctrine bears the mark of it. The *Ascent of Mount Carmel* is full of solicitous care to answer in detail the needs of contemporaries, and most especially to point out the danger of illuminism. In this book Saint John of the Cross treats in a distinct way the purification of the memory and of the will. Mortification of the understanding is taken up only in explanations given on the nature of faith and then, in connection with the dangers of illuminism.

Saint Francis de Sales writes some thirty years later. The Frenchman of the seventeenth century does not differ notably from the Spaniard of the sixteenth century—at least the Frenchman who escaped the Protestant influence. The annals of the Carmelite monasteries of France at that time complacently record the same brilliant excesses that the Spanish Reform made a show of. But Saint Francis de Sales is addressing a special public composed of his Visitandines and ladies of the world. The first, by hypothesis, do not have sufficient physical strength to stand the austerities of Carmel; the second are mistresses of a home and, in their isolated chateaux or in their bourgeois city mansions, lead a life often filled with the obligations of family or of society. Physical mortifications at a violent tempo are impossible for them or at least are not suita-

[32] Saint Teresa is frightened at the austerities of the first Discalced Carmelites at Duruelo and fears that they conceal a ruse of the devil who wants thus to destroy the budding reform (*Foundations,* xiv). Saint John of the Cross, named master of novices at Pastrana, begins by supressing the extraordinary penances that had been established there by his predecessor, the P. Espiñal.

ble. These dear Philotheas cannot, however, be sanctified without doing violence to themselves. They run dangers; they have their unruly tendencies. As a fine psychologist Saint Francis de Sales discerns these very well. And so he is going to impose on them an asceticism of the heart—that Saint Teresa perhaps would have found too severe—which is to secure them against dangers, often numerous, in their situation. They are mistresses of homes with a sense and taste for detail and order, noble souls made to exercise authority. The gentle bishop of Geneva, with a prudent and persevering rigor, will impose a mortification of the will by obedience; and of all their personal tastes by a detachment that will reach to details and even trifles. Souls will thus be liberated for the exercise of perfect love.

Since the seventeenth century, evil has taken other forms. By proclaiming the principle of free thought, the Protestant Reformation withdrew the intellect from the authority of the Church, disengaged it progressively from dogmas and from all restraints. Thus freed, reason was deified under the French Revolution and proclaimed its absolute rights. Queen in all domains, it became successively deist and atheist, and in its isolation ended by doubting itself and all the perceptions of the senses. It renounced the supernatural and lost the taste for metaphysical speculations. It turned to matter to improve the earthly life of man. The scientific discoveries which repaid its new zeal, increased its confidence in itself; but by increasing comfort and decreasing effort they contributed to making the body which they were to serve, anemic. A proud individualism, the enemy of every restraint of authority, exalting personal egosim, became implanted in manners and in morals; a restless individualism, for even continually new pleasures could not satisfy the profound need of our soul created for the Infinite. Such is the modern malady which has its source in a pride of intellect that we are hardly aware of, so completely has it passed into our way of life, and which, placed at the service of the senses, has drained our moral and sometimes our physical energies. Is it possible to bring the supernatural to these maladies so grave and so profound?

Saint Therese of the Child Jesus came to bring light to our time, to indicate to us, first, the asceticism that is proper for our ills. She will tell us, then, that the violent physical asceticism of the sixteenth century is not generally suited to our anemic temperaments; that any desire that we might have for it could well proceed in us either from that spiritual pride which wants to reach the summits quickly and takes delight in the effort, or from the unhealthy melancholy, rather frequent in our day, which seeks suffering for itself. Saint Therese of the Child Jesus does certainly not condemn physical mortification, necessary in our time as in all times. Her fidelity in enduring all those that the rules of Carmel and providential circumstances offered her, shows us clearly her thought. She blames only the excess, too often stressed in the lives of the saints and in the history of the beginnings of the reformed Carmel. The violence that the Gospel requires of us, we must exercise on pride in all its forms, for our souls are filled with it as with a noxious gas. Perfection, she proclaims, is in humility of heart.

In order to combat a generalized pride, Saint Therese constructs a spirituality of humility, her "way of spiritual childhood." To remain a child, to cultivate carefully in oneself the awareness of one's littleness and trusting weakness, to rejoice in one's poverty, to display it gladly before God as an appeal to His mercy; such, in her opinion, is the most proper attitude to attract God's glance and the plenitude of His transforming and consuming love. Really to acquire this attitude and to keep it, demands a complete immolation. And so Saint Therese requires of her disciples an energy no less persevering, a gift no less absolute than do the reformers of Carmel themselves. She is of their race and of their blood, their authentic daughter, the faithful interpreter of their thought. It pleases us to think that

Saint Teresa and Saint John of the Cross would not have given for our time an interpretation of the principles of spirituality other than the one they gave for all time, adapted to our special needs.

Saint Therese of the Child Jesus, independently of her personal merits and her particular mission in the world, thus makes us admire the living suppleness of the spirituality of Carmel, which, in order to fulfil its task throughout the centuries and keep its fecundity, bends maternally over the souls of each epoch and, to cure their ills, draws from its treasures riches both new and old.[33]

## C. Progressive asceticism

In the book of her *Life,* Saint Teresa tells that, when supernatural prayers became habitual with her, she felt the need of finding a director who would help her, for "I was attached in certain ways to things which, though not wrong in themselves,

---

[33] A religious order can conserve its spirit and fulfil its mission throughout the centuries only by adapting its external forms to the changes and vicissitudes of the different epochs. Saint Teresa was able to revive the primitive spirit of Carmel in the sixteenth century only by creating a form of eremitic life adapted to the customs and the needs of her time.

Among the external forms that envelop the spirit of an order that must survive the vicissitudes of time and the subversion of civilizations because it embodies an essential function of the priesthood of Christ, there are some which must change and there are others which are immutable because inseparable from the very spirit. Thus, Saint Teresa re-establishes the silence of the desert in her monasteries; but she is clothed with drugget and sets up a cloister, while the prophet was clothed with animal skins and went here and there.

The cult of what is ancient and fidelity to tradition, which would remain indifferently attached to all the primitive forms of the spirit, would risk crystallizing that spirit in a mortal rigidity and, by hindering it from adapting itself and flowering, would cause it to lose the very thing that it wants so strongly to keep.

To distinguish between the external forms to be kept and those that must disappear at any given epoch, belongs neither to inexperienced fervor nor to that lazy routine that constantly tends to minimize effort; it is not a right, either, of the authority of the superior, who is charged with conserving rather than with modifying; it is the exclusive privilege of sanctity, which is alone capable of moulding into a living and authentic form the spirit, of which it possesses the plenitude.

were sufficient to spoil all my efforts." [34] They told her of a holy priest of Avila who, as she said,

> began with the holy determination to treat me as if I were strong (and so I ought to have been, considering the extent to which, as he saw, I practise prayer), so that I should give no offense of any kind to God. But when I saw . . . that I had not courage enough to live more perfectly, I became distressed, and realizing that he was treating me in spiritual matters as though I were going to become perfect immediately, I saw that I should have to be more careful. . . . I, though advanced in Divine favors, was, as regards virtues and mortification, still quite a beginner. Really, if I had had nobody else to consult, I think my soul would never have shown any improvement.[35]

The holy priest of Avila, Master Daza, had considered only the absolute exigencies of the supernatural favors received, and not at all the strength of soul. Saint Teresa reproaches him for this, a fact that indicates to us clearly the thought of the Saint on this subject. The asceticism that tends to absolute detachment must proceed progressively, by degrees; if not, it will fail completely. A prudent and enlightened director must regulate this progress by considering the actual strength of a soul and the exigencies of God, which, they too, are progressive. During three years of His public life, Jesus bore with the moral and spiritual rudeness of His apostles, their slowness of mind; in increasing degrees, He let the light as to the kingdom of God penetrate their souls.

In expounding her spiritual doctrine, Saint Teresa insists from the beginning on the nature of the divine exigencies and the necessity for generous resolutions in the soul; but throughout the Mansions, she will show herself to be always maternal, understanding, encouraging to weak souls, emphasizing the merits of efforts made and the value of results obtained, thus inciting to new generous resolutions for higher attainments, following a continuous and ordered progression.[36]

[34] *Life*, xxiii; Peers, I, 147.
[35] *Ibid.*; 148.
[36] On the chart printed on the end sheet in the front of this volume will be found the progression of the Teresian asceticism through the Mansions.

Saint John of the Cross, whose logic of detachment seems to us so terrifying and almost inhuman, is a patient confessor, a condescending director, a father compassionate for human weakness. He frightened on first acquaintance, but when one knew him, "one would have followed him to Turkey."

Saint Therese of the Child Jesus, who was so stern with her novices [37] and gave them the cult of a strong generosity, used to say that there are souls that the divine mercy never wearies of waiting for, and that, among her novices, there were some that she had to take by the tip of the wings; others, by the skin.

The masters of Carmel know the purity of God; and in His light, they discover human weakness. They love the one and the other with the same love. Their practical science does not come only from the logic of their thought; it is also from the compassionate love of their heart. And if in their treatises it is especially a powerful and somewhat harsh light that shines, in their contacts with souls it is loving charity that overflows. Their contemporaries testify to this. Their spiritual science is, in fact, a science of love.

---

[37] In the process of beatification, Soeur Geneviève de la Sainte Face (her sister Céline) deposed that if she had had to mention what pleased her least in Saint Therese of the Child Jesus, it would have been her severity toward the novices.

# CHAPTER VII
# The Devil

*He works like a noiseless file . . .*[1]

In the drama of the spiritual life another personage plays a leading part: the devil. Although his action takes place in the dark, the penetrating gaze of Teresa has discerned its full importance. Frequently she speaks of him in order to draw attention to his presence, to expose his ruses when the soul is at cross roads or in dangerous passes; to point him out, lurking everywhere that there is darkness enough to cover him. For Saint Teresa the devil is not just a mysterious, malicious power; he is a living being, well known because often met, a personal enemy. We can profit by her experience and her teaching in our study of the *nature and the power of the devil, the frequency and modes of his intervention in the spiritual life, the means of discerning his presence and of resisting his attacks.*[2]

[1] I Mansions, ii; Peers, II, 211.

[2] In the works of Saint John of the Cross also, we find many allusions to the devil, as P. Lucien writes in the introduction to the *Dark Night* (Oeuvres complètes):

"Often he makes allusion to the role of the devil: rarely in order to make us fear his extraordinary manifestations, and almost always to show his hidden action, parallel to that of God (like a thief that follows step by step the traveler that he hopes to rob at the right moment). Anyone who would collect all the teachings on the devil, scattered through the work of the mystical Doctor . . . would have a rich treatise on demonology, in which the general principles would neighbor on the most searching psychological descriptions—a rare thing."

See the exhaustive study of the Rev. Father Nilus, O.C.D., "Demonio e Vita spirituale," in *Sanjuanistice* at the Collegium Intern. Carm. Disc.

While relying especially on Saint Teresa in our succinct study, we shall not neglect the rich teaching of Saint John of the Cross.

## A. Nature and power of the demons

The demons are fallen angels. When God created the world, He also created the angels, pure spirits, beings of light endowed with intellect and will, in number incalculable, all different, grouped in hierarchies, graded in perfection according to their power and the light that constituted them, communicating among themselves in the manner of spirits by a simple act of the will. They formed the celestial court of God who destined them to a participation in His life.

That they might merit this glorious destiny, God submitted them to a trial, of which we cannot state the precise nature. The greatest among them, Lucifer, fascinated by his own light, refused to submit. He drew along with him in his revolt a multitude of angels, perhaps the greater number. While the faithful angels found in their submission to God the vision of Him face-to-face and eternal beatitude, the rebel angels, fixed in their attitude of revolt by the simplicity of their nature, found themselves for eternity in the hatred of God, deprived of the sovereign Good and of infinite Love.

To these angels, now become evil spirits and powers of hatred, God gave permission to intervene in the world. They could thus contribute providentially to the trials that men were to undergo, called to replace them in the celestial court. With what power could the demons intervene in this combat? With the power of their angelic nature which, in what constitutes it essentially, has not been diminished by their fall.

In that he is a pure spirit, the devil can dominate the inferior world of matter and the senses. He knows their laws and reactions. He can move them to action and use them intelligently for his own ends. On this score, all that man possesses of the material and sensible—body, sense powers (sensibility, imagination, memory)—does not escape a certain action or influence of the devil.

On the other hand, this fallen angel, although pure spirit,

cannot penetrate into the higher faculties of the soul unless the will gives him entry. He cannot read nor directly act upon thoughts conceived in the intellect. The will, too, is an inviolable and inviolate sanctuary, even in cases of possession, unless of itself it gives way to the devil's domination.

The supernatural world, into which one can enter only with loving faith, is completely closed to him. An evil spirit has, however, a certain knowledge of God and believes in spite of itself in the divine mysteries which torment it. But the laws of the supernatural world that experience alone discloses, the operations of God in souls, the spiritual relations of the soul with God, are for it an impenetrable mystery.

Nevertheless, by means of sensible impressions and images that are presented to the intellect and the will and have normally an influence on their activity, the devil can intervene indirectly in the activity of the soul and the spiritual life. The sense image is sometimes so subtle, and the passage from the image to the idea so rapid, that the soul itself can be easily deceived and not suspect an intervention of the evil spirit. Likewise, the devil can know the thoughts of the intellect, the volitions and desires of the will, and even the supernatural movements of the soul, if he gets hold of the written or spoken expression of them, or succeeds in interpreting the sensible phenomena that accompany them.[3]

Most probably, because of certain external indications, and in virtue of his natural powers of penetration, the devil can guess the habitual orientation of the soul in the supernatural life, the profound efficacy of the graces it has received, its present strength and especially its future, and can conclude

[3] It is quite true that oftentimes, when these very intimate and secret spiritual communications take place in the soul, although the devil cannot get to know of what kind and manner they are, yet the great repose and silence which some of them cause in the senses and the faculties of the sensual part make it clear to him that they are taking place and that the soul is receiving a certain blessing from them (*Dark Night,* Bk. II, xxiii; Peers, I, 477).

consequently as to the necessity of more violent warfare against that soul while it has not yet all its supernatural strength and has not become dangerous to him. It is thus that the devil, ignorant probably of Christ's divinity, discerned nevertheless the singular power of Jesus whom he approached in the desert with temptations that he thought equal to his adversary. Saint Therese of the Child Jesus relates that the mysterious illness from which she suffered at the age of nine,[4] was produced by the devil who, she said, wanted to take revenge on her for the great harm that her family was to do to him in the future.

The power of each demon is proportionate to its nature, and as varied as its personal gifts. The evil spirits do not present themselves as a hostile and uniform force, but like an army; formidable certainly in number, but more formidable still by the distinct intelligent hatred of every one of the enemies that compose it, by the multiple resources and the particular power that that hatred finds in each one of them for carrying on its malicious work.

## B. Intervention of the devil in the spiritual life

Among the parables on "the kingdom of God," there is one that exposes the role of Satan in the life of the Church and of souls. Our Lord says:

> The kingdom of heaven is like a man who sowed seed in his field; but while men were asleep, his enemy came and sowed weeds among the wheat, and went away. And when the blade sprang up and brought forth fruit, then the weeds appeared as well. And the servants of the householder came and said to him, "Sir, didst thou not sow good seed in thy field? How then does it have weeds?" He said to them, "An enemy has done this." And the servants said to him, "Wilt thou have us go and gather them up?" "No," he said, "lest in gathering the weeds you root up the wheat along with them. Let both grow together until the harvest; and at harvest time I will say to the reapers, Gather up first the weeds, and bind them in bundles to burn; but the wheat gather into my barn." [5]

[4] *Autobiography*, iii, 49.
[5] Matt. 13:24-30.

In few words, this parable shows us the ways of the devil, his activity always on the alert to counterfeit the divine activity and destroy it, his skill in profiting by darkness to hide himself; and the divine patience that permits the devil's action to develop at the same time as the work of grace.

It will suffice to refer briefly to the following characteristic features of his intervention:

## 1. FREQUENCY OF THE INTERVENTION OF THE DEVIL

Every evening at the beginning of Compline, the holy Church has us hear the exhortation of the apostle Saint Peter: [6]

Be sober, be watchful! For your adversary the devil, as a roaring lion, goes about seeking someone to devour.

The exhortation is urgent; it is repeated to us each day because certainly the menace is constant.

The hatred of the demons is violent and always on the alert; they use any and every occasion to impede the action of God in souls. The demons moreover are numerous, their resources are various; no one can prudently think himself safe from their attacks. Such is the opinion of Saint Teresa, expressed in many places in her writings. In her own spiritual ascent, there is not a stage where she did not meet them and did not have to fight them. In the very first Mansions she warns us:

As the devil's intentions are always very bad, he has many legions of evil spirits in each room to prevent souls from passing from one to another, and as we, poor souls, fail to realize this, we are tricked by all kinds of deceptions. The devil is less successful with those who are nearer the King's dwelling-place.[7]

The first divine raptures of the fifth Mansions stir up the jealousy of the devil and arouse his fears for the future:

I beseech you, for His sake, not to be negligent, but to withdraw from occasions of sin—for even in this state the soul is not strong enough to be able to run into them safely, as it is after the betrothal

[6] I Pet. 5:8-9.
[7] I Mansions, ii; Peers, II, 210.

has been made—that is to say, in the Mansion which we shall describe after this one. For this communication has been no more than one single short meeting, and the devil will take great pains about combating it and will try to hinder the betrothal.

I tell you, daughters, I have known people of a very high degree of spirituality who have reached this state (V Mansions), and whom, notwithstanding, the devil, with great subtlety and craft, has won back to himself. For this purpose he will marshal all the powers of hell, for, as I have often said, if he wins a single soul in this way he will win a whole multitude. The devil has much experience in this matter.[8]

After the sixth Mansions, the devil becomes less dangerous to the soul:

Afterwards, when he sees that the soul is completely surrendered to the Spouse, he dare not do this, for he is afraid of such a soul as that, and he knows by experience that if he attempts anything of the kind he will come out very much the loser and the soul will achieve a corresponding gain.[9]

Yet it is indeed in these sixth Mansions that the devil works furiously to counterfeit the extraordinary graces; and that, with the permission of God and great frequency, as Saint John of the Cross affirms:

Of those favours which come through a good angel God habitually allows the enemy to have knowledge: partly so that he may do that which he can against them according to the measure of justice, and that thus he may not be able to allege with truth that no opportunity is given him for conquering the soul, as he said concerning Job.[10] This would be the case if God allowed not a certain equality between the two warriors—namely, the good angel and the bad—when they strive for the soul.[11]

The highest divine communications, those that God Himself makes to the soul, could not, however, be known by the devil:

The reason for this is that, as His Majesty dwells substantially in the soul, where neither angel not devil can attain to an understanding of that which comes to pass, they cannot know the intimate and secret communications which take place there between the soul and God.[12]

[8] V Mansions, iv; Peers, II, 265.
[9] Ibid.
[10] Job 1:1.
[11] Dark Night, Bk. II, xxiii; Peers, I, 478.
[12] Ibid.

These affirmations show us that the souls that aspire to perfection are the object of his special attacks. Sinners, given up to their passions, are an easier conquest; thus the devil rules peacefully over an immense throng of souls that he does not disturb in any way. The tepid man too is an easy prey. Only the fervent escape his influence, and it is against them that his raging and persevering hatred is let furiously loose.

Of this fury our Lord gives us an idea when He says:

> When the unclean spirit has gone out of a man, he roams through dry places in search of a resting place, and finds none. Then he says, "I will return to my house which I left"; and when he has come, he finds the place unoccupied, swept and adorned. Then he goes and takes with him seven other spirits more evil than himself, and they enter in and dwell there.[13]

The offensive returns of the devil do not always obtain a like victory; but this description given by our Lord tells us the perseverance of his attacks against those who have conquered him and whose progress can only increase the violence of his hatred.

The action of the devil against souls eager for perfection is not, then, a rare event, reserved for hagiography; it is normal and frequent. It becomes particularly intense "when the devil sees that the soul's character and habits are such that it is ready to make further progress: all the powers of hell will combine to drive it back again," asserts Saint Teresa.[14]

[13] Matt. 12:43-5.
[14] II Mansions, i; Peers, II, 215.
Man was created to replace the fallen angel; that is the foundation for the jealousy of the devil in our regard. The divine plan will be realized in spite of all, and Wisdom has foreseen and organized every detail. It does not seem doubtful that, in the mind of God, such and such a human being is destined to replace in the celestial court, such and such a. fallen angel. Can the demon, by some indications or spiritual affinities, guess this particular design of God—if not for all souls, at least for certain ones among them? If we could affirm this, we could conclude that these souls have a demon personally jealous of their grace, and hence especially bent on their loss.

Without going so far in a domain that scarcely yields itself to our investigations, we can say that there are, between certain demons and certain souls, affinities that facilitate temptations and make them more effective.

But to conclude from these statements that the attacks of the devil will most frequently take an external visible form, would be to misunderstand completely his strategy. The devil is essentially a power of darkness. He works in the dark in order to surprise and trick. The success of his activities to win fervent souls depends on his cleverness in hiding what he is and what he is doing. Hence, he does not reveal himself by external signs except when constrained to do so in order to counterfeit charisms or extraordinary graces that he wants to discredit; or again, when his hatred is so exasperated by repeated defeats that he seems to abdicate all prudence and, letting fall his mask, shows himself such as he is, in a powerless rage, so as to terrify still, if possible, by his very presence. Such manifestations are then the sign of the soul's victories and consequently, of its sanctity.[15] Thus is explained the visible action of the devil in the life of some saints, such as Saint Teresa and the Curé of Ars.

Very rare, too, is a case of possession by which the devil, with the permission of God, enters into a body and its sense faculties, and acts as its master. The will of the soul remains free; but the body is withdrawn from its empire, at least at times. The Church in her prudence exacts certain signs of the presence of the devil before proceeding to public exorcisms.[16] Most of the supposed possessions are reduced to the intervention of the devil in an overexcited imagination, or in senses weakened by illness, or in temperaments given to melancholy.[17]

[15] *Life*, xxxi; Peers, I, 204 ff., where the Saint describes several manifestations of the devil, in which he shows himself powerless and enraged.

[16] We do not here have to treat at length cases of diabolical possession, because they do not directly interest spiritual life. In cases of possession, the devil, by a special permission of God, takes possession of the body and the sense powers and—without penetrating into the will and the intellect (unless the soul has let him)—exercises his empire by suggestion and physical domination.

[17] In these cases the devil exercises his action by imaginary suggestion. At the beginning, making use of the physical weakness of the subject, or a desire for extraordinary graces, he suggests exhausting mortifications. The physical weakness increasing, he finds in the sense powers a greater docility

Satan can the better exercise his power in these souls, since the control of reason in them is weaker. Debility of soul, often pathological, and temptations of the devil are intermingled to such a point that it is almost impossible to distinguish them.

In this connection Saint Teresa notes, speaking of interior words:

Sometimes—often, indeed—this may be a fancy, especially in persons who are melancholy—I mean, are affected by real melancholy—or have feeble imaginations. Of persons of these two kinds no notice should be taken, in my view, even if they say they see or hear or are given to understand things, nor should one upset them by telling them that their experiences come from the devil. One should listen to them as one would to sick persons. . . .

The real solution is to see that such people have less time for prayer, and also that, as far as is possible, they attach no importance to these fancies. For the devil is apt to take advantage of the infirmity of these souls, to the injury of others, if not to their own as well.[18]

Rare at all times, these external manifestations of the power of the devil seem to be even less frequent in our day, perhaps because the charismatic graces are less visible, and especially because atheism so common today, and the apostasy of the masses, assure to the devil a peaceful external domination.[19] This exterior peace must not make us forget that within souls the struggle is carried on hard and bitter, usually silent, daily, against this enemy that is ceaselessly prowling around us and, as Saint Teresa tells us, "works like a noiseless file." [20]

### 2. MANNER AND PURPOSE OF THE ACTION OF THE DEVIL

The devil, our enemy, tries to bring souls to evil by temptation, to hinder them in their progress to God by disturbing and deceiving them.

---

to his suggestions in the imagination and to sense impressions that he produces.

[18] VI Mansions, iii; Peers, II, 279-80.

[19] Doubtless, however, even in our time there are souls or even societies vowed to the devil, professing to render him a cult or at least to serve his interests in the world. These persons enjoy a certain power which makes them particularly harmful.

[20] I Mansions, ii; 211.

### a. *Temptation*

Temptation properly so-called is rarely the exclusive work of the devil. Ordinarily he uses his knowledge of the dominant tendencies of a soul and his power over the senses in order to make an image more enticing, to stir up an impression, to intensify a pleasure, to quicken thus a desire, or make a solicitation more attractive and more actual, so that it will invade the field of conscience and win the consent of the will.

Holy Scripture describes for us the temptation of our first parents in the garden of paradise. The serpent—the most cunning of animals, notes the inspired writer—mixes truth and falsehood, whets the appetite of their senses, feeds the pride of their mind, succeeds in creating a kind of evidence and thus obtains the consent that consummates the sin. Their eyes are then opened; but the sin has been committed.[21] Thus Adam and Eve lost the supernatural gifts of grace and the preternatural gifts of integrity.

Under diverse forms, temptation still remains the same, and sin produces like effects.

Apart from the first three Mansions, Saint Teresa says very little of temptation properly speaking. But she insists on the obstacles that the devil excels in creating in order to hinder the soul from moving towards divine union.

### b. *Disquiet of soul*

Disquiet of soul is the first weapon that the devil uses against a soul desirous of perfection. Disquiet brings it to a halt, at least for a while, and makes it hesitate as to the course to be taken. It paralyzes the soul's activity, lessening its resistance; and its accompanying terrors may even cause a definite stand-still. But above all, this interior disquiet can so envelop the soul in darkness that it becomes an easy prey to the wiles and strategy of the evil one.

[21] Gen. 3:1-7.

Impressions in the senses, phantoms in the imagination, irrational fears in all the sense powers: such are the means that the devil uses to provoke and prolong disquiet. Saint Teresa points out that, with beginners, he instigates all sorts of anxieties about sacrifices to be made, about the future, loss of health, and the like:

For here the devils once more show the soul these vipers—that is, the things of the world—and they pretend that earthly pleasures are almost eternal: they remind the soul of the esteem in which it is held in the world, of its friends and relatives, of the way in which its health will be endangered by penances . . . Oh, Jesus! What confusion the devils bring about in the poor soul, and how distressed it is, not knowing if it ought to proceed farther or return to the room where it was before.[22]

Elsewhere the Saint says:

Beware also, daughters, of certain kinds of humility which the devil inculcates in us and which make us very uneasy about the gravity of our *past* sins. There are many ways in which he is accustomed to depress us.[23]

Sometimes also "when the mind is greatly distracted and disturbed," this is "produced by the devil." [24] Saint Teresa had long experience of this. She tells us how on some occasions, the devil

suddenly lays hold on my understanding, sometimes by making use of things so trifling that at any other time I should laugh at them. He confuses the understanding and does whatever he likes with it, so that the soul, fettered as it is and no longer its own mistress, can think of nothing but the absurdities which he presents to it—things of no importance. . . . It has sometimes seemed to me, indeed, that the devils behave as though they were playing ball with the soul, so incapable is it of freeing itself from their power.[25]

The experience of Saint John of the Cross confirms Saint Teresa's. In the *Dark Night* the holy Doctor describes the tactics the devil uses to produce disquiet:

[22] II Mansions, i; Peers, II, 214.
[23] *Way of Perfection,* xxxix; Peers, II, 169.
[24] *Life,* xi; Peers, I, 70.
[25] *Ibid.,* xxx; 198-9.

As he [the devil] sees that he cannot succeed in thwarting them in the depth of the soul, he does what he can to disturb and disquiet the sensual part, to which he is able to attain—now by means of afflictions, now by terrors and fears, with intent to disquiet and disturb the higher and spiritual part of the soul by this means, with respect to that blessing which it then receives and enjoys

At other times, when the spiritual communication is not made in any great measure to the spirit, but the senses have a part therein, the devil more easily succeeds in disturbing the spirit and raising a tumult within it, by means of the senses, with these terrors.[26]

In the *Living Flame* he sums up and completes the description:

. . . if perchance any soul enters into high recollection, since he cannot distract it in the way we have described, he labours so that he may at least be able to make it advert to sense by means of horrors, fears or pains of the body, or by outward sounds and noises, in order to bring it out and distract it from the interior spirit, until he can do no more and leaves it.[27]

As we see, the noise made by the devil can be external.[28] The agitation that he creates thus can extend to a whole group, to an entire town, and affect very well-intentioned people:

When, in troublous times, he [the devil] has sown his tares, and seems to be leading men everywhere in his train, half-blinded, and (deceiving them into) believing themselves to be zealous for the right, God raises up someone to open their eyes and bid them look at the fog with which the devil has obscured their path.[29]

These words of Saint Teresa are an evident allusion to the commotion that the devil stirred up when the first convent of the Reform, Saint Joseph of Avila, was being founded. The whole town became excited. Its Council convened and called a meeting of all the religious Orders. There was talk of noth-

[26] *Dark Night,* Bk. II, xxiii; Peers, I, 477-8.
[27] *Living Flame,* st. iii; Peers, III, 196.
[28] Saint Teresa writes: On another occasion I was in choir when I felt a vehement impulse towards recollection. I went out, so that the sisters should not observe it, but all who were near me heard sounds where I was, like the noise of heavy blows, and I myself heard voices near me as though people were discussing something. I could not hear what they were saying, however: so deeply immersed was I in prayer that I heard nothing at all and was not in the least afraid (*Life,* xxxi; Peers, I, 206).
[29] *Way of Perfection,* xxi; Peers, II, 92.

ing but destroying the convent. The Saint herself had suffered an attack of the devil who showed her all the difficulties at once, without its being in her power to think of anything else, and made her pass one of the most terrible hours of her life.[30] The devil had guessed the importance of the work that was beginning; and his zeal for destroying it, appears to us today well justified.

### c. A liar and the father of lies [31]

Disquiet is a preparation. It creates an atmosphere favorable to the decisive action of Satan, in the same way as recollection precedes and prepares one for the action of God. The devil effects this decisive action by means of lies. Repeating the words of Jesus, Saint Teresa calls him "a lover of lies and a lie himself." [32] With souls eager for perfection he will have no chance of success unless he covers evil with the appearances of good. Dissimulation, lies, these are the means that he could not do without; they constitute his whole strategy of attack.

In order to ensure every chance of success for his simulation, he depends on the tendencies of the soul and its desires, giving to evil the appearances of the particular spiritual good desired by the soul. Both the blind tendency and the joy of the satisfied desire seem to impede all control of the reason. Hence, the devil gives consolations which will feed the spiritual greediness of a soul, urging it to excesses in exercises of piety and in mortifications; or, at least, will make it find the aridities that follow spiritual joy, so painful that it will be discouraged. Saint Teresa speaks to us of the false humility suggested by the devil, which would paralyze the soul and withdraw it from perfection.

To counterfeit the supernatural graces of God is a more difficult task to which the devil, however, does not fail to devote himself. There are few extraordinary favors that have

[30] Cf. *Life,* xxvi; Peers, I.
[31] John 8:44.
[32] *Life,* xxv; 165.

not their counterfeit; the devil tries to reproduce their sensible
effects as soon as he has observed them.[33] Even if it is promptly
discovered, the trick leaves an uneasiness in the one who is its
victim. Moreover, the devil does not fail to orchestrate noisily
in order to make it known, and thus to cast a certain discredit
and terror over all marvelous phenomena of the kind.

If the counterfeit is not discovered, it can draw the soul
into errors of considerable practical importance for itself and
its entourage. It withdraws the soul progressively from the action of God until, stripped of the spiritual goods that formerly
shone in it, it falls into a discouragement that the devil tries to
aggravate so as to transform it into despair. In the *Living
Flame,* Saint John of the Cross points out how the devil

takes his stand, with great cunning, on the road which leads from sense
to spirit, deceiving and luring the soul by means of sense, and giving
it sensual things, as we have said, so that it may rest in them and not
escape from him.[34]

Here too the devil, taking advantage of the lights and devotion the soul once received in contemplation, seeks to withdraw it from the dark night of faith in which it is united with
God, and to attract it back to the activity of the faculties which
previously were refreshed by supernatural help.

Besides, the devil is, in general, more particularly active in
the periods of transition which, because of the painful obscurity that reigns then and the novelty of the phenomena that
are produced, offer him more numerous occasions and greater
facility to set his traps.

At other times he takes cover under natural causes and little

---

[33] Saint John of the Cross seems to say that there are no extraordinary
graces that the devil is not authoritzed to reproduce:
When the soul has genuine visions by the instrumentality of the good
angel . . . God also gives the wicked angel leave to present to the soul
false visions of this very type in such a way that the soul which is not
cautious may easily be deceived by the appearance that they bear, as many
souls have been. *Dark Night,* Bk. II, xxiii; Peers, I, 479.
[34] *Living Flame,* st. iii; Peers, III, 93.

by little substitutes his own action for them, which becomes thus progressively malicious.

For the moment we do not have to state precisely these diabolical snares and counterfeits; we shall come upon them again in dealing with the different Mansions. But this is enough for us to guess how much attentive and persistent observation these demoniac tricks suppose in their author, how much psychological penetration, skill in counterfeiting, boldness in tempting. *"Serpens erat callidior omnibus animalibus.* Now the serpent was more cunning than any beast," [35] says the inspired writer, speaking of the serpent that tempted Eve. This trait is true of him still and renders him as formidable for us as he was for our first parents.

## C. Means of recognizing the action of the devil

The tricks and deceits of the devil are often difficult to discern. In order to limit and fix the use of public exorcisms, the Ritual gives the signs of diabolical possession. In her treatment of extraordinary graces, Saint Teresa indicates the marks that prove their preternatural origin. A detailed study would not here be in place. For now, let us gather from Saint Teresa's writings a few counsels that will help, in the majority of cases, to discover the interventions of the devil in the spiritual life.

1. In doubt, the Saint asserts, it is better to be mistrustful and to wait:

Both with infirm and with healthy souls there is invariably cause for misgivings about these things until it becomes clear what kind of spirit is responsible. I believe, too, that it is always better for them to dispense with such things at first.[36]

This distrust does not offend God who owes us proof of His supernatural action. It will not harm the soul which, if it is under the action of God, will find in this struggle a means of showing its virtue and of making progress. For "If they are of

[35] Gen. 3:1.
[36] VI Mansions, iii; Peers, II, 280.

God," adds the Saint, "dispensing with them will help us all the more to advance, since, when put to the proof in this way, they will tend to increase." [37]

Time is needed to observe the fruit of these favors, and it is especially by their fruits that one can recognize their origin: "*A fructibus eorum, cognoscetis eos.* By their fruits you shall know them." [38] our Lord warns us.

2. The first fruit that indicates the action of the devil is the lie. Saint Teresa says:

If they [visions] come from the devil there will soon be signs of the fact, for he will be caught out in a thousand lies.[39]

The false angel of light cannot for long sustain his role without betraying himself in some contradiction, whether through his ignorance of the supernatural, his exaggeration in telling the truth, his use of the bizarre, or the particular lies that this "father of lies" feels he must add to trickery doubly feigned.

This sign, the lack of truth, appears very important to Saint Teresa:

Unless it [a locution] agrees strictly with the Scriptures, take no more notice of it than you would if it came from the devil himself.[40]

3. The interventions of the devil could not produce in the soul the effects of peace and humility that the action of God brings. Jesus said "Learn of me for I am meek and humble of heart." [41] Humility and the sweetness of peace are the perfume of His presence and the sign of His direct action. The devil, the enemy of God and deprived of Him, produces normally the contrary effects. Saint Teresa writes:

[37] VI Mansions, iii; Peers, II, 280.
[38] Matt. 7:16.
[39] VI Mansions, ix; 317.
[40] *Ibid.,* iii; 280.
[41] Matt. 11:29.

After experiencing Satanic locutions, the soul is not in the least docile but seems both bewildered and highly discontented at the same time.[42]

And again:

But he [the devil] will not be able to counterfeit the effects which have been described, or to leave in the soul this peace or light, but only restlessness and turmoil . . . It is quite certain that, when it is so (that the favors come from God), the greater the favor the soul receives, the less by far it esteems itself.[43]

Through experience alone, can one grasp the fully precise meaning of these words: light, peace, trouble, disquiet, employed by Saint Teresa. And so a genuine gift of discernment of spirits, a gift allied to experience, is generally necessary to discern the action of the devil, not only in extraordinary phenomena, but even in ordinary manifestations in which he lurks beneath natural causes, using them subtly for his own purposes. The saints were terrible to the devil because, from the first, their fine spiritual sense discerned his presence and his action.

## D. How to combat the action of the devil

The first condition for triumphing over the devil is not to give in to excessive fear. Assuredly, he is an enemy to be dreaded by reason of his power in the domain of sense and his cleverness; but we must not forget his deficiencies, his ignorance of the supernatural world, his powerlessness to penetrate into the higher faculties of our soul, and his status as a reprobate, which allows him only temporary victories and leaves him eternally conquered.

To let oneself be overcome by terror of him would be as unreasonable as dangerous. The devil cleverly has recourse to this wile to conceal his own inferiority and to lay his snares. It would be to lose our advantages and increase his power and chances of success, to fear him beyond measure. This is what

[42] *Life,* xxi; Peers, I, 161.
[43] VI Mansions, iii; Peers, II, 285.

Saint Teresa has taught us, with all the authority that her many contests with evil spirits gave her. After saying that they tormented her very often, and recounting some of their attacks, she adds:

> May what I have said help the true servant of God to make little account of these horrors, which the devils present us with in order to make us afraid. Let him realize that, every time we pay little heed to them, they lose much of their power and the soul gains much more control over them. We always derive great benefit from these experiences . . .
> The fact is, I realize so clearly now how little power the devils have, if I am not fighting against God, that I am hardly afraid of them at all: for their strength is nothing unless they find souls surrendering to them and growing cowardly, in which case they do indeed show their power.[44]

This scorn, so apparent to the devil, must be accompanied by prudence. And prudence, when it has to fight the devil, will use the supernatural weapons that ensure our superiority, namely, the sacramentals; and of these, most especially holy water, as well as prayer and fasting. As often as it can, a prudent soul will refuse battle to the enemy, escaping his attacks by taking itself through acts of faith and humility, where the devil cannot enter.

Let us say a word as to the arms that the soul must use for the combat, and as to when it must have recourse to the tactics of flight.

### 1. ARMS FOR FIGHTING THE DEVIL

#### a. *Prayer and vigilance*

Vigilance in prayer is an indispensable means for struggling against the devil. Saint Teresa says that one reason for which we ought to give ourselves to mental prayer is that the devil no longer has as much of a chance for tempting us. If the evil spirits "see that we are careless,"

> [they] will work us great harm. And if they know anyone to be changeable, and not resolute in *doing* what is good and firmly deter-

[44] *Life,* xxxi; Peers, I, 207-8.

mined to persevere, they will not leave him alone either by night or by day and will suggest to him endless misgivings and difficulties. This I know very well by experience and so I have been able to tell you about it: I am sure that none of us realize its great importance.[45]

The Church, to show the importance of the struggle against the infernal powers, has approved special prayers: prayers for major exorcisms, exorcisms of Leo XIII, prayer to Saint Michael after private Masses.

The invocation of certain saints who have a particular power over the demons is especially recommended. Prayer to one's guardian angel is certainly efficacious: he has been given the mission to protect us; and against whom would he protect us, if not against the fallen angels whom he can oppose with powers of his angelic nature and of the supernatural order.

### b. *Fasting*

To the apostles who were astonished at not being able to cast out a devil, our Lord said: "This kind can be cast out in no way except by prayer and fasting," [46] indicating thus the special efficacy of fasting for the combat against the infernal powers.

Hagiography shows, in fact, that the saints who had a special dominion over evil spirits were very much given to penance: Saint Basil, Saint Anthony, Saint John of the Cross, Saint Teresa, the holy Curé of Ars.

It seems normal that the mortification of the senses, on which the demons ordinarily act, should first free us from their influence. By making us dominate nature, such mortification renders us like the angels and thus confers on us a certain power over the fallen angels.

### c. *Holy water*

The Church has instituted the sacramentals, those rites or objects on which a particular blessing bestows a special virtue

---

[45] *Way of Perfection*, xxiii; Peers, II, 99.
[46] Mark 9:28.

for preservation against the influence of the devil. Among the sacramentals, Saint Teresa favored the use of holy water:

> From long experience, I have learned that there is nothing like holy water to put devils to flight and prevent them from coming back again. They also flee from the Cross, but return; so holy water must have great virtue. For my own part, whenever I take it, my soul feels a particular and most notable consolation. In fact, it is quite usual for me to be conscious of a refreshment which I cannot possibly describe, resembling an inward joy which comforts my whole soul. This is not fancy, or something which has happened to me only once; it has happened again and again and I have observed it most attentively.[47]

In fact, she asks for holy water every time that she is the object of an attack of the devil, and she chases him away. Here is an example:

> On another occasion the devil was with me for five hours, torturing me with such terrible pains and both inward and outward disquiet that I do not believe I could have endured them any longer. The sisters who were with me were frightened to death and had no more idea of what to do for me than I had of how to help myself . . . The Lord evidently meant me to realize that this was the work of the devil, for I saw beside me a most hideous little Negro, snarling as if in despair at having lost what he was trying to gain. When I saw him, I laughed and was not afraid. Some of the sisters       were with me.
> I said: if you wouldn't laugh at me, I should ask for some holy water. So they brought me some and sprinkled me with it but it did me no good. Then I sprinkled some in the direction of the place where the little Negro was standing and immediately he disappeared and all my troubles went, just as if someone had lifted them from me with his hand, except that I was as tired as if I had been dealt a great many blows.[48]

The Church, in the different prayers for the blessing of water, asks insistently that power be given to this water "to put to flight all power of the enemy, to expel this enemy with all the rebel angels, to drive it away, to destroy the influence of the evil spirit and to cast out the venomous serpent." [49]

[47] *Life*, xxxi; Peers, I, 205.
[48] *Ibid.;* 204-5.
[49] "*Ad effugandum omnem potestatem inimici, et ipsum inimicum eradicare et explantare valeas, cum angelis suis apostaticis . . . omnis infestatio immundi spiritus abigatur, terrorque venenosi serpentis abigatur.*" (Ritual, Blessing of water.)

"I often reflect on the great importance of everything ordained by the Church," comments Saint Teresa, "and it makes
me very happy to find that those words of the Church are so
powerful that they impart their power to the water and make
it so very different from water which has not been blessed." [50]

We can understand, then, what the Venerable Ana de
Jesús deposed at the process of beatification, namely, that the
Saint "never started on a journey without taking holy water.
She was greatly distressed if we forgot it. And so we all used
to carry a little gourd of holy water, suspended to our cincture,
and she wanted to have hers." [51]

## 2. TACTICS

To fight with such arms against the powers of evil is to be
assured of victory. But the saints seem not to desire this struggle and do not seek it. The traveler who crosses a desert infested with brigands does not try to meet them, even if he is
sure of defeating them; he is concerned only with reaching
the end of his journey. Neither does the soul en route to its
God seek out the demons that might stop it, or at least retard
it in its progress by causing it injuries. It stays out of their way.

An excellent strategy is that of flight which shelters the
soul from the attacks, the blows, and the tricks of the devil.
One accomplishes this by moving, through faith and humility,
into the supernatural regions where the devil has no entrance.

### a. *The exercise of faith or anagogical acts*

In the Epistle to the Ephesians, the apostle Saint Paul, describing the armor that the Christian must put on for the spiritual combat, especially emphasizes faith as a defensive arm
against the devil:

Put on the armor of God, that you may be able to stand against the
wiles of the devil. For our wrestling is not against flesh and blood, but

[50] *Life*, xxxi; Peers, I, 205.
[51] *Ibid*. (Cf. French translation by P. Grégoire, Ed. de la Vie Spirituelle,
note, p. 149).

against the Principalities and the Powers, against the world-rulers of
this darkness, against the spiritual forces of wickedness on high. Therefore take up the armor of God, that you may be able to resist in the
evil day, and stand in all things perfect. Stand, therefore, having
girded your loins with truth, and having your feet shod with the readi-
ness of the gospel of peace, in all things taking up the shield of faith,
with which you may be able to quench all the fiery darts of the most
wicked one.[52]

In the *Dark Night,* Saint John of the Cross has an apt commentary on this teaching of the apostle. On entering into contemplation by the exercise of faith, the soul, he says, disguises
itself under a new livery. This livery, made of the theological
virtues, hides it from its enemies. It is the white vestment of
faith that protects it from the devil, for:

Faith is an inward tunic of a whiteness so pure that it completely
dazzles the eyes of the understanding. And thus, when the soul journeys in its vestment of faith, the devil can neither see it nor succeed
in harming it, since it is well protected by faith—more so than by all
the other virtues—against the devil, who is at once the strongest and
the most cunning of enemies.
It is clear that Saint Peter could find no better protection than faith
to save him from the devil, when he said: *"Cui resistite fortes in fide.[53]*
Resist him, steadfast in the faith." [54]

Faith lifts the soul above the domain of the senses, over
which the devil can exercise power, and introduces it into the
supernatural world, into which he cannot enter. Here then, the
soul is inaccessible to its enemy; and consequently, safe from
his attacks and blows.

In his *Souvenirs,* Father Eliseus of the Martyrs, a confidant
of Saint John of the Cross, recalls that the holy Doctor used to
recommend the method of "anagogical acts," or acts of the
theological virtues in order to escape all temptations. He gives
us the teaching of the Saint:

As soon as the first movement or the first attack of a vice makes
itself felt . . . one need not oppose it by an act of the contrary virtue,

[52] Eph. 6:11-6.
[53] I Pet. 5:9.
[54] *Dark Night,* Bk. II, xxi; Peers, I, 471.

according to the first method, but should have recourse immediately to an act or movement of anagogical love which is opposed to the attack. By thus uniting our affection to God, it happens that the soul—by elevating itself—quits the things of earth, presents itself before God, and is united to Him. By this fact, the vice, the temptation of the enemy are frustrated, the temptation fails, the idea of doing evil lacks an object. The soul, stronger there-above where it is loving, than in the body that it animates, divinely withdraws the flesh from temptation, so that the adversary no longer knows how to attack it or to harm it; it is no longer there where it counts on striking it and ruining it. A marvelous thing! the soul seems then to be a stranger to the vicious movement; near its Beloved and united to Him, it is entirely free from that movement on which the devil founded its hopes.[55]

Ordinarily these anagogical acts can succeed in withdrawing the soul and lifting it to supernatural regions only after some exercise in their use. And so the holy Doctor added, according to the same author, that if it happens to beginners that:

in spite of the anagogical act and movement, they notice that the vicious force of the temptation is not completely averted, let them be sure, in order to resist it, to have recourse to all the arms and considerations in their power . . .
Saint John of the Cross emphasized "the excellence and efficacy of this method" which "unites all that strategy offers that is necessary and essential to triumph." [56]

This strategy, which secures at the same time the psychological advantage of diversion and the supernatural help resulting from prompt recourse to God, is easily put to practice once the soul has formed the habit. Flight from the enemy will become spontaneous when the soul learns from experience its

[55] P. Elisée des Martyrs, *Souvenirs;* cf. *Oeuvres de Saint Jean de la Croix,* Hoornaert translation, Bk. II, xxxix.
[56] P. Elisée des Martyrs, loc. cit. Saint Therese of the Child Jesus, too, mentions desertion as an excellent means of conquering the devil:
"Sometimes when the temptation was very severe, I would run like a deserter from the battlefield if I could do so without letting the Sister [a religious who was the occasion of her temptation] guess my inward struggle. . . .
"I spoke just now, dear Mother, of the flight that is my last recourse to escape defeat. It is not honourable, I confess, but during my noviciate, whenever I had recourse to this means, it invariably succeeded" (*Autobiography,* ix, 152).

beneficial results. In the *Dark Night,* Saint John of the Cross writes of the purified soul:

When it feels the disturbing presence of the enemy, then—wondrous thing!—without knowing how it comes to pass, and without any efforts of its own, it enters farther into its own interior depths, feeling that it is indeed being set in a sure refuge, where it perceives itself to be most completely withdrawn and hidden from the enemy. And thus its peace and joy, which the devil is attempting to take from it, are increased.[57]

A specialist in this method, Saint John of the Cross has recourse to it not only against the attacks of the devil, but also against unruly movements of the sense faculties.

### b. *Humility*

In order to escape the ruses of Satan, Saint Teresa recommends especially the *virtue of humility.* This virtue seems to enjoy a sort of immunity: in fact, it excels in discerning the devil's action and suffers no harm from it: "He [the devil] can do little or no harm if the soul is humble," [58] declares Saint Teresa, speaking of locutions of the evil spirit. And elsewhere she says: "God will not permit him to deceive a soul which has no trust whatever in itself." [59]

Satan is fixed in an attitude of pride by his revolt against God. He does not know how to be humble nor does he understand humility. All his counterfeits, even counterfeits of humility, always bear visible marks of pride. The person who is humble, habituated to the sweet perfume of Christ, promptly detects them by this sign. But the regions in which the humble man lives are not known to the devil. He is ignorant of the reactions of humility; he is always disconcerted and vanquished by it.

On the eve of her profession, Saint Therese of the Child Jesus suffered attacks from the devil:

[57] *Dark Night,* Bk. II, xxiii; Peers, I, 477.
[58] VI Mansions, iii; Peers, II, 285.
[59] *Life,* xxv; Peers, I, 161.

The devil—for it was he—made me feel sure that I was wholly un-suited for life in the Carmel, and that I was deceiving my superiors by entering on a way to which I was not called . . . I cannot describe the agony I endured. What was I to do in such a difficulty?

She sends for her Novice Mistress to come out of the choir, tells her of her temptation and, she adds, "the devil was put to instant flight by my humble avowal." [60]

There is, under God's grace, no adversary more formidable to the devil than souls that are both weak and humble, for:

The weak things of the world has God chosen to put to shame the strong, and the base things of the world and the despised has God chosen, and the things that are not, to bring to naught the things that are.[61]

Hence, Saint Teresa has no fear of the evil spirits in spite of the power they can use:

Not a fig shall I care then for all the devils in hell: it is they who will fear me. I do not understand these fears. "Oh, the devil, the devil!" we say, when we might be saying "God! God!" and making the devil tremble. Of course we might, for we know he cannot move a finger unless the Lord permits it. Whatever are we thinking of? I am quite sure I am more afraid of people who are themselves terrified of the devil than I am of the devil himself. For he cannot harm me in the least, whereas they, especially if they are confessors, can upset people a great deal.[62]

To chase off the terrors is not, however, sufficient. We must recognize the providential role of the devil in our trials on earth. Certainly, he can draw us to evil, but, as Saint John of the Cross notes:

It must be known in this connection that, when the good angel per-mits the devil to gain this advantage of assailing the soul . . . he does it to purify the soul and to prepare it by means of this spiritual vigil for some great spiritual favour and festival which he desires to grant it, for he never mortifies save to give life, neither humbles save to exalt.[63]

[60] *Autobiography*, viii, 119.
[61] I Cor. 1:25 f.
[62] *Life*, xxv; Peers, I, 165.
[63] *Dark Night*, Bk. II, xxiii; Peers, I, 480.

It is, then, to increase our merits, to make our virtues more pure and more strong, our progress towards Him more rapid, that God permits the devil to tempt us and try us.[64]

[64] In a vivid and powerful page, Tauler describes thus the advantages of temptations and the means of conquering them:

"When the deer is closely hounded by dogs through forests and mountains, the heat of excitement brings on a thirst and desire to drink, keener than in any other animal. Just as the deer is pursued by dogs, so the beginner (in the ways of charity) is hounded by temptations. Especially when he turns away from the world, he is closely pursued by seven strong mastiffs, vigorous and agile. . . . The more spirited and impetuous the chase, the greater ought to be our thirst for God and the ardor of our desire. It sometimes happens that one of the dogs catches the deer and puts its teeth into the stomach of the beast. When the deer cannot get rid of the dog, it drags it along near to a tree and knocks it so hard against the tree as to break its head and thus is freed. . . . That is precisely what man must do. When he cannot master his dogs, his temptations, he must in great haste run to the tree of the Cross and of the Passion of our Lord Jesus Christ, strike his dog, his temptation, against it and break its head. That is where he triumphs over every temptation and frees himself of them completely" (*Sermons* of Tauler, Monday before Palm Sunday, from the French of Hugueny, I, 258).

*Spiritual advancement grows love for the spiritually lost*
*link to the prophet Elijah*

*Link between spirituality and apostolate*
*Key in Theresa's work*

# CHAPTER VIII
# The Teresian Spirit

> As the Lord liveth in whose sight I
> stand . . . With zeal have I been zeal-
> ous for the Lord.[1]

A mother of spiritual souls, *Mater spiritualium,* Saint
Teresa addresses herself only to those who are cultivating the
interior life, to those "who do eventually enter the castle." [2]

"Aristocratic spirituality," this is sometimes called. But can
we truly say that Saint Teresa is unconcerned about the souls
that are living spiritually inactive and paralyzed in sin as that
man physically was, "who had lain beside the pool for thirty
years;" [3] or like those even who "remain in the outer court of
the castle, which is the place occupied by the guards; they are
not interested in entering it, and have no idea what there is in
that wonderful place, or who dwells in it, or even how many
rooms it has"? [4] Such a reproach would testify to a complete
misunderstanding not only of the soul of Teresa but of the
spirit that animates all her work.

Saint Teresa does not abandon the souls that she cannot draw
after her because sin holds them fixed in the immobility of
death. Indeed, the farther she advances, the more frequently she
looks back to them with a glance tenderly kind. By the time she
reaches the summits, her compassion has become immense and
her love so great that it absorbs her. A new spirit springs from

[1] Elias's battle cry (III Kings 17; 19:10) adopted as a motto by the
Order of Carmel.
[2] I Mansions, i; Peers, II, 204.
[3] *Ibid.*
[4] *Ibid.;* 203.

it, a spirit of zeal which transforms the life of Teresa and passes into her spirituality.

To ignore this, would be to misunderstand the richness of the Teresian soul and the vivifying principle which gives power to her spirituality, as well as its movement and orientation.

## A. Zeal of the Prophet Elias

In founding the reformed Convent of Saint Joseph of Avila, Saint Teresa thought only of satisfying her own aspirations for perfect union with God; enclosing herself within so strict a cloister, she dreamed only of intimacy with Jesus.

But, in this atmosphere so apt to raise the soul to God and unite it with Him alone, hearts were so soon set aflame that Saint Teresa began to suspect that God had His own special designs in it all.

And then news came to them from France where the wars of religion were raging; stories were told of the moral and spiritual misery of the Indians in the New World. News and stories together did more than supply fresh fuel for the increasing ardors of divine love; they opened up new horizons and surpassingly high desires for intimacy with Christ Jesus:

At about this time there came to my notice the harm and havoc that were being wrought in France by these Lutherans and the way in which their unhappy sect was increasing. This troubled me very much, and, as though I could do anything, or be of any help in the matter, I wept before the Lord and entreated Him to remedy this great evil.[5]

It breaks my heart to see so many souls travelling to perdition, she continues. I would the evil were not so great and I did not see more being lost every day.[6]

The zeal that consumed Teresa at the account of the Protestant devastation was the same as that which burned in the soul of the prophet Elias, the father of Carmel: "What are you doing, Elias?" the angel of the Lord says to him. And the

[5] *Way of Perfection*, i; Peers, II, 3.
[6] *Ibid.*; 4.

prophet answers: "With zeal have I been zealous for the Lord God of hosts: for the children of Israel have forsaken thy covenant. They have thrown down thy altars, they have slain thy prophets, *zelo zelatus sum pro Domino Deo exercituum.*" [7] The avowal of the prophet became the motto of the Teresian Carmel.

Thus Saint Teresa recovered the fullness of the spirit of Elias. If it is true that the prophet was consumed by the ardors of justice and Teresa by the ardors of love, that difference reflects the different laws under which they lived: Elias belonged to the law of fear, Teresa lived under the law of love. But an identical attitude of contemplative prayer before God, enkindled in them the same divine fire that the shock of similar events caused to burst forth in consuming flames.

These ardors of love are illumining for Teresa. They enlarge her spiritual horizons. She passes on from Christ Jesus, whose intimate love she had come to seek in Carmel, and finds the whole Christ, the Church, the souls who are part of it, even those who are outside but nevertheless called to it. She experiences what takes place in Christ; she feels the suffering of love refused, of the redemptive blood shed uselessly; great pity for the souls who go down to hell for having scorned the love of their God. She lives the dogma of the Church; she enters into the sufferings and anguish of the Church militant, penetrating into the depths of the heart of Christ.

Love of the Church is going to dominate thereafter the whole life of Teresa. It becomes a powerful passion, absorbing all her personal desires—her thirst for intimacy and need for union. It takes into its service all the energies of her soul and her external activity, and inspires all her works until it finds in her last breath its simplest and most sublime expression: "I am a daughter of the Church."

To work for the Church is the vocation of Teresa, the purpose of her Reform:

[7] III Kings 19:10.

> If your prayers and desires and disciplines and fasts are not per-
> formed for the intentions of which I have spoken, reflect (and believe)
> that you are not carrying out the work or fulfilling the object for
> which the Lord has brought you here.[8]

These clear words with which Saint Teresa concludes Chapter III of the *Way of Perfection* fix our attention on what we
have called her spirit, the dynamism of her spirituality, and
the aim of her work.

Christ Jesus Himself gave to these words a magnificent
clarity the day on which He united Teresa to Himself by the
bonds of spiritual marriage. As a sign of His definitive union,
He gave her a nail and caused her to hear these words:

> Behold this nail. It is a sign that from today onward thou shalt be
> My bride . . . henceforward thou shalt regard My honour . . . as that
> of My very bride.[9]

At the summit of Carmel, one is crucified with Christ, and
one is entirely given to works for His glory. It is towards this
summit glimpsed in the light, that Teresian spirituality directs from the very beginning the gaze of those who come to
its school, orientates their efforts and their desires: "I have
come to Carmel in order to pray for priests and for the conversion of sinners," said Saint Therese of the Child Jesus
upon entering Carmel. The little saint had understood her
vocation. It is necessary for us, too, to understand the Carmelite vocation, in order to place in its proper perspective the
whole teaching of Saint Teresa.

## B. Prayer and sacrifice

Now, it is no longer question of joys to be had in loving
contact with the Master, but of struggles to be endured for
the love of Christ and the salvation of souls. But how, in so
strict a cloister, could one satisfy such desires and serve the
Church usefully? The Saint herself wonders: "Seeing that I

[8] *Way of Perfection*, iii; Peers, II, 15.
[9] *Relations*, xxxv; Peers, I, 352.

was a woman and a sinner, and incapable of doing all I should like in the Lord's service." [10]

Because it is supernatural, her love is not led astray by its ardor. The Saint is more realistic than ever; in order to make reparation and to serve, she will begin by accomplishing perfectly her duties as a religious:

As my whole yearning was, and still is, that, as He has so many enemies and so few friends, these last should be trusty ones, I determined to do the little that was in me—namely, to follow the evangelical counsels as perfectly as I could, and to see that these few nuns who are here should do the same, confiding in the great goodness of God.[11]

The passion that had arisen in her soul obliges her now to rethink in some way her ideal of religious life and the obligations that flow from it.

Prayer was already the principal function of Carmel in the Church. How necessary it is for those who fight for the Church, Saint Teresa shows all through Chapter III of the *Way of Perfection* from which we are quoting. This prayer must obtain for them "the qualities needed for the struggle" and preservation from the dangers of the world.

Without ever leaving her cloister, Saint Teresa will be able to take part in those battles of the Church and give her whole strength for the victory of Christ:

All of us by busying ourselves in prayer for those who are defenders of the Church, and for the preachers and learned men who defend her, should do everything we could to aid this Lord of mine.[12]

The apostolic role thus assigned to prayer contributes to its higher perfection. For if prayer is to be powerful, it must in fact be perfect, so true is it that the efficacy of prayer depends especially on the degree of sanctity of the soul who makes it. Thus love for souls is an incentive to strive for union with God. "Let us strive to live in such a way," writes the Saint,

[10] *Way of Perfection*, i; Peers, II, 3.
[11] *Ibid.*
[12] *Ibid.*

"that our prayers may be of avail to help these servants of God." [13]

Instead of distracting the Carmelite nun from her contemplative prayer, zeal for souls becomes a spur to greater union with God. It urges her to use all the natural and the supernatural means that technique and grace offer, in order to possess God more closely and to draw on His omnipotence.

This zeal opens up horizons of sacrifice that were unknown when desire was set only on intimate union with God. Certainly, Teresa had said, "to see God we must die." And yet she herself admitted that when she founded the Convent of Saint Joseph of Avila, she had not at all thought of practising austerities there:

> When this convent [Saint Joseph's, Avila] was originally founded . . . it was not my intention that there should be so much austerity in external matters, nor that it should have no regular income: on the contrary, I should have liked there to be no possibility of want.[14]

First then, zeal for souls immolates a certain measure of self-seeking that still remained when the soul was seeking personal intimacy with God.

But more than that, with Christ Jesus who entered into His Passion for the supreme sacrifice after offering His priestly prayer, it understands that prayer for the Church finds its efficacy only in sacrifice.

After Teresa discovered the Church, and after a great compassion for souls in consequence took possession of her, penance at Carmel became more austere and complete immolation became a need and a law.

## C. Apostolic works

The great prophet whose spirit Saint Teresa rediscovered in its plenitude used to leave his solitude sometimes to go into action. In fact, among those prophets that are called prophets

[13] *Way of Perfection*, iii; Peers, II, 11.
[14] *Ibid.*, i; 3.

of action, in contrast to the writer prophets, Elias is the greatest. His interventions in the life of Israel are frequent and resounding.

What is Saint Teresa going to do? Is she going to throw herself into action? How could she not feel the desire?

> I was so distressed at the way all these souls were being lost that I could not contain myself. I went to one of the hermitages, weeping sorely, and called upon Our Lord, beseeching Him to find me a means of gaining some soul for His service . . . How I envied those who could spend their lives ministering to others for the love of Our Lord, even though they might suffer a thousand deaths! [15]

To these ardent desires for apostolic work, Jesus Himself gives the answer:

> While suffering this terrible distress, I was praying one night when Our Lord appeared to me in His usual way, and said to me very lovingly, as if He wished to bring me comfort: "Wait a little, daughter, and thou shalt see great things." [16]

What is the meaning of this promise? What will the great things be? The visit of P. Rubeo, superior general of the Carmelites, will make known the answers. The Father General, during his sojourn at Avila (1566), manifests to Saint Teresa a most affectionate interest in the Convent of Saint Joseph which is realizing his dearest desires as father of the Order. He commands the Saint to found on the same model as many convents as will be asked of her.

God has spoken through the superior of the Order. Teresa cannot hesitate. Besides, this command corresponds with her new-born desires. The world is on fire, and Christ is not loved. Since numbers are an element in strength, the fortresses must be multiplied where courageous Christians will gather, and from which will rise the hymn of that perfect prayer that will save souls and contribute to the triumph of the Church.

She sacrifices, then, the joys of solitude and the sweet peace

[15] *Foundations,* i; Peers, III, 3-4.
[16] *Ibid.;* 4.

of the first years of Saint Joseph of Avila, for the hard task of her foundations which she begins in 1567 with a convent at Medina del Campo.

She kindles her own ardor in the soul of her daughters and communicates to them her intentions at the same time as her science of prayer. They will be contemplatives and intercessors whose prayer is all given to the Church:

> Oh, my sisters in Christ! Help me to entreat this of the Lord, Who has brought you together here for that very purpose. This is your vocation; this must be your business; these must be your desires; these your tears; these your petitions.[17]

As for Teresa, she will travel over all the roads of Spain, and valiantly persevere in her austere task until death comes to her at Alba de Tormes on her way back from the foundation of Burgos, the most difficult of all according to her testimony. Thus this sublime contemplative became a woman of action whose competence in all matters, whose effective daring and prodigious works are the equal of the most enterprising of the apostles.

But in the "great things" promised by our Lord, Saint Teresa saw something more than the foundation of convents of Carmelite nuns. These did not suffice for her zeal. She dreamed of prolonging her conquering action by extending the Reform to the friars of the Order.

Rubeo, who during his visit had given wide permissions for the foundations of nuns, becomes hesitant when there is question of the friars. But the Saint shows herself to be an insistent advocate. The Father General will send after his departure, then, the permissions asked for. They are limited and yet they fill the Saint with joy.

Without delay she sets to work on the dearest of her projects, the one whose realization will cost her the most suffering and will raise the worst tempests. But the work seems to her so important. Is it not through the Discalced Carmelite

Fathers that her whole plan will be realized, that her conquering zeal will be satisfied, and her ideals will take final form?

"Being a woman and a sinner," she says, she sees herself powerless to do what she would like for the glory of God. In her plan, her sons—who will be priests, learned men, contemplatives, and apostles—are to supply for her lack and extend her action. She wants them to be such that they can sustain her daughters, govern her convents, but also do combat for the Church and cross seas for the conquest of souls. She surrounds them with respect and maternal solicitude. She had trembled before the austerities of Duruelo, in the thought that the devil wanted perhaps to destroy her dream by these excesses; but now her joy is boundless when she finds in P. Gracián the talents and the grace of Carmel such as her zeal desired.

In little time, Gracián will be the first superior of the separated province of Discalced Carmelites. The divine promises are realized. In the great things that have been done by the creative genius of Saint Teresa, the plenitude of her spirit and of her zeal fructifies.

## D. Summary of characteristic elements

We have dealt at length with the plans of Saint Teresa and their realization, only in order to understand better her spiritual doctrine. A work of reform and a spiritual doctrine sprang simultaneously from her soul: they are both fruits of the same living spirit, the one completing and throwing light on the other. In comparing them, we can understand more clearly the characteristic elements and the aim of Saint Teresa's spiritual teaching.

1. Her writings and the external organization of the Reform show us in the first place that the Saint leads the soul to the summits of perfection by the way of prayer and of contemplation. There is no other way for her and her disciples. All must be contemplatives.

2. These contemplatives must all become apostles. Saint Teresa does not receive among her following those souls who would come only to learn the ways of prayer and the secret of divine intimacy: beyond Christ Jesus, she discovers to all the Church and dedicates them all to its service. The transforming union or spiritual marriage fructifies in spiritual maternity. It is the fecundity of divine union that Saint Teresa emphasizes as the principal and last end to be attained. The texts cited above, as well as the works of Saint Teresa, prove this abundantly.

Saint Therese of the Child Jesus, the most illustrious of the daughters of Saint Teresa, declares that she found her vocation the day that she understood that in the Church she would be love and would thus fulfil the vital function of the heart.

3. This fecundity will at first be that of prayer, powerful because perfect and immolated. After offering His priestly prayer for the Church, Jesus goes into the garden of Gethsemane and gives Himself up—He, infinite purity—to the torments of sin. Prostrate on the ground under the weight of the sin of the world He frees us of it, praying in painful anguish; and sweating blood, He secures the efficacy of His prayer of union for the apostles and for us. Elias, the father of Carmel, had already groaned painfully, too, in the cave of Horeb under the weight of the sin of Israel: "They have destroyed thy altars and have slain thy prophets," he answered the angel; "and I, I have been zealous for the Lord God of hosts." [18]

Teresa, in the choir at Saint Joseph of Avila or in the hermitages, wept and moaned also for the sin of the world:

I was so afflicted by the loss of so many souls that I did not know what to do. I withdrew into a hermitage and wept tears in abundance.[19]

[18] III Kings 19:14.
[19] *Foundations*, i; Peers, III, 3.

Saint Teresa and her daughters are to continue for the Church the prayer of Jesus at Gethsemane. Their way of life and their particular spirituality prepare them for this function of Christ's priesthood. Fidelity to their vocation should lead them where their souls, now purified, are at the same time consumed in the flames of divine love and, like their divine spouse in His Passion, clothed in the oppressive mantle of the world's sin; and where, like the Lamb who takes away the sins of the world, they offer to God's Majesty that ardent agonizing prayer which brings purification and salvation to other souls.

It is thus that Saint Therese of the Child Jesus, at the end of her life, bathed in the floods of the divine mercy that penetrates and surrounds her, eats the black bread of modern incredulity by undergoing violent temptations against faith.

This prayer, highly contemplative and eminently efficacious, is the first form of the Teresian apostolate, the first end of Teresian spirituality.

4. Could it be the only end? Could the spiritual doctrine of Saint Teresa be apt only for forming great contemplatives, perfect pray-ers in the service of the Church? Some seem to think so.

In fact, the marvelous success and profound influence that the Carmelite monasteries have had in France for three centuries have contributed to create the impression that the whole of Carmel is contained within the high walls and stern grilles that shut out the noise and contact of the world; and that the spiritual doctrine of Saint Teresa is destined only for contemplatives who can create for themselves a special setting for recollection, and is not at all adapted to an apostolate of action. This error is all the more regrettable in that it hides from the eyes of many a spiritual doctrine of the apostolate that is at the same time most simple and most elevated, particularly suited to form perfect apostles.

Saint Teresa was a remarkable woman of action. Her spirituality found her quite prepared for the life of exterior works that she led for fifteen years. And it was during that period, that her doctrine received its perfect formulation. Moreover, in order to draw into the ways of perfection those whom she considered as her fathers and her sons, all of whom were leading an apostolic life, (the Discalced Carmelite Fathers whom she had engendered to the perfect Carmelite life, and her directors who had commanded her to write: the Jesuits Balthazar Alvarez and Gaspar de Salazar, the Dominicans Báñez and García de Toledo) she had only to give them, as to her own Carmelites, the spiritual science she had lived.

But where can one find this spiritual doctrine, and in what way is it distinguished from her contemplative doctrine? To answer those questions, one could underline here and there in her writings some counsels particular to those who have a mission to work for the Church, and note that in the book of her *Life* and the *Way of Perfection,* written before the extension of the Carmelite Reform, it is the contemplative that is explaining her doctrine on prayer; while in the *Interior Castle* it is the contemplative apostle, become the spouse of Christ, who speaks and gives a doctrine that is higher, wider, and more complete on the spiritual life.

In reality, the spiritual doctrine of the apostolate in the Teresian teaching cannot be separated nor distinguished from her contemplative doctrine. In this spirituality, contemplation and the apostolate are solidly united; they are fused into one life of the soul and happily complete each other. They are two aspects of a harmonious whole, two manifestations of the same profound life.[20]

At most, some will say, they correspond to two phases of the spiritual life. At first the soul is invited especially to keep itself for God, for it is important above all that it be

[20] Here, we can only state the fact. These statements will have their development and proof in the exposition of the Teresian doctrine, and will be indicated in the general outline at the beginning of this volume.

united with Him; later it is permitted, and finally it has the duty, to work for the good of souls. Contemplative phase and active phase, it would seem. Let us not be too quick to classify by using labels that we should recognize at once as inexact. The recollection of the first period is destined only to accumulate forces for the apostolate. As to the activity of the second period, it in turn is profitable in the first place for contemplation which it purifies from all egoism; and it prepares the soul for the transforming union.

Having sprung from her soul and from her life, the spirituality of Saint Teresa takes from these its double character, highly contemplative and astoundingly active. It forms spiritual souls who are still apostles with a consuming zeal when they have learned to remain constantly in the presence of the living God, according to the twofold word of the prophet which became the motto of the Teresian Carmel: *The Lord liveth in whose sight I stand . . . With zeal have I been zealous for the Lord of hosts!*

# CHAPTER IX

# Spiritual Growth

> *The soul does not grow in the way the body does, though we speak as if it did, and growth does in fact occur.*[1]

The divine life develops like "a grain of mustard seed which, when sown upon the earth is the smallest of all the seeds, but . . . it grows up and becomes larger than any other herb, and puts out great branches";[2] or again, like "leaven which a woman took and buried in three measures of flour, until all of it was leavened."[3] These parables of the Gospel symbolize the growth of grace in the soul and lay emphasis on its power to enlarge the whole substance. Yet one may ask how that growth takes place, and by what signs it shall be recognized. That is a mystery of which Saint Teresa fathomed the depths uncommonly well, familiar as she was with the complexities of our nature and the divine obscurities. Her teaching, which we shall try to synthesize, does not dispel the obscurity of the mystery; but, because with the aid of some elucidating signs it fixes the classical stages of progress towards God, it is eminently precious.

## A. Different aspects and stages

The vision of the *Castle* or of a holy soul, helps to clarify the essential point of Teresian teaching as to spiritual growth. Teresa saw a globe of crystal, with apartments more and more brilliant the nearer they were to the center where God is,

[1] *Life*, xv; Peers, I, 94.
[2] Mark 4:31-2.
[3] Matt. xiii:33.

the inner fire. Thus from its outer spheres, the soul goes to its inner center, to be there united perfectly with God, to live in His light, submissive to His action.

1. Perfection, then, consists in perfect union with God, transforming union or spiritual marriage. Spiritual progress is marked by a progress in union, which is indicated in a symbolic way in the vision by a growing intensity of light. Such is the teaching of Saint Teresa, firm and precise: God is our end; to attain to Him is perfection; the soul is perfect in the measure in which it is near to Him.

In this movement towards God—from the union of grace in its minimum of vitality, which is the point of departure, until transforming union, which is the term—Saint Teresa distinguishes seven stages or mansions, marked in the vision of the *Castle* by increase of light; in reality, by progress in union with God. "I have spoken here only of seven Mansions," she says, "yet in each there are comprised many more, both above and below and around." [4] And elsewhere she remarks that the sixth and seventh Mansions "might be fused in one: there is no closed door to separate the one from the other." [5] She could have decreased or increased the number of mansions; but she had to choose, and the number seven, which is the perfect number, permits a logical and rational division.

Among these seven Mansions, if we omit the first which can be considered as the point of departure, we distinguish three that mark clearly characterized states of union: the third Mansions, where the natural activity of the soul, aided by grace, triumphs; the fifth Mansions, in which union of will takes place; the seventh Mansions, enlightened by the transforming union. The three other Mansions are periods of transition; or better, of preparation.

The later ones are normally more painful and more obscure than the preceding. Dryness dominates in the second Man-

4 VII Mansions, iv; Peers, II, 351.
5 VI Mansions, iv; 287.

sions; the night of the senses in the fourth; and the night of the spirit in the sixth. More painful and more dangerous, the trials of the soul here sometimes detain it for a long time, or cause it to fall, so many are the stumbling-blocks to be met. The solicitude of the director will then have to be more attentive and more paternal. For enlightenment, he will find helpful the descriptions and counsels of Saint John of the Cross who became the doctor of the nights in order to lead souls to the union of love. In the spiritual itinerary, these stages of ascent become thus the most important.

2. It would be an over-simplification, however, to limit the study of spiritual growth to a consideration of progress in union, which is its essential characteristic. This growth presents many other aspects; in the first place, the activity of the two living forces that bring it about: the love of God for the soul, and the love of the soul for God.

These two loves progressively harmonize their action which becomes gradually more powerful in the course of spiritual growth. Two very distinct phases appear in the progress considered under this aspect. In the first phase, which includes the first three Mansions, God, assuring the soul of His ordinary grace or general help, leaves to it the initiative and direction in its spiritual life. In the second phase, which extends from the fourth Mansions to the seventh, God intervenes progressively in the life of the soul by a help called particular, which makes itself more and more potent, takes the initiative away from the soul, imposes upon it submission and abandonment, and finally establishes the perfect rule of God; and the soul, now a true child of God, is moved by the Spirit of God.

This double activity of God and the soul is modified, though always harmonizing, throughout the different Mansions. The action of God becomes more and more profound and marked in the soul, manifesting His Christ progressively to it. During the first phase—that is, during the first three Mansions—God assures the soul of the general help of His

grace and leaves the faculties their full independence, offering to them the humanity of Jesus Christ, that they may be
nourished with it and be attached to the unique Mediator who
alone can lead them to the summits. During the second phase,
God intervenes with His special help which is His direct action in the soul. At the beginning, the fourth Mansions, He
introduces the soul into the light of the Word who, in manifesting Himself, veils our images and thoughts. By means
of recollection, quiet, or contemplative dryness, He orientates
sense towards spirit, adapts it to the supernatural operations
which are in the latter, and habituates it to bear peacefully
the mystery that is still dark and often painful.

The union of will is effected in the fifth Mansions by the
Wisdom of Love which will be able thereafter, thanks to its
hold on the master faculty, to purify and to form the soul for
the realization of the eternal design of God. This eternal design is the whole Christ or the Church. It inspires all God's
action in souls and envelops each individual soul.

In the sixth Mansions, Wisdom brings the soul into the
mystery of the Church and communicates to it the riches of
Christ as well as His redemptive sufferings. These are both
shared in the depths of the spirit by delightful substantial
touches or by cruel abandonments; and in the operative faculties by favors and by exterior trials. This double work of
enrichment and purification—the cruel suffering of which is
assuaged by the presence and action of the Blessed Mother
ever Virgin—prepares directly for the summits of contemplation and for the fecundity of the apostolate exercised under
the impulsion of God.

In the seventh Mansions, in the transforming union, where
his purified gaze can enjoy the divine Presence, the contemplative has found his place in the Church; and in it, fulfills
perfectly his mission.

The soul's own activity goes hand in hand with the sanctifying action of God in order to cooperate with it, in prayer

as well as in the practice of the virtues. In the course of its development, the soul's action too will take different forms. During the first phase, the initiative of the soul in prayer consists in a quest for God by ways that become progressively simplified. Attention to prayer is predominant, even to the point that asceticism here resolves itself into efforts at recollection and whatever can favor it. The soul will also labor at correcting its exterior faults. During the second phase, asceticism will become more interior and more energetic in order to destroy the capital sins that appear on the spiritual plane; while during contemplative prayer, the soul will have to cooperate energetically with the action of God by self-surrender in a silence often painful.

In these regions where the divine exigencies become at the same time more imperious and more delicate, the virtues of the soul are more spiritual, more profound, and more docile. The changing forms of these exigencies and of these virtues, and the atmosphere so to speak that seems to reign in each of the Mansions, can be characterized by attributing faith as the special virtue of souls in the fourth Mansions; obedience and love of God, in the fifth; hope and charity, in the sixth; perfect chastity and charity in the seventh.[6]

---

[6] We do not find formulated, with Saint Teresa, the division into the purgative, illuminative, and unitive ways. If we wanted to apply this convenient classification to the plan of the Teresian progression, it would be necessary to distinguish three purgative and illuminative periods preparatory to the three states of union that have been indicated. Thus we should have:

Purgative period:

| | | |
|---|---|---|
| Aridities of the second Mansions. | Night of the senses, fourth Mansions. | Night of the spirit, sixth Mansions. |

Illuminative period:

| | | |
|---|---|---|
| Prayer of simplicity, third Mansions. | Contemplative prayer of quiet and illumination. | Spiritual marriage. Substantial touches. |

Unitive period:

| | | |
|---|---|---|
| Union of the third Mansions. | Union of will. | Transforming union. |

The action of God and the co-operation of the soul, in such close dependence on each other, produce a real transformation; Saint Teresa is pleased to point out its profound effects, and she illustrates it by comparison with the silkworm:

You have heard of the wonderful way in which silk is made—a way which no one could invent but God—and how it comes from a kind of seed which looks like tiny peppercorns (I have never seen this, but only heard of it, so if it is incorrect in any way the fault is not mine). When the warm weather comes, and the mulberry trees begin to show leaf, this seed starts to take life; until it has this sustenance, on which it feeds, it is as dead. The silkworms feed on the mulberry-leaves until they are full-grown, when people put down twigs, upon which, with their tiny mouths, they start spinning silk, making themselves very tight little cocoons, in which they bury themselves. Then, finally, the worm, which was large and ugly, comes right out of the cocoon a beautiful white butterfly.[7]

This comparison, "very appropriate" according to Saint Teresa, and one to which she returns several times, shows the transforming action of charity which divinizes as it develops, creates new virtues, perfects the natural powers, and produces a new and perfect type of humanity, a soul transformed in God.

One of the most notable effects of this transformation is the formation of the apostle, realized progressively. In the first phase, corresponding to the first three Mansions, the soul exercises its apostolic mission with its natural activity aided by grace; in the second phase God takes hold of it to make of it a perfect instrument for His designs. While His reign is being established in it in the fourth Mansions, it would be harmful for the soul to try to share with others the spiritual treasures it is receiving. It is not yet so fully in possession of them that it can so give without danger of losing all. In the fifth Mansions, God, having established His reign in the will, can already use the soul as an instrument and confide to it a mission—an imperfect instrument that the exterior trials and interior purifications of the sixth Mansions will bring to perfection. The transforming union makes the

[7] V Mansions, ii; Peers, II, 253.

perfect apostle, burning with zeal, docile to the divine motions, and hence astoundingly powerful.

These interior transformations have echoes that can be perceived in the psychological consciousness. Independently of the extraordinary favors that produce in it real shocks and leave their salutary wounds, through passing and sometimes overflowing joys, through sufferings often violent and by means of them, grace silently and slowly creates in the depths of the soul a region of peace. Here is a refuge to which noise and tempests attain only rarely, an oasis with springs of strength and of joy whose benefits are progressively extended, assuring stability and balance, until the plenitude and flowering of the seventh Mansions.

Spiritual growth presents itself, we can see, as a living and complex development of which one can distinguish but not disengage the multiple aspects. The desire of showing at the same time the living unity and the living richness, made us draw up a synthetic chart which will indicate also the division of our work and will justify the choice of the subjects treated.[8]

### B. Mystery of growth

An attentive study of the chart which, by various and precise characteristics, indicates the regular process of spiritual growth, might give the impression that it is easy to discern the progress of a soul and to situate it in this progression. On the contrary, the examination of numerous concrete cases yields evidence of the complexity of souls and the mystery of spiritual growth.

[8] The chart will be found in the beginning of this volume. More often than not, the teaching given is of interest not only for the period of spiritual life to which it has been attached. We put it, however, at the place where it seemed the most necessary and answered to the dominant note of the moment. Thus, the soul will not wait for the fifth Mansions in order to practise obedience; but in this period, the union of will makes it practise this perfectly. Likewise, recourse to the Blessed Virgin is at all times indispensable, but the desolate poverty of the sixth Mansions makes the Blessed Virgin exercise her providential role as Mother of Mercy.

Every growth, from that of the plant which draws from the mould of the earth organic elements which it transforms and assimilates, up to the growth of the Infant Jesus in whom were manifested progressively the riches of wisdom and of grace that were in Him, remains mysterious.

1. In spiritual growth, the mystery is more complete. On the one hand, in the growth of material things it is only the mode according to which life assimilates and uses for its vital functions inanimate matter, that is obscure. The external signs of organic development are apparent. But in the case of the spiritual growth of the soul, grace, like the very life of God of which it is a participation, is altogether hidden from us. In heaven we shall be able, with the light of glory, to see God as He is and ourselves as we shall then be with our divine riches. Meanwhile, these spiritual realities remain, for us, buried in the shadow of mystery, for lack of a power to seize them directly.

There exist, however, authentic manifestations of grace; and the gifts of the Holy Spirit give us a certain experience of it. But, how difficult they are to observe, these manifestations of the supernatural, so irregular are they, so mixed with foreign elements! How incomplete and intermittent, even for the most favored contemplatives, is this experience that we have through gifts of the Holy Spirit.

When it becomes incarnate in human nature, the supernatural assumes the forms of the individuals who receive it. It appears to us, then, under aspects as diverse as the individuals themselves. The exterior actions which it produces are as different as the temperaments that are their instruments.[9] Rarely in fact, it seems to us, does the action of God produce directly a sensible phenomenon. Like the white light of the sun that shines upon the landscape and makes all its colors

---

[9] Virtue presents itself exteriorly with the particular forms of the temperament: here, smiling; there, more austere; elsewhere timid or daring, without our being able to conclude, by considering these external traits alone, whether charity is more or less great.

brilliant, the action of God in the soul, most of the time, has no determinate form, but receives it from the temperament of the subject in whom it is produced.[10]

If we admit with Teresa and John of the Cross that the sensible manifestations of the action of God diminish in frequency and intensity as the faculties become purified, we shall have to recognize that, even if certain manifestations permit us to affirm the existence of grace in a soul, they cannot indicate the strength and the quality of the spiritual cause that produces them.[11]

The mystery that surrounds the supernatural and its external signs explains why the inhabitants of Nazareth did not recognize the divinity of Jesus, any more than the high sanctity of Mary and of Joseph; and why Saint Therese of the Child Jesus could be unknown to most of the religious of her convent, watchful nevertheless for any indications of holiness. God did not have to veil miraculously the marvels that were realized in these souls; it sufficed to leave to grace the mystery that envelops it and to assure to the external manifestations of the supernatural the veil of simplicity which is the characteristic of the highest and most pure souls.

2. Interpretation of the signs of the soul's spiritual growth is rendered more difficult by the mobility of the soul which—according to the testimony of Saint Teresa—by turns, under the action of God or of various causes, lives in very different states and, with an astonishing facility, goes from elevated

[10] This remark, that we no more than state, will be developed at greater length in connection with the first contemplative prayer (God-Love and God-Light) and the psychical reactions under the shock of the divine.

[11] In order to appreciate the value of these exterior manifestations, we must recall that spiritual progress is made in quality much more than in intensity. A sentiment—or even a spiritual state—may reappear at the different stages; it will perhaps be more intense in its manifestations in the lower degrees, but it will certainly be more purified and better in quality at the summits.

An error as to quality can create and entertain dangerous illusions, as for instance in a soul that, being inundated with sensible consolations, would think it had received a substantial touch of the sixth Mansions.

*or, for example St. Silouan*

regions to the most inferior; hence, from an interior Mansion to the most exterior. So often does the Saint return to this point, and with such force, that we cannot neglect to heed what she says:

> As I have already said—and I should not like this to be forgotten—in this life of ours the soul does not grow in the way the body does, though we speak as if it did, and growth does in fact occur. But whereas a child, after attaining to the full stature of a man, does not diminish in size so that his body becomes small again, in spiritual matters the Lord is pleased that such diminution should take place—at least, according to my own observation, for I have no other means of knowing. . . . There come times when those whose will is so completely subjected to the will of God that they would let themselves be tortured rather than be guilty of one imperfection and die a thousand deaths rather than commit sins, find it necessary, if they are to be free from offending God, when they see themselves assaulted by temptations and persecutions, to make use of the primary weapons—that is, of prayer—and thus to recall to themselves that everything comes to an end, that there is a heaven and a hell, and other truths of the same kind.[12]
> No soul on this road is such a giant that it does not often need to become a child at the breast again. (This must never be forgotten: I may repeat it again and again, for it is of great importance.) [13]

This instability of the soul which prevents it from remaining stable in any definite degree or mansion, will make it still more difficult to judge in which Mansion it habitually dwells.[14]

3. But beyond a doubt, it is the action of God Himself that contributes most to the complexity of this problem. Divine mercy, the source of all sanctification, jealously safeguards its sovereign liberty. Christ "called unto Him whom He would

[12] *Life,* xv; Peers, I, 94.
[13] *Ibid.,* xiii; 80.
[14] The movement from higher to lower pointed out by Saint Teresa, or the descent of a soul from a superior region to lower Mansions, can be, in other cases—especially at the beginning of the spiritual life—a movement from lower to higher. A soul that is a beginner can have a grace of union proper to the fifth Mansions, or a vision of the sixth, even when it is habitually in the second or fourth Mansions. It would be very naive if it judged that this favor elevated it definitively to the fifth or the sixth Mansions. In fact, one can not say of a soul that it is in such or such a Mansion unless habitually it gives sign of it and lives its states.

Himself," [15] says Saint Therese of the Child Jesus, on reading
the page of the Gospel that describes the scene of the choosing of the apostles, and considering her own privileges. The
Holy Spirit gives to each one, grace in the measure that He
has chosen.

This liberty of the divine mercy calls forth the admiration
of Saint Teresa: speaking of a person who had a great deal of
experience in spiritual things in a short time, she said:

> . . . these being gifts bestowed by God when He wills and as He
> wills and having nothing to do either with time or with service. I do
> not mean that these latter things are unimportant but that often the
> Lord grants to one person less contemplation in twenty years than to
> others in one.[16]

It may be that God has prepared a special mission for a particular soul; or, the divine prodigality may be the response to
some powerful intercession made on its behalf. Or again, it
may perhaps be that God thus expresses His own good pleasure. But generally in actual experience God's designs are unknown to us, and we are nonplussed:

> But, O my God, how is it that even in spiritual matters we often
> try to interpret things in our own way, as if they were worldly things,
> and distort their true meaning? We think we can measure our progress
> by the number of years during which we have been practising prayer.
> We even seem to be trying to set a measure to Him Who bestows on us
> measureless gifts, and Who can give more to one person in six months
> than to another in many years. This is something which I have so
> often observed, and in so many people, that I am amazed to find we
> can act so pettily.[17]

Human reason, therefore, must not apply to the ways of divine mercy its own standards. It can only state as a fact that
God calls to His intimacy, in short time, some souls that were
notably unworthy; that others seem to be unaware of certain
stages and find suddenly that they have passed them; that Saul

[15] *Autobiography*, i, 15.
[16] *Life*, xxxiv; Peers, I, 237.
[17] *Ibid.*, xxxix; 283.

the persecutor was struck down on the road to Damascus and became, shortly, Paul, the great apostle of the Gentiles.

The direct intervention of divine mercy in the sanctification of souls sets aside the regular and logical process of spiritual growth established by theological reason. According to Saint John of the Cross, it transforms the regions where it reigns into regions without paths where the ways are as numerous and personal as the souls. Each one moves on without leaving any more trace than the ship that is crossing the ocean, or the bird that cleaves the air in its rapid flight.

These findings end in a question. Since the signs of spiritual growth are so uncertain, or at least so difficult to observe; and the soul moves forward and back so easily through the Mansions; and since on the other hand, divine Wisdom seems to take joy in baffling our reason by going counter to our conceptions in this domain, what then is the value of the beautiful Teresian progress of the soul through the seven Mansions? Is there any use in studying it and trusting in it?

## C. Lights in the darkness

Before answering this question, let us emphasize the merit of Saint Teresa who, with insistence, has set forth the mystery of spiritual growth and put us on guard against any interpretation by facile but erroneous analogy:

As I have already said—and I should not like this to be forgotten—in this life of ours the soul does not grow in the way the body does, though we speak as if it did, and growth does in fact occur.[18]

She wants us to come into contact with the mystery that surrounds spiritual growth. Awareness of this mysterious darkness makes one more prudent, more humble in one's judgments, teaches one to respect the rights of God, to give due share—incontestably the first—to His power and His liberty in the work of our sanctification. To ignore or to neglect this divine intervention, to systematize everything according

[18] *Ibid.*, xv; 94.

to one's reason so as to explain in clear formulas and apparently luminous charts, is to fall into the error of a great number who "think they can learn to discern spirits without being spiritual themselves." [19] One could not be spiritual while failing to recognize the mystery that surrounds the action of God.

In thus treating with insistence, of the obscurity that always veils God's action in the soul, Saint Teresa happily completed her teaching on spiritual growth and, far from diminishing its interest, increased its value by indicating in what sense it must be interpreted. The accuracy of her teaching is in no wise dimmed by this divine obscurity. On the contrary, her doctrine stands out in its various details as so many beacon lights along the road at night, to guide the soul and lead it through its various stages to the summit of the mountain.

This is because not everything is, in fact, irregular and obscure in the sanctifying action of God. Divine Wisdom, although transcendent, does not always appear at variance with our human reason. It has its habitual modes of acting, founded on laws that we can discern. Rather easily we discover that God moves beings according to their nature, using the laws that are proper to them. The stars gravitate in space and sing the glory of God by obeying the law of the mutual attraction of bodies. By the blind submission of instinct God causes the animal to reach the natural end that He has fixed for it. God indicates the way for man by the moral law which respects his liberty.

In the case of man, the action of God becomes much more delicate in the supernatural domain. Grace is engrafted in nature. It is poured, in a way, into the soul and the faculties. Thus by grace, God leads the soul to its supernatural end by using its natural modes of acting, respecting the hierarchy of the faculties, without violence, sweetly and strongly. God's action disappears more often than not under the natural activity and

[19] *Life,* xxxiv; Peers, I, 237.

seems to come out with regret from this burial in the human where its simplicity permits it to move with ease and entire liberty.

Familiar with God, and an incomparable psychologist, Saint Teresa penetrates the depths of the Spirit of God and the depths of our nature. She knows the ways of God who respects our nature, and she discerns the effects of His action in our faculties. It is on this double knowledge that the logical progress in the advance of the soul towards God, is based. The Saint shows us how God leaves the soul at first to its own initiative, manifests Himself to it in a far-away but sweet fashion, then captures its will, profits by this hold to purify it profoundly, to use it, and finally to unite it to Himself perfectly. Running through the particular acts or extraordinary graces, she indicates a logical progress of stages, founded on the constitution of our human nature and the progressive domination of God.

The divine mercy may dispense with the steps, upset here or there the order of the purifications, create new forms of sanctity, break up the fine regular ordering of the Teresian ascent; yet the logical and classical process remains with its luminous signs which, marking the stages of growth, permit us to note, here, the slow and profound work of grace, and there to wonder at the brilliant play of mercy that takes account neither of time, nor of work, nor of obstacles.

Such is the teaching of Saint Teresa on spiritual growth, supple and living, precise yet respectful of the mystery. All the Teresian grace and genius are very happily displayed in it: her marvelous knowledge of man and her eminent intuition of God, her penetrating power of analysis which discerns the slightest psychological events of the soul and the most delicate unctions of God, her power of synthesis that details do not blind and which, under the divine light, always keeps a large and clear view of the way to be run on the road that leads to the Infinite. And so, this teaching goes beyond an epoch and a school of spirituality. It seems to us to have a universal import. It alone would suffice to place Saint Teresa among the greatest masters of all time.

# The First Stages

# Entrance to the Mansions

PERSPECTIVES having defined the program of Teresian spirituality, has opened to us the Teresian way of perfection. We can now enter upon it and follow our guide step by step.

On this way there are seven stages or "mansions" that one goes through in two periods or phases. In the first phase, which includes the first three Mansions, God intervenes in the spiritual life of the soul by a help called "general" which is no different from the ordinary helping grace. The divine aid becomes "particular" in the second period and indicates the direct intervention of God by the gifts of the Holy Spirit. In the first phase, the spiritual movement proceeds from the soul and, with the aid of grace, ends in God; the water that fills this basin of the soul is brought from afar by the aqueducts of human making.' In the second phase, the movement begins in God and comes to its fullness in the soul; the water arises from an interior source that quickly and quietly fills the basin.[1]

THE FIRST STAGES will treat of the first phase. Saint Teresa does not linger in these first Mansions. Of the one hundred and fifty pages in Peers' edition of the *Interior Castle,* only thirty are given to the first period. The Saint herself explains this brevity, pointing out that the works are numerous that have described those well-known regions and have spoken excellently on the manner of going through them. The rule and organization of her convents give her daughters all the practical directives necessary for that phase. It is still more true to say that the mind and the heart of the Saint were already lifted up to more elevated summits, because in her opinion the ways of perfection begin where the first stages end. Her special domain, the one in which she is an uncontested master, extends from the fourth Mansions and beyond.

We must not, however, pass over the teaching of Saint Teresa for the first period. The Teresian thought is original here as elsewhere. Certain pages, such as the symbolic descriptions of the state of grace, of sin, of hell, are unique. All are precious because they give us the true perspective on the spiritual life and maintain us in it. The final end—God, to whom we must attain—is constantly present. The importance of the first efforts is emphasized; but they are only the first in a long struggle and a long course. We must from the beginning be decided to go to the end, even should we die on the way. A dangerous temptation is to be satisfied with the first victories which are in reality only half-successes; or, to progress like a toad, so much involved in external details as to forget the end which is to drink at the Source of living water that is God Himself.

From the very first pages of the *Interior Castle,* Saint Teresa is equal to herself; she asserts the immense desires of her great soul and reveals herself a master, directing towards the summits. Although she leaves to others the care of setting down in detail what we must do, she tells us powerfully in what spirit and with what vigor we must carry on the first combats, and towards what luminous and distant goal we must be advancing.

[1] IV Mansions, i; Peers, II, 231 f.; *ibid.,* ii; 237.

# CHAPTER I
# The First Mansions

*Let us rather think of certain other souls, who do eventually enter the castle.*[1]

We are now in the first Mansions with those souls "who do eventually enter the castle." The Saint finds them very worthy of her maternal solicitude, for they are indeed weak. Let us listen to her describe their state and speak to them in affectionate terms, fearful for their safety, inviting them to advance to regions that are less exposed.

## A. Description of the first Mansions

The first Mansions are vast anterooms that radiate out to the whole periphery of the castle:

Think of them as comprising not just a few rooms, but a very large number. There are many ways in which souls enter them.[2]

There are throngs in these spacious apartments. Some do no more than enter; many remain in them and go no farther. Perhaps the great majority of Christians are there. To judge of this, let us consider the description that Saint Teresa gives of the state of these souls:

1. They are in the state of grace. This is so evident for the Saint that she merely notes it with a vigorous stroke:

We were saying just now how black and noisome are the streams that flow from souls in mortal sin. Similarly, although this is not the same thing—God forbid! It is only a comparison.[3]

[1] I Mansions, i; Peers, II, 204.
[2] *Ibid.*, ii; 210.
[3] *Ibid.;* 209.

Only those who are in the state of grace can enter the castle, for grace alone permits one to establish with God that exchange of friendship that is prayer and the spiritual life.

2. Grace is alive to a certain extent in such souls, but how anemic! They come with good intentions,[4] "very much absorbed in worldly affairs; but their desires are good." [5] Good intentions and good desires which manifest themselves from time to time by an appeal to God:

> Sometimes, though infrequently, they commend themselves to Our Lord; and they think about the state of their souls, though not very carefully. Full of a thousand preoccupations as they are, they pray only a few times a month, and as a rule they are thinking all the time of their preoccupations.[6]

As is evident, their spiritual life is not intense. It is reduced to the minimum that keeps it from dying. Did not Saint Alphonsus Liguori say that the vital minimum of charity, lest it die of starvation, is at least one act a month? The supernatural life in the first Mansions gravitates around this minimum.

3. What is it that prevents the leaven of the Christian life from developing?

> The soul is still absorbed in worldly affairs, engulfed in worldly pleasure and puffed up with worldly honours and ambitions.[7]
> They are very much attached to them [their preoccupations], and, where their treasure is, there is their heart also.[8]

We can guess with what difficulty these souls turn to God; nevertheless, their movement is sincere:

> From time to time, however, they shake their minds free.[9] . . . Eventually they enter the first rooms on the lowest floor, but so many reptiles get in with them that they are unable to appreciate the beauty of the castle or to find any peace within it. Still, they have done a good deal by entering at all.[10]

[4] I Mansions, ii; Peers, II, 210.
[5] *Ibid.*, i; 204.
[6] *Ibid.*
[7] *Ibid.*, ii; 210.
[8] *Ibid.*, i; 204.
[9] *Ibid.*
[10] *Ibid.*

4. This minimum of spiritual life that the Saint insists on with maternal compassion, this spark that is scarcely aglow, is not enough to enlighten the soul and give it the awareness of life. In fact, it does not see the light of God that is in it. And Saint Teresa, habituated as she is to the clear and pure light that fills her soul, lays stress on this deficiency:

You must note that the light which comes from the palace occupied by the King hardly reaches these first Mansions at all; for, although they are not dark and black, as when the soul is in a state of sin, they are to some extent darkened, so that they cannot be seen (I mean by anyone who is in them); and this not because of anything that is wrong with the room, but rather (I hardly know how to explain myself) because there are so many bad things—snakes and vipers and poisonous creatures—which have come in with the soul that they prevent it from seeing the light. It is as if one were to enter a place flooded by sunlight with his eyes so full of dust that he could hardly open them. The room itself is light enough, but he cannot enjoy the light because he is prevented from doing so by these wild beasts and animals, which force him to close his eyes to everything but themselves.[11]

This state of semi-darkness excludes not only all mystical experience properly so-called, but also any habitually felt need of turning to God; it impedes practically any power to rest in the thought of Him for some time, or of entering more deeply into one's own soul; although, adds the Saint:

as a matter of fact it would like to gaze at the castle and enjoy its beauty, it is prevented from doing so, and seems quite unable to free itself from all these impediments.[12]

5. In this semi-darkness, in the confusion of these first Mansions, which is caused by the upsurge of evil tendencies and the freedom given to them, the devil finds a terrain altogether favorable to his strategy:

As the devil's intentions are always very bad, he has many legions of evil spirits in each room to prevent souls from passing from one to another, and as we, poor souls, fail to realize this, we are tricked by all kinds of deceptions.[13]

[11] I Mansions, ii; Peers, II, 210.
[12] Ibid.; 211.
[13] Ibid.; 210.

And Teresa points out some of the tricks of the devil who turns to his advantage even the good desires that the soul is cultivating.[14]

In the higher Mansions, the faculties of the soul have enough "strength for the fight." [15] But in the first ones, on the contrary, the milieu is so favorable to the action of the devil, and the soul is so "easily vanquished, although it may desire not to offend God," [16] that in the opinion of the Saint, it cannot remain in these Mansions without "great peril . . . for, being among such poisonous things, it cannot, at some time or another, escape being bitten by them." [17] This bite, as one can guess, is sin; and grave sin.

## B. Mortal sin

The fear of seeing souls fall into mortal sin seems to haunt Saint Teresa while describing the first Mansions. She could not, in fact, be aware of a soul so near to the precipice without trembling for it with maternal solicitude. And so she has not yet ended the description of the state of the soul in the first Mansions when she speaks of mortal sin. She wants, by arousing fear of it, to help avoid it.

> I know of a person to whom Our Lord wished to show what a soul was like when it committed mortal sin. That person says that, if people could understand this, she thinks they would find it impossible to sin at all, and, rather than meet occasions of sin, would put themselves to the greatest trouble imaginable. So she was very anxious that everyone should realize this.[18]

We too know of this person: it is Teresa herself, as her other writings testify.[19] She draws on her mystical experience to give us a description of mortal sin of such precision and imagery that not only does it satisfy theologian and poet but

[14] I Mansions, ii; Peers, II, 211-2.
[15] Ibid.; 211.
[16] Ibid.; 210.
[17] Ibid.; 211.
[18] Ibid.; 205.
[19] Cf. Life, xi; Relations, xxiv; Peers, I, 345.

it also inspires every one with the greatest horror of committing sin.

First, as to the state of the soul:

No thicker darkness exists, and there is nothing dark and black which is not much less so than this.[20]

And again: "How black and noisome are the streams that flow from souls in mortal sin." [21]

How are we to explain this ugliness and darkness?

You need know only one thing about it—that, although the Sun Himself, Who has given it all its spendour and beauty, is still there in the centre of the soul, it is as if He were not there for any participation which the soul has in Him.[22]

God, in fact, remains present in the soul. It could not continue in existence without that active presence of God sustaining it:

Of the soul that is not in grace, I grant you . . . there is some kind of darkness not, however, from any defect in the Sun of Justice, Who is within it and is giving it being, but because . . . this soul is not capable of receiving the light.[23]

It should be noted here that it is not the spring, or the brilliant sun which is in the centre of the soul, that loses its splendour and beauty, for they are always within it and nothing can take away their beauty.[24]

God, then, is not directly touched by sin. Sin affects only the relations of the soul with God; the soul alone suffers absolute losses.

Created by God, we must return to God. God is our end. In returning to Him by the way that He has indicated, we fulfil His Will and procure His glory, and at the same time we find our happiness. This way is pointed out to us by the general obligations or the particular precepts that are imposed on us. Through obedience, the soul keeps to the right direction

[20] I Mansions, ii; Peers, II, 205.
[21] Ibid.; 209.
[22] Ibid.; 205.
[23] VII Mansions, i; 330.
[24] I Mansions, ii; 206.

and goes forward to God. With face turned towards Him, it
receives His light, His warmth, His life. When on the contrary,
the soul knowingly and willingly refuses to obey God in order
to satisfy a passion or seek a selfish good, it is no longer orientated towards Him. The sin that it commits then is constituted
by this voluntary choice, and the attitude of estrangement that
results from it, by which one prefers a particular good to
God.[25] As long as the soul has not, by contrition and firm purpose, retracted its attitude of sin and returned to God, it remains deprived of all the spiritual advantages that ensure its
right orientation and union with Him.

These simple ideas show us the precision and the richness
of the Teresian description.

Here is how the Saint explains the effects produced in the
soul by this withdrawal from God by the breaking of the bond
of charity:

If a thick black cloth be placed over a crystal in the sunshine, however, it is clear that, although the sun may be shining upon it, its
brightness will have no effect upon the crystal.[26]

And in her *Life* she writes:

When a soul is in mortal sin, this mirror [i.e. itself] is covered with
a thick mist and remains darkened.[27]

A soul in the state of grace resembles the "tree of life,
planted in the living waters of life—namely, in God." [28] If it
commits mortal sin, it loses that life:

It is completely devoid of power, like a person securely tied, bound
and blindfold, who, desire to do so as he may, can neither see nor
hear nor walk, but is in great darkness.[29]

This powerlessness is to be understood, evidently, of the
supernatural order, for the soul can continue to act in the nat-

[25] "Aversio a Deo per conversionem ad creaturas." This is the definition
of sin given by theology, following Saint Thomas.
[26] I Mansions, ii; Peers, II, 206.
[27] *Life*, xl; Peers, I, 292.
[28] I Mansions, ii; Peers, II, 205.
[29] *Relations*, xxiv; Peers, I, 345.

ural order, and even to perform acts that are naturally good. But these good works are without merit:

> While in a state like this the soul will find profit in nothing; . . . none of the good works it may do will be of any avail to win it glory.[30]

Charity alone can vivify good works; without it, every work is dead. But a soul in the state of sin has lost contact with the divine source of Love; charity is no longer poured out within it. In very truth, it "gives no shade and yields no fruit." [31]

A principle of evil, the devil, is substituted for the source of life and of light which is God:

> After all, the intention of a person who commits a mortal sin is not to please Him but to give pleasure to the devil; and as the devil is darkness itself, the poor soul becomes darkness itself likewise.[32]

Such privation of light is only the first of the effects of the destruction wrought by sin. The soul also loses the other spiritual advantages of the presence of God who was its life and its fruitfulness. Dead to the supernatural life, it is condemned by its state to a complete sterility:

> None of the good works it may do will be of any avail to win it glory; for they will not have their origin in that First Principle, which is God, through Whom alone our virtue is true virtue.[33]
> After all, what kind of fruit can one expect to be borne by a tree rooted in the devil? I once heard a spiritual man say that he was not so much astonished at the things done by a soul in mortal sin as at the things not done by it.[34]

Withdrawn from the action of God, the soul is then nothing but darkness, sterility, ugliness, wickedness; and this, in the midst of a confusion and interior disorder that move Saint Teresa to exclaim:

[30] I Mansions, ii; Peers, II, 205.
[31] *Ibid.;* 206.
[32] *Ibid.;* 205.
[33] *Ibid.*
[34] *Ibid.;* 206.

What a state the poor rooms of the castle are in! How distracted are the senses which inhabit them! And the faculties, which are their governors and butlers and stewards—how blind they are and how ill-controlled! [35]

The Saint lays stress on the profit she had gained from the vision of a soul in the state of mortal sin; the principal benefit was that she "had learned to have the greatest fear of offending God." [36]

But for the multitude who are less favored than is Teresa, our faith offers a vivid and sad spectacle that sets before us the terrible horror of sin: the agony of Jesus in the Garden of Gethsemane. Jesus had come to deliver us from sin by taking it on Himself: *Ecce agnus Dei, ecce qui tollit peccatum mundi;* [37] "Behold the lamb of God, who takes away the sin of the world!" In these words, John the Baptist presented Him to the crowd on the banks of the Jordan. The holy humanity of Christ, anointed with the oil of divinity—and by that fact, impeccable—had assumed the sin of the world.

On coming into the world, Jesus had taken on Himself this weight of sin. Like a cloak of ignominy, it covered the Holy One *par excellence* and made of Him a victim. Between the floods of light and of happiness that were His by reason of the beatific vision of the Divinity that dwelt within Him, and the weighty burden of ignominy that was upon Him, the Christ Jesus walked bravely onward, journeying towards His Passion.

After the Last Supper, when He had crossed the Cedron, Jesus makes known a change in His soul: "My soul is sorrowful unto death. It is the hour of the power of darkness." On hearing this cry of sadness, we are led to think of the word of Saint Paul: *Stipendium peccati mors est.* "The wages of sin is death." [38]

What has happened? In some mysterious way, the soul of

[35] I Mansions, ii; Peers, II, 206.
[36] *Ibid.*
[37] John 1:29.
[38] Rom. 6:23.

Jesus has become upset. He has allowed the floods of sin—
hitherto contained by the floods of His beatific vision—to in-
undate His soul in a destroying onrush. His senses are submerged; His faculties, intellect and will, are engulfed in it.
Christ never knew sin, yet God makes Him into sin for us
(II Cor. 5:2). His holy humanity becomes the battle ground
of the two most powerful forces: that of the divinity which
sanctifies it, and that of the sin of the world of all time. Hell
rises to the attack of Heaven, to spread its darkness, its hatred,
its death. In order to measure the suffering of Christ, His loath-
ing disgust, His darkness, the weight of the hatred that He
carried, we would have to be able to measure the distance that
separates His sanctity from the sin whose ravaging floods sweep
over Him. The suffering is in the contrast and in the vigor
with which the two forces come to grips—holiness remaining
passive, hatred seeming to have alone the right to vie and to
destroy. It is the hour of the power of darkness.

Jesus, who without weakening had borne the weight of the
divinity, falls to the ground, groans, and sweats blood under
the weight of sin. Humanly, He would have died if God had
not sent an angel to sustain Him and to assure Him of sufficient strength to go through all the stages of His sacrifice.

More eloquently than all speeches and all visions, the drama
of Gethsemane discloses the destructive power of sin.

## C. Hell

But sin that has been conquered by Christ can also be by us
as long as we are here below; for, in spite of the dense veil that
surrounds the soul, it "is as capable of enjoying His Majesty
as is the crystal of reflecting the sun." [39] When it recovers
charity by a humble confession or an act of love, it is at once
under the warming influence of the divine Sun which gives life,
light, and beauty.

But if death sets free from the body a soul still charged

[39] I Mansions, ii; Peers, II, 205.

with mortal sin, it will never again be able to remove that "pitch which blackens the crystal." [40] The soul then remains eternally fixed in its estrangement from God. This is eternal hell, a normal consequence of sin and of the soul's immutability in eternity. In this world, the powers of the soul can find in particular goods a certain satisfaction which assuages the pain of the privation of God, or renders them indifferent to it. In eternity, there is no good outside of God. Apart from Him, the soul is destitute; and its powers, made to find their rest and their refreshment in God, suffer from an insatiable and endless hunger and thirst. Such is the pain of the loss or privation of God, the principal pain of hell, created by sin itself and by the attitude of opposition that it has imposed on the soul. This loss of God makes Saint Teresa shudder and cry out:

O souls redeemed by the blood of Jesus Christ! Learn to understand yourselves and take pity on yourselves! Surely, if you understand your own natures, it is impossible that you will not strive to remove the pitch which blackens the crystal? Remember, if your life were to end now, you would never enjoy this light again.[41]

To the pain of loss is added the pain of the fire that burns without consuming, of an intelligent fire that measures its flames to the gravity and number of sins, and applies them variously according to the kind of sin. A vision permits Saint Teresa to illustrate this description; for she had a vision of hell which she counted among "the most signal favours which the Lord has bestowed upon me." [42] She gives us the detail of it in the book of her *Life*.

I was at prayer one day when suddenly, without knowing how, I found myself, as I thought, plunged right into hell. . . . This happened in the briefest space of time, but, even if I were to live for many years, I believe it would be impossible for me to forget it. The entrance, I thought, resembled a very long, narrow passage, like a furnace, very low, dark and closely confined; the ground seemed to be

[40] I Mansions, ii; Peers, II, 206.
[41] *Ibid.*
[42] *Life*, xxxii; Peers, I, 217.

full of water which looked like filthy, evil smelling mud, and in it were many wicked-looking reptiles. At the end there was a hollow place scooped out of a wall, like a cupboard, and it was here that I found myself in close confinement. But the sight of all this was pleasant by comparison with what I felt there. What I have said is in no way an exaggeration.

My feelings, I think, could not possibly be exaggerated, nor can anyone understand them. I felt a fire within my soul the nature of which I am utterly incapable of describing. My bodily sufferings were intolerable . . . to say nothing of the knowledge that they would be endless and never-ceasing. And even these are nothing by comparison with the agony of my soul, an oppression, a suffocation and an affliction so deeply felt, and accompanied by such hopeless and distressing misery, that I cannot too forcibly describe it. To say that it is as if the soul were continually being torn from the body is very little, for that would mean that one's life was being taken by another; whereas in this case it is the soul itself that is tearing itself to pieces. The fact is that I cannot find words to describe that interior fire and that despair, which is greater than the most grievous tortures and pains. I could not see who was the cause of them, but I felt, I think, as if I were being both burned and dismembered; and I repeat that that interior fire and despair are the worst things of all.

In that pestilential spot, where I was quite powerless to hope for comfort, it was impossible to sit or lie, for there was no room to do so. I had been put in this place which looked like a hole in the wall, and those very walls, so terrible to the sight, bore down upon me and completely stifled me. There was no light and everything was in the blackest darkness. I do not understand how this can be, but, although there was no light, it was possible to see everything the sight of which can cause affliction. At that time it was not the Lord's will that I should see more of hell itself, but I have since seen another vision of frightful things, which are the punishment of certain vices. To look at, they seemed to me much more dreadful; but, as I felt no pain, they caused me less fear.

The Saint terminates her description:

I was terrified by all this, and, though it happened nearly six years ago, I still am as I write: even as I sit here, fear seems to be depriving my body of its natural warmth.

And she concludes:

Since that time, as I say, everything has seemed light to me by comparison with a single moment of such suffering as I had to bear during that vision. I am shocked at myself when I think that, after having so often read books which gave some idea of the pains of hell, I was neither afraid of them nor rated them at what they are.[43]

These descriptions, taken from the *Life* of the Saint, are quite in keeping with the atmosphere of the first Mansions and suited to inculcate in the souls that inhabit them the fear they should have of losing the treasure of sanctifying grace, so threatened in those regions. We have not hesitated therefore to quote at length.

The vision of hell arouses in Saint Teresa an immense pity:

This vision, too, was the cause of the very deep distress which I experience because of the great number of souls who are bringing damnation upon themselves    It also inspired me with fervent impulses for the good of souls: for I really believe that, to deliver a single one of them from such dreadful tortures, I would willingly die many deaths.    I do not know how we can look on so calmly and see the devil carrying off as many souls as he does daily.[44]

Hence, she begs souls in the first Mansions to get rid of, or stay free of, this sin that brings on such harm:

O souls redeemed by the blood of Jesus Christ! Learn to understand yourselves and take pity on yourselves! Surely, if you understand your own natures, it is impossible that you will not strive to remove the pitch which blackens the crystal? [45]

And she adds:

May God, in His mercy, deliver us from such great evil, for there is nothing in the whole of our lives that so thoroughly deserves to be called evil as this, since it brings endless and eternal evils in its train.[46]

Such is the language that is appropriate for speaking of the souls in the first Mansions. May salutary fear prod them on to an effort to leave the regions they inhabit and enter resolutely into a more profound interior life. Unless they do so,

[43] *Life,* xxxii; Peers, I, 215-7.
[44] *Ibid.;* 217-8. Cf. also VII Mansions, i; Peers, II, 220, where the Saint, after speaking of the dark prison where souls in the state of mortal sin are bound, says that to pray for them is the best kind of alms-giving.
[45] I Mansions, ii; Peers, II, 206.
[46] *Ibid.*

a terrible danger threatens them, the evil of mortal sin with its train of further evils. But let the soul understand the teaching of the Saint; let it make an energetic resolution; and it will find itself already in the second Mansions.

# CHAPTER II
# At the Point of Departure

*At the beginning one must not think
of such things as spiritual favours.*[1]

Spiritual anemia, tumult, faint light: these are the impressions left by the first Mansions. There the soul is an easy prey. It has only one means of escape: to retire into the inner Mansions where the light shines more brightly, where life is envigorated, where peace reigns and fruit is gathered in.

The soul must flee towards God. And so the Teresian spirituality has no other end than to organize that flight. Flee to God. Such is the first resolution that Saint Teresa imposes on the soul. For this, a resolute will, discretion, and great desires, are required from the very beginning. The Saint demands these dispositions of her disciple.

## A. Orientation towards God

"I want to see God!" the child Teresa had exclaimed. And this was not a passing whim, the sigh of a moment of fervor; it was the aspiration of her whole soul, the passion of her entire life, the longing that dominated all of her spiritual attitudes. Moreover, perfection consists in being perfectly united with God, our end. Hence, the realistic logic of the Saint, teaching others the ways of sanctity, imposes on the soul from the beginning, as its first attitude and first movement, the need of tending to Him with whatever modest strength it can dispose of. The quest for God must guide its steps and inspire all its actions. This fundamental point of Teresian spirituality

[1] II Mansions, i; Peers, II, 216.

deserves emphasis because of its practical importance and its originality.

In the first pages of her treatise on the Mansions, Saint Teresa, her mind altogether bathed in the light of her vision, describes for us the "beautiful and delightful Castle" that is the soul; especially the great Reality that fills it, the Sun that shines in it, and the Fountain of life springing up within it. With infectious enthusiasm, she tells its splendors, returning to it repeatedly, now to add a detail or clarification, and again to lament of the Sun's disappearance behind the black veil of sin—the "Sun Who has given it all its splendor and beauty, and is still there in the centre of the soul." [2]

It is, in fact, important that the soul know from the beginning that it is "nothing but a paradise, in which, as God tells us, He takes His delight." [3] Not to know this, would be "great stupidity"; it would be not to know who we are.

The Saint at once invites the soul to enter into itself by the door of "prayer and meditation," [4] to come to know and to admire the marvelous spiritual realities that it contains. Those who do not want to take this step and whose whole "interest is centered in the rough setting of the diamond, and in the outer wall of the castle—that is to say, in these bodies of ours," [5] are spiritually crippled or paralyzed, and have taken on a likeness to the reptiles and beasts in the midst of which they have grown accustomed to living.[6] Perhaps they really have the supernatural life; but what is to be said of a life that does not show any sign of its existence?

To know God in Himself and the riches that he pours out into the soul, is beyond doubt for Saint Teresa the first knowledge to be acquired, the first act of the spiritual life. One can enter into it only by the door of prayer.

[2] I Mansions, ii; Peers, II, 205.
[3] *Ibid.*, i; 201.
[4] *Ibid.;* 203.
[5] *Ibid.;* 202.
[6] *Ibid.;* 203.

I told you, however, at the outset . . . that the door by which we can enter into this castle is prayer. It is absurd to think that we can enter Heaven without first entering our own souls—without getting to know ourselves, and reflecting upon the wretchedness of our nature and what we owe to God, and continually imploring His mercy." [7]

But let there be no mistake. It is in order to find God that one enters by the door of prayer and self-knowledge. The knowledge of self depends on the knowledge of God:

The soul must sometimes emerge from self-knowledge and soar aloft in meditation upon the greatness and the majesty of its God. Doing this will help it to realize its own baseness better than thinking of its own nature. . . . For although, as I say, it is through the abundant mercy of God that the soul studies to know itself, yet one can have too much of a good thing, as the saying goes, and believe me, we shall reach much greater heights of virtue by thinking upon the virtue of God than if we stay in our own little plot of ground and tie ourselves down to it completely.[8]

*reason for contemplativ in lectio divina*

This knowledge of God and this loving converse with Him in prayer, is the source of all we need in the spiritual life. Through it, we discover the end to be attained, the divine demands, the virtues to be practised, and the strength that is needed:

The Lord Himself says: "No one will ascend to My Father, but by Me" . . . and "He that sees Me sees My Father." Well, if we never look at Him or think of what we owe Him, and of the death which He suffered for our sakes, I do not see how we can get to know Him or do good works in His service.[9]

It is to prayer therefore that Saint Teresa invites beginners; and it is by their fidelity in seeking God, that she is going to measure their progress. The souls in the first Mansions "pray only a few times a month, and as a rule they are thinking all the time of their preoccupations." [10] Appreciable progress has been made by those in the second Mansions because they "have already begun to practise prayer . . . [and] can understand

[7] II Mansions, i; Peers, II, 218.
[8] I Mansions, ii; 208.
[9] II Mansions, i; 218.
[10] I Mansions, i; 204.

the Lord when He calls them; for, they gradually get nearer to the place where His Majesty dwells." [11] This progress could only have been realized by an asceticism of detachment. It is easy to see that this is so, if we think back to the condition of the soul in the first Mansions. There, the unmortified tendencies, "snakes and vipers and poisonous creatures" [12] were so numerous that they blinded it and prevented it from seeing anything but themselves. Many cares dominate such a soul "still absorbed in worldly affairs, engulfed in worldly pleasure, and puffed up with worldly honours and ambitions." Legions of evil spirits have no difficulty—because of the disorder and darkness—in making the poor soul fall. For "if we fill the palace with vulgar people and all kinds of junk, how can the Lord and His Court occupy it." [13]

What is the soul then to do? It is not strong enough to clear away such obstacles and brave such enemies. Saint Teresa advises it to fly from the occasions so that it may find God:

Everyone, however, who wishes to enter the second Mansions, will be well advised, as far as his state of life permits, to try to put aside all unnecessary affairs and business. For those who hope to reach the principal Mansion, this is so important that unless they begin in this way I do not believe they will ever be able to get there. Nor, indeed, even though it has entered the castle, is the soul free from great peril in the Mansion which it actually inhabits.[14]

Speaking to her daughters, the Saint insists: "Beware, my daughters, of cares that have nothing to do with you." [15]

Saint Teresa makes use of all the good will of the soul and whatever strength it has in these beginning stages, for this effort at flight which is indispensable in one who would find God. And so our Saint notes with joy any growing detachment from exterior things, as one of the characteristic signs of the progress made by souls in the second Mansions:

[11] II Mansions, i; Peers, II, 213.
[12] I Mansions, ii; 210.
[13] *Way of Perfection*, xxviii; Peers, II, 118.
[14] I Mansions, ii; 211.
[15] *Ibid.*

Even when we are engaged in our worldly pastimes and businesses and pleasures and hagglings, when we are falling into sins and rising from them again . . . in spite of all that, this Lord of ours is so anxious that we should desire Him and strive after His companionship that He calls us ceaselessly, time after time, to approach Him . . . and the poor soul is consumed with grief at being unable to do His bidding immediately.[16]

The effort at detachment must be persevering and will go hand in hand with progress towards union in the following Mansions. It needs to be sustained by a certain organization of the exterior life. The Carmelite daughter of Saint Teresa will find this help in the monastic setting and rule that channel and regulate all her activities. The spiritual person in the world will have to find it normally in a rule of life, a plan that is stable, yet flexible, which will fix precisely the obligations of his state and his times for prayerful converse with God. This will safeguard him not only from solicitude for external things and the stubborn violence of his passions, but also from the whims of his own fancy and excessive preoccupation.

As we see, Teresian asceticism, in this first period, is entirely subordinated to the search for God. In fact, this is so all along the way of spiritual progress. Teresa has only one desire: to see God and to serve Him in His Church; perfection, for her, consists in being united with God. The simple and rigorous logic of this desire and this conception requires that it be so.

Let us note here, however, that in the second phase, which begins at the fourth Mansion, she seems to place asceticism ahead of the search for God. In the *Way of Perfection* she devotes the first twenty chapters to an exposition of the virtues necessary for the contemplative. She writes:

You will ask, my daughters, why I am talking to you about virtues . . . when you want me to tell you only about contemplation. My reply is that, if you had asked me about meditation, I could have talked to you about it, and advised you all to practise it, even if you do not possess the virtues. For this is the first step to be taken towards the acquisition of the virtues . . . But contemplation, daughters, is an-

[16] II Mansions, I; Peers, II, 214.

other matter. . . . This king does not allow Himself to be taken except by one who surrenders wholly to Him.[17]

Thus the beginner must first engage in mental prayer before acquiring the virtues; and the contemplative must practise virtue in order to progress in his contemplation.

Like the daughters of Saint Teresa, we too are a little surprised at these statements; we are so accustomed to hearing that the beginner must struggle along in the hard work of asceticism, and that the contemplative must lose himself in the depths of his contemplation. And yet, what admirable logic! For after all is it not normal that the beginner, in the midst of his dangers should first try to find God; and before entering upon the struggle with his faults, seek, in the intimacy of prayer, the light to see God's demands on him and his own defects; and that he should beg for strength to carry on the fight?

When, having arrived at the second phase, he has found God and has learned by experience that after his first advances "the King does not allow Himself to be taken except by one who surrenders wholly to Him," he will put all his care to making the total gift of himself and practising that absolute asceticism which is to purify him and win the perfect gift of God.

Saint Teresa and Saint John of the Cross, who are almost silent on the asceticism of the first phase, write the *Way of Perfection* and the *Ascent of Mount Carmel* respectively, in order to expound in detail that liberating asceticism of the second phase, which by detachment and absolute poverty, humility and perfect charity, draws down the outpourings of divine love and prepares the soul for divine union.[18]

---

[17] *Way of Perfection*, xvi; Peers, II, 63-4.
[18] The ascetical teaching of the *Way of Perfection* and the *Ascent of Mount Carmel* can be useful for every soul. But it was written and is eminently suited by reason of its absolute character, for contemplatives who have discovered the all that is God and His absolute demands. In fact, for the first phase, Saint Teresa suggests (*Life*, xii) a work entitled the *Art of Serving God*, which tells how the soul must act to favor growth of the

In the second as well as in the first phase, Teresian asceticism is subordinated to the search for God, and has no other end in view than to facilitate this and make it successful. If asceticism is more thorough and unrelenting in the second phase, if it be dwelt upon with so much precision by the Carmelite Masters, this is because the soul is then able lovingly to respond to the divine advances, and because such response is inexorably required by God as a condition for union. On the other hand, if in the beginning this asceticism seems minimized and given only a secondary role, that is because the soul is as yet weak; and because, in the eyes of Saint Teresa, the all important thing for the soul is to set itself firmly in its quest for God, and employ in that all its energies.

Let us not be mistaken, however. In comparing it with the bitter war on our faults recommended by other spiritual writers, we must guard against judging the asceticism recommended by Saint Teresa to beginners, as only half-hearted and of little account. "At the beginning one must not think of such things as spiritual favours," proclaims Saint Teresa.[19] Suffering is the rule in the second Mansions. To enter them and pass through them, requires a virile courage, and this is the first disposition that Saint Teresa exacts of beginners.

## B. Dispositions necessary for beginners

Before starting out, Saint Teresa examines those who are desirous of following in her path. The examination is not hard; it is, however, serious and profound. It bears less on results already attained and exterior qualities, than on the basic dispositions of a soul.

---

virtues. It is her thought, then, that her disciple will go to other works to complete her teaching on the practice of the virtues. This teaching will always have to be inserted in line with her doctrine which subordinates asceticism to the seeking of God.

[19] II Mansions, i; Peers, II, 216.

## 1. A RESOLUTE WILL

Saint Teresa demands courage above all things from her disciple. And this courage is necessary from the very beginning. The Saint says and repeats it insistently, it seems to her so important:

Let him play the man and not be like those who went down on their knees in order to drink when they went to battle . . . but let him be resolute, for he is going forth to fight with all the devils and there are no better weapons than the Cross.

There is one thing so important that, although I have said it on other occasions, I will repeat it once more here: It is that at the beginning one must not think of such things as spiritual favors . . . For it is not in these Mansions . . . that it rains manna.[20]

Far from glossing over the trials, Teresa reviews them in detail. She is plain-dealing and candid. The soul that is forewarned can prepare for the combat; it will not be taken by surprise.

At first, we find a rather general warning. The souls that are in the second Mansions "suffer more than in the preceding Mansions." [21] If the soul is gifted, the Saint adds, its trials will probably be particularly acute:

The soul will certainly suffer great trials at this time, especially if the devil sees that its character and habits are such that it is ready to make further progress.[22]

We might ask what these sufferings will be. First of all, the struggle that must be kept up against one's evil tendencies. It requires a certain violence, to turn to God, to renounce bad habits, to fight perhaps against one's family and social environment, to be more alone in order freely to seek God and live according to His light.

Assuredly, the grace of God sustains the effort of the soul; but that grace has not the nourishing sweetness and pervading

[20] *Ibid.*
[21] *Ibid.;* 214.
[22] *Ibid.;* 215.

delight that God will give later. Ordinarily it does not lift up the soul, but leaves it to its painful task! The Saint writes:

> It is in these early stages that their labor is hardest, for it is they themselves who labor and the Lord Who gives the increase.[23]

It is not only in exterior action that the work is painful, but also in the relations with God. We ought to speak here of aridities in prayer, as these are one of the most difficult ordeals of this period; but their importance in the spiritual life obliges us to treat them separately. Here we shall only emphasize the remark of the Saint that the suffering of the soul in its relations with God is greater in the second Mansions than in the first. The reason she gives seems subtle, and yet it is so right. In the first Mansions the soul was, as it were, anaesthetized in its spiritual paralysis; in the second, the supernatural life that has come out of its torpor, makes it more sensitive:

> I say they have a harder time because the souls in the first Mansions are, as it were, not only dumb, but can hear nothing, and so it is not such a trial to them to be unable to speak; the others, who can hear and not speak, would find the trial much harder to bear." [24]

This more awakened sensibility perceives better the calls of the Master; but it also discovers better the numerous defects of the soul:

> These souls, then, can understand the Lord when He calls them; for, as they gradually get nearer to the place where His Majesty dwells, He becomes a very good Neighbor to them. And such are His mercy and goodness that . . . even when we are falling into sins and rising from them again . . . this Lord of ours is so anxious that we should desire Him and strive after His companionship that He calls us ceaselessly, time after time, to approach Him; and this voice of His is so sweet that the poor soul is consumed with grief at being unable to do His bidding immediately; and thus, as I say, it suffers more than if it could not hear Him.
>
> I do not mean by this that He speaks to us and calls us in the precise way which I shall describe later; His appeals come through the conversations of good people, or from sermons, or through the reading of

[23] *Life*, xi; Peers, I, 64.
[24] II Mansions, i; Peers, II, 213.

good books; and there are many other ways, of which you have heard, in which God calls us." [25]

To the suffering that comes from personal struggles and contrition, is added that which comes from *the demons.* The evil spirits cannot let that soul escape to God without exerting all their efforts to bring it back or to bar its way, especially when they understand that "its character and habits are such that it is ready to make further progress." [26] They come in multitudes into these Mansions, and, although from now on they are not always victorious, they keep the upper hand against a soul that is still weak and fettered by the senses which are their domain. As long as they have the advantage they profit by it, and so:

The assault which the devils now make upon the soul, in all kinds of ways, is terrible; and the soul suffers more than in the preceding Mansions.[27]

Oh, Jesus! What confusion the devils bring about in the poor soul, and how distressed it is! [28]

There is no question here of extraordinary manifestations, but of interior trials and temptations:

The devils once more show the soul . . . the things of the world—and they pretend that earthly pleasures are almost eternal: they remind the soul of the esteem in which it is held in the world, of its friends and relatives, of the way in which its health will be endangered by penance . . . and of impediments of a thousand other kinds.[29]

In the midst of this interior disturbance, to which the soul is more sensitive than previously because "its understanding is keener," [30] it must hold firm; for the energy shown in bearing the trials of beginners, as Saint Teresa remarks in her *Life,* allows our Saviour to recognize His valiant friends who "can

[25] *Ibid.;* 213-4.
[26] *Ibid.;* 215.
[27] *Ibid.;* 214.
[28] *Ibid.*
[29] *Ibid.*
[30] *Ibid.*

drink of the chalice and help Him to bear the cross before He trusts them with His great treasures." [31]

To these trials are added those that come from the weaknesses of the soul, for at times God, declares Saint Teresa:

even allows these reptiles to bite us, so that we may learn better how to be on our guard in the future and see if we are really grieved at having offended Him.

If, then, you sometimes fall, do not lose heart, or cease striving to make progress, for even out of your fall God will bring good.[32]

Discouragement would have disastrous consequences:

Those who have begun . . . must not allow such warfare to turn them back. They must realize that to fall a second time is worse than to fall once. They can see that it will lead them to ruin: let them place their trust, not in themselves, but in the mercy of God, and they will see how His Majesty can lead them on.[33]

The soul must set its courage to persevere in spite of all, for:

His Majesty is quite prepared to wait for many days, and even years, especially when He sees we are persevering and have good desires. This is the most necessary thing here; if we have this we cannot fail to gain greatly.[34]

Perseverance amid exterior trials and aridities; perseverance when we are "persecuted and afflicted by evil thoughts which we cannot cast out"; [35] perseverance in resuming recollection, for there is no other remedy than to start again when it has been lost; perseverance in the struggle despite all obstacles, not to halt until the goal is reached.[36] For all this, resoluteness alone can ensure success:

There must be many who have begun some time back and never manage to finish their course, and I believe it is largely because they do not embrace the Cross from the beginning.[37]

[31] *Life,* xi; Peers, I, 67.
[32] II Mansions, i; Peers, II, 217.
[33] *Ibid.*
[34] *Ibid.;* 214.
[35] *Ibid.;* 217.
[36] *Way of Perfection,* xxi; Peers, II, 89.
[37] *Life,* xi; Peers, I, 69.

It is a courageous will that Saint Teresa requires from her disciple at the very start, a will that is constant and direct, which, after one simple clearsighted appraisal of the summit of perfection, is resolved to mount it generously:

All that the beginner in prayer has to do . . . is to labor and be resolute and prepare himself with all possible diligence to bring his will into conformity with the will of God. . . . You may be quite sure that this comprises the very greatest perfection which can be attained on the spiritual road.[38]

## 2. DISCRETION AND LIBERTY OF SPIRIT

Having inspired her disciples with this warrior spirit, Saint Teresa is anxious that it be wisely directed. It must be tempered by discretion. Persevering rather than violent and intermittent effort is important and effective in the way of prayer·

Recollection cannot be begun by making strenuous efforts, but must come gently, after which you will be able to practise it for longer periods at a time.[39]

Violence can spoil everything at the beginning by prematurely using up the energies of the soul, and leaving it to founder in discouragement.[40] Beneath the very real generosity that ordinarily animates beginners, their ardors conceal a secret pride. The devil knows this well. And so he works on this point to deceive souls, using for his purpose both their good desires and their pride. Saint Teresa points out some of these temptations:

He inspires a sister with yearnings to do penance, so that she seems to have no peace save when she is torturing herself.[41]

[38] II Mansions, i; Peers, II, 216.
[39] *Ibid.;* 218.
[40] Every beginner has a capital of strength and good will. If at the start he spends this capital in austerities or in violent efforts, the soul risks being broken definitely. It will afterwards be timid and incapable of great things, or again it will be attached to those exterior prescriptions or mortifications that have been so painful to it, to the detriment of the spirit that it will easily sacrifice (Cf. Saint John of the Cross, *Maxims*).
[41] I Mansions, ii; 211.

*good advice for retreats*

She secretly orders her life in such a way that in the end she ruins her health and is unable to do what her Rule demands.[42]

Another sister is inspired with zeal for the greatest possible perfection. . . . She would think any little fault on the part of the sisters a serious failure.[43]

These tricks of the devil have for their aim to use up the energies of the soul in useless and presumptuous efforts, to stifle its good will under constraint, and to take away the strength and freedom it needs in order to go to God with a sure and firm step.

God, certainly, is exacting; but where He is there is freedom, joy, and balance. The road that leads to Him is narrow; but to walk with speed along it, one must not be hampered by vain fears. Saint Teresa thinks it well to remind beginners of this:

*balance*

In the early stages, then, one should strive to feel happy and free. There are some people who think that devotion will slip from them if they relax a little. It is good to have misgivings about oneself and not to allow self-confidence to lead one into occasions which habitually involve offences against God. . . . Yet there are many circumstances in which . . . it is permissible for us to take some recreation, in order that we may be stronger when we return to prayer. In everything we need discretion.[44]

*relaxation*

*recreation*

The Saint has no room for sad devotion. She makes good humored fun of those who are always afraid of losing it, and severely reproves those who would like to pray when it is time to recreate. She judges that recreation is necessary; and before sending Saint John of the Cross to Duruelo, she takes him to the foundation at Valladolid mainly for the purpose of letting him see how the sisters recreated in her convents.

This note of discretion, liberty, and joy is a characteristic of the Saint and her spirituality. To attain to it, common sense and good judgment are necessary; hence she requires these qualities in her daughters. She insists on this more than on devotion, for one can acquire the latter but can neither replace

[42] I Mansions, ii; Peers, II, 211.
[43] *Ibid.;* 212.
[44] *Life,* xii; Peers, I, 74.

nor give the former. She examines her postulants on this point, convinced that one cannot, without danger, engage in the ways of the absolute, a soul whose human equilibrium is not perfectly assured by a straight judgment and sound reason.

### 3. GREAT DESIRES

P. Jean de Jésus-Marie declares that magnanimity is the characteristic trait of Saint Teresa. Báñez expressed the same opinion in a graphic fashion, saying: She is great from foot to head, and from the head on up she is incomparably more so. The quality of greatness appears in all her works, especially in her spiritual doctrine which leads to the sublimest summits.

Saint Teresa wants the beginner, who has as yet done nothing, to be already great in desire. He must look to the heights of the spiritual life and aspire ardently to perfect union with God. She writes:

> I am astounded at how much can be done on this road if one has the courage to attempt great things; the soul may not have the strength to achieve these things at once but if it takes a flight it can make good progress, though, like a little unfledged bird, it is apt to grow tired and stop.[45]

Great desires are the hallmark of a great soul. Great desires alone can inspire courage necessary to surmount the obstacles that beset its way. They are the wind that carries the soul high and far. To convince us, Saint Teresa gives us the testimony of her own experience:

> We must have great confidence, for it is most important that we should not cramp our good desires, but should believe that, with God's help, if we make continual efforts to do so, we shall attain, though perhaps not at once, to that which many saints have reached through His favour. If they had never resolved to desire to attain this and to carry their desires continually into effect, they would never have risen to as high a state as they did. His Majesty desires and loves courageous souls if they have no confidence in themselves but walk in humility; and I have never seen any such person hanging back on this road, nor any soul that, under the guise of humility, acted

[45] *Ibid.*

like a coward, go as far in many years as the courageous soul can in
few.[46]

It might be objected that these great desires spring from
pride. Perhaps, in some cases; but then they will founder in
the first failures and the trials of daily life. Yet *a priori* we
have not the right to judge them so, even though the inexperience of the beginner involves him at the same time in considerable illusions. Grandeur of soul and humility go well together; both rest on an awareness of human weakness and on
faith in the all-powerful mercy of God. The example and testimony of the most illustrious of the daughters of Saint Teresa,
Therese of Lisieux, afford us proof. She writes in her *Autobiography:*

> As I reflected that I was born for great things, and sought the means
> to attain them, it was made known to me interiorly that my personal
> glory would never reveal itself before the eyes of men, but that it would
> consist in becoming a Saint.
> This aspiration may very well appear rash, seeing how imperfect
> I was, and am, even now, after so many years of religious life; yet I
> still feel the same daring confidence that one day I shall become a
> great Saint. I am not trusting in my own merits, for I have none; but
> I trust in Him Who is Virtue and Holiness itself. It is He alone Who,
> pleased with my feeble efforts, will raise me to Himself, and, by cloth-
> ing me with His merits, make me a Saint.[47]

In Chapter XI, the little Saint writes again:

> Alas! I am but a poor little unfledged bird. I am not an eagle, I have
> but the eagle's eyes and heart! Yet, notwithstanding my exceeding
> littleness, I dare to gaze upon the Divine Sun of Love, and I burn to
> dart upwards unto Him! [48]

Great desires and humility can go hand in hand, answering
for one another, and mutually benefiting themselves. Humility
alone can sustain the great desires and keep them fixed on their
goal amid the vicissitudes of the spiritual life. On the other
hand, it would be a false humility that would induce the soul

---

[46] *Life,* xiii; Peers, I, 74.
[47] *Autobiography,* iv, 55.
[48] *Ibid.,* xi, 187.

to renounce its great desires and become a victim to tepidity
or mere respectable mediocrity.

To balance harmoniously one's strength of will, discretion,
and great desires, is an art, one that ordinarily the beginner
does not possess. He will ask a director to teach him. The latter
will normally advise moderation. Saint Teresa fears that he
may sin by excess of discretion and so destroy or diminish the
great desires of the soul. And so she asks the beginner who
takes a director

[to] see to it that he is not the kind of person to teach us to be like
toads, satisfied if our souls show themselves fit only to catch lizards.[49]

The fact that Saint Teresa defends in such energetic terms
great desires, shows that she esteems them as something very
precious to be guarded at all cost.

Thirsty for God, and bringing into service a virile energy,
a true judgment, a desire for great things in order to slake that
thirst, such is the ideal daughter of Saint Teresa at the point
of departure. Perhaps she will seem to the superficial observer
—when she has passed the first stages in the search for God,
following the great Saint—less virtuous, less well regulated
and ordered in her exterior movements than others whose
efforts at the beginning have been dominated by the unique
concern for virtue. Did not the masters of Avila find Saint
Teresa, at the time of her first mystical graces, too lacking in
virtue to receive such favors? The mother will consent provi-
sionally to her daughters' resembling her, provided that, with
their gaze unfailingly fixed on God, urged on by the length of
the road they must cover to arrive at union with Him, they
are not stopped by the obstacles or little lizards they meet along
the way, but hasten on with all the energy of their soul and the
flight of their desires to those summits where shines the light
of God that is drawing them irresistibly on.

[49] *Life*, xiii; Peers, I, 75.

# CHAPTER III
# Prayer in Its First Stages

*If you are to recite the Paternoster well, one thing is needful: you must not leave the side of the Master Who has taught it to you.*[1]

Armed with courage and great desires, freed from its fetters of the first Mansions, the Teresian soul is ready to go further in its quest of God. It stands at the door that opens into the second Mansions, the door of prayer. To enter in requires an answer to the question, how will it make its prayer.

To turn towards God is already to pray, since prayer—a friendly conversation with God—is nothing else than the filial movement of grace towards God who is our Father. Nothing seems more easy and more simple than to follow that filial instinct of grace and, consequently, to pray.

But this filial movement must be regulated, enlightened, and sustained. It must be strong enough to enlist all our energies, continuous enough to vivify all our acts, profound enough to lay hold on our whole soul and unite it to God in prayer that is transforming.

Prayer puts into activity the natural faculties and the supernatural powers. It is an art—one of the most delicate—that requires a technique. It is learned only by a persevering exercise that requires supernatural dispositions and great patience.

Let us consider, then, the first steps of the soul in this way of prayer:

[1] *Way of Perfection,* xxiv; Peers, II, 103.

## A. Vocal prayer

Beginners, of ardent and generous soul, souls filled with those great desires of which Saint Teresa speaks, we find following in the footsteps of the Master. They are the apostles at the beginning of His public life. They have seen Him for long hours completely absorbed in silent prayer, and they would like to learn its secret that they too might thus pray.

Let us read again the gospel narrative:

And it came to pass as he was praying in a certain place, that when he ceased, one of his disciples said to him, "Lord, teach us to pray, even as John also taught his disciples." And he said to them, "When you pray, say:

> Our Father who art in heaven,
> hallowed be thy name.
> Thy kingdom come,
>   thy will be done
>   on earth, as it is in heaven.
> Give us this day our daily bread.
> And forgive us our debts,
>   as we also forgive our debtors.
> And lead us not into temptation,
>   but deliver us from evil." [2]

They asked to be taught the science of prayer, and it is a vocal prayer that Jesus teaches them. But what vocal prayer! Simple and sublime, its concise formulas show clearly the attitude of the faithful Christian before his God, the desires and requests he should present before Him. The *Pater* is the perfect prayer that the Church puts on the lips of the priest at the most solemn moment of the Holy Sacrifice. It is the prayer of child-like souls that know no other, the prayer of saints who taste of the heavenly wisdom with which its formulas are replete.

One day a novice, entering the cell of Saint Therese of the Child Jesus, was struck by the celestial expression of her face. She was busily sewing, and yet seemed lost in deep contemplation. "What are you thinking of?" the young sister asked.

[2] Luke 11:1; Matt. 6:9-14.

"I am meditating on the 'Our Father,' " was the answer. "It is so sweet to call God, 'Our Father' " . . . and tears glistened in her eyes.[3]

In the Our Father can be found the whole art and science of prayer. And so Saint Teresa, in the *Way of Perfection,* proposes simply to "write down a few thoughts on the words of the Paternoster . . . and, if you are studious and humble, you need nothing more." [4]

Often, then, at whatever stage of spiritual life we may be, and whatever may be our fervor or our dryness, let us recite humbly and thoughtfully the Our Father, the prayer that Jesus Himself composed for us, so that we may pray and learn to pray as we should.

In teaching us the Our Father, Jesus has shown for all time the excellence of vocal prayer. He Himself had prayed vocally at the knees of His mother, Mary, in the company of Joseph His foster father; frequently, too, at the synagogue with the children of His age; and in the midst of the assembly of the faithful, the sabbath day. During the course of His public life, Jesus lifted up His voice at times to express His sentiments to God; His gratitude on the occasion of the resurrection of Lazarus, or for the marvels worked by the apostles. He cried aloud His agony in the Garden of Gethsemane.

There are assuredly times when the soul has need of giving external expression to its feelings and of praying with its whole being in order to give to its supplication all the power possible. We are body as well as spirit; and although the exterior act does not change the supernatural value of the interior act, nevertheless it increases its intensity.

This need of associating the senses with interior prayer responds, moreover, to a divine exigency. God who seeks for adorers in spirit and in truth—and consequently, for the prayer that rises, living, from the depths of the soul—wants also to

---

[3] *Autobiography,* Epilogue, 195.
[4] *Way of Perfection,* xxi; Peers, II, 90.

find that external expression which associates the body to interior prayer, for this offers to Him the perfect homage of all, to which He has right.

Because it is exterior and so perfectly human, vocal prayer is *par excellence* the prayer of the multitudes. When it is at the same time simple enough and profound enough to express the convictions of all as well as the intimate feelings of each one, it grips souls, carries them on in its powerful movement, uniting them in a fervent and sublime atmosphere: it mounts up then in a supplication of such grandeur that it seems no longer to spring from this earth, but from Christ Jesus Himself diffused in His members. Thus it is that from the silent invitation of the Immaculate Virgin as she appeared to Bernadette, saying her beads, there came that prayer of the crowds of Lourdes, one of the most impressive and most powerful tributes that can rise from earth to Heaven.

Contemplatives, however sublime be their converse with God, cannot despise or neglect a form of prayer of such value and efficacy with God and with men. They must, then, remain faithful to it, whatever be the difficulties it presents at certain periods. Negligence on this point, which often pleads the excuse of being unable to pray thus, proceeds very frequently from secret pride or a form of passivity which is mere laziness. In that case, vocal prayer will be an energetic exercise in humility and simplicity, fruitful for the soul and pleasing to God.

If vocal prayer is to merit the name of prayer, it must be interior. Saint Teresa reminds us of this:

I want to advise you, or, I might even say, to teach you . . . how you must practise vocal prayer, for it is right that you should understand what you are saying. . . . When I say the Creed, it seems to me right, *and indeed obligatory,* that I should understand and know what it is that I believe . . .

I want you to understand that, if you are to recite the Paternoster well, one thing is needful: you must not leave the side of the Master Who has taught it you.

You will say *at once* that this is meditation, and that you are not capable of it, and do not even wish to practise it, but are content with

vocal prayer. . . . You are right to say that what we have described is
mental prayer; but I assure you that I cannot distinguish it from vocal
prayer faithfully recited with a realization of Who it is that we are
addressing. Further, we are under the obligation of trying to pray
attentively.[5]

Hence vocal prayer is the first form of prayer properly so
called. Beginners will make use of it. Those especially will
have recourse to it more frequently and for a longer time who,
not being familiar with purely intellectual activities, need a
formula to sustain their thought, to arouse sentiments of devotion or take cognizance of them, and cannot give them their
full force of prayer except by expressing them exteriorly.

While for certain souls, frequent recourse to vocal prayer
might encourage a kind of negligence and indolence in face of
the effort to be put forth ·for mental prayer, for other souls
whose habits of activity have created a need for almost continual movement or who "find their thoughts wandering so
much that they cannot concentrate upon the same thing, but
are always restless," [6] vocal prayer can become a way to contemplation, and even the only practical way.

Saint Teresa gives us a typical example of this:

*for some,
remains
primary*

> I know there are many people who practise vocal prayer in the
> manner already described and are raised by God to the higher kind of
> contemplation without *having had any hand in this themselves or even*
> knowing how it has happened. *For this reason, daughters, I attach*
> *great importance to your saying your vocal prayers well.* I know a
> nun who could never practise anything but vocal prayer but who kept
> to this and found she had everything else; yet if she omitted saying
> her prayers her mind wandered so much she could not endure it. May
> we all practise such mental prayer as that. She would say a number
> of Paternosters, corresponding to the number of times Our Lord shed
> His blood, and on nothing more than these and a few other prayers
> she would spend two or three hours. She came to me once in great
> distress, saying that she did not know how to practise mental prayer,
> and that she could not contemplate but could only say vocal prayers
> . . . I asked her what prayers she said, and from her reply I saw that,

[5] *Way of Perfection,* xxiv; Peers, II, 101, 103.
[6] *Ibid.,* xvii; 69.

though keeping to the Paternoster she was experiencing pure contemplation, and the Lord was raising her to be with Him in union.[7]

Who will not recall, listening to Saint Teresa, such or such an invalid bedridden for long years, or some good soul worn out by hard work, using his remaining strength to recite endless rosaries, which, far from fatiguing, calm and fortify him and fill him with sweetness?

To her contemplative daughters, moreover, Teresa says:

> In case you should think there is little gain to be derived from practising vocal prayer perfectly, I must tell you that, while you are repeating the Paternoster or some other vocal prayer, it is quite possible for the Lord to grant you perfect contemplation.[8]

Even if vocal prayer is not used to arrive at recollection, it will at least be a help, in certain circumstances, during mental prayer. There is no contemplative who has not at times experienced, in the aridities of prayer or in trials, how much strength and tranquility the faculties find in repeating slowly some *Ave Maria's* or reciting verses of the *Miserere*. In this regard, Saint Therese of the Child Jesus writes:

> Sometimes when I am in such a state of spiritual dryness that not a single good thought occurs to me, I say very slowly the "Our Father" or the "Hail Mary," and these prayers suffice to take me out of myself, and wonderfully refresh me.[9]

## B. Liturgical prayer

Vocal prayer takes on a special value when it is liturgical prayer. The prayer of the liturgy prepares the way for the Holy Sacrifice, *par excellence* the act of religion; and, in order to surround it with fitting praise, habitually borrows the words of the Holy Spirit, in using inspired texts from the Sacred Scriptures. Its imposing ceremonies, its sublime accents, alone give liturgical prayer a special dignity and efficacy; but these are incomparably increased by the fact that it is the official

[7] *Ibid.*, xxx; 125-6.
[8] *Ibid.*, xxv; 104.
[9] *Autobiography*, x, 163.

prayer of the Church, the prayer of the priesthood of Christ in the Church. And in virtue of this priesthood, in which we share through baptism, we too participate in it.

Because of the beauty with which it invests the sacred rites, the life it breathes into them, but above all by that grace which it makes flow from them, liturgical prayer excels in inspiring crowds to pray and delight in the mysteries being celebrated. It provides individual prayer with most helpful texts, and disposes it to enter into the depths of contemplation. It is like a queen, enthroned in beauty, respected and loved by all.

We might indeed wonder why its very dignity has provoked dissensions. Some would exalt it above all other forms of prayer, while others lament its usurping the rights of silent prayer. The discussions have been sharp at times. A famous liturgist would reproach Saint Teresa with not having the liturgical spirit because she had ecstasies during Mass. On the other hand, contemplatives have sometimes, by their apparent indifference to external forms and nonobservance of liturgical rubrics, justified the indignation of their adversaries who conformed better to pattern and were surely more attentive. Saint Joseph of Cupertino had to be excluded from choir because his ecstasies were disturbing their exercises. Saint John of the Cross, one day at Baeza, was so outside himself during his Mass, that he left the altar after Holy Communion. According to one of her teachers at the boarding school of l'Abbaye, Saint Therese of the Child Jesus could not follow the liturgical texts of the Mass and followed her own thoughts, in spite of the recommendations of her teachers who were Benedictine nuns. Not to mention Saint Philip Neri who allowed himself at the altar the devout but disconcerting liberties of the Roman Oratory.[10]

---

[10] The historians of Saint Philip Neri write:

"Without a companion to recite it with him, he [the saint] would never get to the end of his breviary. At Mass, he forgets everything: collects, epistle, gospel, the elevation of the Host and the Chalice after the consecration. He moves quickly as if to get ahead of the ecstasy. At the Consecra-

Liturgy or contemplation? These saints made a choice, or so it might seem. But actually, is it necessary to set these two against one another and choose?

Assuredly, we must take cognizance of the fact that there are souls who, by attraction and by vocation, draw their sustenance almost uniquely from liturgical prayer; others need silent prayer. But in the two camps there are extreme cases: the liturgist who can pray only with chant, with ancient texts, and in the austere beauty of a monastic church; the ecstatic entirely submissive to the breath of the Spirit, which goes and comes, heedless of rubrics.

Besides these two types, there is the multitude of spiritual minded souls who choose according to their taste and their grace, who take where they find, and see no point to opposing liturgy and contemplation which are in reality different forms of the same prayer and should mutually and charitably serve each other.

Saint Teresa, a master of interior prayer, presents us with a happy reconciliation.

Whatever may have been said, the Saint does in fact value liturgical prayer. She follows the cycle of the liturgy with so much attention as to date her letters, the important events of her life, and even little incidents on her journeys, according to the liturgical feast: "the feast of Saint Magdalen," "the day after the feast of Saint Martin," "November 17, in the octave of Saint Martin." She finishes the *Interior Castle* in 1577, "the vigil of Saint Andrew"; she received very great supernatural favors, "Palm Sunday," or "the feast of the conversion of Saint Paul," or "on the feast of Saint Peter and Saint Paul."

She tastes with delight the texts of the breviary: "How many

---

tion, he has to expedite the words and hurry to elevate and lower the Host and the Chalice, for fear of not being able to bring down his arms. Sometimes he interrupts to walk the length of the altar, makes himself look away, talks to the people, makes observations to the server about the lights."

things there are," she exclaims, "in the psalms of the glorious King David!"

It is certainly among liturgical prayers that she finds the Latin text of the *Song of Songs* that moves her deeply to recollection:

> The Lord, for some years now, has given me a great grace each time that I heard or read a few words of the Song of Solomon, so that without understanding clearly what the Latin words mean in Spanish, this recollects and moves my soul much more than the most devout books that I understand, and this happens very often.[11]

True, the Carmelite liturgy will not have Benedictine splendor. Appropriate to the aim of Carmel, it is a "liturgy of the the poor and solitary"; it is "so bare that for one who comes to it in search of an artistic emotion, or an emotion simply religious, it is impossible to grasp its meaning and its beauty." [12] But this poverty is by no means to be taken as disdain for ceremonial rites. The least of them does not leave the Saint indifferent; she writes:

> I knew quite well that in matters of faith no one would ever find me transgressing even the smallest ceremony of the Church, and that for the Church or for any truth of Holy Scripture I would undertake to die a thousand deaths.[13]

She tells us that her devotions:

> begin by having Masses said for me, and prayers which had been fully approved; for I was never fond of other kinds of devotion which some people practise—especially women—together with ceremonies which I could never endure, but for which they have a great affection.[14]

In order to thank Saint Joseph, she "used to try to keep his feast with the greatest possible solemnity," [15] as being the best way to honor him.

[11] *Life*, xxvii; Peers, I.
[12] Cf. Van den Bossche, *Les Carmes*, pp. 165-7.
[13] *Life*, xxxiii; 226.
[14] *Ibid.*, vi; 34.
[15] *Ibid.*; 58.

She understood especially the value of the Sacrifice of the Mass, which is at the center of all liturgical life, and she desired for her daughters that their participation in the Holy Sacrifice be as active as possible. This is what the Venerable Ana de Jesús reports:

> She (Saint Teresa) wanted us to participate always in the celebration of the Mass and sought out ways by which we could do this every day, even if it were in the same tone in which we recited the Hours. And if now and then this was impossible, for lack of a suitable chaplain, or because we were so few (for we were not more than thirteen), she used to say that it grieved her that we were deprived of that good. Moreover, when the Mass was sung, nothing prevented her from taking part, even though she had just received Holy Communion or was deeply recollected.[16]

This desire for liturgical participation in the Mass will excuse the saint, let us hope, in the eyes of the most exacting liturgists, for having sometimes had ecstasies after Holy Communion; and will entitle her to have their hearing to the end.

The Saint wants liturgical prayer, like every other vocal prayer, to be vivified by interior prayer. If the external movements that it imposes, the art that it cultivates, the sustained attention that it requires, should hinder or even destroy the contemplation that it is meant to serve, the devotion that it should stimulate, or the interior spirit that it wants to express, it would be only a jewel box, very beautiful perhaps but having within no precious stone; or a body without a soul, mere external worship that God could not accept, according to the word of Scripture: "This people honor me with their lips, but their heart is far from me."

There is no doubt that the beginner must learn to pray with the Church, to enter into the sober and majestic beauty of her ceremonies, to penetrate their symbolism and delight at length in her liturgical texts. He must above all seek in liturgical prayer the movements of the soul of Christ in the Church, listen to the groaning of His Spirit of Love, and learn thus in the

[16] Cf. Ribera, *Vida de santa Teresa de Jesús.* Barcelona, 1908, p. 633.

school of Christ Jesus, our Master, what must be each day his intimate and silent prayer.

## C. Meditated reading

Mental prayer is what the beginner wants to learn, and what we must teach him.

It may be that he is already captivated by a sweet and powerful grace to which we can entrust him; for when that comes, everything is simple for him, if not easy, in this exchange of friendship.

But if he feels no supernatural support how could we send him out alone to that intimate converse with God, so simple in its definition but in practice so complex. His love for God is indeed a living one, but his faculties are quite unable to occupy themselves, alone, with subjects so far above him and which, as yet, he badly understands. He is not yet grounded in the truths of faith, or at least is incapable of dwelling on them at length in the presence of the Master; and so he lapses into vague dreaminess or inertion, and the good will of his earlier days gives way to discouragement.

But here is a means suggested by Saint Teresa, one that she herself used a great deal: meditated reading.

Speaking of a soul who cannot form considerations in mental prayer, Teresa writes:

> Reading is none the less necessary for him, however little it may be, as a substitute for the mental prayer which he is unable to practise. I mean that if he is obliged to spend a great deal of time in prayer without this aid it will be impossible for him to persist in it for long.[17]

One can select a book with meditations already developed, ready made affections, resolutions to hand, the whole prayer well planned—impersonal it is true, but still one can make it one's own with the necessary adaptation to one's needs.

The book to be chosen for meditated reading is not the book

[17] *Life*, iv; Peers, I, 24.

that is simply instructive or devotional, nor even the interesting
book that holds one's attention, but the book that suggests and
provokes reflection, arouses the affections, or better still, that
awakens the soul and keeps it in the presence of God.

Simply reading is not meditated reading. Meditated reading
must be interrupted for deeper reflections in the presence of
God, to express to Him our love, to enter into conversation
with Him. It will be short or prolonged according to need and
will be resumed only when one falls again into dreaminess or
inertion.

If the reading should distract from God by stimulating the
thoughts and affections excessively, then it fails in its purpose,
as reading here has only one purpose, the facilitating of mental
prayer. Its sole function is to furnish a subject of conversation
with God, to establish a bond for union with Him. Reading is
in the service of that exchange of friendship with God which
is the essential act of mental prayer; from this, it must never
be allowed to distract. To this end, the soul must ceaselessly
bring it back.

Meditated reading will normally be the form of mental
prayer for the novice in spiritual ways. The contemplative, too,
will return to it in the hours of physical or moral fatigue, to
sustain or relax his faculties; or again, to detach them from
the too lively or obsessing preoccupations that prevent recollection. Let us hear the painful and conclusive experiences of
Saint Teresa on this point: "I myself spent over fourteen years
without ever being able to meditate except while reading," she
writes.[18]

In the book of her *Life,* she tells us precisely the place given
to meditated reading during her eighteen years of aridities:

During all these years, except after communicating, I never dared
to begin to pray without a book. . . . With this help, which was a
companionship to me and a shield with which I could parry the blows
of my many thoughts, I felt comforted. For it was not usual with me

[18] *Way of Perfection,* xvii; Peers, II, 69.

to suffer from aridity: this only came when I had no book, where-upon my soul would at once become disturbed and my thoughts would begin to wander. As soon as I started to read they began to collect themselves and the book acted like a bait to my soul. Often the mere fact that I had it by me was sufficient. Sometimes I read a little, sometimes a great deal, according to the favor which the Lord showed me.[19]

These confidences of Saint Teresa show us the importance of meditated reading in the development of her life of mental prayer. And so we cannot but be astonished at the mistrust of it that exists in certain quarters where they oblige the novices to endure the inevitable dryness of beginners in an almost complete obscurity and without the help of reading to get out of the void into which their inexperience, or even their lack of knowledge, has let them fall. The danger of laziness accompanying the reading does not justify that mistrust. Reading is, in fact, too solid a support for the beginner, and a shield too precious, for anyone to deprive him of it through fear that sometimes he may not know how to use it, or may use it badly.

## D. Meditation

When the faculties are strengthened and nourished enough to do without a support, the soul can enter upon mental prayer in its most traditional form, which is meditation.

Meditation consists in making reflections or considerations on a subject chosen in advance, to arrive at a fruitful conviction or resolution. It can be guided by various methods, all of which include a prelude on the presence of God and humility; the body of meditation, in which convictions are formed by way of reflection; and a conclusion in which sentiments and petitions are expressed, and precise resolutions are made.

There are books of these well arranged meditations that provide models adapted to the needs of various souls. Works explaining the methods of discursive prayer, or giving meditations with the reflections to be made, affections to be formed,

[19] *Life*, iv; Peers, I, 24.

acts to be produced, have been numerous in every epoch. Already, Saint Teresa knew some that were "excellent both as to their teaching and as to the way in which they plan the beginning and the end of the time of prayer." [20] She writes:

For those with orderly minds, and for souls who practise prayer and can be a great deal in their own company, many books have been written, and these are so good and are the work of such competent people. . . .[21]

And others have followed. In the reformed Carmel, certain masters elaborated for the novices methods that indicated the different acts to be produced during mental prayer. The school of French spirituality multiplied books for meditation for the use of priests, religious, and cultured persons of the world. These developed, in a style of classic purity, pious and reasonable considerations that have formed generations of strong and moderate souls, as inimical to the good that creates a stir, as to the evil that gives scandal.

For our modern minds, more intuitive than discursive, more avid for the living and the concrete than for long processes of reasoning, these methods and books became outmoded in short time. And so we are happy to say that Saint Teresa speaks of meditation with temperate praise and an impersonal tone lacking in enthusiasm. This is because she too is one of those souls who have never been able to reason during mental prayer and whose "intellect hinders rather than helps them." [22]

This inability puts us in sympathy with her, and makes it easy for us to agree with her opinions. First, here is the praise:

There is no need to tell anyone who is capable of practising prayer in this way, and has already formed the habit of doing so, that by this good road the Lord will bring her to the harbour of light. If she begins so well, her end will be good also; and all who can walk along this road will walk restfully and securely, for one always walks restfully when the understanding is kept in restraint.[23]

[20] *Way of Perfection,* xix; Peers, II, 77.
[21] *Ibid.;* 76.
[22] *Life,* xiii; Peers, I, 78.
[23] *Way of Perfection,* xix; Peers, II, 77.

The praise is sincere; but anyone accustomed to the vibrating enthusiasm of Teresa will find it without warmth, reasonable and moderated, like the meditation it commends.

Moreover, a danger threatens those whose understanding is too active:

> Returning, then, to those who can make use of their reasoning powers, I advise them not to spend all their time in doing so; their method of prayer is most meritorious, but, enjoying it as they do, they fail to realize that they ought to have a kind of Sunday—that is to say, a period of rest from their labour. To stop working, they think, would be a loss of time, whereas my view is that this loss is a great gain; let them imagine themselves, as I have suggested, in the presence of Christ, and let them remain in converse with Him, and delighting in Him, without wearying their minds or fatiguing themselves by composing speeches to Him, but laying their needs before Him and acknowledging how right He is not to allow us to be in His presence.[24]

*good warning*

Saint Teresa had associated with the intellectuals and knew well their tendencies. The danger for them is that their facility in speculating on revealed truth, the satisfaction and intellectual profit that they draw from it, may fetter them and make them forget that mental prayer is an exchange of friendship with God.[25]

And so the Saint never tires of recalling this truth to "those who use their intellects a great deal and from one subject can extract many ideas and conceptions." [26] These especially must keep in mind her teaching in the *Interior Castle:*

> I only want you to be warned that, if you would progress a long way on this road and ascend to the Mansions of your desire, the important thing is not to think much, but to love much.[27]

[24] *Life,* xiii; Peers, I, 78.
[25] "I have come across some people who believe that the whole thing consists in thought; and thus, if they are able to think a great deal about God, however much the effort may cost them, they immediately imagine they are spiritually minded; while, if they become distracted, and their efforts to think of good things fail, they at once become greatly discouraged and suppose themselves to be lost" (*Foundations* v; Peers, I, 19).
[26] *Life,* xiii; Peers, I, 78.
[27] IV Mansions, i; Peers, II, 233. The Saint says the same thing in the *Book of the Foundations* (Cf. Peers, I, 20): The soul's profit, then, consists not in thinking much but in loving much.

Besides, whatever may be the consolations that come through meditation, one must have no illusions as to their value; they are

like water running all over the ground. This cannot be drunk directly from the source; and its course is never free from clogging impurities, so that it is neither so pure nor so clean as the other. I should not say that this prayer I have been describing, which comes from reasoning with the intellect, is living water—I mean so far as my understanding of it goes.[28]

Meditation—which is a good beginning [29]—does not, however, satisfy Saint Teresa. If we had to sum up her grievances, or rather fears, on this subject, we would say that she is afraid that meditation may detain souls in intellectual activity for itself and not orientate them sufficiently to God, the source of living water.[30]

But has the saint a way of mental prayer to recommend to beginners?

[28] *Way of Perfection,* xix; Peers, II, 80.

[29] *Ibid.;* 77.

[30] According to the testimony of P. José de Jesús-María Quiroga (died in 1629), the methods of mental prayer that were taught to the novices of Carmel at the beginning of the XVII century, shortly after the death of Saint John of the Cross, did not avoid these dangers. In his work on the gift that Saint John of the Cross had for guiding souls, this Father writes:
"When the teaching and influence of our saintly Father John of the Cross ceased, other masters came who taught the discursive and assiduous operations of the soul rather than the very simple spiritual acts which permit one to receive the divine operation and the effects of the divine influence by which perfection is obtained. These masters wrought a very different work in their disciples; these came out from mental prayer with tired heads and rarely gave evidence of enlightened minds. And, since during the novitiate, they did not learn how one must enter into contemplation when ripe for this kind of mental prayer, they left their school of formation without knowing the principal part of their vocation—and they remained all their life without knowing it—working in mental prayer with natural forces, without giving place to the divine operation which introduces perfection into the soul." *Obras del Místico Doctor San Juan de la Cruz,* edicion critica de Toledo, III, 569.

# CHAPTER IV
# The Prayer of Recollection

*i.e. collection of all the faculties*

> *Those who are able to shut themselves up in this way within this little Heaven of the soul . . . may be sure that they are walking on an excellent road.*[1]

If we were to consider only the Teresian definition of mental prayer and the liberty it leaves to souls in this exchange of friendship with God by whom one knows oneself loved, we might think that there was no special teaching to guide beginners and that none was necessary. But a careful study of the *Way of Perfection* and of the single chapter of the Second Mansions clears our minds of any doubt on this subject. Saint Teresa there sets forth the method of prayer that she had always used and that she warmly recommends:

> May the Lord teach this to those of you who do not know it: for my own part I must confess that, until the Lord taught me this method, I never knew what it was to get satisfaction and comfort out of prayer, and it is because I have always gained such great benefits from this custom of interior recollection that I have written about it at such length.[2]

The method of prayer that succeeded so well with Saint Teresa is the prayer of recollection; and beyond a doubt, it is the method that she wants her disciples to adopt.

## A. Description of the prayer of recollection

We are already sufficiently well acquainted with Saint Teresa not to expect from her a didactic treatise, nor even a profes-

[1] *Way of Perfection*, xxviii; Peers, II, 115.
[2] *Ibid.*, xxix; 122.

sorial definition. On the other hand, she excels in describing; in her descriptions, figurative and precise, we find a veritable technique for the prayer of recollection. She says:

> It is called recollection because the soul collects together all the faculties and enters within itself to be with its God.[3]

Farther on, the description is more detailed:

> It is as if the soul were rising from play, for it sees that worldly things are nothing but toys; so in due course it rises above them, like a person entering a strong castle, in order that it may have nothing more to fear from its enemies. It withdraws the senses from all outward things and spurns them so completely that, without its understanding how, its eyes close and it cannot see them and the soul's spiritual sight becomes clear. Those who walk along this path almost invariably close their eyes when they say their prayers; this, for many reasons, is an admirable custom.[4]

It is important to point out that there is no question here of a passive recollection produced by the special intervention of God Himself in the soul; the recollection defined by Saint Teresa is effected by an effort of the will:

> You must understand that this is not a supernatural state but depends upon our volition, and that, by God's favour, we can enter it of our own accord; *this condition must be understood of everything that we say in this book can be done,* for without it nothing can be accomplished and we have not the power to think a single good thought. For this is not a silence of the faculties: it is a shutting-up of the faculties within itself by the soul.[5]

Thus the activity of the powers of the soul, detaching themselves from exterior things in order to turn towards God in the center, is the first phase of the prayer of recollection. Of itself, it is not enough to produce this prayer; it is only the preparatory act, commanded by the presence of God dwelling within. The faculties withdraw to the center of the soul only because God is there in a very special way. The soul is the temple of the Holy Ghost, the temple that Saint Teresa preferred:

[3] *Ibid.,* xxviii; 115.
[4] *Ibid.;* 116.
[5] *Ibid.,* xxix; 120.

Remember how Saint Augustine tells us about his seeking God in many places and eventually finding Him within himself. Do you suppose it is of little importance that a soul which is often distracted should come to understand this truth and to find that, in order to speak to its Eternal Father or to take its delight in Him, it has no need to go to Heaven or to speak in a loud voice? However quietly we speak, He is so near that He will hear us: we need no wings to go in search of Him but have only to find a place where we can be alone and look upon Him present within us.[6]

Recollection has no other end than to lead the soul into the most deeply intimate part of the temple of God. But to penetrate in silence into this temple vivified by so majestic a Presence, does not yet suffice. One must have real contact with God and be lovingly attentive to Him. Prayer at this early stage would normally be only the soul's own active commerce with God: "We must recollect our outward senses, take charge of them ourselves and give them something which will occupy them," writes the Saint.[7]

Saint Teresa fears lest laziness creep into recollection, and many times over in her writings she expresses that fear. It is true that any recollection, by stopping the activity of the faculties, produces a delightful impression of repose. The natural passivity of some souls runs the danger of confusing that sweetness with the peace that comes from the action of God, and hence of giving themselves up to a lazy inactivity and enjoying a tranquility that has nothing divine in it. That is why, our Saint teaches, ordinarily an effort actively to seek God must follow the effort for recollection. A difficult transition this, a delicate manoeuvre especially in the higher states. But let no one oppose her with the teaching of Saint John of the Cross, nor with that of Saint Peter of Alcantara; they do not contradict her.

In these beginnings, no hesitation is possible; the soul must seek to be engaged with God. For this, there is no better way than to seek the company of Jesus and to hold conversation

[6] *Way of Perfection*, xxviii; Peers, II, 114.
[7] *Ibid.*, xxix; 121.

with Him. As the Word, He is present in the soul with the
Father and the Holy Spirit; as the Word Incarnate, He is the
only mediator; He is the Word of God that we must hear in
the silence:

> For, hidden there within itself, it [the soul] can think about the
> Passion, and picture the Son, and offer Him to the Father, without
> wearying the mind by going to seek Him on Mount Calvary, or in the
> Garden, or at the Column.[8]
> It is well to reflect for a time . . . [but then] we must sometimes
> remain by His side with our minds hushed in silence. If we can, we
> should occupy ourselves in looking upon Him Who is looking at us;
> keep Him company; talk with Him; pray to Him; humble ourselves
> before Him; have our delight in Him.[9]

We are, here, at the essential part of the prayer of recollection. The withdrawal of the powers had no other purpose than
to favor this living intimacy with the divine Master:

> Speak with Him as with a Father, a Brother, a Lord and a Spouse—
> and, sometimes in one way and sometimes in another, He will teach
> you what you must do to please Him. Do not be foolish; ask Him to
> let you speak to Him, and, as He is your Spouse, to treat you as His
> brides. *Remember how important it is for you to have understood this
> truth—that the Lord is within us and that we should be there with
> Him.*[10]

On this subject of intimacy with Jesus, the Saint is inexhaustible. But we never tire of listening to her, such is the variety
in her descriptions, the delicacy of her affections, the strength
and richness in that overflowing life:

> See, He is only waiting for us to look at Him, as He says to the
> Bride. . . .
> A wife, they say, must be like this if she is to have a happy married
> life with her husband. If he is sad, she must show signs of sadness;
> if he is merry, even though she may not in fact be so, she must appear
> merry too. . . . Yet this, without any pretence, is really how we are
> treated by the Lord. He becomes subject to us and is pleased to let
> you be the mistress and to conform to your will. If you are happy,
> look upon your risen Lord, and the very thought of how He rose

[8] *Ibid.*, xxviii; 115.
[9] *Life*, xiii; Peers, I, 82-3.
[10] *Way of Perfection*, xxviii; Peers, II, 115.

from the sepulchre will gladden you. How bright and how beautiful was He then! How majestic! How victorious! How joyful! He was like one emerging from a battle in which He had gained a great kingdom, all of which He desires you to have—and with it Himself. Is it such a great thing that you should turn your eyes but once and look upon Him Who has made you such great gifts?

If you are suffering trials, or are sad, look upon Him on His way to the Garden. What sore distress He must have borne in His soul, to describe His own suffering as He did and to complain of it! Or look upon Him bound to the Column, full of pain, His flesh all torn to pieces by His great love for you. . . . Or look upon Him bending under the weight of the Cross and not even allowed to take breath: He will look upon you with His lovely and compassionate eyes, full of tears, and in comforting your grief will forget His own. . . . "O Lord of the world, my true Spouse!" you may say to Him.[11]

Intimacy with Jesus introduces us into the life of the Trinity, for Jesus is our mediator. Through Him we are sons of the Father whom, with Him, we may call "our Father." Saint Teresa cries out:

"Our Father, which art in the Heavens." O my Lord, how Thou dost reveal Thyself as the Father of such a Son, while Thy Son reveals Himself as the Son of such a Father! Blessed be Thou for ever and ever.[12]

United to the Father and to the Son, we shall certainly find the Holy Spirit who proceeds from them: "Between such a Son and such a Father," concludes the Saint, "there must needs be the Holy Spirit." [13]

The divine intimacy that is realized during the regular hours of prayer must be continued during the course of the day:

We must retire within ourselves even during our ordinary occupations. If I can recall the companionship which I have within my soul for as much as a moment, that is of great utility.[14]

In her teaching on mental prayer, very rarely does Saint Teresa distinguish between the time that is especially set aside for it, and the rest of the day. To the presence of God, abiding

[11] *Way of Perfection*, xxvi; Peers, II, 107-8.
[12] *Ibid.*, xxvii; 110.
[13] *Ibid.*; 113.
[14] *Ibid.*, xxix; 121.

# PRAYER OF RECOLLECTION

and always acting in us, there must correspond a striving for
intimacy as constant as possible. The prayer of recollection must
overflow progressively into all of our life. Assuredly, we must
avoid a tenseness that would be exhausting for our faculties
and sterile. But to our discreet and persevering efforts God will
respond with His grace. He manifests Himself to those who
seek Him. Has He not said: "If anyone love me, we will come
to him, and will make our abode with him" (John 14:23).
And this Saint Teresa explains with the aid of her experience:

> I conclude by advising anyone who wishes to acquire it (since, as I
> say, it is in our power to do so) not to grow weary of trying to get
> used to the method which has been described, for it is equivalent to
> a gradual gaining of the mastery over herself and is not vain labour.
> To conquer oneself for one's own good is to make use of the senses in
> the service of the interior life. If she is speaking she must try to re-
> member that there is One within her to Whom she can speak; if she
> is listening, let her remember that she can listen to Him Who is nearer
> to her than anyone else. Briefly, let her realize that, if she likes, she
> need never withdraw from this good companionship, and let her grieve
> when she has left her Father alone for so long though her need of
> Him is so sore.[15]

Such is the prayer of recollection and its end. It is not a passing exercise. It aims at constant union. A method for beginners, yes, but it leads directly towards the summits of divine
union.

## B. How to attain to the prayer of recollection

Ordinarily the prayer of recollection will seem to the beginner to be quite beyond his power and his habits. If he tries to
achieve it, he is aware that his faculties lack facility for it, are
not habituated to discipline, and do not know how to seek
contact with God in the darkness of the soul.

Any experience whatever of the presence of God in the soul
would be a precious help:

> I assure you that for minds which wander it is of great importance
> not only to have a right belief about this but to try to learn it by ex-

[15] *Ibid.;* 122.

perience, for it is one of the best ways of concentrating the mind and effecting recollection of the soul.[16]

It is not necessary that this experience be given by a grace that is mystical in character, a grace of union or any other; a simple interior manifestation of God by a consolation or an appeal can suffice to facilitate recollection and teach it to the soul definitively. These divine manifestations are rather common in the spiritual life. Is there any devout soul who, in a fervent Communion or a prayer, has not felt at least a sweetness that is revealing of a divine presence?

Are we to say, then, that some such experience, however slight, is necessary in order to work at prayer of recollection? Certainly not. For if Saint Teresa assures us that this experience will come later, she also affirms forcefully that "when a soul sets out upon this path, He [the Lord] does not reveal Himself to it [immediately]"; [17] but that He does so at least sufficiently often to keep the soul in the state of recollection, and that the prayer of recollection of which she speaks depends on our own endeavor:

You must understand that this is not a supernatural state but depends upon our volition, and that, by God's favour, we can enter it of our own accord.[18]

The soul must put forth energetic effort. Recollection takes hard asceticism. There is no use hiding this fact, even though it seem frightening. Saint Teresa speaks of the fatigue of beginners, "for the body insists on its rights, not understanding that if it refuses to admit defeat it is, as it were, cutting off its own head." [19]

In the *Interior Castle* she tells us that "the soul will certainly suffer great trials at this time." [20] Her own experience, set down at length in the book of her *Life,* taught her this:

[16] *Way of Perfection,* xxviii; Peers, II, 114.
[17] *Ibid.;* 118.
[18] *Ibid.,* xxix; 120.
[19] *Ibid.,* xxviii; 116.
[20] II Mansions, i; Peers, II, 215.

For many years I endured this trial of being unable to concentrate on one subject, and a very sore trial it is.[21]

Violent attempts, however, are dangerous; for recollection "cannot be begun by making strenuous efforts, but must come gently." [22] The Saint herself considered it a grace, that she found a method of recollection in the *Third Spiritual Alphabet* of the Franciscan, Francisco de Osuna. And she has passed on to us the fruit of her studies and her experience.

First of all, it is important not to separate the diverse times of the prayer of recollection. As soon as the soul is alone, it must seek the company of Jesus and converse with Him:

[After reciting the Confiteor], then, daughter, as you are alone, you must look for a companion—and who could be a better Companion than the very Master Who taught you the prayer that you are about to say? Imagine that this Lord Himself is at your side.[23]

Undoubtedly, the best method of recollection is to fix one's thoughts on the Master who is present. To stretch forward towards the goal is the best way of reaching it and recollection together.

By using these means we may learn to say the Paternoster well and not find ourselves thinking of something irrelevant. I have sometimes experienced this myself, and the best remedy I have found for it is to try to fix my mind on the Person by Whom the words were first spoken.[24]

In order to maintain this prayerful contact with the Master, the faculties must be exercised on whatever other little strategies will serve. Each one will use those that he finds most helpful in keeping him in this loving, intimate converse with God.

Here, we find again all the modes of prayer previously set forth; they no longer constitute independent forms of prayer but are become means to bring about the prayer of recollection.

Some will use the imagination, reconstructing the gospel

[21] *Way of Perfection,* xxvi; Peers, II, 106.
[22] II Mansions, i; Peers, II, 218.
[23] *Way of Perfection,* xxvi; 106.
[24] *Ibid.,* xxiv; 103.

scenes or picturing the person and the actions of the Master; for such persons, this will facilitate a living exchange of friendship with Him.

For others, the reflections of the understanding or discursive meditations may favor the prayer of recollection, but on condition that they do not pass too much time in it, and that reasonings yield place promptly to the living contact that they are to serve:

> We must not always tire ourselves by going in search of such ideas; we must sometimes remain by His side with our minds hushed in silence.[25]

And there will be times when a person will derive aid for mental prayer neither from the imagination nor the understanding. It is still possible to gaze at the Master with a simple regard of faith and to stay in His presence; Saint Teresa assures us of this:

> O sisters, those of you whose minds cannot reason for long or whose thoughts cannot dwell *upon God* but are *constantly* wandering must at all costs form this habit. I know quite well that you are capable of it—for many years I endured this trial of being unable to concentrate on one subject.[26]

This simple gaze of faith establishes a sufficient contact. Often enough, however, it will leave the soul in a painful helplessness. To ward this off—as well as any other powerlessness, from whatever quarter it may come—Saint Teresa suggests a few little practices:

First there is vocal prayer whose advantages we already know; it can provide good food for the prayer of recollection:

> If one prays in this way, the prayer may be only vocal, but the mind will be recollected much sooner; and this is a prayer which brings with it many blessings.[27]

Meditated reading is also a means, and one of the best, for aiding recollection:

[25] *Life,* xiii; Peers, I, 83.
[26] *Way of Perfection,* xxvi; Peers, II, 106.
[27] *Ibid.,* xxviii; 115.

It is also a great help to have a good book, written in the vernacular, simply as an aid to recollection.[28]

To win the attention of the faculties and assist them in considering the person of the living Jesus, one may use an image:

> You will find it very helpful if you can get an image or a picture of this Lord—one that you like—not to wear round your neck and never look at but to use regularly whenever you talk to Him, and He will tell you what to say.[29]

Experience will discover to each one many other attractions and artifices to sustain the activity of the faculties or to supplement it and to hold the soul in contact with the living God.

To those who persevere in making use of these, Saint Teresa promises a rather prompt success:

> If we cultivate the habit, make the necessary effort and practise the exercises for several days, the benefits will reveal themselves, and when we begin to pray we shall realize that the bees are coming to the hive and entering it to make the honey, and all without any effort of ours.[30]

But, according to the mind of Teresa, the prayer of recollection must extend over the entire day and penetrate the whole of a life. In order to pursue this loving intimacy with God throughout our various occupations, the means used for mental prayer will no longer be adequate; others must be found, simple and suitable. Thus, reminders of the presence of God will be connected with certain objects, images, or any familiar things; with a change of occupation, or with any other point of reference that will recall the divine Presence and the act of love to be made. The divine Presence will be sought under the different veils that both hide it and reveal it: in the tabernacle, in the soul, in the persons we meet.

*helps*

By this very simple technique, joined with love, the presence of God soon becomes familiar. At every moment it is signalized by these luminous points of reference, almost everywhere in our

[28] *Ibid.*, xxvi; 109.
[29] *Ibid.*
[30] *Ibid.*, xxviii; 116.

surroundings, in the persons we are meeting, in our tasks and duties; it fills the atmosphere in which we live—in fact, our whole life, and without effort almost or noise of any kind, it becomes for us a tranquil and unfailing light.

Saint Teresa is speaking of this abiding presence of God, this intimacy with Jesus, our inseparable Companion, in short, of the prayer of recollection considered in all of its extension into our life, when she says:

> Nothing, sisters, can be learned without a little trouble, so do, for the love of God, look upon any care which you take about this as well spent. I know that, with God's help, if you practise it for a year, or perhaps for only six months, you will be successful in attaining it. Think what a short time that is for acquiring so great a benefit, for you will be laying a good foundation, so that, if the Lord desires to raise you up to achieve great things, He will find you ready, because you will be close to Himself.[31]

She had already said:

> If a whole year passes without our obtaining what we ask, let us be prepared to try for longer. Let us never grudge time so well spent. Who, after all, is hurrying us? I am sure we can form this habit and strive to walk at the side of this true Master.[32]

In these texts, the Saint seems to say that habitual recollection demands a special grace from God. The method of prayer suggested prepares the soul for such a favor and even enables it to merit it. It is a method that employs all the faculties of the soul to this end and the drawing down upon itself the mercy of God. This in itself bespeaks its excellence and explains its success.

## C. Excellence of the prayer of recollection

The fact that it is a striving for intimate contact with God by union with Christ Jesus is what gives merit and value to the Teresian prayer of recollection. Today, this teaching seems to have no claim to originality. All the methods of prayer that we

---

[31] *Way of Perfection*, xxix; Peers, II, 123.
[32] *Ibid.*, xxvi; 106.

know tend to no other end than this divine union and set no other way than Christ. We must recognize, however, that such unanimity can be traced, in large part, to the influence exercised by Saint Teresa on the French spirituality of the seventeenth ✓ century.

But while the Christocentric orientation in French spirituality was clothed in grand and noble thoughts, with Saint Teresa it was and it remains simple, living, direct. From this point of view, the teaching of Saint Teresa is still original and has special attraction for souls in our day, more intuitive than discursive, more avid for living contact with God than for highly reasoned thoughts.

From the moment that Saint Teresa enters into mental prayer, she is in quest of Christ. Her need for God and for Jesus will brook no delay. No intermediary to attain Christ; no stop on the way; she casts about neither for a thought to penetrate, nor a sentiment, nor a spiritual inspiration to delight in. She consents to consider on her journey only what can lead her straight to the end. Having found Jesus, to talk to Him or simply to look at Him is enough; that is her prayer. The love that is in haste to find is satisfied with this simple contact.

The contact is a living one. Teresa does not make her prayer with the higher part of her soul alone; she goes to Christ with her whole being, supernatural and human. All her powers go eagerly to a profound and complete embrace, for all are hungry for the divine and for God. Inability alone, whether it be from fatigue or God's special action, can arrest the flight of one or other. And Christ Jesus, the Word Incarnate, who took on human nature in order to adapt Himself to our needs and our weakness, responds to these desires. There results a living exchange of friendship in which divine and human energies participate and in which each one and all are enriched by pouring themselves out.

This loving commerce is living and fruitful only because it is a real exchange. Teresian mental prayer is not just simply a school exercise; it is a real exercise of the supernatural life which rests, in all the movements that it prescribes, on dogmatic truth. It establishes therefore a contact between two realities.

The prayer of recollection makes us seek God in the center of our soul. Where could we find Him more intimately, to establish our supernatural relations with Him, than in those inner depths where He communicates His divine life, making each one of us personally His child? God who is present and acting in me is truly my Father, for He engenders me ceaselessly by the diffusion of His life; I can embrace Him myself with a filial embrace, there where He is giving Himself. My Lord and my God really dwells in me; and when my soul will be freed from the prison of the body and purified enough to receive the *lumen gloriae,* the light of glory that enables us to see God as He is, it will find Him penetrating and enveloping these same innermost depths where now it seeks Him with the light of faith. Heaven is in my soul. By keeping me in the company of the Holy Trinity that inhabits it, the prayer of recollection is more than a preparation for eternal life; it is a real beginning of it under the veil of faith.

In this Holy Trinity, whose three Persons act in us by a single, hence common, operation, Saint Teresa asks us to go to the Incarnate Word. This is because our participation in the divine life by grace does not leave us simple spectators of its operations, but makes us enter really into the movement of the triune life. This active and intimate participation cannot come about through superadded persons, for the Trinity is immutable in its infinite perfection. It is possible only by the favor of adoption by one of the three Persons and of an identification with Him, which permits us, by sharing in His operations, to enter into the eternal rhythm of the Three.

It is Jesus, the Incarnate Word, who came to us, saved us, purified and adopted us. He moreover identified us with Himself, so as to have us enter as sons with Him into the bosom of the Holy Trinity, to make us partakers of His splendors and operations as the Word, and, by giving us the same Father and the same Spirit of Love, to secure for us His heritage of glory and beatitude. By Him, in Him, and with Him alone can we live our supernatural life. We belong to Christ, and Christ is in God.

Let us not excuse our abandoning of Jesus by claiming a special devotion to the Father or the Holy Spirit. We can be sons of the Father only through union with Christ, His only Son; and the Holy Spirit can be in us only by reason of our identification with the Word, from whom and the Father, the Spirit proceeds. It is Jesus, too, who gives us Mary; from Him alone derives the veritable filial spirit in relation to her who is our Mother because she is His. In Christ, also, is the Church, and hence all souls.

By attaching us to Christ, the prayer of recollection brings us to our proper place, makes us discover our riches, centers us in Him who is all, and gives us everything in the supernatural order.

Because it makes us live the truth and introduces us into the heart of supernatural realities, the prayer of recollection has a surprising efficacy. Saint Teresa herself tells us some of the practical results that this living contact with supernatural reality produces.

First of all there is a quieting of the faculties which should naturally be agitated in their seeming void but which on the contrary are wonderfully recollected. Besides, Saint Teresa has told us that the best remedy for distractions is to fix our thought on the One to whom we are praying.[33] She also writes:

If one prays in this way, the prayer may be only vocal, but the mind will be recollected much sooner; and this is a prayer which brings with it many blessings.[34]

[33] *Way of Perfection*, xxiv; Peers, II, 103.
[34] *Ibid.*, xxviii; 115.

The habit of fixing our gaze on our Lord produces such effects that the soul returns to it constantly:

If you become accustomed to having Him at your side, and if He sees that you love Him to be there and are always trying to please Him, you will never be able, as we put it, to send Him away.[35]

This habit of the presence of Jesus constitutes, writes the Saint:

a good foundation, so that, if the Lord desires to raise you up to achieve great things, He will find you ready, because you will be close to Himself.[36]

And here is another word of hope:

They are like one who travels in a ship, and, if he has a little good wind, reaches the end of his voyage in a few days, while those who go by land take *much* longer.[37]

This end, to which the Saint is tending and that she wants to make others long for, is the Source of living water, God Himself, giving Himself directly to the soul in contemplation. The prayer of recollection prepares the soul for this:

The sea-voyage, then, can be made; . . . Souls who do so are more secure from many occasions of sin, and the fire of Divine love is the more readily enkindled in them; for they are so near that fire that, however little the blaze has been fanned with the understanding, any small spark that flies out at them will cause them to burst into flame. When no hindrance comes to it from outside, the soul remains alone with its God and is thoroughly prepared to become enkindled.[38]

God in fact, who has infinite desire to give Himself and calls every soul to the Source of living water, cannot fail the soul that seeks Him by so direct and constant a way. Such is the thought of Saint Teresa. She adds to this the assurance that the soul that practises the prayer of recollection such as she teaches it, will certainly arrive at the prayer of quiet:

[35] *Way of Perfection,* xxvi; Peers, II, 106.
[36] *Ibid.,* xxix; 126.
[37] *Ibid.,* xxviii; 115.
[38] *Ibid.;* 117.

It is called recollection because the soul collects together all the faculties and enters within itself to be with its God. Its Divine Master comes more speedily to teach it, and to grant it the Prayer of Quiet, than in any other way. . . . Those who are able to shut themselves up in this way within this little Heaven of the soul, wherein dwells the Maker of Heaven and earth, and who have formed the habit of looking at nothing and staying in no place which will distract these outward senses, may be sure that they are walking on an excellent road, and will come without fail to drink of the water of the fountain.[39]

Such firm reassurance opens up to us horizons that reach far beyond the prayers of the first stages that we are studying. It seems to resolve already the difficult problem of the call to contemplation.

Let us keep this in mind: the prayer of recollection attains to a living contact with God; it is a sure way to deep and delightful intimacies and bears within itself the pledge of them. No promise could be more consoling for the beginner, no encouragement more precious.

[39] *Ibid.;* 115.

# CHAPTER V
# Spiritual Reading

*I will give thee a living book.*[1]

Good will and our own efforts will not suffice fully to establish the soul in the prayer of recollection. Saint Teresa knew from experience that something more was necessary: spiritual reading.

The Saint says that she learned how to recollect herself from the *Third Spiritual Alphabet* of the Franciscan, Francisco de Osuna—a book that her uncle Pedro gave her when she was visiting at his home in Hortigosa.[2] Before that, the high ideals of her adolescent years had been cooled by the reading, at home, of tales of romantic chivalry.[3] It was in the *Letters* of Saint Jerome, on the other hand, that she claims to have found the courage to tell her father of her vocation;[4] and the *Morals* of Saint Gregory, which acquainted her with the story of Job, prepared her to bear her illnesses with patience during the course of her religious life.[5]

Elsewhere she writes: "It seemed to me, in these early stages of which I am speaking, that, provided I had books and could be alone, there was no risk of my being deprived of that great blessing (the favour which the Lord showed me)."[6]

This affirmation aims beyond the Saint's own experience. She is explaining the needs of beginners in the life of prayer: spir-

[1] *Life*, xxvi; Peers, I, 168.
[2] *Ibid.*, iv; 23.
[3] *Ibid.*, ii; 13.
[4] *Ibid.*, iii; 19.
[5] *Ibid.*, v; 30.
[6] *Ibid.*, iv; 25.

itual reading and solitude are equally necessary. Silence creates the atmosphere of prayer; reading gives it sustenance.

## A. Importance

"He who knows in truth, loves in fire!" In these ardent words, Saint Angela of Foligno expresses a law; namely, that love proceeds from knowledge.

In the bosom of the Holy Trinity, the knowledge that God has of Himself and by which He engenders the Son, precedes the mutual love of the Father and the Son whence proceeds the Holy Spirit,ˣ substantial and personal Love. God has written this law too in the heart of man whom He has made to His image: *Nil volitum quin praecognitum,* Nothing is willed that is not first known, proclaimed the Scholastics. In man, love is not always up to the measure of knowledge, although love may indeed exceed knowledge; but without some knowledge, love could not be at all.

This law, at the same time divine and human, governs the life of grace, which is a created participation in the life of the Trinity. The development of charity, which is the very essence of the life of grace, is linked with the development of faith which gives it light; and faith itself, for its own growth, must nourish itself on dogmatic truth.

Thus faith, a supernatural habit, cannot be separated from the intellect in which it is engrafted. It cannot adhere to God, it cannot enter upon its own proper domain of divine mystery, if the intelligence does not first adhere to the dogmatic formulas which express divine truth in human language. However docile the virtue of faith may be in accepting all that God has revealed, it must first have this revelation presented to it before it can, in ordinary circumstances, make an act of faith. And so Saint Paul, after pointing out that faith comes from hearing, adds: "If no one preaches to them, how will they believe?" He thus stressed the fact that faith has its roots in the senses which,

ˣ Augustine, de Trinitas

on receiving the expression of the truth, furnish faith its sustenance.

This nourishment of revealed truth is, in varying degrees, necessary to faith at every stage of its development, but especially at the beginning.[7] It is as yet too little enlightened to be able to keep its gaze firmly fixed, too feeble yet to enter with ease into that obscurity in which divine mystery dwells, and so it must study and reflect much upon those divine truths, that it may lay solid foundations against the time of temptation and doubt.

Thus nourished by divine knowledge, faith grows strong and vigorous; it plumbs the depths of supernatural mysteries, rejoicing in the splendors that shine in the formulas, while awaiting the purifying darkness that is to come, which will lead it into the yet more delectable savoring of divine truth as it is in itself.

Moreover, love begins to yearn to know that which it loves. In the quest of the object of its love, it ceases not to enquire after it and to use all the means it has in its power to attain to it. Our love of God, then, will gather up with avidity whatever He has been pleased to reveal about Himself. It will study revealed truth in order to fathom it; will pick up all the analogies that interpret it, the references that explain it, the authorized commentaries that clarify it, so as to enter still further into the truth itself and draw out food for faith and deeper love. Thus Saint Therese of the Child Jesus sought in words and scenes of the Gospel to know "the character of the good God." Knowledge is the source of love, while in its turn love stimulates knowledge.

This shows us how much mental prayer, especially in its be-

[7] These statements have their full value for the beginners in mental prayer of whom we are speaking. Later, in supernatural contemplation, distinct knowledge fails (*Dark Night*, Bk. II, xii). Love then takes the lead, instructing the soul in the anointings of Wisdom. This delightful wisdom does not dispense the soul from recourse to revealed truth, but it diminishes its need for distinct light.

ginnings, needs revealed truth. It can establish a friendly converse with God only through faith. But if faith can attain to
God only through the medium of those formulas in which revealed truth is contained, it has all the more reason for having
frequent and sustained recourse to them in order to maintain
habitual contact with God in prayer. What support would that
loving commerce with God have other than revealed truth
when as yet it cannot count on the direct action of God through
the gifts of the Holy Spirit? The result could only be long and
painful boredom or lazy inactivity—the one as sterile as the
other.

With good books, on the contrary, the soul can, like Saint
Teresa, go into solitude and be occupied with God. The practices that the Saint recommends to maintain the prayer of recollection are for the most part only various ways of having recourse to revealed truth so as to occupy the faculties and engage
them in this loving converse.

If there be already on the one hand some facility for recollection and affectionate commerce with God, and on the other
a certain disquieting multiplicity of thought arising from reading, then some souls may be led to conclude that spiritual
reading is not only not a help but rather an obstacle to prayer.
From this conclusion there is only one step to omitting all instructive reading or sacrificing it to any other occupation. Such
negligence exposes these souls to danger of a gravity to be
learned only later. For the moment their affective prayer may be
excellent. But normally it will become for want of sustenance
less and less attractive, more languid, more in danger of going
astray and losing itself in egoistic sentimentality. The soul was
thought to be perfectly united to God, so peaceful it seemed;
we later find it lost in itself, in its preoccupations or its resent-
ments, and in the creations of its imagination. The antenna of
the faith was not sufficiently supported by dogmatic truth to be
able to maintain a contact with God that would have saved the

soul from the subtle egoism in which henceforth it seems submerged.[8]

Certainly the needs for distinct lights on particular truths of faith are different according to souls; there are none, however, whose faith can develop without sustenance drawn from the knowledge of revealed truth.

At this point there are some who, in an effort to minimize the importance of spiritual culture, promptly cite the example of great saints who were little gifted intellectually and had little culture. These saints, marvelously enlightened, are an exception. We must remark, moreover, that if the divine assistance supplied for the lack of intellectual means, it did not dispense them from the effort of study. The holy Curé of Ars, for example, worked unrelentingly to qualify for ordination to the priesthood, and then passed long hours in preparing his sermons. The extraordinary lights with which he was later favored can be considered not only as fruits of his sanctity, but as recompense for the intense labor he had done to nourish and clarify his faith.

As a practical corollary to these considerations, we can assert that the first obstacle to be overcome in the way of popularizing today the spiritual life is the religious ignorance of our time. This ignorance leaves in darkness not only hundreds of millions of pagans upon whom the light of the Gospel has never shone, but also millions of minds very near us, in our cities, even though the greatest effort is made to bring the other sciences within reach of all.

Even the educated are not immune from this ignorance; we do not hesitate to say so. The majority of educated men who call themselves unbelievers are ignorant of almost all revealed truth. As to those who have remained faithful to religious practices, too often they have retained from former instructions

[8] These prayers of which we are speaking are prayers simply affective in which there is little or no real contemplation. They fail because they are sustained neither by the action of God nor by the work of the faculties.

only some moral notions, but few or no dogmatic teachings to sustain their spiritual life. Like the others of their class, they embarked upon their studies or their career. Having taken up law, medicine, industry, business, teaching, or art, they live and think and act accordingly. From time to time, perhaps even regularly, they fulfil some external religious duty. But since their adolescence they have had no real contact with revealed truth. They have never thought of it with the mind of mature men, and never considered their soul or their mode of life in the light of Christ's teaching. Thus their religious instruction and their Christian life have remained really inferior to their general culture and their professional formation. The result is that they have become submerged in the natural at the expense of the supernatural. Faith and the tradition of faith remain, but anything like a profound Christian life is lacking. Their Christianity without light, and hence without strength, can have no real influence on human thought and activity.

If it is to be a living force in one's life, faith must be enlightened and strengthened sufficiently to withstand all the weakening influences which threaten it as well as the attacks made against it. It can do this effectively only if the religious culture of the soul is at least in proportion to its culture otherwise. If faith is not nourished according to this wise measure, scarcely can it escape ruin; the more reason then, it cannot hope to develop a deep spiritual life.[9]

## B. Jesus Christ, the "living book"

From Saint Teresa herself we shall ask a directing principle in the choice of our readings.

[9] This religious ignorance produces a phenomenon at first sight rather strange: that of upright souls who, under the pressure of events or of interior disquiet, find in themselves a profound need of spiritual life, and who, to satisfy it, go to oriental religions because they are completely ignorant of the profound life of the Christianity that they have skirted for so long, and that is the religion of their baptism. It comes as a happy but often late surprise to discover the overflowing riches of Christ after quenching their thirst at enticing but impure sources.

In 1559, the Grand Inquisitor of Spain, intent upon stopping
the rising tide of illuminism, thought it his duty to forbid the
reading of most of the spiritual books written in Spanish. This
radical measure threw Teresa into desolation. She complained
affectionately to our Lord:

> When a great many books written in Spanish were taken from us,
> and we were forbidden to read them, I was very sorry, for the reading
> of some of them gave me pleasure and I could no longer continue this
> as I had them only in Latin. Then the Lord said to me: "Be not dis-
> tressed, for I will give thee a living book." I could not understand
> why this had been said to me, for I had not then had any visions.[10]

From then on, she began to have visions of the humanity of
Christ, visions at first intellectual in which the Saint could see
nothing; but, she says,

> I thought He was quite close to me and I saw that it was He Who,
> as I thought, was speaking to me. . . . All the time Jesus Christ seemed
> to be beside me, but . . . I could not discern in what form.[11]

This nearness "lasts for many days—sometimes for more
than a year," [12] not perceived by the senses but clear and certain to the soul with "a feeling of equal certainty, or even
greater" [13] than the senses give. It produces the greatest confusion and humility "yet this brings a special knowledge of
God, and from this constant companionship is born a most
tender love toward His Majesty, and yearnings, even deeper
than those already described, to give oneself wholly up to His
service, and a great purity of conscience." [14]

Then come visions, rapid as lightning, that leave in her imagination an image of the glorified Christ of such beauty that
the Saint thinks it impossible to forget.

> Though the former type of vision which, as I said, reveals God
> without presenting any image of Him, is of a higher kind, yet, if the
> memory of it is to last, despite our weakness, and if the thoughts are

[10] *Life*, xxvi; Peers, I, 168.
[11] *Ibid.*, xxvii; 170.
[12] VI Mansions, viii; Peers, II, 310.
[13] *Ibid.*; 311.
[14] *Ibid.*

to be well occupied, it is a great thing that so Divine a Presence should be presented to the imagination and should remain within it.[15]

This living Book that was thus opening up to the soul of Teresa instructed her marvelously:

> When once I had seen the great beauty of the Lord, I saw no one who by comparison with Him seemed acceptable to me or on whom my thoughts wished to dwell. . . . Once I had seen this Lord, I was so continually in converse with Him that my love for Him and trust in Him began to increase greatly. I saw that, although God, He was also Man, and is not dismayed at the weaknesses of men.[16]

These visions had a very important bearing on the spiritual life of Saint Teresa; she now wanted to seek nothing other than Christ in her prayer.

Saint John of the Cross has the same doctrine in the *Ascent of Mount Carmel.* To show that we must not try to question God and receive instruction from Him in a supernatural manner, he recalls the opening words of the Epistle to the Hebrews: "God, who at sundry times and in divers manners spoke in times past to the fathers by the prophets, last of all in these days has spoken to us by His Son." And the holy doctor comments: [17]

> In giving us, as He did, His Son, which is His Word—and He has no other—He spake to us all together, once and for all, in this single Word.

He develops this thought at some length, saying that to any-one who would now enquire of God or seek any vision or reve-lation, God might answer:

> Set thine eyes on Him alone, and thou shalt find the most secret mysteries, and the wisdom and wondrous things of God, which are hidden in Him, even as My Apostle says: In whom are hidden all the treasures of wisdom and knowledge (Col. 2:3).

All knowledge of spiritual things is contained in Christ Jesus, for He is the eternal Word as well as the Word uttered

[15] *Life,* xxviii; Peers, I, 182-3.
[16] *Ibid.,* xxxvii; 262-3.
[17] *Ascent,* Bk. II, xxii; Peers, I, 173, 175. ✓ *Key passage*

in time. He is the Light that enlightens every mind coming into this world, the Light that shines in our darkness, and that we can follow without fear of going astray.

Thus the apostle wants to know no other thing than Christ, and Christ crucified.[18] He "counts everything loss because of the excelling knowledge of Jesus Christ," [19] and he can wish nothing better for his dear Christians than "to know Christ's love which surpasses knowledge, in order that you may be filled unto all the fullness of God." [20]

Saint Augustine, whose flights of soul soar up to uncreated Wisdom, confesses:

I sought the means of acquiring enough strength to rejoice in Thee, and I did not find it until the day when I embraced the "one Mediator between God and men, himself man, Christ Jesus." [21]

These attestations are no more than commentaries on words spoken by Jesus Himself:

Now this is everlasting life, that they may know thee, and the only true God, and him whom thou has sent, Jesus Christ.[22]

I am the door. If anyone enter by me he shall be safe, and shall go in and out, and shall find pastures.[23]

The doctrine of the universal and unique mediation of Christ, of prime importance in Teresian spirituality, imposes a very clear and very strict obligation on beginners: that of putting themselves at once in the school of Christ Jesus and of seeking in this living Book all the spiritual knowledge that is indispensable for them.

The visions that opened this Book to the spiritual gaze of Saint Teresa disclosed to her the beauty of the resurrected Christ, the sorrowful majesty of Jesus in His Passion, enflamed

[18] I Cor. 2:2.
[19] Phil. 3:8.
[20] Eph. 3:19.
[21] I Tim. 2:5.
[22] John 17:3.
[23] John 10:9.

her with love, enlightened her on the mysterious depths of the human soul and of the divinity of the Incarnate Word. Continuing as they did for weeks and months, they created between Jesus and Teresa those relations of living and respectful familiarity that explain the teaching of the Saint on the prayer of recollection, and the simple and constant union with Christ which is its foundation.

Study must supplement even visions; and it will succeed in any case only if it seeks a living knowledge of Christ. If we are to acquire and maintain in our daily life a loving and constant intimacy with Christ Jesus, which is the food of the prayer of recollection, we must know the living Christ, see Him as He lived, know how and in what interior and exterior conditions He acted and spoke. All our powers, from our senses to the most inward depths of our intellect, must be filled with this living and concrete knowledge. The soul must therefore try to possess what revelation and theology tell us of Christ, of His divinity, of His humanity and the hypostatic union that makes it subsist in the Person of the Word, of His mediation and His priesthood.

Since it is as the God-Man that Christ exercises His mediation, an affectionate curiosity will be directed towards His sacred humanity. It will dwell on the perfections of His body, His beauty, His sensibility; on the riches of His soul, the triple knowledge—intuitive, infused, and experimental—that adorned His intellect; on the rich and ordered life of His imagination and His senses; on the admirable strength and mastery of His will. It will meditate on the harmonious equilibrium and the high perfection of His whole being and His life. It will love to think on His surroundings and His country, the material and moral conditions in which His life here below unfolded and which prepared, by suffering and death, His definitive triumph.

A purely speculative study of the finest treatises on the Person of Christ and the history of His life, would not be sufficient, as one can easily see, to acquire that deep and living knowledge. Constant concern is needed, and untiring perseverance, as well as that special penetration of love that is interested in the least details, that picks out words and gestures that are without apparent importance and sees in them a revealing significance. Thus one brings into clearer light each day the traits already known of the beloved, discovering new riches and entering into a more profound intimacy. Faith and love unite in this way to draw from the living Book which is Christ Jesus "in whom are hidden all the treasures of wisdom and knowledge," [24] whatever it pleases God to reveal to us.

But in the case of the beginner who is in the second Mansions, love is not yet penetrating enough and faith is weak. How, then, is he going to place himself in the school of Jesus Christ? By good reading; a modest and imperfect means, but indispensable for the beginnings.

## C. Choice of reading

The choice of reading must be inspired by this fundamental truth, namely, that all spiritual knowledge is contained in Christ and has been revealed to us in Him. Spiritual books can only and must only make Christ explicit to us and lead us to Him. A reading is profitable for us in the measure in which it gives us knowledge of Christ. Such is the practical principle that determines for each one the value of books and must guide us in the choice of reading.

### I. THE PERSON OF CHRIST: HOLY SCRIPTURE

The desire to find Christ leads us first of all to the Sacred Scriptures and gives them first place among the books to be read and meditated upon. Their incomparable merit is to have God as their principal author. The Holy Spirit has used the human and free activity of an inspired author to tell us whatever He wills and as He wills. The veracity of God, which

[24] Col. 2:3.

can neither be deceived nor deceive us, is the guarantee both for the truth that is proposed and its expression. The inspired word, then, offers us the divine truth itself in its surest and most perfect translation into human language. For the contemplative who is seeking to be united with God in His light, the Holy Scriptures have an inestimable value; for, in giving him the very thought of God under the veil of words, they allow him to commune with the Word, and commit him to the transforming action of His light.

These transcendent merits make of the Bible a divine book; and it has other, lesser merits of unique value. There is no book that compares with it in interest or in usefulness. No other deals with subjects of such elevation and variety, nor presents them in art and poetry so exalted.

The Sacred Scriptures have kept for us the account of the origins of the human race and its calamitous beginning. They tell us the astounding history of the Hebrew people, chosen to preserve the worship of the true God and to prepare the coming of the Messias. Along with broad tableaux of history, with simple and pathetic monographs, with powerful visions, with collections of maxims that sum up the practical teachings of human prudence and divine wisdom, we find formulas of prayer that are the most burning and most sublime, the most humble and most trusting that human lips have ever pronounced.

But we seek especially Jesus Christ in them, from the moment when His redemptive mediation is announced after the fall of our first parents till He finishes, through His apostles, His mission as the Word, revealing the divine truth. The four Evangelists recount in chaste language His earthly life; they repeat His words; they relate His movements, and by a thousand traits even describe His attitudes. Thanks to their observations, there is no celebrated man whose figure and utterances are more living to us at twenty centuries' distance, and with whom intimacy is made easier and more attractive.

Finally, we have the incomparable teaching of Saint Paul, in whose powerful light we fathom the depths and the riches of the mystery of Christ, Mediator, Priest, and Saviour whose life is diffused throughout the Mystical Body of which He is the Head.

There is no other work that can enlighten us in the same degree as Holy Scripture, concerning God and Christ. No other can assure a more substantial nourishment for our meditation, nor be more favorable to a living contact with Jesus and intimacy with Him. It offers food suitable for the beginner; and the perfect want no other book, for it is the only one whose words are filled with lights always new and with savors ever nourishing.

And so there is no contemplative to whom Holy Scripture does not become very dear. Saint Teresa finds that nothing is so conducive to recollection as verses from the Sacred Writings. Saint Therese of the Child Jesus always carries the holy Bible with her; in it she looks for the marks of God and sees in Isaias, the great prophet, the traits of the sorrowful face of her beloved Christ. It is in the company of Saint Paul that Sister Elizabeth of the Trinity lives, in her silent and hidden contemplation.

And yet, in our Christian groups, even the cultured and devout ones, little spiritual nourishment is taken from Holy Scripture. To explain, if not to excuse this neglect and sometimes defiance on their part, they invoke the artlessness in the accounts which seem like crudities to our tastes—not purer, but more refined; the obscurities that result from the variant texts and imperfect translations, and especially from the difference there is between our mental genius and the oriental genius that shaped their composition.

For the person who goes to the Sacred Letters, seeking only light and food for his spiritual life, these difficulties disappear for the most part, if he makes use of good commentaries and books of introduction. Just now there are some excellent ones which, at the price of a little effort, give the key to the books of Scripture. What a magnificent and profitable reward for a soul of prayer when, after a few months of study, he can draw directly from such an unfailing source of light as the Epistles of Saint Paul!

All prayerful souls must nourish themselves with some life of our Lord, which are so happily numerous today and illuminate the Gospels admirably well. These readings make Christ familiar to us. They create in the soul an atmosphere favorable to a life of prayer, and are thus a particularly efficacious preparation for it.

Commentaries on Scripture and the various accounts of the life of our Lord must lead us to the inspired text itself. It alone gives the very word of God. It alone is divine and inexhaustible. To taste it, and especially to be contented with it for prayer, is a sign that one has made progress.

### 2. CHRIST THE TRUTH: DOGMATIC BOOKS

In answer to the deacon Philip who asked him if he understood the passage from Isaias relative to the Messias that he was reading, the eunuch of Candace, queen of Ethiopia, said: "How can I, unless someone show me?" [25]

The Sacred Scriptures require, in truth, a commentary; not only a commentary that explains the meaning of the words, but a wider and more profound one that makes explicit the Christ-light contained in them. This is the role of theology, which analyzes, clarifies, co-ordinates, and sets forth the revealed truths.

The infallible teaching authority of the Church defines the most important truths necessary for our faith, while the theologian continues indefatigably his work on revelation, to make new lights shine out for us from its mystery and to translate it into more precise formulas. Defined dogmas and theological truths express the light of the Word in human and analogical

[25] Acts 8:31.

terms. It is by the assent that we give them that our faith rises up to the Word Himself and attains to Him. We have already mentioned the necessity of this adherence to a dogmatic formula, and of study of the truth, especially at the beginning of the spiritual life. It will be sufficient here to indicate how one must proceed in the study of dogmatic truth, in view of prayer.

1. The first quality a dogma must have is orthodoxy. Only the truth, of which the Church is the guardian and the dispenser, can give to the soul the substantial food and the solid support that it needs to go to God. On the contrary, a theological error, even bearing on a point of detail, can bring about notable deviations on the way. Saint Teresa says she could not tell all the harm that certain false assertions of semi-savants had caused her. Actually a number of spiritual movements have been led astray by spiritual experiences that were badly or insufficiently clarified.

Concern about this must go even to the point of scruple. Saint Therese of the Child Jesus refused to continue the reading of a work when she learned that its author was not submissive to his bishop.

2. It will be excellent for the beginner in spiritual ways, whatever may be his general and religious culture, to consult very simple books on doctrine—the catechism, for instance, whose clean-cut formulas leave to truth its full strength. For faith progresses by penetrating deeply into the truth that is its object, and not by pouring itself out on the beauties of the human word. So much is this so, that for an intense faith, literary artifices and verbosity seem to be obstacles that stop its flight, an annoying crust that hides its treasure. The simplest expression is ordinarily the purest mirror for the lights of the divine Word.[26]

3. This care for simplicity and for the deepening of faith

---

[26] The simplest expression, of which we are speaking, will not be the most banal nor necessarily the least figurative, but that which disappears in some way itself so as to place in relief the truth that it expresses.

must not set limits to its growth in extension. Each dogma is a ray of light, emanating from the divine Word. We have not the right to neglect any one of them; for, besides the riches of light and of grace that each one brings us, it is in the living synthesis of the whole that the affectionate gaze finds the most exact expression of the Word Himself.

4. Not rarely, a dogma is the source of particular grace for a soul before whom it opens up, as it were, a sunlit trail to God. Such a light must be preciously received. Whatever may be the culture of the soul, it must penetrate that truth by a profound study in order to draw out all its nourishing substance.

Likewise, we must not resist the movement that bears the theologians and the faithful of an epoch towards such or such a particular dogma, like the dogma of the Church and the privileges of the divine maternity, in our time. In doing so, one would expose oneself to resisting the Holy Spirit, who guides the Church and secures for it in all the ages of its history the light adapted to its needs.

5. As we see, a soul of prayer must have knowledge of dogma both extensive and profound. Ordinarily, the general culture of the soul, or perhaps the particular needs consonant with its degree of grace, will determine how much. These needs will be different at different periods of its spiritual life. A wise director will decide. And for a faithful soul, it is not rare that God Himself provides for it by special circumstances.[27]

Works that popularize theology are numerous today and

[27] This providential action appears clearly in the life of Saint John of the Cross. He goes to Duruelo after hard studies at the University of Salamanca. His difficult apprenticeship in the contemplative Carmelite life terminated, he organizes the novitiate at Pastrana, and then returns to his studies as rector of the theological college of Alcala. There he stores up provisions of light for the long fruitful silence at Avila (1572–77), which will end in the prison of Toledo. Having attained to spiritual marriage and regained his physical strength, he is named rector of the College of Bacza, and the professors of the University come frequently to the monastery. This new contact with dogmatic truth prepares for the period of literary fecundity which produces all the great treatises of the Saint.

facilitate the learning of dogma. For these one can only be
thankful, and use them on condition that he choose those
adapted to his education and his needs, and not lose himself
in their very multiplicity.

Whenever this is possible, one will gain by consulting the
prince of theology himself, Saint Thomas Aquinas, whose
sound and sober teaching offers to anyone who knows how to
penetrate beyond the surface the strong food of the very depths
of dogma.

Finally, the reading of the Fathers of the Church, those great
masters who were both theologians and contemplatives, places
us at the purest sources of sacred science and Christian life.

### 3. CHRIST THE WAY: SPIRITUALITY

Jesus proclaimed Himself to be the way as well as the truth;
the only one that leads to the Father. This way, which is Christ,
has to be illumined for us. The masters of the spiritual life
fulfil this role, explaining the evangelical precepts and counsels, stating precisely the requirements of the virtues and the
means of practising them, illuminating with the light of theology and experimental science the paths that lead to the
summits of Christian perfection.

The paths are many. The different schools of spiritual life
describe them. How is one to make a choice? A definite. attraction or providential circumstances usually give some indication. Sometimes more investigation is necessary.

Ordinarily a brief study of the different types of spirituality
is very useful. Each one of them affords helpful advice on
particular points. The Ignatian school will show us the importance of asceticism and the means of practising it; the Benedictine school will instruct us on the virtue of religion and the
spiritual value of the liturgy; Saint Teresa and Saint John of
the Cross will teach us the interior cult of prayer and will enlarge our horizons of the spiritual life. This rounding of the

spiritual horizon can also very well prevent the deformations that too narrow or premature a specialization runs the risk of.

Certain souls, destined to become masters of a school, draw something from them all, and thus enriched, form their own spirituality with the grace of their particular mission. Thus Saint Teresa, directed by Jesuits, Franciscans, and Dominicans, grafted all that she received from them into the Carmelite life and constructed the living synthesis that is the Teresian spirit. Saint Therese of the Child Jesus was in touch with all the schools of spirituality of our time; and so she was to adorn with poetry and with attractiveness for souls today her strong and ancient grace as a daughter of Elias, patriarch of Carmel, and of her teacher, Saint John of the Cross.

Ordinarily, however, acquaintance with the various rules for the spiritual life permits the soul to find its way. This way once discovered, there is the further need of making a thorough study of the spirituality that represents it and of knowing the saints who are its masters. Its ideal must polarize all the energies of the soul and make them give their maximum of power and fecundity.

The perfection of the soul is here at stake, as is the good of the Church. This is the way in which the soul will find the graces that God has prepared for its sanctification. And it is by serving the Church in the place that has been indicated, that it will contribute the most efficaciously to the good of the whole. Just as the health of the human body depends on the right functioning of all its organs, so the perfection of the Church requires that each of the faithful be in his place and fulfil the function assigned him. A restless dilettantism that touches everything in order to taste it, is harmful; specialization in one's vocation is the most effective way of serving.

This specialization within a vocation or a type of spirituality still leaves room for particular missions and special graces to develop. The grace of God is multiform; the delicate anointings of the Holy Spirit are so diverse that even in the same group and under the same influences there are not two souls that resemble each other even by half. Hence although a study of the different schools of spiritual thought is necessary in order to find one's way and to walk in it, in the last resort it is the Holy Spirit Himself who guides us to God by the Way that is Christ Jesus.

#### 4. CHRIST THE LIFE IN THE CHURCH

Jesus Christ is the source of divine life, of that life that flows first of all in His sacred humanity, ruling there in its perfection and plenitude, making of it an ever living source of grace and a perfect model whose acts determine the laws of the moral and spiritual order.

This life of Christ goes on in the Church throughout history. It manifests itself in various movements. Thus the Christian is a son of the ageless Church by his baptism but belongs to the Church of a particular period by his temporal life and the mission he has received. It is his duty, therefore, to study the life of Christ in the Church down the centuries, to share profoundly in that life in his own time, to know its exterior movements and interior motions, its joys and trials, its needs and intentions, so as to make them his own: *Hoc sentite in vobis quod et in Christo Jesu;* "Have this mind in you which was also in Christ Jesus." [28] The word of the apostle is to be understood of Christ in the Church.

The reading of a few appropriate reviews or books of current interest will remind one of what is required from a faithful child of the living Church. We might here recall how strongly Saint Teresa was influenced by the accounts of the French Wars of Religion, brought to Spain probably by merchants who had come to the fairs of Medina; or by a conversation with the Franciscan Father, commissary of his Order in the West Indies, who told her of the moral misery of the peoples evangelized by his religious. These accounts brought to a

[28] Phil. 2:5.

focus her vocation as a daughter of the Church, set fire to her zeal, and opened up immense horizons.

The life that comes from Christ triumphs especially in the saints. In them it displays the riches and the power of grace; it appears, living in human forms nearer to us, overcoming difficulties that we know, giving us minute precisions as to the effort it requires, showing us the joys and the triumphs that it secures. The lives of saints explain, complete, bring to a point the Gospel teachings and spiritual doctrines. The value of the principles that these latter set down, their application to various concrete cases, the balance of the whole, are apparent sometimes only in the very deeds of the saint. The rigorous logic of Saint John of the Cross is clothed with a human tenderness when we see the sweet charity that he spread around him; while we understand the strength that the smile of Saint Therese of the Child Jesus conceals when we know of her patience in trials and the standards she set up for her novices.

According to the adage: *verba movent, exampla trahunt,* examples have a force that draws others after them, comparable to no other. To this force that comes to the soul through the peaceful joys of reading, there is added, from reading the lives of the saints, the supernatural grace awakened by their sanctity. Saint Teresa tells of the decisive influence that the *Confessions* of Saint Augustine had on her life.[29]

Varied and numerous, as we see, are the commentaries written on Christ. Certainly, they do not exhaust the treasures of light and of wisdom that are in Him. Yet by their means, the soul makes these treasures progressively its own; and especially, it learns to read in the living Book of Christ. Tremendous is the influence of reading in the development of the spiritual life. We can conclude, then, the necessity of applying oneself to it with care, with a spirit of faith, and with perseverance.

[29] *Life,* ix; Peers, I, 56.

x words move, examples attract

# CHAPTER VI

# Distractions and Dryness

*As it has been such a troublesome
thing for me, it may perhaps be so for
you as well, so I am just going to describe it.*[1]

In speaking of the prayer of recollection, Saint Teresa
makes the following remark:

*It is
inevitable*

> This method of praying in which the mind makes no reflections
> means that the soul must either gain a great deal or lose itself—I
> mean by its attention going astray.[2]

Neither the most vital methods, nor the best ordered prayers,
nor even assiduous spiritual reading can make one wholly secure against distractions and dryness in prayer. This is a heavy
trial, ignorance of which contributes towards increasing the
suffering and the dangers involved in it, notes the Saint. In
this connection she writes:

> The worst of it is that, as we do not realize we need to know more
> when we think about Thee, we cannot ask those who know; indeed
> we have not even any idea what there is for us to ask them. So we
> suffer terrible trials because we do not understand ourselves; and we
> worry over what is not bad at all, but good, and think it very wrong.
> Hence proceed the afflictions of many people who practise prayer, and
> their complaints of interior trials—especially if they are unlearned
> people—so that they become melancholy, and their health declines, and
> they even abandon prayer altogether.[3]

To get more light on so important a subject, we must study
the nature and the causes of distractions and dryness, so as to
discover the remedies.

[1] IV Mansions, i; Peers, II, 235.
[2] *Life*, ix; Peers, I, 55.
[3] IV Mansions, i; Peers, II, 233-4.

234

## A. Nature of distractions and of dryness

"Recollected and distracted are two adjectives that are in opposition," has been correctly said."[4] Recollection is a condition for prayer. Distractions in prayer, then, are in general in inverse ratio to recollection. While recollection is a concentration of the activity of our faculties on a supernatural reality, distraction is an evasion of one or of all the faculties towards another object, which interrupts recollection.

Not every evasion of one or of several powers is, however, necessarily a distraction. On this point, Saint Teresa invites us to a psychological analysis that will help us in finding the precise nature of distractions. Frightened by the wandering of her faculties in various directions, the Saint consulted some learned men who confirmed what her experience had taught her about distraction and the independent activity of the faculties of the soul:

> I have sometimes been terribly oppressed by this turmoil of thoughts and it is only just four years ago that I came to understand by experience that thought (or, to put it more clearly, imagination) is not the same thing as understanding. I asked a learned man about this and he said I was right, which gave me no small satisfaction.[5]

That the powers of the soul may have an independent activity and that certain ones may separately evade recollection yet without destroying it: those are the truths that consoled Teresa.

Which are the powers whose wanderings may be merely annoying, without endangering distraction?

In the first place, the external and internal senses that can

[4] Cf. Dr. Laignel-Lavastine, professor at the Faculty of Medicine of Paris, in his article: "Les distractions dans la prière; étude physio-psychologique," *Etudes Carmélitaines,* April, 1934, pp. 120-42.
We refer to this remarkable study in which the eminent professor, a member of the Academy of Medicine, for the sole purpose of furthering the spiritual life, summed up the results of penetrating physio-psychological analyses, to help us struggle against distractions in prayer.
[5] IV Mansions, i; Peers, II, 233.

perceive or experience impressions without putting a stop to recollection. I might, for instance, while taking a walk in the country, see a familiar landscape, hear the song of birds, experience some physical sufferings or pain of soul, and yet continue my mental prayer on some subject from the Gospels, apart from all these perceptions and sensations. Abstraction from the senses is frequent in recollection. While writing the *Interior Castle,* Saint Teresa notes:

> As I write this, the noises in my head are so loud that I am beginning to wonder what is going on in it. As I said at the outset, they have been making it almost impossible for me to obey those who commanded me to write. My head sounds just as if it were full of brimming rivers, and then as if all the water in those rivers came suddenly rushing downward; and a host of little birds seem to be whistling, not in the ears, but in the upper part of my head. . . . All this physical turmoil is no hindrance either to my prayer or to what I am saying now, but the tranquility and love in my soul are quite unaffected.[6]

The imagination, whose activity is so closely bound up with that of the senses, can also stray away, leaving the soul to the supernatural realities that hold it captive.

Let us turn again to Saint Teresa whose experiences throw such good light on these delicate problems:

> It exasperated me to see the faculties of the soul, as I thought, occupied with God and recollected in Him, and the imagination, on the other hand, confused and excited.[7]

What will be the state of the understanding, that is, the discursive intelligence considered as distinct from the intellect which penetrates its object with a simple and direct intuitive gaze?

Saint Teresa points out that while the will is sweetly bound in the prayer of quiet and enjoying the divine delights, the understanding may be agitated and restless:

> The other two faculties [understanding and memory] help the will so that it may become more and more capable of enjoying so great

[6] IV Mansions, i; Peers, II, 234.
[7] *Ibid.;* 233.

a blessing, though sometimes it comes about that, even when the will is in union, they hinder it exceedingly. . . . These faculties come and go, to see if the will will give them some part of what it is enjoying.[8]

All the texts that we have quoted up to now to show the mutual independence of the activity of the powers of the soul, describe states that are definitely contemplative. In effect, it is in contemplation, when God lays peaceful hold on one or more powers and leaves the others in agitation, that the distinction of the powers appears much more clearly and is perceived experimentally.

Although it becomes more clearly evident during contemplation, the distinction of the faculties is an abiding psychological fact; consequently, it exists at all the stages of the spiritual life. We must note, however, that the direct intervention of God in the activity of the faculties, which produces supernatural contemplation, modifies considerably the laws of recollection during that period.

While it is sufficient during contemplative prayer that the will allows itself to be gently held by God, even though all the other powers are in agitation; yet in the active phase, the voluntary attention of the soul to a supernatural reality that is not experienced, seems not to be possible without an application of the intellect to that object, either by reasoning or by a simple gaze.

In the active phase that we are considering, we can say then, that attention and recollection are dispelled when the intellect is diverted. Moreover, in this same phase, mutual distinction of the activity of the powers—which is less easily perceived— is also less real. The perceptions of the senses and the wanderings of the imagination will more easily hinder the application of the intellect and, consequently, recollection.

Distraction is called voluntary when, willingly and with full intention, the mind turns from the supernatural reality to give its attention to another object. It is involuntary when this

[8] *Life,* xiv; Peers, I, 84.

movement is produced involuntarily or without full intention, ordinarily by yielding to the attraction of a sensation or an image.

When distraction during prayer is no longer just something passing, but, because of the restlessness of the intellect and its inability to remain fixed on any subject whatever, distractions become almost habitual, this constitutes a state of dryness. Dryness is accompanied usually by sadness, a certain helplessness, diminution of the ardors of the soul, and by the disturbance and enervation of the faculties.

Distractions are a trial; dryness gives rise to a state of desolation. Both these sufferings were most keenly felt by Saint Teresa. She shares with us her experiences in this regard, to encourage us. For long years, she says, speaking of the "first way of watering the garden" by drawing the water with a bucket—which corresponds to the first degrees of mental prayer—she knew the fatigue "of lowering the bucket so often into the well and drawing it up empty." It often happened that, even for that work, she was unable to move her arms

. . . unable, that is, to think a single good thought. . . . And when I was able to draw but one drop of water from this blessed well, I used to think that God was granting me a favor. I know how grievous such trials are and I think they need more courage than do many others in the world.[9]

And here is another admission from the sainted mother of mental prayer, which will certainly comfort us in our own painful inabilities:

It was about these things that I used to think whenever I could; and very often, over a period of several years, I was more occupied in wishing my hour of prayer was over, and in listening whenever the clock struck, than in thinking of things that were good. Again and again I would rather have done any severe penance that might have been given me than practice recollection as a preliminary to prayer. . . . Whenever I entered the oratory I used to feel so depressed that I had to summon up all my courage to make myself pray at all. (Peo-

[9] *Life,* xi; Peers, I, 66-7.

ple say that I have little courage, and it is clear that God has given me much more than most women, only I have made bad use of it.) [10]

The suffering inherent in such a state of helplessness and in the weariness that accompanies aridity of the faculties, is intensified by the feeling of the utter futility of all our efforts; we have the impression of definite failure in the ways of mental prayer and consequently in the spiritual life. The soul aspiring to prayer needs to be enlightened and fortified. No way to do this is more useful than an exposition of the causes of dryness and its remedies.

## B. Causes of distractions and dryness

Our inquiry will not bear on the voluntary causes of distractions and of dryness, such, for instance, as negligence in putting them out of mind during prayer or even complacence in entertaining them; notable neglect of spiritual reading and of the preparation necessary to secure for prayer its sustenance; dissipation of life and habitual lack of mortification of the senses. For these, it is easy indeed to state the remedy. Not to apply it, would be to condemn oneself to culpable failure.

We are concerned, rather, with indicating the causes that make the struggle against distractions more difficult and at times ineffectual and which, consequently, do not derive d rectly from the human will.

### I. THE NATURE OF SUPERNATURAL TRUTHS

The very nature of supernatural truths is the primary cause of distractions and dryness. These truths are proposed to us in dogmatic formulas which are their most human expression. The dogmatic formula states in human concepts, analogously, a divine truth that remains a mystery, being of an order superior to those concepts.

In mental prayer, a loving faith assents to the truth itself which is essentially obscure to us; any clearer manifestation of it here below will come only at a later stage, in the experience

[10] *Ibid.,* viii; 51.

of the gifts of the Holy Spirit. But in the first phase, the mystery remains in complete darkness. At the same time, the understanding assents to the dogmatic formula, penetrates the concepts, reasons about them, marvels at them, and tastes them with delight. This occupation of the mind with the most exalted truths is of incomparable interest. And yet, our intellect's power to penetrate them being so strictly limited, it soon enough has drawn from them all the light it can; and so, finding itself once more with the same formulas and without new light, it loses its taste for them: *assueta vilescunt.*

### 2. THE INSTABILITY OF THE POWERS OF THE SOUL

The instability of the powers of the soul is another cause of distractions and dryness. The sense powers as well as the understanding whose activity is so closely bound up with that of the senses, are unstable and fickle. The will can direct them to an object and hold them to it; but as soon as the will lets go its grasp, they reassert their independence and follow their bent. They give themselves up to an apparently disordered activity, yielding to the attractions of external stimuli or phantasms of the memory.

A patient and persevering discipline, the asceticism of recollection, can make them more docile to the action of the will and habituate them to the silence of recollection, but it cannot change their nature. Saint Teresa says in this regard:

> It is the Lord's will that . . . the soul and the will should be given this power over the senses. They will only have to make a sign to show that they wish to enter into recollection and the senses will obey and allow themselves to be recollected. Later they may come out again, but it is a great thing that they should ever have surrendered.[11]

Neither the purification of the senses, which makes the senses amenable to the spirit, nor even the profound purification of the spirit itself—as the statements of Saint Teresa just quoted, prove—bring these fickle powers into complete submission.

[11] *Way of Perfection,* xxviii; Peers, II, 116.

It is only in the sacred humanity of our Saviour and in Our Lady that we find the sense faculties marvelously developed and yet at the same time perfectly submissive to the will.

Original sin created disorder, depriving us of the preternatural gifts which brought harmony into our human nature by making the lower powers subject to the higher, and ordering them all to God. Since then, the independence of the powers declares itself strongly in us. The duality of our nature, composed of matter and spirit, reveals itself in an interior experience that is more and more painful until it is asserted finally in death, the last consequence of original sin: *stipendium peccati mors est.*[12] The wages of sin is death.

Saint Teresa laments this disorder inherent in our nature wounded by sin, that makes recollection difficult:

> I often think of the harm wrought in us by original sin; it is this, I believe, that has made us incapable of enjoying so much good all at once, and added to this are my own sins . . . but sometimes I know quite well that my poor bodily health is having a great deal to do with it.[13]

### 3. ILLNESS

This last observation of the Saint draws attention to the harm that illnesses can cause to mental prayer; and to these, we can add the pathological tendencies or the defects that are imbedded in our character or temperament.

All intellectual activity is influenced to a certain extent by the physical states. Those who must use their minds much, know this well; without experiencing any definite sickness, they feel themselves incapable of carrying on a determinate intellectual work at certain times in the day or at certain periods, and are obliged to distribute it according to the quality of the intellectual energy that it requires.

At mental prayer the mind is occupied with truths that are very high and hidden in mystery. To make this prayer well,

[12] Rom. 6:23.
[13] *Life,* xxx; Peers, I, 202.

one must be in good form. It is true that here, to love is of much more importance than to think; but the affections are more intimately connected with the body than is the understanding and more immediately share in its vicissitudes. And so we are not astonished to hear this testimony from Saint Teresa:

> The other afflictions which we bring upon ourselves serve only to disturb our souls. . . . I have a great deal of experience of this and I know that what I say is true, for I have observed it carefully and have discussed it afterwards with spiritual persons. The thing frequently arises from physical indisposition, for we are such miserable creatures that this poor imprisoned soul shares in the miseries of the body, and variations of seasons and changes in the humours often prevent it from accomplishing its desires and make it suffer in all kinds of ways against its will.[14]

She goes on to say that a change in the time of prayer perhaps gives some relief from these maladies. One could not be more sanely realistic nor more maternally attentive in guiding beginners in the ways of mental prayer.

More troublesome than these passing indispositions, can be the pathological tendencies and defects that are rooted in temperament. Saint Teresa alludes to the tendency some have to melancholy; and also to the "times when our heads are tired, and, however, hard we try, we cannot concentrate." [15] She takes care to divert from mental prayer certain persons who because of psychical weakness cannot stand the least shock without fainting.

Indeed modern psychiatry has made a penetrating study that would have delighted Saint Teresa of constitutional defects that can have a very profound influence on the development of the spiritual life.[16] The clinical cases are almost exclusively the domain of the doctor. But the borderline cases are many. Every

[14] *Life,* xi; Peers, I, 69.
[15] *Way of Perfection,* xxiv; Peers, II, 102.
[16] Cf. the article quoted by Dr. Laignel-Lavastine in *Etudes Carmélitaines,* April, 1934.

one in fact is said to have such or such a tendency more or less evolved.[17]

Although these tendencies are scarcely noticeable in an ordinarily active life, they manifest themselves in all their strength in one given to prayer. The melancholic type who is forever accusing himself; the scrupulous person, continually preoccupied with his doubts; the highly imaginative, who cannot check his mental wanderings; the restless and excitable, whose faculties are always in movement; these find special difficulties in the way of recollection.[18]

### 4. THE DEVIL

"When the distractions and disturbances of the understanding are excessive . . . the devil is their author," declares Saint Teresa. Often, she had experience of this:

In particular it used to come during Holy Week. . . . The devil suddenly lays hold on my understanding, sometimes by making use of things so trifling that at any other time I should laugh at them. He confuses the understanding and does whatever he likes with it, so that the soul, fettered as it is and no longer its own mistress, can think of nothing but the absurdities which he presents to it—things of no importance. . . . It has sometimes seemed to me, indeed, that the devils behave as though they were playing ball with the soul, so incapable is it of freeing itself from their power.[19]

The Saint lays special emphasis on worry, which is a sign of the presence of the devil and causes trouble of mind:

Besides being left in a state of great aridity, the soul suffers a disquiet . . . of such a nature that one cannot discover whence it comes. The soul seems to resist it and is perturbed and afflicted without know-

[17] In the borderline cases of which we are speaking, these tendencies do not vitiate a temperament nor destroy the fruitfulness of a life. It is important that the soul adapt itself to them if it cannot destroy them. Supernatural obedience is one of the best compensators to check the baneful effects of a tendency.
[18] The purifications, which cause these tendencies finally to disappear or at least notably attenuate them, bring them first to their maximum tension, and these pose a delicate problem in religious psychology.
[19] *Life,* xxx; Peers, I, 198-9.

ing why. . . . I wonder if one kind of spirit can be conscious of another.[20]

The presence of the impure spirit could be perceived only by a spirit already purified. It seems, too, that this violent action of the devil is very rare; that he reserves it for strong souls from whom he has much to fear. Nevertheless, these descriptions are most useful, for they indicate to us his habitual tactics and mode of action.

It is natural enough that the devil should use his great power and take advantage of the relative weakness of beginners in prayer, to stop them in their journey towards God by causing in them, as far as he is able, as much dryness and distractions as he can. That he thus intervenes—often successfully—in the prayer of beginners seems certain; and, although using on them much more benign procedures than on Saint Teresa, these are probably much more effective.

### 5. THE ACTION, AT LEAST PERMISSIVE, OF GOD

The action of these natural and preternatural causes enters into the plan of God who uses everything for the good of those whom He loves. Supernatural light and grace, fruits of the Passion and death of Christ, cannot penetrate deeply within a soul unless it shares in that redemptive suffering and death. Such sufferings give it light on its own self and establish it in humility:

I believe it is for our good that His Majesty is pleased to lead us in this way so that we may have a clear understanding of our worthlessness; for the favours which come later are of such great dignity that before He grants us them He wishes us to know by experience how miserable we are, lest what happened to Lucifer happen to us also.[21]

They are a trial that brings to light the valiant:

I believe myself that often in the early stages, and again later, it is the Lord's will to give us these tortures, and many other temptations which present themselves, in order to test His lovers and discover if

[20] *Life*, xxv; Peers, I, 160.
[21] *Ibid.*, xi; 67.

they can drink of the chalice and help Him to bear the Cross before He trusts them with His great treasures.[22]

These words of the Saint set before us the providential design that governs and uses wisely all activities, even those that are free and hostile, for the sanctification of souls.

Even in the case of beginners this dryness is often accompanied by an intermittent ray of divine light which itself produces contemplative dryness.

For this reason we think it certain that, in the case of Saint Teresa, the powerlessness of the understanding came from the graces of union that she had previously received; for those who have been elevated to perfect contemplation "can no longer meditate upon the mysteries of the Passion and the life of Christ." [23] Her long seasons of aridity in prayer, with the sentiments of humility and sadness that afflicted her, could not but be states illumined by a strong divine light that was adjusting sense to spirit and preparing her soul for the marvelous graces that she was to receive.

Certainly, one could not say as much for all the aridities of beginners; yet, it does not seem too presumptuous to consider that contemplative dryness is possible, intermittently, in the majority of fervent souls, even in their early stages in the ways of prayer.

## C. Remedies

It is to souls that have proved their good will by faithfulness to recollection, to spiritual reading, and to prayer, that Saint Teresa addresses her advice as to the remedies for dryness. She wants to teach them how to fight against the involuntary causes of distractions and aridity.

### I. DISCRETION

An examination of the causes of distraction shows us that there are several that we cannot overcome even by violent ef-

22 *Ibid.*
23 VI Mansions, vii; Peers, II, 305.

fort. When there is question of the weakness of the faculties in the face of supernatural truths, of their natural instability, of physical maladies, or of the action of the devil, we understand that violent efforts would be foolish. This conviction will serve to direct the whole struggle against distractions and will make us cultivate discretion which alone can overcome the obstacles. But let us listen to our wise spiritual mother:

> The very suffering of anyone in this state will show her that she is not to blame, and she must not worry, for that only makes matters worse, nor must she weary herself by trying to put sense into something—namely, her mind—which for the moment is without any. She should pray as best she can: indeed, she need not pray at all, but may try to rest her spirit as though she were ill and busy herself with some other virtuous action.[24]

Elsewhere she says:

> The more we try to force it [the soul] at times like these, the worse it gets and the longer the trouble lasts. But let discretion be observed so that it may be ascertained if this is the true reason: the poor soul must not be stifled. Persons in this condition must realize that they are ill and make some alteration in their hours of prayer; very often it will be advisable to continue this change for some days.
>
> They must endure this exile as well as they can, for a soul which loves God has often the exceeding ill fortune to realize that, living as it is in this state of misery, it cannot do what it desires because of its evil guest, the body.[25]

The Saint sums up her advice thus:

> At such times the soul must render the body a service for the love of God, so that on many other occasions the body may render services to the soul. Engage in some spiritual recreation, such as conversation (so long as it is really spiritual), or a country walk, according as your confessor advises. In all these things it is important to have had experience, for from this we learn what is fitting for us; but let God be served in all things.[26]

We quote at length, less to gather precise counsel on what to do—for cases differ widely—than to learn from Saint

[24] *Way of Perfection*, xxiv; Peers, II, 102.
[25] *Life*, xi; Peers, I, 69.
[26] *Ibid.*; 70.

Teresa in what spirit to carry on the battle against distractions. One can easily see that to overcome certain obstacles to prayer, more than discretion in prayerful efforts may at times be needed. The collaboration of a spiritual director and a medical doctor may, in some cases, become necessary and contribute effectually to health of body as well as to the progress of the soul.

### 2. PERSEVERANCE

Prudence in our efforts at prayer should result in persever-ance and not in idleness. "This is the most necessary thing here," [27] proclaims Saint Teresa; and she never tires of repeat-ing it. Had she not written on a bookmark: "Everything passes.
Patience obtains all things." This is true especially of mental prayer. It was through perseverance that she herself obtained her supernatural riches: "Not many days would pass without my spending long periods in prayer, unless I was very ill or very busy."

The greatest temptation of her life was to remain a year or more without praying, because to refrain from prayer seemed to her more humble.[28]

Perseverance will have for its object not only the exercise of prayer itself, but also the asceticism of recollection that must accompany it. We must keep a guard over the senses during the day, abstain from dissipating frivolities, and turn our minds and hearts to the Master as frequently as possible by ejacula-tory prayers or acts of the theological virtues.

Distractions and dryness in prayer enlighten the soul. They show it its deep-seated weaknesses and the precise causes of its distractions. There may be some recurring attachment or antipathy; an impression that is troubling still; such or such an image that clamors for attention; or a memory that is hin-dering recollection. Better than by detailed examens, the soul

[27] II Mansions, i; Peers, II, 214.
[28] *Life,* vii; Peers, I, 42.

thus discovers the exact point to which it must apply the efforts of its asceticism to acquire recollection.

Let the soul persevere, Saint Teresa assures us, and even though one be a sinner, God will be merciful:

> I cannot conceive, my Creator, why the whole world does not strive to draw near to Thee in this intimate friendship. Those of us who are wicked, and whose nature is not like Thine, ought to draw near to Thee so that Thou mayest make them good. They should allow Thee to be with them for at least two hours each day, even though they may not be with Thee, but are perplexed, as I was, with a thousand worldly cares and thoughts. In exchange for the effort which it costs them to desire to be in such good company (for Thou knowest, Lord, that at first this is as much as they can do and sometimes they can do no more at all) Thou dost prevent the devils from assaulting them . . . and Thou givest them strength to conquer.[29]

In short, only perseverance can make sure of success in prayer.

### 3. HUMILITY

A patient and trusting humility must accompany perseverance:

> What, then, will he do here who finds that for many days he experiences nothing but aridity, dislike, distaste and so little desire to go and draw water that he would give it up entirely if he did not remember that he is pleasing and serving the Lord of the garden; if he were not anxious that all his service should not be lost, so say nothing of the gain which he hopes for from the great labour of lowering the bucket so often into the well and drawing it up without water? . . . What, then, as I say, will the gardener do here? He will be bold and take heart and consider it the greatest of favours to work in the garden of so great an Emperor; and, as he knows that he is pleasing Him by so working (and his purpose must be to please, not himself, but Him), let him render Him great praise for having placed such confidence in him; . . . let him help Him to bear the Cross and consider how he lived with it all His life long; let him not wish to have his kingdom on earth or cease from prayer; and so let him resolve, even if this aridity should persist his whole life long, never to let Christ fall beneath the Cross. The time will come when He shall receive his whole reward at once.[30]

[29] *Life,* viii; Peers, I, 50-1.
[30] *Ibid.,* xi; 66-7.

Such dispositions of loving and patient humility are already one of the fruits of spiritual dryness. Because they bring the soul to share in the providential design that permits and uses aridities for the sanctification of the elect, they very soon obtain high favors from God:

> These trials bring their own reward. . . . It has become clear to me that, even in this life, God does not fail to recompense them highly; for it is quite certain that a single one of those hours in which the Lord has granted me to taste of Himself has seemed to me later a recompense for all the afflictions which I endured over a long period while keeping up the practice of prayer.[31]

Jesus conquered by a humble and loving patience. And this same disposition will assure the soul a triumph over the interior and exterior obstacles that hinder it from union with God.

In the *Interior Castle,* Saint Teresa sums up this doctrine:

> As it has been such a troublesome thing for me, it may perhaps be so for you as well, so I am just going to describe it, first in one way and then in another, hoping that I may succeed in making you realize how necessary it is, so that you may not grow restless and distressed. The clacking old mill must keep on going round and we must grind our own flour: neither the will nor the understanding must cease working.
> This trouble will sometimes be worse, and sometimes better, according to our health and according to the times and seasons. The poor soul may not be to blame for this, but it must suffer none the less. . . . And as we are so ignorant that what we read and are advised— namely, that we should take no account of these thoughts—is not sufficient to teach us, it does not seem to me a waste of time if I go into it farther and offer you some consolation about it; though this will be of little help to you until the Lord is pleased to give us light. But it is necessary (and His Majesty's will) that we should take proper measures and learn to understand ourselves, and not blame our souls for what is the work of our weak imagination and our nature and the devil.[32]

[31] *Ibid.;* 67.
[32] IV Mansions, i; Peers, II, 235 f.

# CHAPTER VII
# Spiritual Friendship

*It is a great evil for a soul beset by so many dangers to be alone.*[1]

This tender exclamation from the pen of Saint Teresa, gives us joy. The sublimity and flaming ardor of her desires, the unswerving resolution that she exacts of the soul in quest of God, and the sustained effort that she demands, frighten us at times. But here, the rigorous logician is shown to be a tender mother of souls, understanding and compassionate.

The weakness of the soul is indeed great, especially in beginners of the spiritual life. To find God, it has perhaps left its family and social milieu; the sensible consolations and easiness of the first days have given way to dryness in prayer and difficulties in the practice of virtue. How is it going to remain faithful in its isolation? Later, when God will sustain it by what Saint Teresa calls particular help, it will perhaps be able to bear with solitude. Meanwhile, it certainly needs the company and help of its neighbor.

Besides, God made man social minded. After creating Adam, God, says the Book of Genesis,[2] saw that it was not good for man to be alone and He created a companion who was like him. It is a law and a necessity of his nature: man needs the aid and the society of his kind. Not only would it weigh on his heart to be alone, but it would leave him powerless and sterile. Collaboration is the necessary condition of his personal development; and still more, of the fruitfulness of the creative activity which continues and multiplies him.

[1] *Life,* vii; Peers, I, 46.
[2] Gen. 2:18.

Saint Teresa stresses the particular weakness of woman and her more real and strongly felt need of support and of the help of man who completes and sustains her.

God has extended these laws and exigencies even into the supernatural domain. In order to realize the mysteries in which are founded His relations with humanity, He took a collaborator, the Virgin Mary, whom He associated, as Mother, with His whole work of spiritual paternity. Because they rule over the development of the natural life and the supernatural life as well, these laws are imposed on grace which, engrafted in human nature, must meet their demands. Our sanctification, then, cannot be the exclusive fruit of our personal activity; it requires collaboration. This is a general law, that the difficulties of beginners in the spiritual life bring out more sharply. The soul will find a help that is necessary in spiritual friendships and in direction.

The experiences and writings of Saint Teresa throw singular light on these two important subjects. In fact, this woman, ardent as she was, a captivator of souls and a daring foundress, was all her life long in quest of support and of help. We shall first consider her teaching on spiritual friendships.

## A. Friendships in the life of Saint Teresa

Friendship is an affectionate exchange. Saint Teresa was specially gifted for this. To the external charms that attract, she joined the serious qualities of mind and of heart that hold. Life overflowed from her whole being. Along with that, alert, witty, delicate, lovable and loving—one could win her heart with a sardine—she could not but conquer and become attached herself. We readily see that friendships could be for her a great strength and a grave danger. They were both. Grace made of them a means for spiritual ascent.

After the death of her mother, the adolescent Teresa continued to satisfy her passionate desire for reading. She read books of chivalry:

I thought there was nothing wrong in my wasting many hours, by day and by night, in this useless occupation, even though I had to hide it from my father.[3]

The heroes of these stories became her models and her friends. They created the atmosphere in which her sense powers that were opening to life, were awakened and stimulated:

I began to deck myself out and to try to attract others by my appearance, taking great trouble with my hands and hair, using perfumes and all the vanities I could get—and there were a good many of them, for I was very fastidious.[4]

True, she had no evil intentions and would "never have wanted anyone to offend God" [5] because of her.

Several cousins used to come to her father's house. They were very fond of her. She says, "we always went about together . . . and I would keep our conversation on things that amused them." [6]

She had a sister, María, much older than herself, modest and good. Teresa admired her, but there was no intimacy between them.

On the other hand, she was more attracted to a relative "whom we often had in the house," she tells us, and who was "frivolous in her conversation. . . . I talked and gossiped with her frequently; she joined me in all my favourite pastimes; and she also introduced me to other pastimes and talked to me about all her conversations and vanities. . . ."

"Subsequently my own wickedness sufficed to lead me into sin, together with the servants we had, whom I found quite ready to encourage me in all kinds of wrongdoing. Perhaps, if any of them had given me good advice, I might have profited by it; but they were as much blinded by their own interests as I was by desire." [7]

[3] *Life,* ii; Peers, I, 13.
[4] *Ibid.*
[5] *Ibid.*
[6] *Ibid.*
[7] *Ibid.;* 14-5.

What would come of all this? There was certainly nothing dishonorable in these contacts. They gathered a circle round Teresa, and normally they should lead to an "honorable marriage."

Her father, disturbed by the friendship with that relative, often reproved his daughter. But as he could not prevent her friend from coming to the house, he took a firm hand in the matter: he entered his daughter at the Augustinian convent where children like herself were being educated. The Saint writes that she had been following these vanities for hardly three months.[8]

In this convent, she recalls, "my soul began to return to the good habits of my earlier childhood and I realized what a great favour God does to those whom He places in the company of good people." [9] Thus, a change of surroundings was enough to change the dispositions of Teresa.

It was the affectionate influence of one of the nuns that completed the work of conversion and brought Teresa to the horizons of the religious life. This nun, "very discreet and holy," who "slept with those of us who were secular," was María de Briceno.

> She began to tell me how she had come to be a nun through merely reading those words in the Gospel: Many are called but few are chosen. She used to describe to me the reward which the Lord gives to those who leave everything for His sake. This good companionship began to eradicate the habits which bad companionship had formed in me, to bring back my thoughts to desires for eternal things, and to remove some of the great dislike which I had for being a nun, and which had become deeply engrained in me.[10]

When she left this school she was transformed and had "a little more attraction for the religious life." But she did not want to remain in that convent because of certain difficulties

[8] *Ibid.,* 15.
[9] *Ibid.;* 16.
[10] *Ibid.,* iii; 17.

that it presented. And another friendship attracted her elsewhere:

> I had a close friend in another convent, and this gave me the idea
> that, if I was to be a nun, I would go only to the house where she
> was.[11]

This intimate friend, Doña Juana Suárez, was a Carmelite at
the Incarnation at Avila.

When talking with one of her brothers, Antonio, she makes
her decision:

> We agreed to set out together, very early one morning, for the
> convent where that friend of mine lived of whom I was so fond. In
> making my final decision, I had already resolved that I would go to
> any other convent in which I thought I could serve God better.[12]

Friendship, then, simply furnished an indication in settling
upon the choice of a convent, to enter the religious life.

In the following chapter of her *Life,* Saint Teresa recounts
an experience in friendship that was very painful to her, at
the same time as instructive. Shortly after her profession, she
had to go to her sister's home, at Becedas, for treatment for
an illness:

> There was a priest who lived in the place where I had gone for the
> treatment: he was a man of really good family and great intelligence.
> . . . After I had begun to make my confessions to this priest, . . . he
> took an extreme liking to me. . . . There was nothing wrong in his
> affection for me, but it ceased to be good because there was too much
> of it. . . . Out of the great affection he had for me, he began to tell
> me about his unhappy condition. It was no small matter: for nearly
> seven years he had been in a most perilous state because of his affec-
> tion for a woman in that very place, with whom he had a good deal
> to do. Nevertheless, he continued saying Mass. The fact that he had
> lost his honour and his good name was quite well known, yet no one
> dared to reprove him for it. I was sorry for him because I liked him
> very much.[13]

[11] *Life,* iii; Peers, I, 18.
[12] *Ibid.,* iv; 20. Antonio was to go to the monastery of the Friars Preachers
to ask for the habit. But before going, he was to accompany his sister to
the Convent of the Incarnation.
[13] *Ibid.,* v; 27-8.

In order to deliver him from this spell, the Saint showed him greater affection. In telling this fact, she accuses herself of imprudence: "My intentions here were good, but my action was wrong." [14] She had the joy of completely delivering the unhappy man from the occasion of sin; he did penance and died exactly a year from the day when she had first seen him.

At the Convent of the Incarnation where she lived for nearly thirty years, the Saint did not fall into any of the grave faults to which the absence of cloister exposes one. And yet, she writes:

Now when I began to indulge in conversations, I did not think, seeing them to be so usual, that they would cause the harm and distraction to my soul which I found would be the case later.[15]

There was especially one person for whom she had a growing affection, who distracted her a great deal. Our Lord reproaches her for these conversations by revealing Himself to her with a stern countenance. On another occasion, a huge toad crosses the parlor when she is with that same person; this makes a strong impression on her. God wants no more of these worldly friendships for Teresa.

But she does cultivate some, of the purest and most useful. She knows "a saintly gentleman . . . married, but his life is so exemplary and virtuous . . . he directs all he does to the great good of souls." "So diligent on my behalf was this blessed and holy man that he seems," adds the Saint, "to have been the beginning of my soul's salvation." [16]

It is thanks to this gentleman, named Francisco de Salcedo, that she comes to know Gaspar Daza, "a learned cleric who lived in that place [Avila], and whose goodness and holy life the Lord was beginning to make known among the people"; [17] and that she will later see Saint Francis Borgia. But P. Baltazar

[14] *Ibid.;* 29.
[15] *Ibid.,* vii; 40.
[16] *Ibid.,* xxiii; 147.
[17] *Ibid.*

Alvarez, S.J., who is directing her, finds that certain friendships that she still is keeping, are an obstacle to her spiritual advancement. The question is how to make the Saint decide to break them. She is not offending God, and so, she writes, "it seemed to me that if I abandoned them I should be sinning through ingratitude." In the ensuing discussion, Father Alvarez is doubtless not of a stature to argue victoriously with the Saint in this domain. Let us listen to Saint Teresa:

> I asked him why it was necessary for me to be ungrateful if I was not offending God. He told me to commend the matter to God for a few days, and to recite the hymn *Veni Creator,* and I should be enlightened as to which was the better thing to do. So I spent the greater part of one whole day in prayer; and then, beseeching the Lord that He would help me to please Him in everything, I began the hymn. While I was reciting it, there came to me a transport so sudden that it almost carried me away: I could make no mistake about this, so clear was it. This was the first time that the Lord had granted me the favour of any kind of rapture. I heard these words: "I will have thee converse now, not with men, but with angels."
> The words have come true: never since then have I been able to maintain firm friendship save with people who I believe love God and try to serve Him, nor have I derived comfort from any others or cherished any private affection for them. It has not been in my own power to do so.[18]

The heart of Saint Teresa has been purified; it can cultivate henceforth only purely spiritual friendships. And the transverberation of her heart will soon confer upon her the special grace of maternal fecundity. Friendships, however, keep the same importance in her life.

It is from a circle of friends at the Convent of the Incarnation that there comes the idea of the foundation of Saint Joseph of Avila. In the group were María de Ocampo, who became M. María-Bautista, and Doña Guiomar de Ulloa, who took care of many delicate tasks at the time of the foundation. And yet, in the little Convent of Saint Joseph, Saint Teresa does not authorize particular friendships, however holy they may be.

Such a line of action—which it will be easy to justify when

[18] *Life,* xxiv; Peers, I, 155.

we have explained the Teresian doctrine on friendship—does not destroy affection. Spiritual love overflows from the maternal heart of Teresa, more ardent and stronger than ever. It goes out to souls; and if it discovers in them gifts for working for the kingdom of God, it cannot but love them deeply and desire to see them belong entirely to God.

It is thus that Saint Teresa writes of P. García de Toledo:

> I had always taken him for a man of great intelligence, but now he seemed to me shrewder than ever. I thought what great talents and gifts he had and what a deal of good he could do with them if he gave himself wholly to God. For some years now I have felt like this—I never see a person whom I like very much without immediately wishing that I could see him wholly given to God. . . .
> I shed copious tears, and begged Him that that soul might really give itself up to His service, for, good as I thought him, I was not satisfied but wanted him to be better still. And after praying in that way, I remember saying these words: "Lord, Thou must not refuse me this favour. Think what a good person he is for us to have as our friend." [19]

The friends of Christ, who are also hers, and whom she surrounds with her maternal solicitude, are Father García de Toledo, the Fathers Báñez, Mariano, Gracián, and many others.

To all her daughters she gives a maternal affection; but there are some whom her heart has discerned as more pleasing to God or more apt at rendering Him service. These are María de Salazar, relative of the Duchess de la Cerda, who became María de San José, prioress of Seville, to whom she testifies an affection that lives on in the numerous letters that she wrote her and that we have; and especially Ana de Jesús, her joy and her crown, and Ana de San Bartolomé, the companion of her journeys, her secretary, her confidante, and often her counsellor. Yes, Ana de Jesús and Ana de San Bartolomé, of whom we never tire of talking just as the Saint never tired of loving them, so beautiful they were—the one, by the brilliance of her natural and supernatural gifts; the other, by the simplicity of her soul and her grace—equal, moreover, in their attachment

[19] *Ibid.*, xxxiv; 235-6.

to their mother. The first inherited the spirit of the Reformer; the second, the last beat of her heart; and this is what places them, in our eyes, among the greatest figures of the Teresian Reform.

To these privileged souls Saint Teresa gives an entirely pure and fruitful affection. But she wants to be paid in return, as she writes to M. María de San José:

> I assure you that, if you love me dearly, I for my part return your love and like you to tell me of yours. How unmistakable a trait of our nature is this wish for our love to be returned! Yet it cannot be wrong, for Our Lord wishes it too.[20]

Even at the summits of transforming union, Saint Teresa keeps her specially loved friends, and to justify them she avails herself of the example of Christ.

## B. Her doctrine on friendships

### I. IMPORTANCE OF FRIENDSHIPS

The life of Saint Teresa gives evidence of the decisive influence of friendships. All the great decisions of the Saint were inspired or at least effectively sustained by friendships. But the Reformer of Carmel is a soul exceptionally strong. What, then, will normally be the case with a less vigorous soul whose weakness renders it more passive still under external influences?

There is a general law, that God adapts the distribution of His grace to the conditions of our nature. God became man to bring us His divine life. He instituted the sacraments, sensible signs, to be the channels of grace; He makes habitual and continual use of external events, and still more, of free causes, as messengers of His light and most authentic intermediaries of His grace.

"Faith comes through hearing," says the apostle; and likewise we might add: The senses are to the supernatural life what roots are to the plant; it is through them that nourishment reaches it. Hence, we have some idea of the influence on the development of the supernatural life that the environment in

[20] Cf. *Letters*, II, p. 878.

which the senses are activated, can have; and especially, the friendships by which they are affected in a profound and more constant way.

The beginner will be, ordinarily, more sensitive to the influence of friendship. Saint Teresa stresses and explains how this can be beneficial:

> It is a great evil for a soul beset by so many dangers to be alone. . . . For this reason I would advise those who practise prayer, especially at first, to cultivate friendship and intercourse with others of similar interests. This is a most important thing, if only because we can help each other by our prayers, and it is all the more so because it may bring us many other benefits. Since people can find comfort in the conversation and human sympathy of ordinary friendships, even when these are not altogether good, I do not know why anyone who is beginning to love and serve God in earnest should not be allowed to discuss his joys and trials with others—and people who practise prayer have plenty of both. . . . I believe that anyone who discusses the subject with this in mind will profit both himself and his hearers, and will be all the wiser for it; and, without realizing he is doing so, will edify his friends.
>
> Anyone who could become vainglorious through discussing these matters would become equally so by hearing Mass with devotion in a place where people can see him, and by doing other things which he is obliged to do under pain of being no Christian at all: he cannot possibly refrain from doing these through fear of vainglory. This is also most important for souls which are not strengthened in virtue; they have so many enemies and friends to incite them to do what is wrong that I cannot insist upon it sufficiently. . . .
>
> For people trouble so little about things pertaining to the service of God that we must all back each other up if those of us who serve Him are to make progress. People think it a good thing to follow the pleasures and vanities of the world and there are few who look askance at these; but if a single person begins to devote himself to God, there are so many to speak ill of him that self-defence compels him to seek the companionship of others until he is strong enough not to be depressed by suffering. Unless he does this he will find himself in continual difficulties. It must have been for this reason, I think, that some of the saints were in the habit of going into the desert. It is a kind of humility for a man not to trust himself but to believe that God will help him in dealing with those with whom he has intercourse. Charity grows when it is communicated to others and from this there result a thousand blessings. I should not dare to say this if I had not had a great deal of experience of its importance.[21]

[21] *Life*, vii; Peers, I, 46 f.

## 2. CHOICE OF FRIENDS

The profound influence of friendship suggests at once the need of prudence in the choice of those that we are to cultivate.

It is not out of place, in this respect, to make some distinctions.

Our Lord had friends during His life on earth. To His apostles, He told the secrets of the kingdom of God, the mysteries of His intimate life. And among them, the three preferred ones were the witnesses of His Transfiguration and of His Agony in the Garden of Olives. During the last weeks of His sorrowful struggle at Jerusalem, Jesus used to go in the evening to rest a while at Bethany, in the atmosphere that the affection of Lazarus, Martha, and Mary, made so sweet to His heart. Being a man like us, Jesus cultivates human friendships in order to sanctify ours.

In Christ, friendship is the fruit of a free choice of His merciful tenderness, desirous of giving itself. In the saints, it proceeds both from their divine love that expresses itself in fraternal charity, and from the profound consciousness of their weakness that remains in them beneath the courage of their virtue. In us, it springs from a need of support and of opening our hearts, as well as from a current of sympathy.

As we see, the quality of the friendship depends on the movement from which it proceeds, the love that animates it.

An expert in the art of loving and a penetrating psychologist in analyzing the affections, Saint Teresa will help us in discerning and evaluating friendships by qualifying the love that inspires them. From this practical point of view, the teaching that she gives in the *Way of Perfection* is incomparable.

Let us first note that love is the law of every life, of every being. God has put this law in every creature to regulate its movement towards its providential end; but He has adapted it to the nature of each being. The star gravitates in space by obeying the law of universal gravitation and of the mutual attraction of bodies, which is the law of love for matter. Instinct is another form of the same law of love.

In man we find three forms of the law of love, adapted to the three levels of life in the baptized Christian: sensible love, proper to the life of the body; rational love, which belongs to the soul; and supernatural love, which is essential to the life of grace. Each one of these loves must lead to its perfect development the life to which it belongs. All come from God and so are good in themselves. Considering them separately, we could not despise nor destroy any one of them.

Life does not present to us these different loves separated as in their logical division, but united in various degrees. The practical judgment must be brought to bear on the proportion that each shall have in an individual human being; on the living synthesis realized by their union. It is the dynamism of this ensemble, its movement, its direction, that it is important to evaluate in terms of the supernatural end of a man and the particular vocation of each one. His moral and spiritual value springs from the harmonious unity of his vital energies and their convergence towards his providential destiny.

Saint Teresa speaks to us of friendships and judges them, viewing them under this living and synthetic aspect. She is as little of a logician as possible, in the scholastic sense of the word; it is life that draws and holds her. She analyzes it with a marvelous penetration, and presents it such as she sees it. And so her descriptions are slices of life, cut from the real. And although in discussing friendships, the Saint is addressing her Carmelite daughters, her judgments and her counsels have a human value that gives them a universal bearing.

a. *Sensible love*

We consider here a friendship that the Saint qualifies as a "wrong love," and of which she does not care to speak. It is a matter of a sensible love that has sensual demands; it can be legitimate in marriage. Saint Teresa is talking to religious who have vowed their virginity to God and preserve it as a divine treasure. For them, this love is wrong. They must guard against it with care, for its least breath can tarnish:

> These last affections are a very hell, and it is needless for us to weary ourselves by saying how evil they are, for the least of the evils which they bring are terrible beyond exaggeration. There is no need for us ever to take such things upon our lips, sisters, *or even to think of them,* or to remember that they exist anywhere in the world; you must never listen to anyone speaking of such affections, either in jest or in earnest.[22]

This elimination having been made with an energy that we understand very well for religious, the Saint tells us her plan to explain two kinds of love.

> There are two kinds of love which I am describing. The one is *purely* spiritual, and apparently has nothing to do with sensuality or the tenderness of our nature, either of which might stain its purity. The other is also spiritual, but mingled with it are our sensuality and weakness; yet it is a worthy love, which, as between relatives and friends, seems lawful.[23]

The first is dominated by spiritual love. In the second, the spiritual is united with elements drawn from reason and the senses in diverse degrees, such as make it lawful and even good. Let us call this last love "spiritual-sensible" from the two extremes that it unites; and with the Saint, let us speak of it first.

### b. *Spiritual-sensible love*

Spiritual love is a fruit found at the summits; hence, it is very rare. Spiritual-sensible love is much the more frequent. It is the one that ordinarily nourishes friendships between spiritual persons. As a rule, their spiritual bonds are engrafted in natural sympathies and find in these their strength and their stability. How could they love with a love purely spiritual when their faculties are not purified, and supernatural charity has not yet established its dominion over the lower powers?

[22] *Way of Perfection,* vii; Peers, II, 31.
[23] *Ibid.,* iv; 19.

Saint Teresa reassures us as to the morality of spiritual-sensible friendships by comparing the love that animates them to that which we have for our relatives. Not only are they lawful; they may be beneficial. The apostolate of friendship, that is found so often in specialized movements, will use for the most part this spiritual-sensible type, more adapted as it is to our weakness. By the atmosphere that these friendships create around souls, the persuasive force that they add to counsel, the affectionate support that they afford, they can rescue a soul from loneliness, from bad surroundings, or from the mediocrity of a milieu, to elevate it into purer and more supernatural regions.

The friendships by which Saint Teresa benefited before her entrance into Carmel were of this nature. The affection that she inspired in those about her and that enabled her to attract them, must also have been spiritual-sensible. We cannot suppose that those souls were elevated at once to spiritual love, and that the natural charms of the Saint did not contribute a large part in attaching them to her side.

Might not the same be said with regard to the crowds that forgot their food and drink to follow Jesus even into the desert? They were not only captivated by the divine radiance that shone forth from the sacred humanity of our Saviour; but also, by the kindness, the eloquence, and all the external charms of the Master. Indeed, it was in order to conquer thus, by adapting Himself to our weakness, that the Word became flesh; and by assuming our human nature, He wanted it to be clothed with all the perfection of which it is capable.

In Christ, and also in Teresa, affection was wholly spiritual; and it preserved from danger the less perfect affection of the souls that were captivated by it.

The case will not be the same when both friends bring to their union only an imperfect love. How then can we avoid fearing a loss of balance between the two elements, spiritual and sensible, that are united in this friendship? It is a law that each one of our faculties is drawn towards the good that is presented to it, to taste its proper satisfaction. The satisfactions of the senses are the most violent and risk dominating in the soul that is not purified, and dragging it down.[24] In our nature wounded by sin, love tends to descend to the lower powers and to pour itself out through the senses. This break in balance threatens the most sincere strivings for spiritual good and makes them founder in the culpable liberties of sensuous love, or even the deplorable deviations of mystical sensualism.

Without falling into these excesses, spiritual-sensible friendship can imperceptibly be transformed into an inordinate affection, or an exclusive and particular friendship which is already a disorder. The Saint writes:

> Little by little they deprive the will of the strength which it needs if it is to employ itself wholly in the love of God. . . . even among brothers and sisters such things are apt to be poisonous. . . . The harm which it does to community life is very serious. . . . I am more inclined to believe that the devil initiates them so as to create factions within religious Orders.[25]

They are "wrong in anyone, and, in a prioress, pestilential."

The Saint notes in this connection that "consciences of those who aim only in a rough-and-ready way at pleasing God . . . think they are acting virtuously"; and that in order to check such friendships, "we must proceed diligently and lovingly rather than severely."

It could happen that some element of sensibility might creep into one's relations with the confessor. The question is important and delicate for religious; and so, the Saint treats of it at considerable length. First of all, a person should not fall into exaggerated scrupulosity on this point. If the confessor is holy, zealous, and if he is guiding the soul to greater perfection, Teresa advises:

> What you can do here is not to let your minds dwell upon whether you like your confessor or not, but just to like him if you feel so in-

[24] Cf. *Dark Night*, xiv.
[25] *Way of Perfection*, iv; Peers, II, 17.

clined. . . . Why should we not love those who are always striving and toiling to help our souls? Actually, if my confessor is a holy and spiritual man, I think it will be a real help to my progress for me to like him.[26]

But if the confessor is seen to be tending in any way towards vanity, he should be regarded with grave suspicion. . . . It is a dangerous matter, and can be a veritable hell, and a source of harm to everyone. . . . The devil can do a great deal of harm here.[27]

Perhaps Saint Teresa is thinking of the painful episode at Becedas. Disorders in a cloistered convent cannot develop to such proportions, but there can be grave disturbances, anguish of body and soul. "In what I have said here," testifies the Saint, "I am speaking from experience of things that I have seen and heard and gathered from conversation with learned and holy people." [28] She stresses her hope that "the superior will never be so intimate with the confessor" that the sisters cannot speak freely with the one and the other; and warns "that is the way the devil lays his snares for souls when he can find no other." [29]

There is only one remedy for these evils: let the religious have the liberty of going to more than one confessor, and make use of this privilege from time to time even if the ordinary confessor combines learning and holiness.

We have yet to ask if there is any criterion for discerning whether, in this blend that constitutes spiritual-sensible love, the sensuous predominates and takes the lead in a way that is dangerous. For the answer we cannot depend completely on exterior manifestations in which the temperament of the persons and the customs of the milieu play a notable part. More profound are some psychological signs that Saint Teresa gives: The friendship that is deviating, feeds on trifles:

Some injury done to a friend is resented; a nun desires to have something to give to her friend or tries to make time for talking to

[26] *Ibid.;* 22.
[27] *Ibid.,* iv; 19-20.
[28] *Ibid.,* v; 25.
[29] *Ibid.,* 23.

her, and often her object in doing this is to tell her how fond she is
of her, and other irrelevant things, rather than how much she loves
God. . . . Many imperfections can result from this.[30]

The discernment of good friendships was a problem that had
bothered Saint Therese of the Child Jesus. Saint John of the
Cross gave her the solution. On the back of a holy card that
she kept in her missal, she had copied this passage from the
*Dark Night:*

Some of these persons make friendships of a spiritual kind with
others, which oftentimes arise from sensuality and not from spirituality; this may be known to be the case when the remembrance of that
friendship causes not the remembrance and love of God to grow, but
occasions remorse of conscience. For, when the friendship is purely
spiritual, the love of God grows with it; and the more the soul remembers it, the more it remembers the love of God, and the greater
the desire it has for God; so that, as the one grows, the other grows
also. . . . But, when this love arises from the vice of sensuality afore-
mentioned, it has the contrary effects; for the more the one grows, the
more the other decreases, and the remembrance of it likewise.[31]

The tree is recognized by its fruits. The criterion given by
our Lord for the discernment of true prophets is applicable
here also, and gives certitude. The effects make known the
nature of the affection; or rather, indicate which, in this synthesis, is the force that dominates and imposes its movement
on the other elements. If the spiritual-sensible friendships
make one grow in love of God, they are good and should be
encouraged. Such is the conclusion.

But now Teresa seems to draw back from that conclusion.
She does not accept even those for her convents; she writes:

Where a convent is large I should like to see many friendships of
that type; but in this house, where there are not, and can never be,
more than thirteen nuns, all must be friends with each other, love
each other, be fond of each other and help each other. For the love
of the Lord, refrain from making individual friendships, however
holy.[32]

[30] *Way of Perfection,* iv; Peers, II, 17.
[31] *Dark Night,* iv; Peers, I, 362.
[32] *Way of Perfection,* iv; Peers, II, 17.

The Saint has a more elevated ideal for her daughters, that of spiritual love.

### c. *Spiritual love*

The spiritual love of which Saint Teresa speaks in the sixth and seventh chapters of the *Way of Perfection,* is a highly perfect love: "Few, I fear, possess it; let any one of you to whom the Lord has given it praise Him fervently, for she must be a person of the greatest perfection." [33]

It is enlightened by a clear view on God and on the creature:

... of what it is to love the Creator and what to love the creature ... when one understands by sight and experience what can be gained by the one practice and lost by the other, and what the Creator is and what the creature ... then one loves very differently from those of us who have not advanced thus far.[34]

This love does not rest in external advantages:

Those whom God brings to this state are, I think, generous and royal souls; they are not content with loving anything so miserable as these bodies, however beautiful they be and however numerous the graces they possess. If the sight of the body gives them pleasure they praise the Creator, but as for dwelling upon it for more than just a moment—No! . . .[35]

Do you ask, again, by what they are attracted if they do not love things they see? They do love what they see and they are greatly attracted by what they hear; but the things which they see are everlasting. If they love anyone they immediately look right beyond the body, fix their eyes on the soul and see what there is to be loved in that. If there is nothing, but they see any suggestion or inclination which shows them that, if they dig deep, they will find gold within this mine, they think nothing of the labour of digging, since they have love.[36]

Their great capacities for loving and for serving God, alone justify their preferences for certain souls.

This love is so pure in its object only because it is entirely

[33] *Ibid.,* vi; 26.
[34] *Ibid.;* 27.
[35] *Ibid.;* 28.
[36] *Ibid.;* 29.

spiritual, and it has dominated all the natural tendencies in the soul.

> This is love without any degree whatsoever of self-interest.[37]
> They may from time to time experience a natural and momentary pleasure at being loved; yet, as soon as they return to their normal condition, they realize that such pleasure is folly save when the persons concerned can benefit their souls, whether by instruction or by prayer. Any other kind of affection wearies them, for they know it can bring them no profit and may well do them harm.[38]

Likewise, with regard to spiritual affection for our neighbor:

> Although the weakness of our nature may at first allow us to feel something of all this [natural sensibility], our reason soon begins to reflect whether our friend's trials are not good for her, and to wonder if they are making her richer in virtue and how she is bearing them. . . . If we see that she is being patient, we feel no distress. . . .
> I repeat once more that this love is a similitude and a copy of that which was borne for us by the good Lover, Jesus.[39]

It is ardent and strong like the love of Christ for us:

> It is strange how impassioned this love is; how many tears, penances and prayers it costs; how careful is the loving soul to commend the object of its affection to all who it thinks may prevail with God and to ask them to intercede with Him for it; and how constant is it longing, so that it cannot be happy unless it sees that its loved one is making progress. If that soul seems to have advanced, and is then seen to fall some way back, her friend seems to have no more pleasure in life: she neither eats nor sleeps, is never free from this fear and is always afraid that the soul whom she loves so much may be lost, and that the two may be parted for ever.[40]

But those who possess it are neither blind in their love no too complacent:

> Their heart does not allow them to practise duplicity: if they se their friend straying from the road, or committing any faults, they wi speak to her about it; they cannot allow themselves to do anythin else.

[37] *Way of Perfection*, vii; Peers, II, 31.
[38] *Ibid.*, vi; 28.
[39] *Ibid.*, vii; 31-2.
[40] *Ibid.*, vii; 30.

A person may be indifferent to other people, . . . but she cannot take this attitude with her friends: nothing they do can be hidden from her; she sees the smallest mote in them.[41]

Hence it is that Saint Teresa reprimands Ana de Jesús, Gracián, and Mariano with a frankness that would seem harsh if it did not spring from affection.

To P. Mariano, an ardent nature, she writes:

Oh, dear me, what a trying way you have with you! . . . May God keep you, faults and all, and make you very holy.[42]

To P. Gracián, dejected by the tempest that was rising against the Reform, she wrote:

For pity's sake, don't start meeting troubles half way: God will make everything all right. . . . If you are depressed like that when you are having such an easy time, what would you have been if you had been having a time like Fray John? [43]

As to Ana de Jesùs, who—it was reported to Teresa—failed in discretion when she was making the foundation at Grenada, she received this vigorous reprimand:

I am positively shocked that Discalced nuns should be thinking of such trivialities a propos of the title that the provincial gives to the prioress. . . . And after that (Mother María de Cristo) praises your Reverence and descants on your great worth. . . . May God grant my Discalced nuns to be humble and obedient.[44]

Is there nothing of the human, then, left in this love? To think so, would be to misunderstand it. In fact, it finds in its very purity an exquisite delicacy and a freedom in its expression to which it alone is privileged. It knows how "to sympathize with our neighbor's trials, however trivial these may be." [45] It is gay on occasion and full of solicitude for every need, even material ones.

[41] *Way of Perfection*, vii; Peers, II, 32.
[42] *Letters*, Seville, May 9, 1576; Vol. I, 234.
[43] *Ibid.*, Avila, Aug., 1578; Vol. II, 600.
[44] *Ibid.*, May 30, 1582; Vol. II, 939.
[45] *Way of Perfection*, vii; Peers, II, 34.

The health of Father Gracián worries Teresa. She writes to M. María de San José, prioress of Seville:

> And just now you are making me deeply indebted to you for all the care which our Father tells me you are taking to look after him and which makes me love you more than ever.[46]

She, more than any one else, is affected by the torments that John of the Cross has to endure in his prison, and she writes to the king. But we would have to go through the whole correspondence of the Saint to see how delicately human she remains in her spiritual love of neighbor.

Human? Might not one be tempted to think it too much so, the day when, as a guest in a community of Carmelite friars, her maternal glance singles out a young brother with limpid clear eyes, she calls him and kisses him before the whole community. A spontaneous gesture, truly expressive of a maternal love which can be so free only because it is very pure and spiritual.

She had discerned the worth of Ana de Jesús and perhaps too her future role in the extension of the Reform and so she takes occasion from the restricted site of the foundation at Salamanca to give her a bed in her cell. In the evening she used to go near her to bless her, covering her forehead with the sign of the cross and caresses; then she would look at her for a long time in silence.

This spiritual love is full of divine riches and human delicacy; hence we can understand the exclamation of Saint Teresa:

> Happy the souls that are loved by such as these! Happy the day on which they came to know them! O my Lord, wilt Thou not grant me the favour of giving me many who have such love for me? Truly, Lord, I would rather have this than be loved by all the kings and lords of the world—and rightly so, for such friends use every means in their power to make us lords of the whole world. . . . When you make the acquaintance of any such persons, sisters, the Mother Prioress should employ every possible effort to keep you in touch with them. Love such persons as much as you like. There can be very few of them. . . . When one of you is striving after perfection, she will at

[46] *Letters*, Toledo, Dec. 7, 1576; Peers, I, 362.

once be told that she has no need to know such people—that it is enough for her to have God. But to get to know God's friends is a very good way of "having" Him; as I have discovered by experience, it is most helpful. For, under the Lord, I owe it to such persons that I am not in hell.[47]

We can understand also why Saint Teresa wants for her convents and for her daughters, only spiritual love. This love has the advantage of not causing trouble as do those affections in which sensibility has some part. It is large-hearted, strong, and not at all exclusive. But especially, it is proper to the elevated regions to which the Saint wants to lead her daughters; it is the only one that can permit them to fulfil their vocation in the Church.

They have a vocation to love. All their power of loving is entirely consecrated to Christ and to the Church which is His Mystical Body. They must love perfectly; and the quality is of greater importance for its perfection, than its intensity. Without a doubt, it is spiritual love that is the end of their vocation; it is towards this that they must tend throughout all the purifications, without stopping in the inferior forms of affection that might dazzle them, and whose flames might burn their wings.[48]

While waiting till this love is granted them, for it is a grace, let them prepare themselves to receive it, and merit it by keeping their heart free from every particular affection, and by already manifesting towards all and each one, the affectionate respect that is the external note of the spiritual love for which they are striving.

More than the most glowing descriptions, the scene of the dying Saint at Alba de Tormes makes us long for that spiritual love. The Blessed Ana de San Bartolomé, her inseparable companion, was spending herself at the death bed of the holy mother. After a night of watching—

[47] *Way of Perfection*, vi; Peers, II, 33.
[48] Cf. Saint Therese, *Autobiography*, iv, 63.

Father Antonio sent her to get something to eat. Teresa, not knowing where she had gone, kept looking around for her and did not rest till she saw her returning. Then by a sign, she called her near her, took her hands, and rested her own head on the shoulder of her dear nurse.[49]

At seven o'clock in the morning the agony began, peaceful and radiant as an ecstasy. At nine in the evening, the Reformer of Carmel, still in the same attitude, died in the arms of her dear Ana de San Bartolomé. An apotheosis! The love that carried away the soul of Teresa to God, had kept to the last moment here an attitude and an expression delicately human.

It was with the same perfect love that Teresa loved God and her daughters. While resting during her ecstasy on the heart of Ana de San Bartolomé, she was preparing for her eternal rest in the bosom of God!

[49] Life of Saint Teresa, by a Carmelite.

# CHAPTER VIII
# Spiritual Direction

*I myself, through not knowing what
to do, have lost a great deal of time.*[1]

The soul journeying towards God, finds strength in spiritual friendship; in spiritual direction, light to guide it. The friend is an equal, but the director is a superior to whom submission is due. His function can be distinct from that of the confessor. The confessor is a doctor who cures, who preserves the life of grace against the attacks of sin; the director guides the spiritual progress of the soul. Again, we find in Saint Teresa's writings a complete doctrine on spiritual direction, its importance and even necessity in certain cases, on the choice and qualities of a director, and the dispositions of the one directed.

## A. Importance and necessity of direction

1. The care that Saint Teresa took to procure for herself the help of spiritual direction is sufficient in itself to show the importance that she attached to it. She undertook nothing without consulting theologians and men versed in the spiritual life. The numerous accounts of her life or of graces that she received, tell us the spirit of faith that she brought to consultations and the importance that she assigned to them. She writes:

I praise God greatly, and we women, and those who are not learned, ought always to give Him infinite thanks, that there are persons who with such great labour have attained to the truth of which we ignorant people know nothing. . . .
Blessed be Thou, Lord, Who hast made me so incompetent and unprofitable! Most heartily do I praise Thee because Thou quickenest

[1] *Life,* xiv; Peers, 85.

so many to quicken us! We should pray most regularly for those who
give us light. What would become of us without them amid these
great storms which the Church now has to bear? [2]

Her gratitude was indeed justified. Among the secular and
regular priests and religious of all orders that she consulted at
Avila and in the cities to which she went for her foundations,
we find the greatest theologians of the time, such as the Dominicans, Ibáñez Bartolomé of Medina, and the great Báñez,
her regular theologian; those best qualified to speak on the
spiritual life, as for instance the first Jesuits of Avila, among
whom was Baltazar Alvarez; and four now canonized Saints:
Saint Peter of Alcantara, a Franciscan; Saint Louis Bertrand,
a Dominican; Saint Francis Borgia, commissary general of the
Society of Jesus; and Saint John of the Cross, the first Discalced
Carmelite Father.

In her writings she returns frequently to the importance or
even the necessity of direction. In one instance she says:

My opinion has always been, and always will be, that every Christian should try to consult some learned person, if he can, and the
more learned this person, the better. Those who walk in the way of
prayer have the greater need of learning; and the more spiritual they
are, the greater is their need.[3]

Direction is necessary at the beginning of the spiritual life:

The beginner needs counsel to help him ascertain what benefits him
most. To this end a director is very necessary; but he must be a man
of experience.[4]

To provide against the first difficulties of recollection, she
writes:

I will say no more about this now, except that it is very important
for you to consult people of experience.[5]

The need for a director will make itself especially felt in the
periods of darkness which are periods of transition; that is, in
the second, the fourth, and the sixth Mansions.

[3] *Life,* xiii; Peers, 81.
[4] *Ibid.;* 79.
[5] II Mansion, i; Peers, II, 218.

The following observations apply to the soul that has arrived at the prayer of quiet of the fourth Mansions:

> If God leads it, as He led me, by the way of fear, and there is no one who understands it, its trial will be a heavy one; and it will be very glad to read a description of itself which will show clearly that it is traveling on the right road. And it will be a great blessing for it to know what it has to do in order to continue to make progress in any of these states: I myself, through not knowing what to do, have suffered much and lost a great deal of time. I am sorry for souls who reach this state and find themselves alone.[6]

As to the sixth Mansions, where supernatural manifestations may become frequent, direction is indispensable.

2. The Saint gives support to her recommendations by stressing the difficulties of being one's own guide in the spiritual ways. These ways are darksome and will be seen completely only by one with experience. For how could the soul know them without having passed over them? In the Prologue to the *Ascent of Mount Carmel,* Saint John of the Cross declares that he had been moved to write "to relieve the great necessity which is experienced by many souls" who, having set out upon the road of virtue, go no farther often "because they understand not themselves and lack competent and alert directors who will guide them to the summit."

The science of the spiritual life is not enough. If anyone is to find his way and walk in it securely, he must know himself, his good points and his faults. But in any self-examination it is very difficult for us not to be deceived by our passions, or impressions, or by the movements of the faculties that conceal from us the depth of our soul.

Saint Francis de Sales, with delicate precision, underlines the fact that we are so lacking in clear-sightedness as to ourselves because of a certain complacence "so secret and imperceptible that unless one has very good sight he cannot discover it; and the very ones who are tainted with this do not know it,

---

[6] *Life,* xiv; Peers, I, 85.

if it is not pointed out to them." [7] In another place, the holy Doctor explains:

And why should we want to be masters of ourselves in that which concerns the spirit, since we are not so in what concerns the body. Do we not know that doctors, when they are sick, call other doctors to judge as to the remedies that are right for them.[8]

The same statements find a more energetic expression under the pen of Saint Bernard. To Canon Ogier the Saint declares that he who constitutes himself his own master, becomes the disciple of a fool: *Qui se sibi magistrum constituit, stulto se discipulum facit.* And he adds:

I do not know what others think about themselves in this matter: from my own experience I can say that it is easier for me and more sure, to command many others than to direct myself.[9]

The director is more than a guide. He is—again according to the testimony of Saint Bernard—a foster father who must instruct, console, encourage. It is incumbent on him to discern the particular grace of the soul, to withdraw it from false attractions, to preserve it from all dangers, especially at times of spiritual darkness, and to make it triumph by using all its energies.

This enlightened and persevering action is, in every circumstance, of incomparable value for a generous soul; understanding sympathy can be the most efficacious help to it during periods of darkness and trial.

3. Direction enters into the divine economy for the guidance of souls.

God, in fact, established His Church as a hierarchical society. He guides and sanctifies the souls in it by the authority of the pope and the bishops for matters of ecclesiastical jurisdiction, and the ministry of the priest in matters of conscience. Christ gave to them His power: He binds in heaven what they bind on earth; He looses in heaven what they have loosed on earth.

[7] *Devout Life*, Bk. III, xxviii.
[8] *Sermons*, Feast of Our Lady of the Snows.
[9] *Letters*, lxxxvii; 7.

Pope Leo XIII points out this important truth in his letter, *Testem benevolentiae* (January 22, 1899); he writes:

> We find at the very origins of the Church a well-known manifestation of this law: although Saul, breathing out threat and carnage, had heard the voice of Christ Himself and had asked Him: Lord, what do you want me to do? he was sent for the answer to Damascus, to Ananias: Enter into the city, and there it will be told you what you must do.

Christ does not take back the powers that He has given; He sends to those who have received them, the souls that He Himself lays hold on.

This is the argument that Saint John of the Cross develops in the *Ascent of Mount Carmel:* [10]

> For God is so desirous that the government and direction of every man should be undertaken by another man like himself, and that every man should be ruled and governed by natural reason, that He earnestly desires us not to give entire credence to the things that He communicates to us supernaturally, not to consider them as being securely and completely confirmed until they pass through this human aqueduct of the mouth of man. And thus, whenever He says or reveals something to a soul, He gives this same soul to whom He says it a kind of inclination to tell it to the person to whom it is fitting that it should be told. Until this has been done, it gives not entire satisfaction because the man has not taken it from another man like himself.[11]

The Saint goes on to stress the fact that the word of God, addressed directly to Moses and to Gideon, had no strength for them until it had passed through a human instrument.

It is to this human instrument that God confides the care of interpreting and completing His message. Woe then to the man who, even though enlightened directly by God, would want to remain alone: Saint Paul went to the apostles to be confirmed in his faith; Saint Peter by himself, although taught by God, went astray with regard to a ceremony concerning the Gentiles; Moses received excellent counsel from Jethro, his father-in-law; and many who worked wonders in testimony of our Lord,

[10] *Ascent*, Bk. II, xxii; Peers, I, 177.
[11] *Ibid.*

will not be recognized by Him in the day of judgment, although they may have done marvels in His name.

4. Hagiography and the history of the Church give further evidence of the excellence and benefits of direction.

Direction was held in honor by the Fathers of the Desert, who gathered around an elder to receive his counsels. Cassian tells us that the most detestable monks were the sarabaïtes who gave themselves up to extraordinary mortifications but would obey no one, or were constantly changing masters.

It is also in honor, and sometimes obligatory, in religious Orders, especially during the period of formation.

For the majority of the saints, it appears as an important element in their spiritual life. In the case of some, the relationship between director and directed led to an intimate union in which both souls found, besides light for their ascent, a marvelous spiritual enrichment and fruitfulness in works of mercy. We think of Saint Clare and Saint Francis of Assisi, Saint Francis de Sales and Saint Jane de Chantal. And it is hard to imagine what the Foundress of the Visitandines would have been without the holy Bishop of Geneva.

From these considerations must we draw the conclusion that a special spiritual director, in the modern sense of the word, is necessary? The answer to this question requires a few distinctions.

Let us first take cognizance of the fact that the problem presents itself only for the Christian who is solicitous for his perfection. The ordinary Christian would not ask and, practically, would not know what to do with advice other than that which comes to him through preaching or through the reception of the sacraments.

On the other hand, the spiritual man properly speaking certainly needs counsel and direction appropriate to his state. But the Church has foreseen this need and provided for it. Consequently it seems normal that the religious should find sufficient directives in the means put at his disposal: regular confessors, superiors, the rule, and providential events that touch him. Perhaps it was because she was walking in an ordinary way, but we note that Saint Therese of the Child Jesus had no other direction than that of the ordinary or extraordinary confessors of the community, and that God seems to have wanted to keep her from any other influence.

It happens nevertheless rather frequently that in the religious life, and especially in the contemplative life, the soul does not have at hand the direction that it needs, particularly at certain more difficult periods. In that case, it would fail in prudence and risk compromising its spiritual progress if it did not exercise diligence to find the special help that it needs.

As to the soul living in the world, without a precise rule, it is difficult to see how it could advance along the spiritual way without the help of regular direction.

Whether we are satisfied with the helps placed at our disposition, or whether we have recourse to a special director, it is necessary to be helped by some one who has a concern for the care of our soul.

If anyone should think he can dispense with this ordinarily, it would at least be necessary for him to submit to a guide any supernatural action of God in his soul.

## B. Choice and qualities of a director

The influence that spiritual direction can have in a soul, gives a very great importance to the choice of a director. Saint John of the Cross says of this:

It is a difficult thing to explain how the spirit of the disciple grows in conformity with that of his spiritual father, in a hidden and secret way.[12]

The orientation of a life, the rapidity of its spiritual ascent, its sanctification and perhaps even salvation, can depend on the choice of a spiritual guide. Hence we readily understand why

[12] *Ascent*, Bk. II, xviii; Peers, I, 146.

Saint Francis de Sales recommends that a director be chosen, not among a thousand but from ten thousand.

To choose a director simply on the basis of a natural sympathy could be plain imprudence. Reason and faith must guide the choice. Saint Teresa states the criteria:

> It is of great importance, then, that the director should be a prudent man—of sound understanding, I mean—and also an experienced one: if he is a learned man as well, that is a very great advantage.[13]

And the Saint sounds a grave warning in this regard:

> Anyone, I repeat, who surrenders his soul to a single director, and is subject to him alone, will be making a great mistake, if he is a religious, and has to be subject to his own superior, in not obtaining a director of this kind. For the director may be lacking in all the three things, and that will be no light cross for the penitent to bear without voluntarily submitting his understanding to one whose understanding is not good. For myself, I have never been able to bring myself to do this, nor do I think it right. If such a person be in the world, let him praise God that he is able to choose the director to whom he is to be subject and let him not give up such righteous freedom; let him rather remain without a director until he finds the right one, for the Lord will give him one if his life is founded upon humility and he has the desire to succeed.[14]

The influence of direction is such that divine Wisdom, so full of care for our needs, shows a particular concern in the choice. God Himself sometimes indicates the right director to a soul that He has charged with a special mission: Saint Paul is sent to Ananias; Saint Margaret Mary is told to go to Père de la Colombière. Divine Wisdom gives to all souls, if not precise indications, at least a light for this choice.

Saint Teresa does not mention holiness among the criteria; but we shall add it. Evidently she wants to insist on the moral qualities of the director. In actual fact, although it is a function of the priesthood, spiritual direction is bound in especially with the personal qualities of the priest, and draws from these its efficacy. One could sin through imprudence—except in case

---

[13] *Life,* xiii; Peers, I, 80.
[14] *Ibid.;* 81-2.

of urgency or necessity—by counting uniquely on the sacerdotal grace of a priest to ask him for important advice or regular direction, without considering his aptitude for this special ministry.

### 1. HOLINESS

To find a director who is a saint, is indeed a precious grace. To require or even to desire, however, that his holiness shine out in external manifestions, or that he be enlightened by extraordinary lights, is a dangerous whim that would expose one to many errors. It must suffice for us, that humility and charity attest to his holiness. These two virtues that mutually complete and enlighten one another, make good directors.

Supernatural charity, free of all self-interest, seeks only God in souls and refers everything to Him as to the absolute Master. In the director, it is an outpouring of the paternity of the Father of light and of mercy; it makes him patient and understanding, compassionate with misery and confident in every good will.

Humility enlightens charity by drawing down those outpourings of the divine mercy. It makes the director find his place between God and the soul, assures to him the light and docility he needs to fulfil his mission as instrument of God and human collaborator in the work of grace.

Having deeply at heart this role assigned him in the divine economy, the director will often put himself into the hands of God to beg for His light, His inspiration, and His grace to carry on perfectly the work he is to do. A humble mistrust of self and a great confidence in God will, through the gift of counsel, draw forth the divine responses that he needs for the accomplishment of his mission.

A collaborator of God, he must work to bring into effect the will of God. The soul belongs to God; it is to God that it must journey, and by the way that God determines. It is for the director to discern the divine will with regard to a particular soul, and help this soul in its fulfillment.

Souls are as diverse as flowers. "Hardly could we find one that even half resembles another," [15] according to John of the Cross. Each one has its mission in the divine plan, its place in heaven; and, here below, there is a power in its graces, a beauty, certain exigencies, that correspond to the design of God for it. The same divine Sun warms and enlightens all: they all quench their thirst at the same living Source and are fed with the same Bread of Life that is Christ. Yet Wisdom stoops like a mother over each soul, calling it by its divine name, and varying admirably the effects of light in each one, its tastes of grace, the ardor of its desires, and the movements of its love.

Oh, the profound and inscrutable mystery of souls and of God's life in them! Who could say what divine destiny will unfold from the grace that such and such a child has received in baptism? Will this germ of the spiritual life bloom into a flower whose whole adornment will be in its modesty, and whose charm, in the secrecy of its perfume? Will it be a small verdant tree, embellishing the field of the Church and nourishing the children of God with its fruits; or will it rise up like a lofty tree of the forest whose topmost branches reach into the skies?

The director will regard this mystery with respect. The action of grace in the soul will reveal to him the divine name by which it is called. It will do so in a way not easy to express in words but yet clearly. The director, while unable to unveil its future to the soul, will show it God's designs upon it, the way grace is leading it and the significance of what happens to it. He will be its guide through the maze of life's complications and, in the regular movement of the ordinary life as well as in the trouble of disconcerting events, he will make known the present duty, will determine the attitude to be taken, and will help to trace the line of the providential plan.

[15] *Living Flame*, st. iii.

Charity and humility will be the director's sole support in the journey into darkness. They will enable him to move about with ease there and carry on the work of the divine Artisan, leading the soul to the full realization of His designs in its regard. These virtues alone can save the director from the dangers that threaten him, namely: the monopolizing of souls and using them for personal ends, petty jealousies, a narrow authoritarianism that makes him impose his own views and methods and diminishes the liberty of the soul under the action of the Holy Spirit.[16]

Holiness alone knows how to respect perfectly the absolute rights of God over a soul and to serve these utterly even by withdrawing, if need be, to entrust the soul to better advised counsels.[17] It seeks no other joy and no other reward than the privilege of contemplating, at times, the work of God in souls and of collaborating discreetly—always in the shadow—so that the power, the wisdom, and the mercy of God, admirable in all His works but especially in His saints, may shine forth and be glorified.

## 2. PRUDENCE

*Ars artium regimen animarum,* the direction of souls is an art, and one of the most delicate. Its domain is the darkness of the Divine and the complexity of human nature. To it, it be-

---

[16] In the *Living Flame* Saint John of the Cross flays vigorously the directors who fall into these faults: "These directors . . . from motives of their own interest or pleasure . . . are placed as barriers and obstacles at the gate of Heaven; they hinder from entering those that ask counsel of them. . . . Some do it knowingly, others unconsciously; but neither class shall remain unpunished" (St. iii; Peers, III, 194).

[17] And again: "Not all directors have sufficient knowledge to meet all the possibilities and cases which they encounter on the spiritual road. . . . Not everyone who can hew a block of wood is able to carve an image; nor is everyone who can carve it able to outline and to polish it; nor is everyone that can polish it able to paint it; nor can he that is able to paint it complete it with final touches. . . . Spiritual directors, then, ought to give these souls freedom, for, when they would seek to better themselves, their directors have an obligation to put a good face upon it, since they know not by what means God desires such a soul to make progress" (*Ibid.;* 192-3).

longs to reconcile the demands of God with human weakness. In this, prudence plays a very important role. A director, then, could not be without it.

1. Prudence will be exercised first of all in seeking to know the will of God, in discerning the signs that authenticate it. It must know how to wait for certain manifestations before engaging itself in actualities that can be perilous. God, who is our Master, could not require the accomplishment of His will before having made it clearly manifest to us. He gives to Moses proofs of the mission He is entrusting to him. He is not angry when Gideon asks for repeated assurances of his new vocation. If it would truly be presumptuous, according to Saint John of the Cross, to ask for extraordinary signs, nevertheless we have the right to ask of God the manifestation of His will by the means of His choice. Where there is uncertainty, prudence has the duty to wait.

It is moreover an art, to know how to wait; not to interpret too hastily a strong attraction, an event that seems to be a providential sign. It is also an art to know how to make a soul wait without discouraging it, without diminishing its ardor. Waiting cools fervor that is too impetuous, and unveils the obstacles to be met with; it thus avoids those failures that would crush the spirit. It tries and strengthens whatever attractions are deep, obliges God to give His light, and prepares the way for fruitful realizations. The great doers, such as Saint Vincent de Paul, were often patient temporizers.

Prudence puts the soul at the pace of God who has His time for every work and does not want to be outrun. When the time is come—and sometimes it comes suddenly—prudence is prompt and energetic as God Himself, and demands that there be neither hesitation nor delay in the accomplishment of a divine will that is henceforth certain, and for which the grace that is received could well be only for a day.

2. Prudence chooses the means for the work to be done—not those suggested by the zeal of beginners nor by the desire

for quick execution, but those required by the limited strength of the soul and the long perseverance necessary for success. Saint Teresa tells us how the aims of her director, the master Daza, to elevate her virtue at once to the height of the divine favors that she was receiving, was almost disastrous for her.[18]

The prudence of which we speak, which is discretion, is neither timidity nor laziness. It knows the divine exigencies and never consents, even in the face of difficulties, to diminish the ideal that has been glimpsed. It aims simply at adapting the actual possibilities of the soul to the demands of God, and at not using up prematurely the forces that are necessary for a long journey. It puts forth a constantly sustained effort; and, when confronted by a greater obstacle, it knows how to mobilize all the energies of the soul for the violence that success requires.

If the director, as Saint Teresa insists, must not command impossible things such as imposing numerous fasts and severe penances on a weak person, neither must he merely teach us how "to be like toads" and to be "satisfied if our souls show themselves fit only to catch lizards." [19]

3. The secrets of the soul are the secrets of God. The director to whom they are confided must keep them with care. Prudence puts this duty upon him.

God, in fact, cloaks His actions with silence and obscurity. The Incarnate Word buries thirty years of His earthly life in the shadow of Nazareth and then reveals Himself only in the measure that His mission requires. The Holy Spirit acts silently in souls and in the Church in the midst of the agitations of the world. God loves silence and discretion. At times He would seem to cease action when indiscreet eyes are looking at Him. Saint Therese of the Child Jesus tells us that the joy caused by

---

[18] "Really, if I had had nobody else to consult, I think my soul would never have shown any improvement" (*Life*, xxiii; Peers, I, 148).
[19] *Life*, xiii; 75.

the apparition of the Blessed Virgin changed into sadness when her secret was revealed.[20]

Several times in her writings Saint Teresa speaks of the sufferings and the serious trials that the indiscretions of her directors caused her:

> They [women] should be advised to keep their experiences very secret and it is well that their advisers should observe secrecy too. I speak of this from knowledge, for I have been caused great distress by the indiscretion of certain persons with whom I have discussed my experiences in prayer. By talking about them to each other they have done me great harm, divulging things which should have been kept very secret. . . . The fault, I believe, was not theirs.[21]

In Chapter XXIII of her *Life*, the Saint recounts some of these trials. She got to the point of fearing that she could no longer find any confessor who would be willing to hear her, and of seeing everyone avoid her. And so she could do nothing but weep.[22]

4. Prudence, which imposes discretion, will also at times place upon the director an obligation to seek authorized counsel in order to solve a particular case.

It will also prevent him from going outside the province of the director to interfere in other domains, even at the request of the one he directs. Such a confusion could only be prejudicial to spiritual authority properly so-called; it tends to a subjugation rather than to the progressive liberation of the soul, and consequently runs counter to the end of spiritual direction.

### 3. EXPERIENCE

Experience in the spiritual ways will be the wise guide of prudence. All the masters of the spiritual life have spoken from their own experience or from that of the souls that they had been able to observe closely.

[20] *Autobiography*, iii.
[21] *Life*, xxiii; Peers, I, 150.
[22] Cf. also VI Mansions, viii; Peers, II, 313: "In such a case what should by rights be a close secret gets noised abroad and the penitent is persecuted and tormented . . . and this leads to many sore trials, which, as things are at present, might affect the Order."

The action of God in the soul is regulated by the divine mercy which baffles our human logic. Techniques and methods do not suffice to follow it; these may even put a stop to its beneficent outpourings, or at least restrict them.

All explanations possible will not dispel the mystery enveloping God's action in a soul. How then can the director go straight beyond the descriptions and explanations offered him, and indicate to the soul what line of conduct to follow, if he does not know experimentally this particular form of the action of God, or at least the spiritual realms where it takes place and the effects that it produces? Without experience he can be a benevolent and passive witness; but it does not seem that he can—unless he be supernaturally enlightened—encourage and direct with authority as his function obliges him.

These remarks have application especially to certain states and to supernatural graces. But they keep their full value even in the most modest domains of the practice of virtue, of mortification, and of the difficulties that are met from the beginning of the spiritual life.

Saint Teresa tells us that she was fully reassured as to her visions and interior words only by Saint Francis Borgia and Saint Peter of Alcantara, who could draw from their own experience. It seems certain, also, that the interpretation of the signs of contemplation given by Saint John of the Cross and their application to a concrete case require some experience.

Likewise, the Saint advises the beginner to find a director who has had experience of his difficulties and of the graces with which he has been favored:

> The beginner needs counsel to help him ascertain what benefits him most. To this end a director is very necessary; but he must be a man of experience, or he will make a great many mistakes and lead souls along without understanding them or without allowing them to learn to understand themselves; for the soul, knowing that it is a great merit to be subject to its director, dares not do other than what he commands it. I have come across souls so constrained and afflicted because of the inexperience of their director that I have been really

sorry for them. And I have found some who had no idea how to act for themselves; for directors who cannot understand spirituality afflict their penitents both in soul and in body and prevent them from making progress. One person who spoke to me about this had been kept in bondage by her director for eight years; he would not allow her to aim at anything but self-knowledge, yet the Lord was already granting her the Prayer of Quiet, so she was suffering great trials.[23]

Such inexperience as this is in danger of thwarting once and for all the soaring spirit of a soul, either through its lack of understanding or its timidity; or, again, of exhausting it prematurely by excessive mortifications, not having had experience of their rigor and effects.

### 4. LEARNING

Can it be said that Saint Teresa prefers learning to experience in a director? She writes:

And although learning may not seem necessary for this, my opinion has always been, and always will be, that every Christian should try to consult some learned person, if he can, and the more learned this person, the better.[24]

The learning that Teresa requires in a director is not just ordinary knowledge. In several passages [25] she recalls the harm that those semi-savants caused her, who could not explain the manner of God's presence in the soul nor the gravity of her faults; and she contrasts them to the truly wise who enlightened her.

Those really learned men were, for the most part, professors who, possessing a thorough knowledge of dogma, could examine the most elevated spiritual experiences and not be frightened by them because new. In fact, mystical experiences rest ordinarily on dogmatic truths which, alone, men given to study grasp with enough mastery to draw from them all their light and spiritual value:

[23] *Life,* xiii; Peers, I, 79-80.
[24] *Ibid.;* 81.
[25] Cf. *Ibid.,* v; xviii; also VI Mansions, i; Peers, II, 250-1.

In difficult matters, even if I believe I understand what I am saying and am speaking the truth, I use this phrase "I think," because, if I am mistaken, I am very ready to give credence to those who have great learning. For even if they have not themselves experienced these things, men of great learning have a certain instinct to prompt them. As God uses them to give light to His Church, He reveals to them anything which is true so that it shall be accepted; and if they do not squander their talents, but are true servants of God, they will never be surprised at His greatness. . . . In any case, where matters are in question for which there is no explanation, there must be others about which they can read, and they can deduce from their reading that it is possible for these first-named to have happened.

Of this I have the fullest experience; and I have also experience of timid, half-learned men whose shortcomings have cost me very dear.[26]

The director must have knowledge of moral theology and mystical theology; that is, must possess the science of the ways of God and the principles that govern them. This study is indispensable. It can in some instances make up for experience, and it will always be valuable in examining the facts of a given case.

The director should not be completely in ignorance of religious psychology and psychiatry, both of which supply him with directives for the guidance of souls. Opening to him, as they do, the mysterious realm of the subconscious, they will make him more prudent in his judgment of supernatural phenomena and his evaluation of abnormal cases.

Saint Teresa considers learning so important in a director that she does not hesitate to proclaim it useful even when it is not accompanied by the spirit of prayer:

Let us not make the mistake of saying that learned men who do not practise prayer are not suitable directors for those who do. I have consulted many such; and for some years past, feeling a greater need of them, I have sought them out more. I have always got on well with them; for, though some of them have no experience, they are not averse from spirituality, nor are they ignorant of its nature, for they study Holy Scripture, where the truth about it can always be found. I believe myself that, if a person who practises prayer consults learned men, the devil will not deceive him with illusions except by his own desire; for I think devils are very much afraid of learned men who are

[26] V Mansions, i; Peers, II, 250.

humble and virtuous, knowing that they will find them out and defeat them.[27]

We can feel that these assertions express a deep conviction and spring from the heart of the Saint. Could one conclude from them that she prefers learning in a director, to experience? Let us see how she makes her thought on it more precise; she adds:

> I have said this, because some people think that learned men, if they are not spiritual, are unsuitable for those who practise prayer. I have already said that a spiritual director is necessary, but if he has no learning it is a great inconvenience. It will help us very much to consult learned men, provided they are virtuous; even if they are not spiritual they will do us good and God will show them what they should teach and may even make them spiritual so that they may be of service to us. I do not say this without proof and I have had experience of quite a number.[28]

Saint Teresa is not here establishing a comparison between the value of experience and that of learning. She has in mind only the precise case of a choice to be made between a director who is devout but ignorant, and a learned and virtuous director who might not be a man of prayer. The affinities between the soul of prayer and the devout director must yield; the learned director is the one to consult.

Other passages from her writings and her personal example give us still more exact details as to the thought of the Saint on the choice of a director.

At the beginning of the spiritual life, the soul needs a director endowed with prudence and discretion who will make it avoid the excesses of the beginner and will advise moderation without, however, destroying its great desires. The soul in these stages needs also to be understood:

> The beginner needs counsel to help him ascertain what benefits him most. To this end a director is very necessary; but he must be a man of experience.[29]

[27] *Life*, xiii; Peers, I, 81.
[28] *Ibid.*
[29] *Ibid.;* 79.

Learning without experience would be less beneficial for the soul at this stage:

I mean that learning is of little benefit to beginners, except in men of prayer.[30]

It is again an experienced director that a soul wants at the beginning of contemplative prayer, or when receiving some of the more sublime supernatural favors:

It will be very glad to read a description of itself which will show clearly that it is traveling on the right road. And it will be a great blessing for it to know what it has to do in order to continue to make progress in any of these states.[31]

Saint Teresa herself, who had recourse at Avila to the counsel of Father Ibáñez, Father Báñez and Father Baltasar Alvarez, was fully reassured as to her supernatural favors, especially the visions, as we have said, only by Saint Peter of Alcantara and Saint Francis Borgia who had, themselves, been thus favored.

When the soul has arrived in the higher states of the spiritual life, as Saint Teresa had when she wrote the *Interior Castle*, it has learned to discern the activity of God within. It then calls especially for the lights of the science of theology to clarify its experience. We find Saint Teresa, during the last period of her life, showing a marked preference for men who were learned in sacred doctrine. Although her directors—Saint John of the Cross and Father Gracián—had all the qualities required, she did not neglect appealing from time to time to the theologians that she knew; and especially to Father Báñez, her theologian adviser.

Teresa sums up her counsels as to the choice of a director by this advice:

It is of great importance, then, that the director should be a prudent man—of sound understanding, I mean—and also an experienced one: if he is a learned man as well, that is a very great advantage. But if all these three qualities cannot be found in the same man, the first two

[30] *Ibid.;* 80.
[31] *Ibid.,* xiv; 85.

are the more important, for it is always possible to find learned men to consult when necessary.[32]

## C. Duties of the one directed

### 1. SPIRIT OF FAITH

The director is a human instrument in the service of God's work in souls. This truth, which imposes duties on the director, must also regulate the attitude of the one directed.

Faith alone can give contact with God through the veils with which He hides Himself here on earth: the veils of His creation, of the Holy Eucharist, of the personality of His instruments. "He who wants to approach God, must believe," says the apostle. It is thus by faith that the one who is directed will come to the divine sources of grace in his director, and will make them flow out upon his soul. Faith will inspire his attitude towards the director. He will multiply his positive acts of faith, especially when the veil seems heavier; or again, when very close bonds of affection might introduce too much natural facility or passivity into his obedience.

### 2. AFFECTIONATE CONFIDENCE

The director fulfils his mission not only by virtue of his priesthood, but also with his personal qualities. The one who is directed must therefore add to faith, which sees in the director God whom he represents, a confidence in him personally and his good qualities, and the grateful affection that his devotedness merits. Saint Teresa calls her directors the great benefactors of her soul. With simplicity and often with enthusiasm, she speaks of the consolation she finds in talking with them, her joy in meeting them again after an absence, the solicitude and delicate attentions with which she surrounds them, her deep and faithful affection especially when she finds in them the natural and supernatural gifts which permit them

[32] *Life*, xiii; Peers, I, 80.

to serve the Lord very well. There are some who appear a
little surprised at hearing her express her sentiments in their
regard with so much warmth and simplicity. To these she gives
reassurance and admits that she smiles at their fears. Her simplicity is not ignorance; it comes from her purity and mastery
over her heart. What she has written in the *Way of Perfection*
on precautions to be taken in relation to one's confessor, is
proof of this; but she also wrote "that a great means for making notable progress is, in her eyes, to love one's confessor." [33]

### 3. SIMPLICITY AND DISCRETION

The spirit of faith and of confidence will manifest themselves first of all by a sincere and complete opening up of the
soul, in a form as simple as possible. The director could not
direct a soul without knowing it as perfectly as possible. The
one directed can expect to receive the lights and graces of
direction only insofar as he has himself provided the director
with all that can enlighten him. He should, then, make known
his aspirations and his temptations, his weaknesses and his acts
of virtue, the working of God in his soul and his own generous
response; in short, whatever in the present or the past can reveal his inner dispositions and the designs of God for him.
Saint Francis de Sales gives this advice:

Treat with him [the director] openheartedly, in all sincerity and
fidelity, revealing clearly to him the good in you and the evil, without
pretence or dissimulation . . . Have extreme confidence in him, mingled
with a holy reverence, in such a way that the reverence does not lessen
the confidence, and confidence does not hinder reverence.[34]

The same advice is to be found from the pen of Saint
Teresa:

The really essential thing, sisters, is that you should speak to your
confessor very plainly and candidly—I do not mean here in confessing
your sins, for of course you will do so then, but in describing your
experiences in prayer. For unless you do this, I cannot assure you that

[33] *Way of Perfection*, v; Peers, II, 48, note.
[34] *Devout Life*, Bk. III, iv.

you are proceeding as you should or that it is God Who is teaching you. God is very anxious for us to speak candidly and clearly to those who are in His place, and to desire them to be acquainted with all our thoughts, and still more with our actions, however trivial these may be.[35]

The Saint stresses the importance of such opening up of the soul when there is question of supernatural favors:

The safest course is that which I myself follow: if I did not, I should have no peace—not that it is right for women like ourselves to expect any peace, since we are not learned. . . . I mean that we must describe the whole of our spiritual experiences, and the favors granted us by the Lord, to a confessor who is a man of learning, and obey him. This I have often done.[36]

Our Lord warned her one day, not to follow the counsels of a confessor who had asked her to keep complete silence concerning divine favors. Concerning this she tells us:

I then found out that I had been very badly advised by that confessor and that when I made my confession I must on no account keep back anything, if I obeyed that rule I should be quite safe, whereas otherwise I might sometimes be deceived.[37]

Saint John of the Cross also insists so strongly on this, that we cannot neglect to sum up his teaching:

. . . anything, of whatsoever kind, received by the soul through supernatural means, clearly and plainly, entirely and simply, must at once be communicated to the spiritual director. . . . It is very necessary to give an account of them all, although it may seem to the soul that there is no reason for so doing. And this for three causes.[38]

The first of these reasons bears underlining:

God communicates many things, the effect, power, light and security whereof He confirms not wholly in the soul, until, as we have said, the soul consults him whom God has given to it as a spiritual judge.[39]

The holy doctor notes that:

[35] VI Mansions, ix; Peers, II, 317-8.
[36] *Life*, xxvi; Peers, I, 167.
[37] *Ibid.;* 168.
[38] *Ascent*, Bk. II, xxii; Peers, I, 182.
[39] *Ibid.;* 183.

There are some souls who greatly dislike speaking of such things, because they think them to be of no importance. And they know not how the person to whom they are to relate them will receive them; which is lack of humility. . . . And there are others who are very timid in relating them, because they see not why they should have these experiences, which seem to belong to saints . . . but for this very reason it is well for them to mortify themselves and relate them.[40]

These counsels of Saint John of the Cross are addressed specially to contemplatives. Nevertheless, they retain their value for all souls. In fact, one cannot receive direction appropriate to one's needs without providing the director with reasonable material for evaluation.

These precious directives do not, however, justify any sentimental outpourings in which there would be more display of feeling than of faith, more concern to call attention to one's self—even by excessive insistence on one's faults—than sincere desire to be directed. It is true that at the beginning a rather complete opening of the soul is ordinarily necessary; but after that, frequent communications, especially written ones, are rarely free of tendencies that risk making them fail of their best purpose. Such would be that passivity which, wanting precise lights on everything, paralyzes personal reflection and initiative; or on the other hand, the avowed, or perhaps unconscious, desire of having one's own views approved, of imposing one's feelings, and possibly even of directing the director himself.

The one who is being directed must not ignore the fact that his habitual attitudes, his spontaneous reactions, reveal better to the director the depths of his soul and the harmony of the divine designs over it than do whatever he can ordinarily grasp of these himself through the veil, often deceiving, of his own impressions and judgments. And so a certain discretion must accompany simplicity in opening his soul, and dictate the measure. Simplicity itself would be lost if, in its disclosures, it became talkative and pretentious.

[40] *Ibid.*

### 4. OBEDIENCE

Obedience it is that makes certain the efficacy of direction, for it makes the counsels and commands of the director pass over into one's conduct. It is thus the most important duty of the one directed.

Saint Teresa likes to insist on this obedience, to show its import:

> Whenever the Lord gave me some command in prayer and the confessor told me to do something different, the Lord Himself would speak to me again and tell me to obey Him; and His Majesty would then change the confessor's mind so that he came back and ordered me to do the same thing.[41]

This extremely precious teaching of the Saint establishes the hierarchy of powers. Christ left His power over souls to the Church. He respects the order that He Himself establishes and subordinates to it His action within souls. The desires that He inspires in them directly, must be submitted to the director, who represents the Church. The soul must not undertake anything of what has been prescribed to it by God Himself, as long as the director has not commanded it. Saint Teresa affirms this with vigor in the case of interior words:

> If the locutions are accompanied by the signs already described, one may be very confident that they are of God, although not to such an extent that, if what is said is of great importance and involves some action on the part of the hearer, or matters affecting a third person, one should do anything about it, or consider doing anything, without taking the advice of a learned confessor, a man of clear insight and a servant of God, even though one may understand the locutions better and better and it may become evident that they are of God. For this is His Majesty's will, so by carrying it out we are not failing to do what He commands: He has told us that we are to put our confessor in His place, even when it cannot be doubted that the words are His. If the matter is a difficult one, these words will help to give us courage, and Our Lord will speak to the confessor and if such is His pleasure will make him recognize the work of His spirit; if He does not, we have no further obligations. I consider it very dangerous

[41] *Life,* xxvi; Peers, I, 168.

for a person to do anything but what he has been told to do, and to follow his own opinion in this matter; so I admonish you, sisters, in Our Lord's name, never to act thus.[42]

This line of conduct is based on the divine authority of the director representing the Church, whose will expressed externally must always be preferred to all interior manifestations, even should they be certain and authentic. It puts in sharp relief the obedience that is due the director, and at the same time the sovereignly important role of direction for the spiritual ascent.

[42] VI Mansions, iii; Peers, II, 283.

# CHAPTER IX
# Regulated Life
# and Simplified Prayer

*Now let us return to these carefully-
ordered souls.*[1]

To those who by the mercy of God have overcome in these combats, and by dint of perseverance have entered the third Mansions,
what shall we say but "Blessed is the man that feareth the Lord"? . . .
We shall certainly be right in calling such a man blessed, for, unless
he turns back, he is, so far as we can tell, on the straight road to
salvation.[2]

The joy with which Saint Teresa hails the arrival of souls
at the third Mansions indicates that an important stage has
been reached. In what does the victory consist? The Saint will
make this explicit both in the domain of virtue and in that of
prayer. She warns us, however, that such a soul does not yet
seem to be engaged upon the way of perfection.

The teaching of Saint Teresa as to the third Mansions, is
very precious.

## A. Regulated life

To have arrived at the third Mansions is, Teresa emphasizes,
"a very great favour"; but, thanks to the goodness of God,
"there are, I believe, many such souls in the world."

Here, with a few clear strokes, is given a vivid description
of these souls:

They are most desirous not to offend His Majesty; they avoid committing even venial sins; they love doing penance; they spend hours

[1] III Mansions, i; Peers, II, 222.
[2] *Ibid.;* 219.

in recollection; they use their time well; they practise works of charity toward their neighbors; and they are very careful in their speech and dress and in the government of their household if they have one. This is certainly a desirable state.[3]

The spiritual mansion seems to be well kept; everything breathes order and correct appearance. But let us not be satisfied with a glance at the ensemble; we shall look to the details.

The fine order is apparently due to a perfect organization of the exterior life. These souls have a rule of life that sets the time for exercises of piety and their duration, the part of the day that will be given to works of charity. We would call them today, persons of piety devoted to charity. They do not let their works or their devotions interfere with their duties of family life or of society. There is no negligence in their essential duties since the same wisdom directs the government of their home and the organization of their personal life. Their religion is of good quality; it has been able to harmonize very happily the externals of the duties it imposes towards God, the family, and society.

And what do we find, back of this lovely façade? Has the fine order gained the interior of the dwelling? It seems so. These souls "are most desirous not to offend His Majesty; they avoid committing even venial sins." Such are their interior dispositions.

We cannot but share in Teresa's admiration for such excellent results, especially if we call to mind the state of the soul when it was in the first Mansions. Then, saturated with the maxims of the world and given up to its evil tendencies, it thought seriously of God scarcely more than a few times a month.

We can guess the tenacity of effort it required, the length of the struggle against self and others to avoid occasions of sin, to mortify evil tendencies, to put order into one's life, to introduce into it some regular exercises of piety, to accomplish

[3] *Ibid.;* 221.

with care all the duties of one's state, to give to works of charity the time that pleasures or distractions formerly took, to avoid sin in every way, to acquire the virtues, in short, to regulate one's whole exterior, one's words and actions, so that in them there might shine a discreet reflection of good interior dispositions.

One stage in the spiritual life is over. Good habits have been acquired and are practised in daily life. By its virtuous living, its preoccupations—of which it makes no mystery—by its good works which are disclosed with discretion but without human respect, by its whole exterior, this soul is established in the group of those whose serious piety, wide and charitable, demands esteem and respect.

This is a triumph that is due to the persevering energy of the will enlightened by reason. But before drawing conclusions, let us see what progress has been made in prayer.

## B. Simplified prayer

These souls "have their hours of recollection," Saint Teresa says succinctly, speaking of the third Mansions; adding, however, that they have periods of aridities. The *Way of Perfection* and her *Life* will instruct us better on the development of prayer in these souls.

The efforts that have been put forth so perseveringly, have created a certain facility for recollection:

When we begin to pray we shall realize that the bees are coming to the hive and entering to make the honey, and all without any effort of ours. For it is the Lord's will that, in return for the time which their efforts have cost them, the soul and the will should be given this power over the senses. They will only have to make a sign to show that they wish to enter into recollection and the senses will obey and allow themselves to be recollected. Later they may come out again, but it is a great thing that they should ever have surrendered, for if they come out it is as captives and slaves and they do none of the harm that they might have done before. When the will calls them afresh they respond more quickly.[4]

[4] *Way of Perfection*, xxviii; Peers, II, 116.

The acquired facility for recollection is accompanied by a simplification in the activity of those powers that were carrying on the exchange of friendship with God. Whereas formerly, long vocal prayers were necessary in order to remain near the Master, now:

after we have begun to force ourselves to remain near the Lord, He will give us indications by which we may understand that, though we have had to say the Paternoster many times, He heard us the first time. For He loves to save us worry; and, even though we may take a whole hour over saying it once, if we can realize that we are with Him, and what it is we are asking Him, and how willing He is, *like any father,* to grant it to us, and how He loves to be with us, *and comfort us,* He has no wish for us to tire our brains by a great deal of talking.[5]

The work of the imagination also is simplified. Details are left out of the representations of Christ, the contours of the images become less precise, in order to let the presence of our beloved Master become more vivid and more attractive.

As to the intelligence, ordinarily it loses its taste for multiplied reasonings, for repeated meditations on a variety of subjects. It loves to enter more deeply into such or such a truth, or to return to large syntheses rich with many elements that it knows, encompassing them now with a simple regard, apparently confused, but in reality penetrating and affectionate, as it draws from them deep and vitalizing impressions.

Profusion of words and noisy activity of the faculties have given way to the language of signs, to interior movements and the simple gaze of the soul, to peaceful rest near the Master.

This silence and repose are attitudes expressive of love; they favor excellently exchanges of friendship:

The fire of Divine love is the more readily enkindled in them [these souls]; for they are so near that fire that, however little the blaze has been fanned with the understanding, any small spark that flies out at them will cause them to burst into flame.[6]

[5] *Ibid.,* xxix; 121-2.
[6] *Ibid.,* xxviii; 117.

In what measure shall we say that this prayer, with a sim-plified activity of the faculties, is contemplative? Let us not, for the moment, take up that complex problem. Let us call it simplified prayer—or better, prayer of simplicity—and define it as: a gaze of the soul in silence.

This gaze of the soul on a distinct truth or a living form of Christ is active; the attractiveness of the object renders it peaceful and silent. Consequently, we can distinguish in the prayer of simplicity a double element: the gaze fixed on its object, and the calm or silence that this produces. One seems to follow from the other; they are in reality concomitant.

Ordinarily the soul, according to the times or its tempera-ment, will be more or less conscious of one or the other ele-ment. It will be aware of the object of its gaze, giving little attention to the peace it brings; or, it will give itself up to peaceful and sweet repose, giving to the object only the atten-tion necessary to prolong the impression and renew it. In the first case, we shall have the prayer properly called "of simple regard"; in the second, the simplified prayer of recollection.

The prayer of simple regard, might we say, is made with the eyes of the soul open; in the prayer of recollection, the impression of light obliges one to close the eyes. The seraphim, they say, veil their faces in the presence of the Eternal God. Saint Therese of the Child Jesus declares that she will not do as they, but will gaze into the eyes of the good God. Sister Elizabeth of the Trinity, on the contrary, seems to lower her gaze before the dazzling light. Different attitudes that require a different name; but they seem to be only different forms of the prayer of simplicity, or different acts of advertence to it.

How is one who has arrived at the prayer of simplicity, to conduct oneself? The answer to this important and practical question is suggested by the definition of the prayer of simplic-ity. It is an active gaze of the soul, in silence: rightly, then, one must have regard both for the activity and for the silence. The repose of soul comes from the simplified activity of the faculties. This calm is more beneficial and nourishing than all the chains of reasoning: and so it must be respected and maintained. But at best, it cannot be continued for long because of the very mobility of the intellect whose attention is soon distracted from its object. Hence it becomes necessary to bring the faculties back to the object under consideration, or towards some other, in order to renew the peaceful impression and to find again the life that flows from it.

Repeatedly, as we have said, Teresa recommends making the faculties work during prayer, as long as they are not held captive by the divine Master. Nevertheless, this necessary activity must not trouble the fruitful silence that pervades certain regions of the soul. Such is the double recommendation that she develops in the fourth Mansions, a propos both of the passive recollection which leaves liberty of action to the powers of the soul, and of the quietude which binds the will and which the understanding must not disturb. She says:

> God gave us our faculties to work with, and everything will have its due reward; there is no reason, then, for trying to cast a spell over them—they must be allowed to perform their office until God gives them a better one.[7]

This rule, given for the state of passive recollection, applies all the more to the prayer of simplicity. Here, however, th activity will be more peaceful. Normally, the soul that has achieved some simplification, profits accordingly by it. Besides, any undue activity would destroy the silent rest that gives value to that prayer and opens the soul to the influences of grace.

In this kind of prayer, made up of successive pausing at certain scenes rather than of reasoned thought, the work of the soul consists in moving from scene to scene, delaying before each in an admiring comprehensive gaze, and then passing to the next peacefully when interest in the previous one fails.

A slow progress, by a series of leaps so to speak, with certain marked times for stops, we might say of the prayer of

[7] IV Mansions, iii; Peers, II, 243.

simplicity in contrast to the regular and continued march of meditation. But it is not the distance covered nor the multiplicity of ideas that matter; it is uniquely the strength that is left in the soul by reason of its contact with the realities that the ideas represent. The peace that results seems to indicate that such a contact is established and that the soul is drawing fruit from it. Hence it can be said that this prayer is incomparably richer than all the more active forms, even should they be more ardent and more luminous.

The prayer of simplicity is the fruit of higher and finer forms of the activity of the intellect. The penetrating intuition to which it is related is superior to discursive reasoning.[8] It marks the triumph of intellectual activity in prayer, just as regularity in one's exercises of devotion, mortification of evil tendencies, fulfillment of one's duties, and all the good order that we have admired, mark the triumph of the will in asceticism and in the organization of the life of religious practice.

The soul entered upon the way of perfection by putting to the service of its ideal all its intellectual and moral energies. Sustained by the general help of God, which is His ordinary grace, it has conquered. The third Mansions show us the triumph of human effort in the search for God. We can understand why Saint Teresa rejoices in it, and hails with enthusiasm such a result:

> In enabling these souls to overcome their initial difficulties, the Lord has granted them no small favour, but a very great one. . . . This is certainly a desirable state and there seems no reason why they should be denied entrance to the very last of the Mansions; nor will the Lord deny them this if they desire it, for their disposition is such that He will grant them any favour.[9]

[8] We have already noted that the modern mind is more intuitive than it is fond of reasoning. It likes vivid syntheses, full and compact formulas. Is this a sign of decadence or of vitality? Genius is in fact intuitive, as is a mind that is served by anemic organs. However that may be, intuition is a higher form of the activity of the mind and is one of the graces of our time. It brings souls very quickly to the prayer of simplicity, and is an excellent natural aptitude, favorable to the development of contemplation.

[9] III Mansions, i; Peers, II, 221.

There is encouragement and promise in these praises; consequently, they imply that the third Mansions are still far from the summit. Moreover, the description given by Saint Teresa convinces us of this fact.

## C. Deficiencies and difficulties

The verse from the psalm with which Saint Teresa begins her description, expresses very well the atmosphere of the third Mansions: "Blessed is the man who fears the Lord." There is joy in his heart; and yet, too many dangers threaten him, for him not to be armed with fear. The progress of the soul is not yet stabilized:

> However determined such persons may be not to offend the Lord, they will do well not to run any risk of offending Him; for they are so near the first Mansions that they might easily return to them, since their fortitude is not built upon solid ground like that of souls who are already practised in suffering. These last are familiar with the storms of the world, and realize how little need there is to fear them or to desire worldly pleasures. If those of whom I am speaking, however, had to suffer great persecutions, they might well return to such pleasures and the devil well knows how to contrive such persecutions in order to do us harm.[10]

The devil can find allies right at hand, for the evil tendencies of such persons are just barely mortified in their most exterior manifestations. The well regulated exterior might deceive us, as unfortunately it deceives the soul itself, as to the quality of the virtues that serve as its basis.

On discovering this truth, Teresa declares herself painfully surprised:

> I have known a few souls who have reached this state—I think I might even say a great many—and who, as far as we can see, have for many years lived an upright and carefully ordered life, both in soul and in body; and then, after all those years, when it has seemed as if they must have gained the mastery over the world, or at least must be completely detached from it, His Majesty has sent them tests which have been by no means exacting and they have become so restless and depressed in spirit that they have exasperated me, and have

[10] *Ibid.*, ii; 228-9.

even made me thoroughly afraid for them. It is of no use offering them advice, for they have been practising virtue for so long that they think they are capable of teaching others and have ample justification for feeling as they do.[11]

Pride enters into this attitude; in fact, speaking of humility, the Saint asserts: "it is the lack of this, I think, if you see what I mean, which prevents us from making progress." [12]

Certainly, God grants to souls in these Mansions "a spiritual sweetness much greater than we can obtain from the pleasures and distractions of this life"; [13] but they have become conscious of their virtue, and on this conviction, they rest many pretensions to the most elevated graces:

> These souls know that nothing would induce them to commit a sin —many of them would not intentionally commit even a venial sin— and they make good use of their lives and their possessions. So they cannot be patient when the door is closed to them and they are unable to enter the presence of the King, Whose vassals they consider themselves, and in fact are. Yet even on earth a king may have many vassals and they do not all get so far as to enter his chamber. . . .
> Oh, humility, humility! I do not know why I have this temptation, but whenever I hear people making so much of their times of aridity, I cannot help thinking that they are somewhat lacking in it.[14]

What a mixture of virtue and of pride, of sincere good will and of illusion! It is certainly normal that, as the soul makes progress towards sanctity, there continue to exist within it side by side evil tendencies and sublime virtue. Flesh and nature, grace and sin, throw each other into greater relief. "Unhappy man that I am!" Saint Paul cries out, under the double weight of his human misery and his spiritual riches. And Saint Therese of the Child Jesus avows that she finds herself more and more imperfect in the measure that she advances; but she finds her joy in this, because misery draws down mercy.

But the situation is different in the souls in the third Mansions. While Saint Paul groans in the experience of his misery,

[11] III Mansions, ii; Peers, II, 223-4.
[12] *Ibid.;* 226.
[13] *Ibid.;* 227.
[14] *Ibid.;* 222.

these poor souls do not see theirs and will not let anyone show them. Hence Saint Teresa makes this observation:

It is no use offering them advice. . . . They consider they have acted in a highly virtuous way, as I have said, and they wish others to think so too. . . . Well, I cannot find, and have never found, any way of comforting such people, except to express great sorrow at their trouble, which, when I see them so miserable, I really do feel. It is useless to argue with them, for they brood over their woes and make up their minds that they are suffering for God's sake, and thus never really understand that it is all due to their imperfection. And in persons who have made so much progress this is a further mistake.[15]

The problem is no easy one. How is it possible to rescue these souls from their illusions and to enlighten their good will? She tells us about some of them so that "we may learn to understand and test ourselves"—

A rich man, who is childless and has no one to leave his money to, loses part of his wealth; but not so much that he has not enough for himself and his household—he still has enough and to spare. If he begins to get restless and worried, as though he had not a crust of bread to eat, how can Our Lord ask him to leave all for His sake? It may be, of course, that he is suffering because he wants to give the money to the poor. But I think God would rather I were resigned to what His Majesty does, and kept my tranquillity of soul, than that I should do such acts of charity as these.[16]

Teresa chides this man for his lack of freedom of spirit, says he should pray for it, and turns to another case:

Another person has means enough to support himself, and indeed an excess of means. . . . but if he strives after more and more, however good his intention may be, he need not be afraid that he will ever ascend to the Mansions which are nearest the King.[17]

And she adds that such people become restless if they are despised in any way or lose some of their reputation—although they do meditate on what a good thing it is to suffer as our Lord did.

Can we say that these reproaches and examples have clarified

15 *Ibid.;* 224.
16 *Ibid.;* 224-5.
17 *Ibid.;* 225.

perfectly the position of the souls in the third Mansions? How can we reconcile their serious failures with the genuine progress they have made; or the merited reproaches, with the esteem and respect that their exterior conduct and good works win for them? The matter is still somewhat obscure. And so Saint Teresa writes:

> Consider carefully, daughters, these few things which have been set down here, though they are in rather a jumbled state, for I cannot explain them better.[18]

The exhortation to go over these points meditatively indicates that the problem is serious. It will help, carefully to re-read the two chapters of the third Mansions. We notice that, in the presence of souls there, Saint Teresa seems embarrassed, almost ill at ease. She gives them definite praises, a number of rather general reproaches, explanatory digressions, and a touch of restrained irony about those persons who are:

> very careful in their speech and dress. . . . (and) have for many years lived an upright and carefully ordered life, both in soul and in body.[19]

Are we right in gathering together these indications of uneasiness and attaching importance to them? We know that Saint Teresa writes without a preparatory outline, letting her pen run on. She does not read over what she has written. She sees and she describes. Sometimes she does not make clearly explicit the impression that a tableau makes on her, and yet that impression dominates the whole description.

In the first Mansions, for instance, we felt that she was trembling at the sight of those souls whose supernatural life was so weak, falling into sin and into hell. And then we saw her discreetly serious with those who can make an orderly meditation, and who, thinking with order, are off to a good start. When she comes to the persons of devotion of the third Mansions, Saint Teresa tarries longer. She shows us that these

[18] III Mansions, i; Peers, II, 223.
[19] *Ibid.;* 221, 224.

souls are not on her side, do not live under the same light, do not judge as she does.

Is it a question of difference in temperament, different ways of life—those persons, living in the world and Saint Teresa, in the cloister. No, certainly not. Saint Teresa's impressions are neither superficial, nor purely natural. We must trust in her judgment, and examine the problem more closely.

We find that these souls are established in spiritual positions that a wide trench separates from those of Saint Teresa, a trench that they have not yet crossed. The distress that the Saint feels at their state, opens up to us a general spiritual problem of great importance. She puts it in a few words:

Words are not enough, any more than they were for the young man when the Lord told him what to do if he wished to be perfect. Ever since I began to speak of these Mansions I have had that young man in mind, for we are exactly like him.[20]

Need we recall the gospel scene?

And behold, a certain man came to him and said, "Good Master, what good work shall I do to have eternal life?" He said to him, "Why dost thou ask me about what is good? One there is who is good, that is God. But if thou wilt enter into life, keep the commandments." He said to him, "Which?" And Jesus said,
"Thou shalt not kill,
Thou shalt not commit adultery,
Thou shalt not steal,
Thou shalt not bear false witness,
Honor thy father and mother,
and, Thou shalt love thy neighbor as thyself."
The young man said to him, "All these I have kept; what is yet wanting to me?" Jesus said to him, "If thou wilt be perfect, go, sell what thou hast, and give to the poor, and thou shalt have treasure in heaven; and come, follow me." But when the young man heard the saying, he went away sad, for he had great possessions.[21]

"We are exactly like him," says Saint Teresa, humbly placing herself in the third Mansions.

These souls have not yet entered upon the way of perfection.

[20] *Ibid.;* 221.
[21] Matt. 19:16-22.

# CHAPTER X

## Supernatural Wisdom and Christian Perfection

*They are eminently reasonable folk!*
*Their love is not yet ardent enough to*
*overwhelm their reason.*[1]

"We are acting like the young man in the Gospel," this is the thought that resounds painfully in our soul when we come to the third Mansions. Like the young man, many souls have for a long time conscientiously kept the precepts of the Law; they desire perfection, but when faced with the requirements of the Master, they hesitate and sadly go away. Their sadness weighs upon us as well as upon them. "Truly, such misery is to be pitied," Teresa laments.

These souls have come to a halt or turned back in face of the exigencies of Christian perfection. "If you will be perfect . . ." our Lord has said to them as to the young man. Hence here is the parting of the ways for those who would really be perfect. Such is the thought of Saint Teresa. If anyone doubted this, a look into her treatise, the *Way of Perfection,* would suffice for an answer. In the first pages, one would find her chapter on absolute poverty, which is her commentary on the word of Jesus to the young man.

As to Saint John of the Cross, he addresses himself only to those who have already accepted absolute detachment and want to know the direct way to the summits. They are beginners when they engage themselves to set out courageously on the

---

[1] III Mansions, ii; Peers, II, 226.

road of "nothing"; they are proficients when notable results are manifest in their prayer; and under that name, they will continue their journey until the transforming union.

The Saints of Carmel accept the words of Christ at their full meaning. "If you want to be perfect, sell all you have." A soul is on the way to perfection only when it has made this first renouncement.

## A. Folly and perfection

Are we, then, to think that a definitive detachment from all our possessions is really the decisive and necessary gesture that opens the way to evangelical perfection? The words of our Lord, the teaching of Saint Teresa in the *Way of Perfection,* the typical examples that she gives to show the imperfection of souls in the third Mansions and that illustrate the rich young man's attachment to his goods, would lead us to think so.

But this would seem to make the perfection of the gospel impossible for all those whose position in life could not admit of such absolute poverty. The souls in the third Mansions, who are at the head of a house, could not hope to attain perfection?

Evidently, this could not be so. The problem of perfection lies elsewhere. Complete detachment from possessions is imposed only on certain souls; but it is the sign of a more intimate and more general renouncement within the reach of all, adapted to each one, and crucifying all equally.

In order to discover what this renouncement is, we shall analyze a few testimonies; their diversity will show the complexity of the problem and then will serve to solve it.

1. Let us first return to what Saint Teresa has said on this point. It has particular interest for us, and is what we are trying to clarify.

We know her reproaches to the souls in the third Mansions: lack of humility and of detachment, together with excessive distress and sadness over little trials. But those are apparent faults in comparison with another that is more profound, that

touches the interior comportment of the soul, affects the whole
spiritual life, and explains all the other faults. The Saint exposes it:

> The penances done by these persons are as carefully ordered as their
> lives. They have a great desire for penance, so that by means of it
> they may serve Our Lord—and there is nothing wrong in that—and
> for this reason they observe great discretion in their penances, lest they
> should injure their health. You need never fear that they will kill
> themselves.[2]

We already knew that these souls were well ordered and
that everything about them was perfectly regulated. The affable
irony of Teresa does not surprise us either, for she is too spontaneous and too vital a person not to smile at an order so precise in all its details. But now here is one of those statements
that we sometimes find in her writings thrown as if by chance
into the midst of apparently jumbled explanations, and which,
opening up new horizons, gives the key to the problem:

> They are eminently reasonable folk! Their love is not yet ardent
> enough to overwhelm their reason. . . .

The truth of this seems so evident to herself. She seizes
upon it and develops it with some warmth:

> How I wish ours [our reason] would make us dissatisfied with this
> habit of always serving God at a snail's pace! As long as we do that
> we shall never get to the end of the road. And as we seem to be walk-
> ing along and getting fatigued all the time—for, believe me, it is an
> exhausting road—we shall be very lucky if we escape getting lost. . . .
> Would it not be better to get the journey over and done with? . . .
> When we proceed with all this caution, we find stumbling-blocks
> everywhere; for we are afraid of everything, and so dare not go
> farther. . . . For the love of the Lord, let us make a real effort: let us
> leave our reason and our fears in His hands and let us forget the
> weakness of our nature which is apt to cause us so much worry. . . .
> Our task is only to journey with good speed so that we may see the
> Lord.[3]

This is plain enough: the souls whose reason has so well
regulated their life, are now too reasonable to go farther. What

[2] III Mansions, ii; Peers, II, 226.
[3] Ibid.

was a very useful means, has now become an almost insurmountable obstacle; and these souls cannot see that their reason is blocking for them the way of perfection.

Reproach of this kind, and in so downright a form, astonishes us a little, coming from Saint Teresa. We know her, energetic and quick, and consequently annoyed by too minute prescriptions: she shuddered on merely reading the numerous rules that a religious imposed on one of his monasteries for the days of Holy Communion. But even so, we were not expecting reason to be brought to trial by this mother who is so spiritual and so wise, this genius so well balanced in her doctrine as in her life, this saint who remains so human in the expansiveness of her natural faculties even in the transforming union. Is a little folly, then, required for sanctity?

2. The apostle Saint Paul clearly affirms that it is, in his Epistle to the Corinthians.

The apostle had come to Corinth after the almost complete failure of the magnificent discourse that he had pronounced at the Areopagus of Athens, of which the *Acts* have kept for us the outline.[4]

In the face of the difficulties of another kind that he found at Corinth—violent opposition from the Jews and moral depravation in the city—the apostle had felt more imperiously than ever the need of relying solely on the strength of Christ. Besides, his manner of preaching, being that of a simple artisan who wove goat's hair, had made converts only among the humble. Recalling to them these events, he wrote them in his first letter:

For Christ did not send me to baptize, but to preach the gospel, not with the wisdom of words, lest the cross of Christ be made void. For the doctrine of the cross is foolishness to those who perish, but to those who are saved, that is, to us, it is the power of God. For it is written,

[4] "Now when they heard of a resurrection of the dead, some began to sneer, but others said, 'We will hear thee again on this matter.' So Paul went forth from among them. Certain persons however joined him and became believers" (Acts 17:32-3).

> "I will destroy the wisdom of the wise,
>     and the prudence of the prudent I will
>     reject."

Where is the "wise man?" Where is the scribe? Where is the disputant of this world? Has not God turned to foolishness the "wisdom" of this world? For since, in God's wisdom, the world did not come to know God by "wisdom," it pleased God, by the foolishness of our preaching, to save those who believe. For the Jews ask for signs, and the Greeks look for "wisdom"; but we, for our part, preach a crucified Christ— to the Jews indeed a stumbling-block and to the Gentiles foolishness, but to those who are called, both Jews and Greeks, Christ, the power of God and the wisdom of God. For the foolishness of God is wiser than men, and the weakness of God is stronger than men.

For consider your own call, brethren; that there were not many wise according to the flesh, not many mighty, not many noble. But the foolish things of the world has God chosen to put to shame the "wise," and the weak things of the world has God chosen to put to shame the strong, and the base things of the world and the despised has God chosen, and the things that are not, to bring to naught the things that are; lest any flesh should pride itself before him. From him you are in Christ Jesus, who has become for us God-given wisdom, and justice, and sanctification, and redemption; so that, just as it is written, "Let him who takes pride, take pride in the Lord."

And I, brethren, when I came to you, did not come with pretentious speech, or wisdom, announcing unto you the witness to Christ. For I determined not to know anything among you, except Jesus Christ and him crucified. And I was with you in weakness and in fear and in much trembling. And my speech and my preaching were not in the persuasive words of wisdom, but in the demonstration of the Spirit and of power, that your faith might rest, not on the wisdom of men, but on the power of God.[5]

In this long quotation in which testimonies are heaped up and antitheses abound, one idea stands out clear and strong; there is a radical opposition between the wisdom of the world in which Saint Paul is living, and the wisdom of God who is guiding him in his apostolate and presiding over the development of Christianity.

Saint Teresa reproached the souls in the third Mansions with being too reasonable to enter upon the ways of perfection, and wished them love to the point of folly. Saint Paul underlines

[5] I Cor. 1:17; 2:1.

that the wisdom of Christ is folly to the eyes of the world. These two assertions complete one another and express well the idea that is commonly entertained of high sanctity.

3. The great Saints, as we know from the story of their lives, were not only heroes—as, for instance, Saint Lawrence who from his burning hot gridiron laughed at his executioner—but also on occasion showed themselves subject to a higher law.

Saint Francis of Assisi strips himself of his clothing in the public square to satisfy the demands of his father, and begins his heroic adventure in the service of Lady Poverty.

No less foolish is the task begun by Saint John of the Cross at Duruelo and continued by Father de Foucauld under the blazing sun of the Sahara until he sprinkles with his blood that land that he wanted to make fruitful for God.

As to the holy Curé of Ars during the last years of his life, the power of the cross is displayed as much in the patience and penances of the holy Curé as in the marvelous gifts with which he is favored.

The good common sense of the faithful is quick to canonize these men and surround them with enthusiastic veneration. It takes as a sign of sanctity that very folly of the cross that runs through their lives and issues marvelously in supernatural fruits.

The observations of Saint Teresa and Saint Paul, the living examples that leave no doubt as to the identification of the folly of the cross with sanctity, these pose a very important practical problem: in what does this folly of the cross consist? Is sanctity really in opposition to human reason? In what measure must one be foolish in the eyes of men in order to be a saint?

Several distinctions concerning the three wisdoms which are at the foundation of the moral and the spiritual order will throw light on this problem and will permit us to state more accurately the teaching of Saint Paul and Saint Teresa.

## B. The three wisdoms

Divine Wisdom directs all things sweetly to their final end by subjecting them to laws in conformity with their nature, and so establishes order in the universe.

God inscribed in matter the law of the mutual attraction of bodies and in this way rules over the marvelous evolutions of the stars that sing, in space, the glory of God. Again it is by obeying the law of instinct that each animal assures its own development and the multiplication of the species, and fulfils its providential role in the world of living beings.

God directs man to his ultimate end by the moral law; but while matter and animal nature submit necessarily and passively to the laws that God imposes on them, without being conscious of them or being able to depart from them, the moral law is made manifest to the intelligence of man and respects his liberty. For him, it is an expression of the will of God; it solicits his free cooperation in the execution of God's plan for the world.

Divine Wisdom leads man to his supernatural perfection by manifestations of the divine will that appear in three different modes. Hence, for the Christian there are three orders of wisdom, three planes of morality and perfection that continue to supplement one another.

1. God has imposed on all men a natural moral law whose first principles are inscribed in the heart of man are evident to him: the distinction between good and evil, the obligation to do good, not to do to others what one would not want done to oneself, and so on. Although these notions are immediately known by the natural light of reason, they leave man free not to follow the prescriptions that flow from them.

From the fundamental principles human reason deduces other obligations which are the more or less immediate consequence of them. On these derivative obligations, it continues its work of research and unfolding; for example, it determines what justice is, and shows how it teaches respect for our neighbor and for ourselves. It fixes for our needs and our desires the measure of satisfaction that keeps a right balance in the whole person. This reason codifies the precepts of the natural law, and gives light to the natural virtues by making explicit the motives and the measure that must govern their observance.

The ensemble of these various prescriptions that reason has drawn, by logical deduction, from the fundamental prescriptions of the natural law constitutes the code of natural rights which fixes, in the domain of the individual as well as of society, the duties and the rights of each one and of all in the universal human society.

This natural moral order has an incontestable divine origin, in respect both to the basic principles that Wisdom has inscribed in every human being, and to the power of reason that constructs it, and is itself a light with which the Word has endowed us to guide us back to Him.

The natural moral order is, moreover, the first manifestation of the order established by Wisdom. True, it is the most humble manifestation, but—because founded on the nature of things—it is at the base of the whole moral edifice. No one can lay claim to respecting the divine order and aspiring to higher virtues, who does not first observe the prescriptions of the natural law. To assert that there can be no order which does not rest on it, is to state sufficiently the value of this natural wisdom.

2. In the Sermon on the Mount, Jesus Christ warns those listening to Him:

Do not think that I have come to destroy the Law or the Prophets. I have not come to destroy but to fulfil.[6]

Such is in fact the role of the new manifestation of the divine order that Wisdom shows through revelation.

[6] Matt. 5:17.

Revelation makes known to man his supernatural end, the participation in the life of the Holy Trinity to which he is called. It indicates to him the means that he must take, the higher virtues that he must practise in order to attain this more elevated end to which he is destined. Since we are the children of God, we must be perfect as our Father in heaven is perfect. And since Jesus Christ has been sent to show us the way that leads to God, and to be an exemplar of the perfection we are to realize, we must follow Him and model our actions on His.

Corresponding to the new order that is revealed to us and to the supernatural vocation that is ours, there are not only new obligations but also the means adapted to their fulfillment. At the same time as a new light shines for us upon the eternal plan of Wisdom, there is given us the grace that adapts us to live it, and the infused supernatural virtues which permit us to enter into this plan and to work within its sphere.

Revelation does not destroy reason but strengthens it in its conclusions and enlightens it by opening up undreamed of horizons. Likewise, the infused supernatural virtues—which are engrafted in all the human faculties, whose operations they use for their own acts—fortify at the same time the natural virtues, enlarging their domain and providing them with new motives. Saint Thomas says:

Now it is evident that the mean that is appointed in such like concupiscences according to the rule of human reason, is seen under a different aspect from the mean which is fixed according to the Divine rule. For instance, in the consumption of food, the mean fixed by human reason, is that food should not harm the health of the body, nor hinder the use of reason: whereas, according to the Divine rule, it behooves man to *chastise* his *body, and bring it into subjection* (I Cor. 9:27), by abstinence in food, drink and the like.[7]

Thus by revelation and by our participation in the life of the Trinity, we are raised to a new order of morality which requires us to tend towards our supernatural end by the prac-

[7] *Sum. Theol.*, I-II, q. 63, a.4.

tice of virtues proper to the supernatural order, and of the natural virtues themselves, supernaturalized and enlarged by a new light.

3. The virtues proper to the supernatural order are specially the theological virtues, infused virtues that regulate our supernatural relations with God. These virtues are engrafted in the human powers and use the operations of the faculties to perform their own acts. Being theological, and as such having God for their object and motive, they tend normally toward liberation from all that is human in order to find in God alone their nourishment and their support. Their operations will be perfect only when they are purely God-centered, that is, free from every inferior element and fixed more purely in the divine object and motive.

Usually in the beginning the theological virtues need to be sustained and developed by meditation on the truths of faith and theological truths derived from them. This is an indispensable and very precious help which contributes eminently to their growth.

But reason alone will not place within reach of these virtues the hidden mysteries which are their proper object. It can occupy itself only with the dogmatic formulas which express these truths in human language and with analogous truths. Reason is an instrument inadequate to the supernatural, and if they rely only on it, the theological virtues will stagnate in imperfect modes of acting. In order that these virtues may bring their operations to their perfection, adhere to their divine object and rest in it alone, a light and help must come to them from that object which is God Himself, to enlighten them and stabilize them in Him. This light and this help come to them actually through the gifts of the Holy Spirit.

It is through the gifts of the Holy Spirit that divine Wisdom, who dwells in the sanctified soul, produces illuminations and movements that sustain the activity of the theological virtues and bring them to the perfection of their proper acts. Take a soul that makes an act of faith in the presence of the Blessed Trinity within it. While disposing intelligence to return once more to the dogmatic truth for this new act of faith, the soul finds that, in entering by faith into the darkness of the mystery, it is beginning to experience a certain sweet delight, to be drawn by a certain confused light to rest peacefully on the mystery, or even to penetrate it more deeply. Or, a nurse might be caring for a sick person with a supernatural devotedness inspired by her sense of duty; then suddenly it comes to her in a concrete and living way that this patient is a member of the suffering Christ. From then on, she sees in him only her beloved Christ, and, sweetly moved by a love that makes her forgetful of self, she continues her charitable mission with incomparable gentleness and delicacy.

In the one case and the other, an illumination and movement from the Holy Spirit joined to bring about an act of contemplative faith and an act of perfect charity.

By those illuminations that give light to the intellect and at the same time disconcert it or bring it face to face with a transcendent light; by those sweet and delicate promptings that move the will to acts that surpass its natural strength and cause it to accomplish them with a perfection of which it was not capable, divine Wisdom intervenes directly in the supernatural operations of the soul.

Let us hear Saint Thomas explain to us this subtle and marvelous play of the divine action in the spiritual man:

As the bee and the migrating bird, impelled by instinct, act with an admirable sureness which reveals the Intelligence that directs them, so the spiritual man is inclined to act, not principally by the movement of his own will but by the impulse of the Holy Spirit, according to the word of Isaias (59:19): "He shall come as a violent stream which the Spirit of the Lord driveth on"; and so it is also said (Luke 4:1): "Jesus . . . was led about the desert by the Spirit." It does not follow that the spiritual man does not work by his own will and his free choice; but it is the Holy Spirit who causes in him this movement of free choice and of will, according to the word of Saint Paul: "For it is

God who of his good pleasure works in you both the will and the performance" (Phil. 2:13).[8]

And so, by the gifts of the Holy Spirit, God intervenes in the operations of the spiritual man to the point of becoming the principal agent and thus assuring the perfection of these operations.

Is it not, moreover, entirely normal that God alone can perfectly realize those operations of the life of the Trinity, and that consequently we can participate in them only by placing ourselves under His light and letting ourselves be carried along by His movement: "Those only are the children of God, who are moved by the Spirit of God," says the apostle. In other words, only God can assure the perfection of our divine acts as sons of God.

Having admitted this, we are no longer surprised by the assertions of Saint John of the Cross concerning transformed souls:

And thus, all the first motions of the faculties of such souls are Divine and it is not to be wondered at that the motions and operations of these faculties should be Divine, since they are transformed in the Divine Being. . . . God alone moves the faculties of these souls . . . and thus the works and prayers of these souls are always effectual. Such were those of the most glorious Virgin Our Lady.[9]

## C. The different wisdoms and perfection

The distinctions between the different kinds of wisdom, produced by the manifestations of divine Wisdom in the different planes of morality and of perfection, clarify the teaching of Saint Paul and Saint Teresa, and will permit us to state more exactly the notion of perfection according to our spiritual mother.

1. Saint Paul opposes the wisdom of the cross to that of the world and declared them to be contradictory.

Without any doubt, the wisdom of Christ on the cross that

[8] *In Epistolam ad Romanos,* 8:14.
[9] *Ascent,* Bk. III, ii; Peers, I, 230-1.

the apostle preaches, that which inspired the development of Christianity in its fervent beginnings, is the highest supernatural wisdom and the most pure. It is that of Christ Jesus "who has become for us God-given wisdom, and justice, and sanctification, and redemption; so that, just as it is written, 'Let him who takes pride, take pride in the Lord.' " [10]

The apostle has the care of preserving that wisdom in all its divine purity, of keeping its whole force; and so he fears lest he weaken it by using persuasive words of eloquence which would add to it a human element. It was of prime importance that the faith rest "not on the wisdom of men, but on the power of God."

What is the wisdom of the world that the apostle sets against this so high wisdom of God? Could it be the natural wisdom that we found at the first level of the divine manifestations? One might think so, when the apostle speaks of the persuasive wisdom of words. Such is not, however, the case. This wisdom is that of the world that "profited neither by divine wisdom nor its own wisdom to acquire the knowledge of God." It is a corrupted wisdom which did not remain faithful even to the natural law, and seeks only indulgence in the passions. It is the wisdom of Corinth and of the pagan world which, sunk in idolatry and sensuality, lost the sense of those duties that the natural law imposes on every man.

Between the wisdom of Christ crucified and the wisdom of the world, there is a radical opposition, an irreconcilable hatred: "If the world hates you," Jesus declared to His apostles, "know that it has hated me before you. If you were of the world, the world would love what is its own." [11] And He was to say in His priestly prayer: "Not for the world do I pray." [12]

2. Which wisdom do we find in souls that are in the third

[10] I Cor. 1:30-1.
[11] John 15:18-9.
[12] John 17:9.

Mansions? They do better, certainly, than just observe the natural law; for they avoid venial sin, they have their times of recollection, and practise supernatural virtue.

But reason regulates everything in the practice of their virtues. It is reason that secures the good order of their life, the harmony in their external duties. And this control of reason from which their virtues cannot free themselves, makes for their weakness and hinders their development. These souls have all sorts of good reasons for believing that they are suffering for God, or for dispensing themselves from that violence which would assure their perfection. We recall the two rich persons, of whom one supports with so much desolation the loss of unnecessary goods, and the other puts forth good reasons for trying to increase a fortune of which he has no need.

In these souls, reason is very much in possession of itself, and love is not sufficiently strong to move them to folly. And so they do like the rich young man of the Gospel, who observed the precepts of the law but shrank from the "irrational" exigencies of that complete detachment that marks the entrance into the ways of perfection. These souls can easily be situated at the second stage of wisdom that we have described, where the supernatural virtues ask of reason their light and their measure, and hence remain imperfect.

3. The common notion of high sanctity as a kind of folly of the cross, that obeys transcendent laws and produces superhuman acts, is not without a large part of truth. The saint is, in fact, a person enlightened and moved by the divine Wisdom who assures the perfection of his acts. But the error is, to think that this motion of the Holy Spirit makes the saint produce necessarily, as it were, extraordinary acts. On the contrary, the saint who is moved by the Spirit of God may be to all appearances a man like other men; for we know that sanctity can exist without shining out in any superhuman act, but be simply in the perfection of all the things the saint does.

It is easy for us now, in conclusion, to see more clearly the ideal of perfection according to Saint Teresa.

The good exterior order and supernatural virtue that reason illumines and inspires, are not perfection. There must be that love that reduces reason to folly and submits it to the light and rapture of the Holy Spirit. God alone can make His saints. Before coming under His direct action, one has not entered into the way of perfection. This way opens after the third Mansions, and it is by engaging oneself upon it that one merits the name of beginner.[13]

[13] The act of complete detachment that constitutes entrance into religious life makes one normally pass beyond the regions of the third Mansions. The novitiate, which puts into practice this detachment, ought to fix the soul in higher Mansions. The Carmelite masters (Saint John of the Cross, the Venerable John of Jesus-Mary) stress in fact that religious souls pass rather rapidly through the stages preliminary to the fourth Mansions and receive the graces special to these. But when the period of formation is over, it is very much to be feared that the religious soul falls from its first fervor and returns to spiritual Mansions that are more comfortable because more "reasonable."

# Mystical Life and Contemplation

# CHAPTER I
# The Wisdom of Love

*She reneweth all things and through nations conveyeth herself into holy souls. She maketh the friends of God and prophets.*[1]

We have arrived at the threshold of the fourth Mansions, at the entrance to the realm of Holy Wisdom.

Up to the present, the general help given to the soul has left it the initiative. God has remained in the shadow, in the background of its spiritual life. From now on there will be a particular help which will reveal that presence of God in the soul, of which Saint Teresa speaks. In the inner parts of the castle of the soul, He is the Sun that shines resplendent at the center of the crystal globe, the Fountain ever springing up whose living waters flow into all the apartments, the Holy Trinity of whom the soul is the temple.

Before entering into these holy regions, let us greet their mistress and queen, the Wisdom that is Love, who reigns there and orders all things with light and with love.

## A. What is the Wisdom of Love?

The Old Testament did not know the Incarnate Word, the God who dwelt among us. And so, with solicitude it sought God in creatures, in His works, in the wonderful order that He put into all things. Thus it found the Wisdom of God. It strove to penetrate the mystery of His nature and His action, and it exalted Him magnificently.

Or rather, it is Wisdom who revealed herself and, speaking

[1] Wis. 7:27.

through the mouth of the inspired writers, told of her eternal
origins and extolled, herself, her perfections.

The Lord possessed me in the beginning of his way, before he made
any thing from the beginning.
I was set up from eternity, and of old before the earth was made.
The depths were not as yet, and I was already conceived: neither
had the fountains of waters as yet sprung out.
The mountains with their huge bulk had not as yet been established:
before the hills I was brought forth.
He had not yet made the earth, nor the rivers, nor the poles of the
world.[2]

Wisdom is as eternal as God because she is God. She had a
role in the creation of the world. Wisdom, it was, that ordered
all things; while God created:

When he prepared the heavens, I was present: when with a certain
law and compass he enclosed the depths:
When he established the sky above, and poised the fountains of
waters:
When he compassed the sea with its bounds, and set a law to the
waters that they should not pass their limits: when he balanced the
foundations of the earth:
I was with him forming all things: and was delighted every day,
playing before him at all times;
Playing in the world. And my delights were to be with the children
of men.[3]

Wisdom is "the worker of all things"; [4] "she reacheth
therefore from end to end mightily and ordereth all things
sweetly." [5] But she finds a singular joy in her work that is
the highest of all: the sanctification of souls. It is she who
"through nations conveyeth herself into holy souls. She maketh
the friends of God and prophets." [6]

But who is she, this Wisdom? Is it possible to describe her,
since she is God? Her work reveals her. By a series of trait
after trait, the inspired author endeavors to give us an idea of
her, describing her manifold perfections:

[2] Prov. 8:22-6.
[3] Prov. 8:27-31.
[4] Wis. 7:22.
[5] Wis. 8:1.
[6] Wis. 7:27.

For in her is the spirit of understanding: holy, one, manifold, subtile, eloquent, active, undefiled, sure, sweet, loving that which is good, quick, which nothing hindereth, beneficent,

Gentle, kind, steadfast, assured, secure, having all power, overseeing all things, and containing all spirits, intelligible, pure, subtile.

For wisdom is more active than all active things: and reacheth everywhere by reason of her purity.

For she is a vapour of the power of God and a certain pure emanation of the glory of the almighty God: and therefore no defiled thing cometh into her.

For she is the brightness of eternal light, and the unspotted mirror of God's majesty, and the image of His goodness.

And being but one, she can do all things: and remaining in herself the same, she reneweth all things. . . .

For she is more beautiful than the sun, and above all the order of the stars: being compared with the light, she is found before it.

For after this cometh night, but no evil can overcome wisdom.[7]

The inspired writer who sings of Wisdom with such burning heart, who describes her with so penetrating an insight, is captivated by her beauty:

Her have I loved, and have sought her out from my youth, and have desired to take her for my spouse: and I became a lover of her beauty.[8]

She is a gift from God; it is of Him, then, that we must ask her. We have the example of Solomon's prayer:

Send her out of thy holy heaven and from the throne of thy majesty that she may be with me, and may labour with me, that I may know what is acceptable with thee. . . .

And who shall know thy thought, except thou give wisdom, and send thy Holy Spirit from above.

And so the ways of them that are upon earth may be corrected, and men may learn the things that please thee?

For by wisdom they were healed, whosoever hath pleased thee, O Lord, from the beginning.[9]

Wisdom was given to Solomon, bringing him every good. He sees now that she was always very near to him and that to obtain her, it is sufficient to desire her:

[7] Wis. 7:22 ff.
[8] Wis. 8:2.
[9] Wis. 9:10-18.

Wisdom is glorious, and never fadeth away, and is easily seen by them that love her, and is found by them that seek her.

She preventeth them that covet her, so that she first sheweth herself unto them.

He that awaketh early to seek her shall not labour: for he shall find her sitting at his door.[10]

Wisdom is near to Israel especially, her people of election, the depositary of her promises, the instrument by which she is to accomplish her eternal designs. It is with the people of Israel, helping them unfailingly in spite of their infidelities, that Wisdom finds her delights among the children of men. Solomon describes at length the marvelous work of Wisdom in their favor: [11]

She conducted them in a wonderful way: and she was to them for a covert by day and for the light of stars by night.[12]

But Israel persisted for a long time, unfaithful. The people left the ways of Wisdom, and were taken into doleful captivity to expiate their infidelity. How are they to stop this scourge, return into their land of Israel, and find again prosperity?

Wisdom is still shining in the heavens and remains just as loving towards her people. The prophet Baruch, too, found her, still just as luminous, just as powerful:

Hear, O Israel, the commandments of life. . . .

Thou hast forsaken the fountain of wisdom.
For if thou hadst walked in the way of God, thou hadst surely dwelt in peace for ever.
Learn where is wisdom, where is strength, where is understanding.[13]

The princes of the nations, the most daring navigators, "the merchants of Merrha and of Theman, and the tellers of fables and searchers of prudence . . . giants, renowned men and expert in war" did not find the way of Wisdom. But the God of

[10] Wis. 6:13-15.
[11] Wis. 10 to 19.
[12] Wis. 10:17.
[13] Bar. 3:9-14.

Israel who exercises a sovereign power over the light, who "sendeth forth light, and it goeth: and hath called it, and it obeyeth him with trembling," [14] exercises that same authority over Wisdom and keeps her at the disposition of His people. Let Israel, then, turn back to his God and to that Wisdom that is "the book of the commandments of God, and the law that is for ever."

Return, O Jacob, and take hold of it: walk in the way by its brightness, in the presence of the light thereof.

Give not thy honour to another, nor thy dignity to a strange nation.

We are happy, O Israel: because the things that are pleasing to God are made known to us.[15]

The Wisdom of the Old Law has entered also into the economy of the New. She has taken possession of the Church and of souls, and continues in them her beneficent action. In order to reveal her to the faithful, the Church rightly loves to use those texts in which the Old Testament displayed, to speak of Wisdom, all the riches of Hebrew poetry, the power to suggest of its symbols, the picturesque charm of its words, filling them with the radiance of inspiration. And because she is the self-same throughout endless ages, we find her again, and with what joy, beautifully set forth in the magnificent descriptions that our Christian spiritual life offers us of that Wisdom. We find her so full of mystery—one and yet many, swifter than any movement, penetrating everywhere because of her purity, the spirit of the power of God, more beautiful than the light, supple and active, the worker of all things, the divine power directing everything with might and with sweetness.

The New Testament stresses that this is a loving Wisdom which gives love unceasingly. It is love that inspires all her designs, all her movements, all her deeds. Her sanctifying work in us is highly a work of love; the embrace by which she takes hold of us and clasps us to herself, to bring us into the Trinity of divine Persons, is surpassingly an embrace of love.

[14] Bar. 3:33.
[15] Bar. 4:2-4.

In order to designate Wisdom as worker of love, we call her "Loving Wisdom." Loving or Holy Wisdom unites the Old and the New Testaments. It is the divine name that expresses all that is worked by God in man and for man from the beginning of creation to the end of time.

Loving Wisdom is not, properly speaking, a divine Person. She is the three Persons, the Trinity that dwells in our soul and whose single operation "conveyeth her into holy souls and maketh the friends of God and prophets." [16]

At the threshhold to the realm of Holy Wisdom, the fourth Mansions, let us note a few traits of her action.

## B. What does Holy Wisdom do?

### I. SHE ORDERS AND DISPOSES ALL THINGS FOR THE ACCOMPLISHMENT OF THE DESIGN OF GOD

1. In order better to dispose ourselves for her action in us, it is to be emphasized that Wisdom is intelligent. She has a plan; to realize it, she employs the resources of her understanding and her power. The world was created only for the realization of the design of God, and each one of us has a definite place in it. It was not to disport ourselves at whim or to attain to our personal ambitions that we came into the world. God has placed us here to be the human agents of His eternal plan and to work out the precise task that He has assigned to us.

Agents we shall certainly be—lovingly submissive or in revolt, that depends on us—but whatever be our attitude, the plan of God will be realized with our co-operation or in default of it. When the last details are finished, the course of time will stop; the world will be no more, for Wisdom will have accomplished the work for which it was created.

We have been told what this eternal design of God is. It is a purpose of mercy, hidden from past ages, the divine purpose that Saint Paul was chosen to reveal to us, the design decreed

[16] Wis. 7:27.

before the foundation of the world to be realized in the fullness of time, God's loving plan to unite all things in Christ.[17] The eternal design of God that Holy Wisdom is to realize is the Church of God, the end and reason for all things.[18]

Dictators and empires, peoples and individuals, come and go. Their deeds enter into the fulfillment of the great plan of God and are ordered to it by Wisdom who penetrates and disposes all things from one extremity of the world to the other. They pass away; and their works subsist in eternity only in so far as their wills lovingly directed them towards the accomplishment of the design of divine Wisdom.

Thus it is in order to realize the eternal design of God in us and through us, that Holy Wisdom intervenes in the soul with particular help in the fourth Mansions. The work to be done in the soul is of so high and delicate a nature, that Wisdom must apply herself to it and direct it with her own lights and movements.

2. The plan of God, for which we know the formula, is for us inscrutable. Infinite Wisdom conceived it and brings it to fulfillment. The thoughts of God surpass our thoughts as does the sky, the earth. Their mystery is as unfathomable as God Himself.

The regions to which the reign of Wisdom extends are dark regions, because the brilliance of her light and action shines forth upon them. The transcendence of the divine light it is that creates the darkness, not as a passing accident, but as an effect that is normal for our weak spiritual sight.

We could not, then, penetrate or grasp with our intelligence the design of God in its ensemble, nor even the part of it that falls upon us, nor the ways by which we shall be led. The lights that shine in the darkness could even delude us if we interpreted them too exactly. In founding the Convent of Saint

[17] Eph. 1:9-10.
[18] Saint Epiphanius, a Greek bishop of the fourth century, reputed for his holiness and learning.

Joseph of Avila, Teresa was led by a divine attraction for solitude and intimacy with Jesus; from there, Holy Wisdom had
her set out several years later to furrow the roads of Spain, as a
foundress. She wrote her treatises for the spiritual help of her
daughters; she was far from thinking that divine Wisdom was
preparing in them spiritual help for souls of all times. Saint
Francis de Sales wanted to found the Visitation to provide for
the needs of the people; and it ended as a contemplative institute that was to receive the revelations of the Sacred Heart.

In these regions, dark to us because Wisdom reigns in them,
light is given at each step to the soul who believes and surrenders itself to that loving Wisdom whom it has taken as
guide and mistress.

In saying that Wisdom gives light while causing darkness,
we seem to be involved in a contradiction. Yet every spiritual
experience attests to the co-existence of both. And because of
the resulting peace and the good fruit they produce in the
soul, we can divine their supernatural origin. Wisdom is light
and darkness. Here below she abides in the shadows. Faith
alone will enable us to find her there; and love, to dwell in
peace with her.

### 2. SHE ORDERS ALL WITH LOVE

This Wisdom is of love. She is at the service of God who is
Love. Now, love is goodness communicating itself. It needs to
pour itself out, and finds its joys in giving self—a joy that is
in the measure of the gift it makes, and the quality of that
gift. Because she is entirely at the service of God, Wisdom uses
all her resources to communicate love.

1. It is not surprising then that Wisdom rejoices to be with
the children of men, for in their souls she can pour out grace,
the best of created gifts, a participation in the nature and the
life of God.

Love that pours itself out so abundantly is a torrent of sweetness. It shares its happiness with souls, creating in them light

and peace and joy. Hence it is said that the reign of Holy Wisdom is a reign "of justice, of love, and of peace." [19]

2. But this love descends on souls not yet fit to receive it, souls still tarnished with the stains of sin. Love must set its kingdom up in a world given over to sin. There ensue struggle and suffering; its conquests are made only at the price of hard combat; its peaceful reign brings upon it blows and hatred. "The disciple is not above the Master . . . the world has hated me and it will hate you." Holy Wisdom is here like a lamb in the midst of wolves; for the world is evil, and she condemns the world by her very presence. There is a law of strife and of interior and exterior suffering that follows, here below, all the developments and triumphs of the Wisdom that is Love. She lives and extends her conquests on earth in a Church that is militant and sorrowful even in its victories. "Did not the Christ have to suffer these things before entering into his glory?" [20] Jesus proclaims after His Resurrection. The same necessity is imposed on all who follow Him.

3. Sweet and painful, the Wisdom of Love is essentially active. This activity is not merely transient; it is abiding. If love ceased for one instant to communicate itself, it would be no longer love; for love that becomes static degenerates into egoism. God ceaselessly engenders His Son; from the Father and the Son, the Holy Spirit constantly proceeds; that is why God is eternal Love.

The love which has been poured out on us cannot remain static in our souls. It must ascend once more whence it came, having made us the instruments of a further giving of itself. Taking us captive, the Wisdom of Love introduces us into the inner current of the divine life in the bosom of the Trinity, enlisting us as her co-operators in attaining her divine designs, making us channels of grace and instruments of her action. Love is essentially dynamic and dynamogenic.

[19] Preface for the Feast of Christ the King.
[20] Luke 24:26.

The apostolate is not a work of supererogation. It is the normal sequel to contemplative love. To think only of intimate union with God is to be ignorant of the nature of love, to arrest its movement. For it would be the destruction or at least the diminution of love to confine it within any kind of selfishness no matter how spiritual this might seem.

Holy Wisdom is concerned with souls less for themselves than for her own divine purpose. And this only purpose is the Church. She chooses us as members of the Church, that we may hold a place in it and fulfil a mission. We have to recall this frequently, so prompt is our egoism and our pride—encouraged by the feeling of our personal intimacy with God—to persuade us that we are an end in ourselves, the last end in the sanctifying work of divine Wisdom in our soul.

The sacred humanity of Christ was created, adorned with marvelous privileges and hypostatically united with the divinity, for the sake of the Church and the redemption of souls.* He knows this as soon as He comes into the world: "Sacrifice and oblation thou wouldst not, but a body thou hast fitted to me . . . 'Behold I come to do thy will, O God.' " [21] And the creation of the Blessed Virgin, with all her privileges, finds its justification in the divine maternity and the maternity of grace.

Like Christ Jesus and His divine Mother, all the saints are for the Church. Holy Wisdom sanctifies them to bring them into unity with the Church and use them for her works. When Saint Teresa was elevated to spiritual marriage, Christ gave her a nail of the crucifixion and added: "Henceforth you will be my spouse. . . . Henceforth you will take care for my honor . . . because you are truly my spouse." [22]

The words are clear. This permanent union does not vow her to intimacy in solitude, sealed with a sign and a plighted

* Cf. the *Credo: qui propter nos homines et propter nostram salutem descendit de coelis,* "who for us men and for our salvation came down from heaven."—Translator's note.
[21] Heb. 10:5-7.
[22] *Relations,* xxviii; Peers, I, 352.

word, but to action for Christ. Christ takes her for His spouse and gives her to the Church that she may be, in it, the mother of spiritual souls.

Holy Wisdom has only one design, for the realization of which she employs all the resources of her wisdom and her power: a single end that explains all her works, and that is the Church.

The masterpiece of divine Wisdom is incontestably the sacred humanity of Christ. And this humanity, united to the Word by the bonds of the hypostatic union, marvelously adorned with all the gifts, in possession of the beatific vision even here below—Holy Wisdom delivers it up to suffer the Agony of Gethsemane, to die the death of the cross, and to be the bread of life for those she has made her own. The Incarnation, Calvary, the Eucharist: these are the most beautiful triumphs of the Wisdom that is Love. Christ on the cross is a model that she lifts up before us as the perfect exemplar of all her works here. She wants to immolate us too, to make us beautiful that we may become purified and magnificent temples. She wants to prepare an altar in us, to offer us up to the glory of God and cause to spring from our wounds, floods of light and of life for souls.

Wisdom built herself a dwelling and adorned it with seven pillars; there she has prepared an altar, she immolates her victims, and calls everyone to the feast that follows the sacrifice. This abode of Wisdom is Christ Jesus; it is the Virgin Mary . . . it is ourselves.

# CHAPTER II
# The Gifts of the Holy Spirit

*Whoever are led by the Spirit of God,*
*they are the sons of God.*[1]

It is through the gifts of the Holy Spirit that Wisdom directly intervenes in the life of the soul and establishes complete dominion over it. The role of these gifts is therefore of capital importance in the spiritual life.

And yet Saint Teresa does not name them. Saint John of the Cross makes only a few passing allusions to them. Even theologians themselves are wary in their approach to them, so wrapt in mystery is the field of their operations and so incomplete is our knowledge of them.

But a study, however brief, of the gifts of the Holy Spirit can be of such practical help that we venture to attempt it. What are the gifts of the Holy Spirit; and what is the nature of God's action, to receive which, they dispose the soul? What is the experience of which they are the instruments? What use are we to make of them? These are the problems that we now take up in the sole hope of throwing some light on them.

## A. Nature and role of the gifts of the Holy Spirit

### I. DEFINITION

According to Saint Thomas, the gifts of the Holy Spirit are abiding supernatural habits or qualities which perfect man and

---

[1] Rom. 8:14.

dispose him promptly to obey the inspirations of the Holy Spirit.[2]

The definition given by Saint Thomas is happily explained by Father Gardeil.[3] The gifts, he says, are "passive powers engendered in the soul by divine love, and transformed by the Holy Spirit into permanent bases for His direct operations in the soul." Supernatural charity, because it is love of friendship, establishes relations of reciprocity between God and the soul. In turn active and passive, it gives and it receives. It is made for these exchanges, and exists only for them. Upon this essential aptitude of charity to receive, upon its receptive capacity, the gifts of the Holy Spirit are established as habits or permanent supernatural qualities constantly open to the action of the Holy Spirit present in the soul. As passive qualities, the gifts receive and transmit the lights, motions, and action of the Holy Spirit; they thus permit direct and personal intervention of God in the moral and spiritual life of the soul, even to the least details. As permanent qualities, the gifts place the soul at the constant disposal of the Holy Spirit, and can surrender it at any moment to His lights and His inspiration.

The gifts are to the soul as the sail is to the boat that the efforts of the oarsman move forward with difficulty. Should there come a favorable wind that swells the sail, the boat skims rapidly along to its destination, even though the oarsman relax his effort.

Thus it appears how the gifts of the Holy Spirit are, according to the definition of Saint Thomas, "habits, or permanent supernatural qualities, by which man is perfected to obey readily the promptings of the Holy Spirit."

They are usually called "gifts"; but Saint Thomas prefers the way in which Scripture speaks of them, as "spirits": "And the

---

[2] Cf. *Sum. Theol.*, I-II, q.68, a.3.

[3] In order to write this chapter, I used extensively the masterly study of P. Gardeil on *"Les dons du Saint Esprit"* (Dictionnaire de théologie Catholique, Vol. IV, Pt. 2, 1728–81), and his book, *La structure de l'âme et l'expérience mystique;* and in places I have borrowed his own expressions.

spirit of the Lord shall rest upon him," we read in Isaias,[4] "the spirit of wisdom and of understanding, the spirit of counsel and of fortitude, the spirit of knowledge and of godliness. And he shall be filled with the spirit of the fear of the Lord."

The term "gift" is, in fact, equivocal, for it suggests a power that is sufficient of itself. And even the word "spirit," especially if it is accompanied by the precise enumeration of the supernatural riches that come to us through the gifts: wisdom, understanding, fortitude, and so on, runs the danger of obscuring the nature of the gifts by permitting a confusion between the gift itself, "a passive or receptive power," and the action of God that it receives and transmits.

This confusion is all the more regrettable, since the action of God through the gifts is essentially gratuitous and depends on His free will. God pours out His grace as He wills, declares the apostle. The gifts are only aptitudes for receiving that action. Developing at the same time and tempo as the supernatural organism of grace and the virtues, they become capacities that are more vast, more delicately attuned to the inspirations and delicate motions of the Holy Spirit, more docile instruments, more pliant and powerful under the action of God for His personal interventions; but they never carry in themselves a strict right to a more frequent or more profound action of God. God does not give to him "who runs, but to him to whom He wants to show mercy," proclaims the apostle, speaking clearly of the gratuitous action of God through the gifts.

But if we consider them, as we ordinarily do, not only in themselves as passive instruments but as instruments animated by the actual spirit of God, we can say with Msgr. Gay that they are "supple and energetic, docile powers and strong forces that render the soul more passive under the hand of God, and at the same time more active in following Him and accomplishing His works." [5]

[4] Isa. 11:2-3.
[5] Msgr. Gay. *Vie et vertus chrétiennes.*

## 2. VIRTUES AND GIFTS

In the supernatural organism, the gifts rank near the virtues. Virtues and gifts are different and distinct, but are closely related. A study of their differences and relationship will allow us to state more precisely still, the nature of the gifts and of the divine action for which they are the instruments.

### a. *Differences*

Virtues and gifts are exercised in the same domain of the moral and spiritual life. The acts in which they intervene are not essentially distinct. Yet those that proceed from the gifts usually have the special mark of difficulty which justifies the divine intervention; and they always bear a seal of perfection that reveals it. Thus it is their mode of operation that differentiates them essentially.

The virtues are powers, of which each one has acts proper to itself. To posit its own act, the supernatural virtue borrows from the faculty into which it is grafted, its operations. A tributary of the human faculties, the supernatural virtue is controlled by the reason which directs them all, and its activity has reason for its guide. Another point important to the question at issue is that an act of supernatural virtue not only does not exclude but rather presupposes the intervention of God who, as First Cause, sets it in motion. Virtue then acts as a free secondary cause receiving from God its active power and an impulse which leaves it however its independence.

Through the gifts of the Holy Spirit, the intervention of God in the activity of the soul becomes direct and more complete. God substitutes His light for that of reason, His motion for that of the will, without suppressing its liberty; He descends to the faculties to direct and sustain their action. The soul's activity is taken over by God, and the faculties become His instruments. He is no longer simply the universal First Cause as in the activity of the virtues; through the gifts, He descends into the habitual domain of secondary causality, acting through the faculties of the soul that He holds in bondage to His light and His motion.

### b. *Relations between the virtues and the gifts*

Their different ways of acting do not set virtues and gifts in opposition but permit them to complete one another and to unite harmoniously for the perfection of the spiritual life.

In so far as their operations depend on the operations of the faculties in which they inhere, the supernatural virtues—especially the theological virtues—have at their services instruments inferior to their supernatural status and their divine object. The motives of credibility and all that the intelligence can supply faith with regard to revealed truth do not permit faith perfectly to adhere to infinite truth itself, nor to rest in it for the love of itself alone; in a word, to make in all its perfection an act that is proper to itself and to attain to its divine object with all its force. The lights furnished by the intelligence are concerned only with "the silvered surfaces" (that is, the dogmatic formula itself) and do not reveal "the gold of its substance" (that is, infinite truth itself), that the eye cannot see nor the ear hear nor the heart of man conceive.

The consequences of sin—evil tendencies and imperfections with their cortege of dullness, of weakness, of indelicacy, and of slowness in doing good—are added to the already deep-seated powerlessness of the faculties when faced with the Infinite. They increase the disproportion between the divine end to be attained and the help that supernatural virtue can count on from human powers.

The intervention of God through the gifts of the Holy Spirit remedies these deficiencies and provides the appropriate help. It brings to the soul a light that transcends the analogical notions of the intellect, a motion that dominates sweetly and strongly the will and the passions. It liberates the supernatural virtues from their dependence on the natural faculties and causes them to posit, with perfection, their proper acts. Thus it is that faith, receiving a higher light as to God through the gift of understanding, assents perfectly to its divine object and rests peacefully in the darkness that becomes its delight. This faith whose activity has been brought to its perfection by the gifts is the "living" or contemplative faith, explained by the Carmelite P. Joseph a Spiritu Sancto as faith illumined by the gifts: *fides illustrata donis*.[6]

The interventions of God through the gifts of the Holy Spirit can become so frequent and so interior that they establish the soul in an almost continual dependence on the Holy Spirit. From then on, the human faculties almost never direct the spiritual life; they have part in it now ordinarily only as instruments. The very activity of the supernatural virtues seems to pass into the background, to such an extent has the spiritual life become divine under the motion of the Spirit who supports and guides it. It is in this sense and in the light of such an experience that Saint Therese of the Child Jesus said at the end of her life: "I have not yet had a minute of patience! It is not mine! They are always mistaken!" [7] This complete dependence on God which rests at the same time on an absolute spiritual

---

[6] "Fides illustrata donis est habitus proxime eliciens divinam contemplationem . . ." P. Joseph a Spiritu Sancto, *Cursus theologiae mystico-scholasticae*, T. II, praed. II, disp. XII, q.1, n.15, p.657. Edition, P. Anastase, Beeyaert, 1925.

This learned writer studies at length the co-operation of faith and the gifts in contemplation. We shall translate a few of his statements that give light on this difficult problem: "The gifts of the Holy Spirit do not produce the act of supernatural contemplation, but modify the contemplation produced by enlightened faith (living)." *Ibid.*, q.1, n.66, p.684. "The gifts act only insofar as the soul is united to God; but this union is effected by the theological virtues: which proves that the latter are superior to the gifts; and this is in fact what Saint Thomas teaches when he says: 'The theological virtues are more excellent than the gifts . . . they are those whereby man's mind is united to God' (I-II, q.68, a.8). "The act of the gifts, of the gift of understanding for example of which we are speaking, does not terminate in God as known in Himself, but in Him as tasted. . . . It is in the sweetness experienced by the will, which is something created, that God is seen by the gift of understanding and the other intellectual gifts, especially the gift of wisdom." *Ibid.*, III, n.83, p.694.

[7] *Novissima Verba*, Aug. 18, p. 143.

poverty and on the continual help of God, constitutes the perfection of filial grace and marks the perfect reign of God in the soul; for it is written that "whoever are led by the Spirit of God, they are the sons of God." [8]

In this highly elevated spiritual state, the soul seems to remain habitually attentive to God's action and co-operates with it in a sweet abandonment. But it also happens that God intervenes in the soul without its having the least consciousness of it. The divine rapture sometimes produces a shock that suspends the activity of the faculties, as in mystical union, and during this suspension of the senses the soul is marvelously enriched.[9] But God can also enrich a soul in the same way and give it treasures that it will discover only later, without suspension of the senses or rapture.[10] Or again, He seizes a faculty and, without in any way revealing to it His seizure, causes it to posit an act that appears to be natural or even indeliberate, but whose supernatural effects reveal with certitude the efficacious divine motion that produced it.[11]

God's hold on a soul that is unaware of it, seemed to Saint Therese of the Child Jesus the most desirable form of sanctity because the most simple. Is it not also the highest? At least, it is the one that shows best how the Spirit of God is "more active than all active things: and reacheth everywhere by reason of her purity."

The touches of the Holy Spirit on the soul can therefore be perceptible to the senses or altogether spiritual. They may be

[8] Rom. 8:14.

[9] Cf. the description of the mystical union, Fifth Mansions, i and ii; also, of the rapture and flight of the spirit, Sixth Mansions, i and ii.

[10] "When it is the case [this vision], I believe that we ourselves do nothing and accomplish nothing—the whole thing seems to be the work of the Lord. It is as if food has been introduced into the stomach without our having eaten it or knowing how it got there. We know quite well that it is there, although we do not know what it is or who put it there" (*Life*, xxvii; Peers, I, 172).

[11] Cf., for example, in the *Autobiography*, viii, the revelation with which Mother Genevieve was favored concerning Saint Therese of the Child Jesus; the latter said: "Such holiness seems to me the most true, the most holy; it is the holiness I desire, for it is free from all illusion."

powerful or delicate. Without suppressing the freedom of man, the Holy Spirit can constrain his faculties painfully or sweetly. He can move them in so subtle a manner that they are unaware of the sovereign power that is bringing them to do a work that will be all the more fruitful and more divine.

Such are the marvelous resources, the delicate art that Wisdom employs to make souls "the friends of God and the prophets."[12] In studying these interventions of the Holy Spirit through the gifts, we have sometimes the impression of a lifting of the veil of mystery which hides God's action in the soul and in the Church. We are soon to find out that we are touching on a mystery that lies deeper still. But at least our faith is now enlightened enough to gaze with eagerness and delight into the new depths of darkness that it knows to be filled with the most lofty and admirable works of divine power and wisdom and mercy.

### 3. DISTINCTION OF THE GIFTS FROM ONE ANOTHER

Isaias enumerates seven spirits, or rather forms of the Spirit of God that rest upon the Messias: "the spirit of wisdom and of understanding, the spirit of counsel and of fortitude, the spirit of knowledge and of godliness, and the fear of the Lord." Theology, following Saint Thomas, has seen in this sacred septenary both the plenitude of the divine Spirit that rests upon Christ and an enumeration of the seven distinct gifts of the Holy Spirit.

The distinction of the gifts, like that of the virtues, is based upon the distinction of their proper objects.

The gift of wisdom penetrates divine truths, not to dispel their essential obscurity, but to relish them as by a connatural attraction created by charity.

The gift of understanding, an intuition of divine things, renders clear the divine truth regardless of the objections and obstacles that conceal it, keeps the soul at peace under the

[12] Wis. 7:28.

blinding light of mystery, and causes distinct lights to shine on the secondary objects of faith; that is, on what is ordered to the manifestation of the mystery, to its credibility, and to its regulative power over morals.

The gift of knowledge clarifies the relations of created things with divine Truth and judges them in the light of that Truth.

The gift of counsel intervenes in the deliberations of prudence, giving light as to decisions to be made.

The gift of piety makes one render to God the duties that are due Him as to a loving Father.

The gift of fortitude secures strength to triumph over the difficulties in the way to the accomplishment of good.

The gift of fear creates in the soul the respectful and filial attitude towards God, demanded by His transcendence and quality of Father.

Among these gifts, four are of the intellect: wisdom, understanding, knowledge, and counsel; three, of the will: fortitude, piety, and fear of the Lord.

Three are contemplative: wisdom, understanding, knowledge; four are active: counsel, fortitude, piety, and fear of the Lord.

Theology has explored the relations of the gifts with the virtues, with the beatitudes, and the fruits of the Holy Spirit. Thus, wisdom is united with charity; understanding and knowledge, with faith; fear of the Lord, with hope; piety, with justice; fortitude, with the virtue of fortitude; counsel, with prudence.

Peace and the beatitude of the peacemakers belong to wisdom. The beatitude of the clean of heart, and the fruit of faith, belong to the gift of understanding. The beatitude "Blessed are they who mourn" is proper to the gift of knowledge, while the beatitude of the merciful follows the gift of counsel. The gift of piety takes in the beatitude of the meek (Saint Augustine), or that of the merciful and of those who hunger (Saint

Thomas). To the gift of fortitude belong patience and lon-
ganimity; and to the gift of fear, the fruits that are modesty,
continency, and chastity.

These precise distinctions and classifications have permitted
an analysis of each one of the gifts and their properties, together with detailed explanations. Such studies satisfy the mind
avid for clarity and logic; but when one applies them to concrete cases, they give the impression of departing from reality
in the measure that they become more precise and clear.[13]

Take for example the case of Saint Therese of the Child
Jesus whose spiritual life was directed from childhood by the
gifts of the Holy Spirit. Exact definitions of the gifts and their
properties ought to make it easy to find the gift that predom-
inated in her. But on the contrary, opinions are astonishingly
diverse on that important question. "The gift of piety," some
say, considering her filial attitude towards God. "The gift of
wisdom," others assert, struck by her experience of the divine
mercy, which explains her whole way of spiritual childhood.
"The gift of fortitude," declares her sister who knew her intimately and followed her in all her spiritual life.

The distinctions so clear in theory seem to be of little help
in this actual case with its abundance of data. Logic seems powerless in the presence of reality.

Should we then leave aside logic and its distinctions? We
do not think so; the distinctions and classifications are founded
not only in reason but in fact. Yet we think we can show, in
the light of the teaching of Saint John of the Cross, that the
distinction of the gifts, although a real one, must not be af-

[13] It seems to us first, that beyond the gifts of the Holy Spirit which are
ordained to receive a particular form of the action of God, there is place
to distinguish the receptivity or passivity of charity itself which is not ordered to any precise object. It is thanks to this receptive capacity of charity,
which is itself grafted into the essence of the soul as an entitative quality,
that God can act in the soul itself by substantial touches; in other words by
touches of the substance of God on the substance of the soul—touches incomparably more fruitful than the action of God through a particular gift.

firmed so absolute and so complete that one could study them in isolation and separate sharply their effects.

In his commentary on the third stanza of the *Living Flame,* explaining the communications of God to the soul that has attained to transforming union, Saint John of the Cross compares the divine attributes to resplendent lamps which touch the soul with their shadows or splendors which partake of the nature and properties of the attributes from which they emanate. According to this principle, the shadow cast upon the soul by the lamp of the beauty of God will be a fresh beauty, of the nature and proportions of the beauty of God. The shadow cast by strength will be fresh strength of the proportions of the strength of God. And so with the shadows of all the other lamps or attributes. The doctor of mysticism is expounding a general law concerning divine communications in the supernatural order: God communicates to the soul a real participation in His nature and His life; grace, inferior to God because created, nevertheless makes us true children of God; the participation in the divine nature that it gives is entire although created.

The Saint here stresses that each attribute is the very being of God and contains, consequently, the richness of all the others:

> Now, inasmuch as these virtues and attributes of God are enkindled and resplendent lamps, and are near to the soul, as we have said, they will not fail to touch the soul with their shadows, which will be enkindled and resplendent likewise. . . . Oh, abyss of delights, that art the more abundant in proportion as thy riches are gathered together in the infinite simplicity and unity of Thy sole Being, so that each one is known and experienced in such a way that the perfect knowledge and absorption of the other is not impeded thereby.[14]

In other words, the communications that the soul receives passively from God are clothed in the form and special properties of the divine attribute from which they emanate; but, since this attribute is the very essence of God and bears within

[14] *Living Flame,* st. iii; Peers, III, 168, 170.

it the riches of all the others, the communication that the soul receives of it bears also a created participation in the whole being of God and in all the divine riches of the other attributes.

In this exposition that we have abridged with regret, taking only what concerns our subject, Saint John of the Cross does not explicitly name the gifts of the Holy Spirit; it is evident, however, that these divine communications come to the soul through the gifts. The diversity of the communications, or overshadowings of different divine attributes, causes distinct gifts to intervene. One can glimpse already the conclusion that we wish to be drawn: the overshadowings of different attributes, which come to the soul through distinct gifts, produce in it different delights and are ordered to distinct practical ends; but substantially they are identical, for the different attributes from which they emanate are all the same essence of God. In His direct and personal communications to the soul under a distinct form or for a particular end—as light or strength, sweetness or beauty—God is not divided; it is a participation in His whole richness that He communicates through each one of the gifts.

To push the distinction of the gifts to the point of assigning to each one of them an essentially different action of God, is to misunderstand the divine character of that action, reducing it to the human level and introducing unwarranted distinctions.[15]

[15] One might object in a rather specious way that, just as the different virtues are ordered to specifically distinct acts, so the obediential powers are each ordered to a single effect to the exclusion of every other; just as the sense of hearing can perceive only sounds.

We must indeed recognize that virtue and gift, active power and passive power, are determined to a determinate object. But while the act produced by an active power gives the measure of the activity put forth, a passive power perceives in the causality acting upon it, only the special effect to which it is ordered as a power. Hearing perceives the music of an orchestra; but that orchestra offers to the other senses (sight, for example) other perceptions. Likewise when a gift of the Holy Spirit perceives the particular effect of an intervention of God, it does not exhaust the power of the latter, which produces other effects in the soul by other gifts or by the receptive passivity of charity.

It seems to us that most of the errors and confusions in the study of the gifts of the Holy Spirit come from the fact that we measure the action

On the other hand, the complete identity of the divine communications under the various gifts—whose distinction is sufficiently safeguarded by the diversity of perceived effects and of ends attained—well explains both the difficulty of deciding which particular gift predominates in a certain case, and that unity of holiness achieved by ways and under the action of gifts that are so different. The last point should be underlined. An example will bring it out more.

Take Saint John Bosco and Saint Teresa, both of whom are moved by the Holy Spirit, but certainly in very different ways. Don Bosco, given to the active life, manifests the influence of the gifts of counsel and fortitude. Teresa is a contemplative who lives by the gifts of wisdom and understanding. If these gifts were completely distinct, they ought normally to produce quite different forms of sanctity and of mystical life. But let us consider the two saints at the summit of the spiritual life. We find Saint John Bosco enjoying prophetic visions of the future and the development of his Institute, to a greater extent than the contemplative Saint Teresa herself. As to Saint Teresa, she is a marvelously good manager of material affairs and founds convents with a facility and poverty of means beyond the experience of Saint John Bosco. Active and contemplative meet in a sanctity which is one; and also in mystical gifts that are astonishingly alike. How explain these resemblances if, under the exterior diversity of the ways and gifts that led them both to the same summits, the action of God were not identical in its most profound effects? [16]

---

of God by what we perceive of it, and the receptive power of the gifts by the perceptions that they register. We forget that divine action, while adapting itself to us and our needs, is not itself reduced to a human measure, but that it remains transcendent in itself and in its effect.

It is our intellect which, because of its need for clarity and precision, reduces everything to the measure of what it can dominate and understand. There are very few, says Saint Teresa, who do not measure the divine action by the measure of their thoughts.

[16] There are other questions concerning the gifts such, for example, as the frequency of the divine interventions through the gifts, which will be treated in other chapters.

## B. Experience of the gifts

A study of the gifts of the Holy Spirit brings us, at each step, to new problems. We have now come to one that is both theological and psychological, one of the most difficult and least explored, and yet most useful in the direction of souls: the problem of mystical experience or of psychological consciousness of the action of God through the gifts.

How does that awareness take place? What are its different modes? Does it accompany every action of God through the gifts, and in what measure does it reveal such action? These are questions whose answer would quiet many anxieties and encourage the progress of many souls.

But these problems are too complex to be embraced in this brief study. We shall simply set down a few remarks that will suggest partial answers.

1. There is a tendency to identify mystical life and mystical experience, the action of God through the gifts and the experience of that action, as if they were inseparable.[17] This confusion is the source of important practical errors. In actual fact, it is evident that the action of God through the gifts is clearly distinct from the experience that we can have of it, so that the first may exist without the second.

Saint John of the Cross stresses the fact that at the beginning of the mystical life the soul, quite desolate at the loss of its former consolations, does not perceive the subtle sweetness of the contemplation that is being given it. The Saint notes too that when divine communications come to a purified soul, they do not produce in it any perceptible effect, just as a ray of sunlight entering a room with perfectly pure air and going out by an opposite window, would not be seen at all because it encountered no material particles to reflect its light.

[17] Likewise the name of mystical life is sometimes reserved to that which is exercised under the action of the contemplative gifts (wisdom, understanding, knowledge). It seems to us more normal to understand it of all life that is under the action of the gifts of the Holy Spirit.

As has been already remarked, God can infuse into a soul His sublimest favors without the soul's being experimentally conscious of receiving them. In his *Spiritual Canticle,* Saint John of the Cross asks for communications of which the senses know nothing. And Saint Teresa speaks of very great lights she discovered in her soul without knowing exactly when she received them.

The direct communications of God are not, then, always accompanied by awareness of them. Consequently, one could not affirm that there is no mystical life without mystical experience.

2. With regard to mystical experience, one can first put this question: Is it possible to experience the gifts of the Holy Spirit in themselves, that is, apart from the divine communications which actuate them?

A gift would normally enter into consciousness only through its exercise. How could one know that he had the sense of hearing, if no sound ever struck his ear? Similarly, every experience of one of the gifts has reference to an experience of its use through a divine communication.

Nevertheless, in the third stanza of the *Living Flame,* Saint John of the Cross observes, speaking of the deep caverns of the senses, that when the faculties—

are empty and clean, the hunger and thirst and yearning of their spiritual sense become intolerable; for, as the capacities of these caverns are deep, their pain is deep likewise; as is also the food that they lack, which, as I say, is God.[18]

This suffering from emptiness which has been preceded by divine communications, seems to be a kind of experience of the capacity of the gifts of the Holy Spirit, which bears painfully their privation. The experience is not reserved, it seems, to souls already near to transforming union. It is found with less

[18] *Living Flame,* st. iii; Peers, III, 70. Saint John of the Cross emphasizes the fact that this pain of emptiness is particularly intense after the divine visits of espousals, to prepare the soul for spiritual marriage.

intensity in souls that have been under the action of the gifts of the Holy Spirit, and who in certain circumstances experience their poverty and misery. This great feeling of pain, or experience of the gift of the Holy Spirit, ordinarily precedes divine communications, and prepares the soul for them by inciting it to acts of humility and of confidence that draw upon it the outpourings of mercy.

3. Another remark that helps to clarify the problem of mystical experience: in divine communications, the soul experiences neither God nor His action, but only the movements produced within by that divine action. The mystical experience is not, then, a direct experience but a quasi-experience of God through the movement that His intervention produces.

4. In this quasi-experience, there is one central impression. Most of the time, this is the dominant one and the strongest; sometimes even the only one, exclusive of any other: namely, the perception or the experience of the contrary of what is given by the divine communication, an experience that we might call negative.

When communicating Himself to the soul, God cannot dissimulate either what He is in Himself or the quality of His gift. His transcendence manifests itself. His presence imposes profound respect; His dazzling light produces darkness in the intellect not adapted to receive it; His strength overwhelms human weakness. The very sweetness that comes with the gift of wisdom makes the soul rejoice in its littleness. God thus puts the soul in an attitude of truth by creating in it humility.

Hence, this negative experience, however disconcerting it may be,[19] is the most constant and most authentic sign of the

[19] Disconcerting especially because it seems to run counter to ordinarily accepted notions. Usually, in fact, the intervention of God is pointed out as assuring the exterior triumph of the action of God.

Saint Lawrence on his grille is presented to us as the perfect type of the gift of fortitude. And yet, which should one prefer: Saint Lawrence on his grille, setting at defiance his executioners, or Jesus Christ on the cross, triumphing over suffering and death, but reciting the psalm: My God, my God, why hast thou forsaken me? The evident design of God was to strengthen by divine action. The positive experience of the gift may be lacking, as we have said.[20] If the negative experience is wanting, one may legitimately doubt the reality of God's action in the soul.

Being united to the divine communication of which it is the sign and the effect, the negative experience explains those antimonies often pointed out as characteristic effects of the gifts, and is the basis for the relations of the gifts with the beatitudes. Blessed are the poor in spirit, the meek, the clean of heart, the peacemakers, those who hunger and thirst for justice . . . because their dispositions of poverty, of purity, of gentleness, their hunger and thirst after justice are the fruit of God's action in them and dispose them for new divine effusions. In order to offer oneself to the divine illuminations by humiliation, as Pascal counsels, one must first have been touched by divine light; and the littleness that calls down Wisdom is also its fruit. Here is a paradox of apparent oppositions divinely evoking and fulfilling the one the other: the littleness of the creature and the transcendence of God, man's sin and God's mercy, must become more and more manifest in the proportion that God reveals His action and His truth in the soul.[21]

---

the exterior fortitude of Saint Lawrence, the fortitude of His Spirit and of His Church against the external power of Rome; but the experience of the gift of fortitude in Christ on the cross—even from the exterior point of view—is more perfect and more complete. We might make the same remark concerning the gift of fortitude in Saint Therese of the Child Jesus on her deathbed. "I did not think it was possible to suffer so much," she said. "The cup is filled to the brim. . . ." This plaint is not corrected but completed by her heroic patience and this other word: "I do not regret having surrendered myself as a victim of love."

[20] One can then admit as a consequence, that a very high degree of contemplation can habitually be manifested only by an impression of darkness and powerlessness. This remark casts light on the contemplative experience of Saint Therese of the Child Jesus.

[21] This antimony is found not only in the experience of the soul at the moment when it is under the action of a gift; it creates an habitual state of soul. Thus the gift of wisdom maintains an habitual impression of littleness and humility; the gift of understanding seems to make the soul live in an atmosphere of obscurity. We observe, too, that the gift of counsel belongs

5. To this negative experience of privation, there can be added a positive and delectable experience of the action of God through a gift of the Holy Spirit.

To be sure, only the gift of wisdom gives the wholly delightful experience of the gift of God. The supreme gift, perfecting all the others just as charity from which it proceeds perfects all the virtues, the gift of wisdom introduces a "taste," its own and more or less subtle, into all the other gifts, in all souls docile to the action of the Holy Spirit; and it creates that peaceful humility which is the sign of contact with God.

Apart from the gift of wisdom and its subtle influence on all the others, the positive experience of the gifts is extremely variable. At times the gift of understanding fills the soul only with darkness; and again, it throws penetrating light on a truth of faith. The gift of fortitude permits Saint Lawrence to defy his executioners—and makes Saint Therese of the Child Jesus heroic without feeling at the same time any reserve of strength. It causes Jesus to yield to His agony on the cross; and is expressed by a more than human cry that makes the executioners beat their breasts. The gift of counsel sheds light on a decision to be made—or it leaves the soul hesitant until some event sets it, as it were in spite of itself, in the direction it should take. The gift of knowledge can produce a distaste for creatures—or show, on the contrary, their value in the plan of God.

The recipient's reaction to this experience as well as his appreciation of it will be influenced by his temperament. Under the impact, so to speak, of the power or the light of God, the reactions of one will differ from those of another; in the same grouping of impressions, the optimist will lay stress on those that are pleasant; the pessimist, indicate only the painful. And

to temporizers who might give the impression of being hesitant. We also know that the Church, following the apostle Saint Paul, loves to show forth the gift of fortitude in children and young girls: "the weak things of the world has God chosen to put to shame the strong" (I Cor. 1:27).

if we add that certain divine interventions can themselves create such or such impressions, produce in a faculty such or such precise effect, we can see that in this domain of the positive experience of the action of God through the gifts of the Holy Spirit, we are in a complex and obscure realm, in which one can progress only with prudence and form judgments only with extreme circumspection.

To escape from these uncertainties and obscurities, let us go to the surest and most visible sign of God's action through the gifts. *A fructibus eorum cognoscetis eos:* You shall know them by their fruits. Such is the standard given us by our Lord to distinguish the preachers and prophets inspired by the Holy Ghost from the shepherds who are only hirelings. Spiritual fecundity always accompanies the action of the Holy Spirit. His fruits are not limited to miracles; they may be charity, benignity, patience, and the others. Yet the discernment of the fruits of the Spirit of God will not in every case be easy; for, even in a holy man, good works are accompanied by defects and faults; and their fecundity is manifest only at a long date. The Spirit of God will Himself provide for this and will make Himself recognized when the time comes, by that humble patience that will have known how to wait and to pray.

## C. Utility and utilization of the gifts

All that has been said on the nature and the role of the gifts of the Holy Spirit reveals to us their importance in the spiritual life.

The gifts of the Holy Spirit are doorways on to the Infinite, letting into the soul breezes for its illimitable spaces, the soft utterings of the Spirit of Love. This Spirit, it is true, breathes "where it will and no one knows where it comes from or where it goes." [22] But we know that it is the Spirit of loving Wisdom, of the divine Mercy who longs to pour out His love, who has created us in order to give Himself to us and to bear us away

[22] John 3:8.

in the powerful movement and the burning intensity of His overflowing life.

The Spirit is infinitely wise and infinitely powerful. To serve His designs, He uses all the resources of His wisdom and His strength. He it is who realized the hypostatic union, enriching the humanity of Christ with the unction of the divinity. Again, it is this Holy Spirit of infinite mercy who preserved the soul of the Virgin from the consequences of original sin and made her all pure and full of grace.

For the realization of His designs in us, our good will is too slow and too weak. The Holy Spirit will use the doorways that are open before Him. Through these entrances, He will blow His divine breezes through the soul, "touching" its virtues and perfections, "refreshing them and moving them so that they may diffuse wondrous fragrance and sweetness." [23]

Thus by the gifts of the Spirit, those passive powers whose capacity is adapted to the force of the inflowing that they receive, God takes possession of the soul and there gives it to will and to do, perfecting its virtues. He takes control of it either progressively or at one stroke according to the manner and the measure He has decreed. Saint Therese of the Child Jesus testifies that one day our Lord took her and placed her there. And Saint Paul declares that by the grace of God he is what he is.

It is by doors open on to the Infinite, by sails set to breezes of the Spirit, that omnipotent Mercy enters into souls and makes of them prophets and friends of God.

But the doors must be open with confidence, and the sails raised by love, if they would be full with the winds of the deep. Yet how can this be, if the soul knows not of the gifts of the Holy Spirit nor what God can accomplish through them?

In the first centuries of the Church, the action of the Holy Spirit in souls and in the Church showed itself exteriorly, manifesting itself in broad daylight. On the Feast of Pentecost,

[23] *Spiritual Canticle,* st. xxvi; Peers, II, 135.

the Holy Spirit came under the form of tongues of fire to take possession of the apostles and, through them, of the Church. He disclosed His presence by the transformation effected in the apostles; and His power, by all their works. He frequently intervened in the life of the Church, enlightening, impelling, guiding it. He was a Person living in the bosom of the Church and recognized as such: *Visum est enim Spiritui Sancto et nobis*.[24] . . . For the Holy Spirit and we have decided, wrote the apostles. They often invoked His light and His authority and were rewarded with a visible granting of their prayers.

Since then, the Holy Spirit would seem to have hidden Himself more and more in the depths of the Church and souls, only rarely manifesting Himself exteriorly. This certainly does not mean that there has been a decline in His power and His activity. The change merely has to do with His modes of acting. He is still living in us, ready to give Himself; and we ever have His gifts enabling us to be set in motion by Him. But is it because He is hidden, or is it rather that men have become too much bent on things of this earth, that they no longer dispose themselves to receive His sanctifying action in them? At all events the Holy Spirit has become to a large extent not only a hidden God but also a God unknown; and the teaching of spiritual writers on His sevenfold gifts has long been unknown to Christians in general.

Mystical theology—to give this science its technical name— fell some time ago into discredit, if not disrepute, with many otherwise good Christians. The bogey of the imagination and unhealthy illusion was everywhere raised, especially when the graces of the Holy Spirit were accompanied by sensible phenomena. The masters of the spiritual life strove uniquely to develop the virtues, neglecting the gifts or feigning not to know of their existence. The Holy Spirit, dwelling in our souls, having come to live in them His ardent, captivating life, was proscribed from a life that wanted to be Christian without

[24] Acts 15:28.

Him. He seemed at times to escape from His prison, but the soul in which He manifested Himself, having become His joyous victim, became also the victim of those well-meaning reasonable people with whom it associated. It was judged suspect, and sometimes even dangerous by the group in which it moved; it became a kind of outcast. Who among us could not add names to these reflections, and perhaps great names, today happily reinstated.

But mystical science has been restored to honor. The chilling winds of Jansenism have died down. The Spirit of Love is free once more to brood over souls. The heart of the Saviour has opened itself wide. Saint Therese of the Child Jesus has taught a way of spiritual childhood that leads to the furnace of love, placing herself at the head of a legion of little souls, victims of God's merciful love. The Holy Spirit is living in the Church; His life is spreading. Fervent Christians, even unbelievers, are seeking for that life; the first, with an enlightened and already enkindled love; the others, in affliction and unrest. But how can they find entrance to this haven of peace without a guide, without method, without doctrine?

The Church provides us these guides in mystical science, teachers of loving knowledge. They are Saint Teresa of Avila, the spiritual mother; Saint John of the Cross, the mystical doctor; Saint Therese of the Child Jesus, their spiritual daughter, the greatest mistress of the spiritual life in modern times, and one of the greatest of all time.[25]

[25] It seems to us that a thorough study of the spirituality of Saint Therese of the Child Jesus should advance admirably the science of the gifts of the Holy Spirit. The action of the gifts predominates in her from the age of three; from then on, she refuses nothing to the good God. God's action in her through the gifts appears disengaged not only from extraordinary phenomena, but also from the overpowering sensible reactions to which it is rather generally thought to be indissolubly linked. Very simple and very pure action, it reveals to us the essential.

When one studies Saint Therese of the Child Jesus, one must not forget this predominance of the gifts of the Holy Spirit in her spiritual life. Her generosity is entirely submission to the light of God; her strength is in her docility to God's movements. It is therefore inexact to be unwilling to see in her anything but a violent effort to triumph over herself in order to ac-

Starting from the fact that perfection consists in the perfect reign of God within us through the Holy Spirit, mystical theology is totally concerned with finding a solution of this practical problem: How to draw upon us the inflowing of the Spirit, and how then to abandon ourselves and co-operate with His conquering action? Assuredly, the Holy Spirit is sovereignly free in His gifts, and nothing could constrain or diminish His divine liberty. Yet certain dispositions of soul have a seemingly irresistible attraction for Him; and there are certain others that He demands for active co-operation with His action.

The whole teaching of the masters of Carmel tends to put in relief those dispositions, to define the asceticism adapted to the action of God through the gifts. One will find nothing else in the *Ascent of Mount Carmel,* or in the *Way of Perfection,* nor in the *Interior Castle.* It reappears in the doctrine of Saint Therese of the Child Jesus. Their whole spiritual science concerns itself with the utilization of the gifts of the Holy Spirit. To forget this in reading their works, would be to misunderstand the end in view and to falsify the perspectives.

There are three dispositions which are basic to this asceticism and correspond to three laws or exigencies of every action of God in the soul. These fundamental dispositions which command the full co-operation of the soul and will go on being perfected as the divine action develops in it, are the gift of self, humility, and silence.

We shall study them in this third part as certain conditions and general effects of God's action in the soul. These preliminaries will cast light on the study that will follow, on the particular modes of the progressive action of the Holy Spirit, and the co-operation that it requires in each one of its phases.

-----

quire virtues. In reality, she works under the movement of the Holy Spirit only to make God's strength triumph in her. It is for this reason that she will be able to say that she has no virtues, and that God gives her each instant what she needs.

# CHAPTER III
# The Gift of Self

*What power this gift has! . . . It cannot fail to draw the Almighty to become one with our lowliness.*[1]

According to Saint Teresa, all the asceticism that she proposes in the *Way of Perfection* can be summed up in the perfect realization of the gift of self:

> The aim of all my advice to you in this book is that we should surrender ourselves wholly to the Creator, place our will in His hands and detach ourselves from the creatures. . . .
> We are preparing ourselves for the time, which will come very soon, when we shall find ourselves at the end of our journey and shall be drinking of living water from the fountain I have described. Unless we make a total surrender of our will to the Lord, *and put ourselves in His hands* so that He may do in all things what is best for us in accordance with His will, He will never allow us to drink of it.[2]

The close relation between contemplation and the gift of self is many times over affirmed by the Saint. The soul must respond to the first contemplative graces by this complete gift; otherwise, the graces are renewed only at passing intervals:

> If we do not give ourselves to His Majesty as resolutely as He gives Himself to us, He will be doing more than enough for us if He leaves us in mental prayer and from time to time visits us as He would visit servants in His vineyard. But these others are His beloved children.[3]

But of what reservations and slowness are we guilty in the realization of this gift of self, which must be absolute if it would draw down the plenary gifts of God:

[1] *Way of Perfection,* xxxii; Peers, II, 138.
[2] *Ibid.;* 137-8.
[3] *Ibid.,* xvi; 66.

We think we are giving God everything, whereas what we are really offering Him is the revenue or the fruits of our land while keeping the stock and the right of ownership of it in our own hands.[4]

This practical truth claims our attentive consideration and reflective thought:

Being unable to make a full surrender of ourselves, we are never given a full supply of this treasure.[5]

These statements are clear and downright, but too general to suffice where illusion can so easily insinuate itself. We must strengthen our conviction as to how necessary is this gift of self and what precisely God demands from us in regard to it.

## A. Necessity and excellence

1. Saint Teresa herself indicates the first and fundamental motive which makes of the gift of self a necessity:

As He refuses to force our will, He takes what we give Him but does not give Himself wholly until *He sees that* we are giving ourselves wholly to Him. This is certain, and as it is of such importance, I often remind you of it. Nor does He work within the soul as He does when it is wholly His and keeps nothing back. I do not see how He can do so, since He likes everything to be done in order.[6]

Being the absolute master of all things as their Creator, God could use His rights to constrain creatures to do His will. But He leads them by laws in conformity with their nature, respecting the gifts with which He has endowed them. To man, to whom He has given intellect and free will, God dictates His will through the moral law which is addressed to the intellect; and thus he respects man's liberty. "God does not force our will," Saint Teresa emphasizes. Rather than compel it, He prefers to face the risk of a partial failure of His designs and modify their ordering, as happened after the revolt of the angels and the fall of man.

[4] *Life,* xi; Peers, I, 63.
[5] *Ibid.;* 64.
[6] *Way of Perfection,* xxviii; Peers, II, 118.

Man sometimes tyrannizes over his fellow-man; but God respects the faculties with which He has endowed our nature. The part that He leaves to their action even in His most sublime designs is so important that we are baffled by it, when it is disclosed to us. The free co-operation of man is truly a necessary condition for the fulfillment of the eternal decrees of the divine mercy.

Thus before realizing the Incarnation of His Word—the first link in the admirable chain of Christian mysteries—God asks the consent of Mary whom He has chosen as co-operator. He sends the archangel Gabriel to announce to her the mission that He has foreseen for her. His decrees will be realized only with her consent. All heaven listens and waits, attentive to the words of the Virgin. It thrills with joy at the *Fiat* of Mary, which may also be called the *Fiat* of human nature to its assumption by the Divinity in the hypostatic union. It makes of Mary a co-operator with God. Thereafter she is to be effectually and actively Mother, wherever God will be Father in His relations with men.

Likewise, in order to be united perfectly with souls, God will exact of each one its personal consent and active co-operation. His grace is predisposing, certainly, but it pursues its work and comes to full flowering in us only with our good will. A first consent, a first gift of self, even though complete, is not enough; for our free will is an inalienable good. After giving it, we keep and use it still. The work of God in us follows the vicissitudes of our hesitations and our refusals which unfortunately check it, as well as of our fervent yieldings to it which set us free for the inflowing of grace. "God takes only what we give; but He does not give Himself completely as long as we have not given ourselves to Him absolutely." Saint Teresa thus enunciates a law of the spiritual life. God takes possession of us only in the measure that we give ourselves up to Him. Perfect union requires as its first condition the complete gift of self.

2. The gift of self is a deep need of love, and its most perfect act. Love, which is goodness communicating itself, tends to this loss of self in the beloved and finds thus its satisfaction and its plenitude. God finds His infinite beatitude in the generation of His Word who is His perfect expression and in the spiration of Love which is the Holy Spirit into whom He passes completely.

In us also charity attains to its plenitude and perfection when, taking full possession of us, it bears us with it once more to God in a movement of filial love towards the Father.

Further, that complete purification which according to Saint Thomas is effected by religious profession is not a privilege, a sort of plenary indulgence, granted on such an auspicious occasion; but is the normal effect of that perfect charity which covers a multitude of sins. Every complete giving of self, made with the same fervor of love, purifies the soul in the same way.

We are sometimes tempted to seek in poetry or sublime language the expression of perfect love; but this love is best expressed in the complete and earnest gift of self.

3. The gift of ourselves is the most perfect sacrifice we can offer to God.

Sacrifice, the act of religion *par excellence,* the one that alone recognizes the sovereign dominion of God and makes reparation for sin, includes the oblation of a victim, followed ordinarily by an immolation. The oblation is, according to some theologians, the only essential act of the sacrifice; in the opinion of all, it is the most important. The oblation surrenders the victim to God, makes it His and permits Him to dispose of it as He desires, either to immolate it or to use it for other ends.

The gift of self is such an oblation, offering as it does to God all that we have and all that we are, accepting in advance His every will and His good pleasure. By offering for the present and the future the faculties of intellect and will, the highest and the specifically human powers, man makes the noblest of human sacrifices, the greatest possible for him, and the one most acceptable to God. "Obedience is better than sacrifice," [7] the Holy Spirit teaches us, comparing the oblation that obedience imposes with the bloody immolations of the victims of the Old Law.

4. By the prophet Malachias, God also said:

> I have no pleasure in you, saith the Lord of hosts: and I will not receive a gift of your hand. For from the rising of the sun even to the going down, my name is great among the Gentiles: and in every place there is sacrifice and there is offered to my name a clean oblation. For my name is great among the Gentiles, saith the Lord of hosts.[8]

God thus testified to His eagerness to see the figures finally give way before the reality. The reality is the oblation of Christ. This oblation, which gave all their value to the figurative sacrifices under the Old Law, can alone, under the New Law, give full meaning to the gift of self as made by the Christian.

On coming into this world, the sacred humanity of Christ saw at once, because of His intuitive vision of God, all the divine riches that were His. He knew the admirable perfections of His human nature, formed by the Holy Spirit in the womb of the Virgin; the overflowing life of each one of His faculties and the harmonious balance of that human complex, comparable to no other. Christ also saw directly, face to face, the divine nature dwelling within Him, anointing Him with the oil of its gladness and strength and, while making Him meek and humble of heart, transporting Him to the summits of holiness and beatitude. He had vision too of that hypostatic union by which His sacred humanity subsists indissolubly in the Second Person of the Blessed Trinity. In the same light He discovered God's plan for Him: by the sacrifice of Calvary, He was called to unite all that sin had divided, and He was to be an inexhaustible source of grace for regenerated humanity. These

[7] I Kings 15:22.
[8] Mal. 1:10-11.

riches and this incomparable mission, which were revealed to
the first glance of Christ, were given to His humanity entirely
gratuitously, without any antecedent merit, since an instant
previous it did not exist and it never existed until assumed by
the Word. What was to be the first movement of His soul under the sweet and beatifying burden of the divine light and
unction? The psalmist has noted it, and the apostle Saint Paul
has underlined it in the Epistle to the Hebrews, in order to
mark its importance:

> In coming into the world, he says,
>> Sacrifice and oblation thou wouldst not,
>>> but a body thou hast fitted to me:
>> In holocausts and sin-offerings thou hast
>> had no pleasure.
>> Then said I, "Behold I come—
>>> (in the head of the book it is written
>>> of me)—
>> to do thy will, O God.[9]

Christ, in this first act of His humanity, offers Himself as an
oblation to His Father. The complete gift of Himself is a loving adherence to the Word and to the design of God who
created Him for sacrifice. By this oblation, the sacrifice of
Calvary begins; from then on, Jesus is priest and victim, and
the Redemption is taking place.

This oblation is not an isolated act; it is a deeply rooted
disposition of the soul of Christ, as constant as His bond with
the Word and as actual as His union with the divine will
which regulates all He does. In this continual offering of Himself, Jesus finds His nourishment, as He tells the apostles who
besought Him to eat after His conversation with the Samaritan
woman: "I have food to eat of which you do not know. . . .
My food is to do the will of him who sent me, to accomplish
his work." [10] The humanity of Christ subsists in the Person of
the Word; if it were separated by a sin, it would fall into nothing. But no, that is not possible: the union is indissoluble and

[9] Heb. 10:5-7.
[10] John 4:31-4.

consequently the impeccability of Christ is absolute. But since the sacred humanity subsists in the Word, it is in the Word that it finds its life; and the human will of Christ lives spiritually by its adherence to the divine will.

The offering is sincere and complete; the realization of the will of God is perfect. Jesus lets Himself be directed by the divine will. He goes of Himself where it leads Him, here and there, at the time and according to the manner fixed by it, into the desert, to Thabor, to the Supper Room, to Gethsemane, and to Calvary; not one iota was to be omitted of its decrees. His work finished, He Himself wants to ascertain that it is truly so. From the height of the cross, He lets His gaze rest on the long roll of divine decrees in which God, by the hand of the prophets, fixed the detail of the events in the life of His Christ. Yes, everything has been done. Jesus is certain of this and has it recorded:

Therefore, when Jesus had taken the wine, he said, "It is consummated!" And bowing his head, he gave up his spirit.[11]

The whole life of Christ is enclosed between two glances at the book of God's decrees concerning Him. Between the silent oblation at the beginning that the piercing gaze of the prophet foresaw, and the consummation at the end related by the evangelist, there is place only for a continual offering and complete gift of Himself to the will of God.

The gift of self, which makes perfect the obedience of Jesus Christ, also achieves our redemption and becomes the principle of His glory. The apostle stresses this:

He humbled himself, becoming obedient to death, even to death on a cross. Therefore God also has exalted him and has bestowed upon him the name that is above every name, so that at the name of Jesus every knee should bend of those in heaven, on earth and under the earth.[12]

[11] John 19:30.
[12] Phil. 2:8-10.

We must place our gift of self in the light of the oblation of Christ to understand its necessity and fecundity. What we have said up to the present, are only scattered truths which are brought into harmony under that light and find in it a new cogency.

An essential disposition of Christ, the complete gift of self is an essential disposition of every Christian. It identifies one profoundly with Christ; without it, any imitation of Him could not but be superficial, and perhaps empty external formalism. In order to belong to Christ, one must surrender to Him as He surrendered to God, for we are Christ's and Christ is God's.

Christ's offering of Himself to God is His response to the Word who assumed His humanity. It is vital for Him and assures Him His spiritual sustenance. The gift we make of ourselves surrenders us to the grace of Christ which is in us; it is a call to be more completely possessed by Christ. In Christ, the oblation is a loving adherence to the mystery of the Incarnation, already realized; in us, the gift of self incites the divine Mercy to new donations of His grace. Mercy cannot but respond, for Mercy is Love stooping down irresistibly to our suppliant poverty.

Christ's oblation delivers Him up to the divine will and especially to the sacrifice of Calvary. Identified with Christ through the inflowing of His grace, the soul, ever renewing its oblation, truly becomes for Him an additional humanity in which He can extend the realization of His mysteries. Thus the soul is continually present on the altar as the material for sacrifice, as an instrument of redemption for souls. The gift of self that unites it with Christ causes it to enter into the states of Christ and to participate intimately in His mysteries, introducing it into the very depths of the mystery of the Redemption and of the Church.

Just as the fruitfulness of Christ's whole mission stemmed from His oblation on the cross, so do the fruits of His grace in the soul derive from this complete surrender of self, which is the chief part of the soul's co-operation with grace.

In the *Way of Perfection,* Saint Teresa lays stress on the effects of union and identification brought about by the total gift of self:

> The more resolute we are in soul and the more we show Him by our actions that the words we use to Him are not words of mere politeness, the more and more does Our Lord draw us to Himself and raise us above all petty earthly things, and above ourselves, in order to prepare us to receive great favours from Him, for His rewards for our service will not end with this life. So much does He value this service of ours that we do not know for what more we can ask, while His Majesty never wearies of giving. . . .
> He begins to make such a friend of the soul that not only does He restore its will to it but He gives it His own also. For, now that He is making a friend of it, He is glad to allow it to rule with Him, as we say, turn and turn about.[13]

But, declares Saint Teresa:

> So niggardly and so slow are we in giving ourselves wholly to God that we do not prepare ourselves as we should to receive that precious thing. . . .[14]
> So, being unable to make a full surrender of ourselves, we are never given a full supply of this treasure.[15]

## B. Qualities of the gift of self

### 1. ABSOLUTE

That our gift of self may obtain such high favors, Saint Teresa requires only that it be absolutely complete. Such a gift is a veritable renunciation of self in favor of God. The renunciation will be felt very painfully on one or another point, according to the attachments of the soul, but it must be complete. The young man in the Gospel, to whom Jesus presents the ways of perfection, saying: "Sell your goods, give them to the poor and follow me," is stopped by the prospect of parting with his goods, for he was rich. The sale of all that

[13] *Way of Perfection,* xxxii; Peers, II, 138-9.
[14] *Life,* xi; Peers, I, 63.
[15] *Ibid.;* 64.

he had was only the first act—probably the most painful and most significant—but the first in a drama that was to lead him to the complete abandonment of himself to Christ, expressed in "follow me."

Religious profession, in its essential aspect as a radical and solemn consecration made to God, can be compared with the gift of self. Both include the same complete renunciation of self and absolute surrender into the hands of God of all that one is and has, for the present and the future. Profession takes its value especially from the plenitude of the gift of self that animates it. Nevertheless, to the complete gift of self it adds that character of solemnity that makes of it an exterior act inspired by the virtue of religion, and places the religious in a state apart, in the Church. On the other hand, the gift of self made independently of external forms does not determine it towards any of them. Inspired uniquely by charity, supple and fervent, broad and simple, it leads each soul to the perfect realization of its particular vocation and opens it to the plenitude of its special grace.

Again we must place the gift of self in the perspective of the oblation of Christ, to see what the word absolute means. United to the divinity by the hypostatic union, the human nature of Christ subsisted in the Person of the Word. The acts elicited by it were attributed to the Person of the Word who made them His own. It was thus completely despoiled, since its whole existence and all its operations belonged to the Second Person of the Blessed Trinity. The first consequence of Christ's oblation was His assent to that complete possession of His human nature by His divine personality, its entire self-renunciation.

We cannot think of realizing by the gift of ourselves a renouncement of our person; that would be to dream of a hypostatic union for ourselves, or of some sort of pantheism. But, that reservation made, our union with God—and consequently, the gift of self on which it is founded—involves no other limits.

This union is effected through grace, a participation in the divine nature; and the model that is set before it is the union of the Father and the Son in a single nature. Hence the gift of self must tend to unity with Jesus Christ, and must accept all the exigencies of such a union.

What these demands are, is made manifest to us in a concrete way in the life of Christ from Bethlehem's crib to Calvary, with its continual subjection to the Spirit of God and the immolation on the cross that terminates it. It is to all that, that God's conquest of us leads, and the complete gift of self, in anyone who accepts it.

Among the possible realizations and the immolations, God will make a choice for each one of us, for we are not of the stature of Christ; and God, who shares with us the graces of Christ, divides also the immolations that accompany them. What part will be ours? We do not know. This ignorance along with the certitude that our participation in the sacrifice of Christ will be only partial, is the occasion for some illusions. It seems to authorize us to envisage only a part of the sacrifice, and perhaps to choose it. To escape this illusion and everything that would render our self-sacrifice less absolute, there is just one remedy: to habituate ourselves to make whatever sacrifice comes our way.

### 2. INDETERMINATE

In reality, the aspect of indetermination is not a new quality of the gift of self; its purpose is uniquely to protect the plenitude of the gift against all reservations more or less conscious. It seems that even among the most generous, the souls are actually rare whose gift of self is not limited by precise determinations. God even seems to favor these determinations in the beginning of the spiritual life. He attracts us to Him and to self-surrender by enticing perspectives, or by particular lights that harmonize well with our natural tastes or our grace. A particular boy for instance sees in the priesthood only its preaching; another, the Holy Mass. Again, some of us enter the religious life simply with the idea of saving our soul. But once we have entered deeply into the spiritual life, we discover its marvelous splendor and the demands it makes for perfection. And yet we continue to set bounds; generally these are established on another spiritual plane, and obey new ideas and tastes which have arisen.

Notions and tastes as to what sanctity is are as varied as individuals. Generous souls will attach great importance to suffering, often undertaking penances of their own choice, sometimes indiscreet ones, as every spiritual director knows from experience. Or the soul plans its own spiritual life, its daily itinerary, detailing all its sacrifices which the imagination multiplies enormously. The soul itself is at the center of this dream-construction which envisages God standing by as a kind Father whose role it is in His fatherly goodness to help the soul realize this particular form of perfection that it has chosen for itself, and the special kind of apostolate that it fancies.

Handsome constructions whose irremediable vice is to have been made by the hand of man and outside the divine plan! To consecrate one's energies to such realizations is usually to depart from the will of God.

Meanwhile, God's real designs in our regard declare themselves, upsetting our own preconceived ones. The result, at least momentarily, is discouragement and disillusionment, unless we begin to reconstruct at once in our own fashion. And perhaps God will permit us to work things out as we foresaw, and to enjoy a success which might even appear brilliant, but which is always only mediocre because superficial and human under a supernatural veneer. Our generosity was spent for ourself and our own projects; it missed the plan of God because it did not make an undetermined gift.

It is truly in the dark that one must look for the design of God; for His thoughts are above human thoughts as heaven, earth. Our God dwells in darkness; the transcendent light of

His Wisdom blinds our poor eyes. What is our part, what is our place in His divine plan? He alone knows. The part that we must do, the place that we are to fill, in these is our perfection. The gift of self—which is meant to be made in view of the part and the place reserved to us in the divine work and edifice—must seek them in mystery and surrender to that mystery which hides and guards them jealously, awaiting the hour for realization. Thus the gift of self must be indeterminate in order not to go astray in purely human projects, but to be at one with the divine reality and truth.

It might be thought that this indetermination, by calming the constructive activities and withdrawing every precise, immediate object from the will, diminishes one's energies for willing and acting. Nothing of the kind. Such a gift, with no fixed reservations, is not an attempt at communion with the void, but an effective means to the fulfillment of the divine volitions which are certain but unknown to us at the moment. It entails a renunciation of all personal projects, and thus reserves all the energies of the soul for the accomplishment of those duties and tasks which Providence each day assigns us. Those of the future remain hidden in mystery. Hence the indeterminate gift of self, far from diminishing one's forces, prevents their dispersion, and applies their full strength to the doing of the present will of God. The holy indifference which is its fruit frees the soul from those bitter disappointments that paralyze it for a moment and sometimes break one's spirit definitively.

Finally, a positive, incomparable benefit is derived from this unlimited gift, become habitual. It surrenders the soul to the action of the Holy Spirit. In the darkness of faith where it holds the soul, it keeps it alert to the least manifestation of the divine will. It refines its spiritual senses, making them delicately attuned to the sweet anointings of the Holy Spirit and the most subtle of His motions; it sustains and develops the suppleness of the soul, keeping it apt at every instant for any good work. Thus the soul becomes attentive to God's voice and docile; and these dispositions make the best instruments of the Holy Spirit.[16]

### 3. OFTEN RENEWED

For the gift of self to produce all the effects we have indicated, it must be not just a transitory act, but a constant disposition of soul. This it can become only on the condition of being frequently renewed.

The offering of oneself must rise up without ceasing from the soul as the most perfect expression of its love, and as a continual challenge to the divine Mercy. By it, the soul breathes love in and yearns for it still further; it is purified and united to its God. But the soul is ever taking back something of what it gave, and can only repair this failure by offering itself anew.

Besides, as events take place and interior lights increase, new horizons open up to the gift of self, revealing other forms for practical activity. Hence it must be renewed often and even constantly if it would be ready for new demands.

By such renewals, the soul creates within itself what we might call a psychological disposition of self-giving, a disposition which acts like a reflex. Let anything whatsoever happen that touches that soul, be it with sorrow or with joy, and it renews this gift at once under the impulse of the apparently unconscious yet voluntary reflex. The powers of the soul that are

---

[16] When faced with the mystery of the divine exigencies to which the complete gift abandons us, there are souls who are not only timorous, but frightened. They recoil from the darkness and all it holds that is terrifying. What is there in that mystery where the tempest rumbles, of which the Passion of Christ gives us a picture? In truth, in that darkness there will be suffering—a share in the Passion of Christ in some form—there will be death. But let them be reassured: by casting oneself into that darkness by the gift of self, one falls necessarily into the arms of divine Mercy. The Mercy that is God receives the soul, bathing it in His peace and His strength. "The chalice is full to the brim," Saint Therese of the Child Jesus will say," but I am in an astonishing peace. . . . I would not want to suffer less. . . . I do not regret having been a victim of Love."

Such is the testimony of all the saints, testimony which ought to dispel the cloud of terrors that the devil stirs up before an act of capital importance in the spiritual life.

painfully affected will perhaps protest at times against the offering; the soul has the impression that the more turbulent powers will not acquiesce. What matter! The gift is made; it is maintained by the will; the soul has spoken its love, and the gift attains to God. By the bond that is established, grace will descend, efficacious certainly and progressively tranquilizing. Without this habitual disposition of self-giving, the soul might have to await the complete pacification of its unruly powers before it could make the perfect surrender of itself to the will of God.

All these truths are difficult to express because they are supernatural, of delicate perception, and profound. A glance at the Virgin Mary on the day of the Annunciation will help us more effectively to discover them than will the best-directed analyses.

The Virgin Mary, filled with grace as she was by the Holy Spirit and lost in the simple light of God, had all her energies peacefully intent on the realization of the divine will. The archangel Gabriel appears and salutes her. The Virgin is for an instant troubled by his presence and his praise. She listens to the message: "Thou shalt conceive in thy womb and shalt bring forth a son; and thou shalt call his name Jesus. He shall be great, and shall be called the Son of the Most High; and the Lord God will give him the throne of David his father, and he shall be king over the house of Jacob forever; and of his kingdom there shall be no end." Mary has understood; the angel is indeed asking her to become the mother of the Messias. She had never dreamt of this, for she had never thought of self. The simplicity of her grace veiled from her its immensity. She knew only God and His will. Facing the perspectives that were opening suddenly before her, she has only one question, for she is concerned for her virginity: "How shall this happen, since I do not know man?" Reassured by the angel who answers: "The Holy Spirit shall come upon thee and the power of the Most High shall overshadow thee," the Virgin

Mary, without hesitation, without asking for several days to think about it and consult, nor even a few minutes to prepare herself, gives—for herself and all humanity—her consent to the most sublime and most terrifying of contracts: to the union in her virginal womb of humanity and divinity, to Calvary, and to the mystery of the Church. And the Word was made flesh at the *Fiat* of the Virgin, whom a disposition of complete and undetermined offering had long since prepared in her supple and docile soul.

In our souls also, the gift of self invites the divine visitations and prepares us for the same fruitful *Fiat*. Saint Teresa writes:

Oh, my sisters, what power this gift has! If it be made with due resolution, it cannot fail to draw the Almighty to become one with our lowliness and to transform us into Himself and to effect a union between the Creator and the creature.[17]

It must enter into our whole life, take possession of our soul, creating in it an abiding disposition, keeping us ever in an attitude of profound humility.

[17] *Way of Perfection,* xxxii; Peers, II, 138.

# CHAPTER IV
# Humility

*But in the sight of Infinite Wisdom,
believe me, there is more value in a
little study of humility and in a single
act of it than in all the knowledge in
the world.*[1]

Beginning with the First Mansions, Saint Teresa continuously speaks of the necessity of self-knowledge in order to advance in the spiritual life. We summarized her teaching on this in one of the first chapters.[2] But knowledge of what we are before God and of our evil tendencies, even though exact, is not enough. It must pass over into our life and into our soul, creating a disposition and an attitude, a bearing of the soul in all its spiritual life. Only by being transformed into humility can knowledge of self acquire its whole efficacy.

Saint Teresa never wearies of proclaiming the necessity of the virtue of humility. When she finds it in a soul, she is reassured—whatever be the form of prayer that accompanies it. If she does not find it, she is anxious about the soul, even though it have the most brilliant natural and supernatural gifts; for, she says, speaking of pride and vainglory: "there is no poison in the world which is so fatal to perfection." [3]

But in this stage of the spiritual life, humility is particularly necessary. Because they lack it, many souls in the third Mansions do not progress farther. Here, Saint Teresa says:

[1] *Life,* xv; Peers, I, 92.
[2] Cf. PERSPECTIVES, iii, "Knowledge of Self," p. 33.
[3] *Way of Perfection,* xii; Peers, II, 52.

What the journey which I am referring to demands is great humility, and it is the lack of this, I think, if you see what I mean, which prevents us from making progress.[4]

And again, at the threshold of the fourth Mansions:

As well as acting, then, as do those who have dwelt in the Mansions already described, have humility and again humility! It is by humility that the Lord allows Himself to be conquered so that He will do all we ask of Him.[5]

This insistence of the Saint indicates that we cannot make further progress without considering more thoroughly her teaching on humility. When convinced of its necessity, we shall see its degrees and the forms of pride to which it is opposed; and we shall say a word as to the means of acquiring it.

## A. Necessity of humility

The soul in these Mansions must dispose itself for the inflowing of loving Wisdom. If the gift of self calls to that Wisdom, humility it is that attracts her irresistibly. The conduct of our Lord in the Gospel gives evidence of this in an illuminating way.

If we follow Jesus in His public life, we cannot fail to notice the wise discretion that He observes in manifesting the nature of His mission and His doctrine. He ordinarily uses parables; and although their symbolism was certainly more clear to the Oriental mind than it is to ours, yet He left so many obscurities that the apostles usually asked in private for a detailed explanation.

One day when He was walking along with His apostles in Caesarea Philippi, Jesus asked them: "Who do men say that I am?" And they answered Him: "Some say John the Baptist; and others, Elias; and others, one of the prophets." "But you," He said, "who do you say that I am?" Peter answered: "Thou art the Christ, the Son of the living God." Jesus said to him:

[4] III Mansions, ii; Peers, II, 226.
[5] IV Mansions, ii; 239.

"Blessed are thou, Simon Bar-Jona, for flesh and blood has not revealed this to thee, but my Father in heaven. . . ." And then He charged His disciples not to tell anyone that He was the Christ.[6] This scene shows us that Jesus had not as yet fully revealed to His apostles His messianic mission; and that, even in this second year of His preaching, He did not want it to be publicly disclosed.

The multitude, moreover, tried to fathom the mystery that surrounded the origin of Jesus and His mission. Saint John lets us hear an echo of their excited discussions at the time of the Feast of the Tabernacles, the last year of our Saviour's public life. On one occasion: "Some of the crowd, when they had heard these words of his, were saying: 'This is truly the Prophet.' Others were saying, 'This is the Christ.' Some, however, were saying, 'Can the Christ come from Galilee? Does not the Scripture say that it is of the offspring of David, and from Bethlehem, the village where David lived, that the Christ is to come?' So there arose a division among the crowd because of Him." [7] Jesus did not dispel their doubts.

During the intimate conversation after the Last Supper, the apostles finally declared with joy: "Behold, now thou speakest plainly, and utterest no parable. Now we know that thou knowest all things, and dost not need that anyone should question thee. For this reason we believe that thou camest forth from God." [8]

Yet, while Jesus left some of His own followers in darkness concerning the most important truths about Himself, we find Him in the first year of His public life, revealing His secrets to certain souls who seem to force them from Him. We refer here to Nicodemus and the Samaritan woman. Let us consider these two episodes narrated by Saint John in the first chapters of his Gospel.[9]

[6] Matt. 16:13-20; Mark 8:27-30.
[7] John 7:40-3.
[8] John 16:29-30.
[9] John 3:1-21; 4:1-30.

Nicodemus is a doctor of the law; he belongs to the religious and social aristocracy of Jerusalem. Like many of his colleagues, he had listened favorably to Jesus at the time of His first journey to Jerusalem. Now, however, he must be specially troubled and moved, for he decides—he, a doctor of the law—to find Jesus and put questions to Him, although He was an unlettered man. He decides to go at night. The overture is timid, but not without merit, if one considers the position and character of Nicodemus.

A dialogue ensues: "Rabbi, we know that thou hast come a teacher from God, for no one can work these signs that thou workest unless God be with him." Jesus answers: "Amen, amen, I say to thee, unless a man be born again, he cannot see the kingdom of God." Jesus seems thus to anticipate the questions of Nicodemus. The doctor does not understand: "How can a man be born when he is old? Can he enter a second time into his mother's womb and be born again?" Jesus replies: "Amen, amen, I say to thee, unless a man be born again of water and the Spirit, he cannot enter into the kingdom of God. That which is born of the flesh is flesh; and that which is born of the Spirit is spirit. Do not wonder that I said to thee, 'You must be born again.' The wind blows where it will, and thou hearest its sound but dost not know where it comes from or where it goes. So is everyone who is born of the Spirit."

The language is elevated, worthy of such a speaker. Nicodemus understands it less and less: "How can these things be?" Jesus questions him: "Thou art a teacher in Israel and dost not know these things?" The thrust is direct, almost hard, dealt by an unlettered man at a doctor of the law. Nicodemus accepts it without protest. He listens now and understands. The humiliation has opened his mind, and through that salutary wound, Jesus pours floods of light: "No one has ascended into heaven except him who has descended from heaven: the Son of Man who is in heaven. And as Moses lifted up the serpent in the desert, even so must the Son of Man be lifted up, that those who believe in him may not perish, but may have life ever-lasting."

The mystery of the Incarnation and of the Redemption are revealed to Nicodemus in the first months of Jesus' preaching, when all the others are in ignorance of those mysteries. And Nicodemus understood. He will remember this and, on the day when the tremendous drama of Calvary takes place, when the apostles have fled from the mystery of the Cross, he will valiantly come out of the shadows, bringing "a hundred pounds of a mixture of myrrh and aloes," and will join Joseph of Arimathea to render the last duties to the Divine Crucified.

Several days later, Jesus leaves Jerusalem. In order to return to Galilee, he takes the direct route through Samaria. After long hours of walking, He comes about noon to Jacob's well, near the town of Sichar. While the disciples are away in the near-by town getting provisions, a Samaritan woman comes to get water. Jesus asks for a drink. She shows surprise, for she sees in this stranger, a Jew. How dare he, a Jew, ask such a service of a Samaritan; he a man, address thus a woman? Is it possible that he does not know of the implacable hatred that divides Jews and Samaritans? Should he not deem himself fortunate that they leave him in peace? With haughtiness and almost hatred, she answers: "How is it that thou, although thou art a Jew, dost ask drink of me, who am a Samaritan woman?" Jesus does not evince annoyance at this tone and attitude: "If thou didst know the gift of God, and who it is who says to thee, 'Give me to drink,' thou, perhaps, wouldst have asked of him, and he would have given thee living water." The woman banters now, perhaps a little embarrassed: "Whence then hast thou living water? Art thou greater than our father Jacob who gave us the well?" Jesus speaks more precisely: "Everyone who drinks of this water will thirst again. He, however, who drinks of the water that I will give him shall never thirst." This description arouses a desire that is now respectfully expressed: "Sir, give me this water that I may not thirst!"

The Samaritan woman has not yet understood. Besides, she is not ready to receive the marvelous gift that the Master is offering her. The conversation continues: "Go, call thy husband and come here." "I have no husband," she answers. Jesus says: "Thou has said well, 'I have no husband,' for thou hast had five husbands, and he whom thou now hast is not thy husband. In this thou hast spoken truly."

Under the shock of this humiliating revelation, the woman changes her attitude. She was haughty and almost insulting; now she is respectful, humble, submissive. Through the wound and humiliation accepted, light has already entered into her soul: "Sir, I see that thou art a prophet."

The gaping wound opens to receive the healing light. And Jesus is going to give it abundantly. Salvation is from the Jews, not from Samaria, He says. But let this woman be consoled: "The hour is coming, and is now here, when the true worshippers will worship the Father in spirit and in truth." Thus He announces His Church. The Samaritan woman, insatiable, responds: "I know that the Messias is coming, who is called Christ, and when he comes he will tell us all things." And Jesus says to her: "I who speak with thee am he."

In her joy, which makes her forget her water-jar, the woman hurries away to tell her people the good news, and "many of the Samaritans of that town believed in him because of the word of the woman who bore witness." The floods of living water that had been poured into her soul through the deep wound of humiliation, had become at once, according to the promise of the Master, "a fountain of water, springing up into life everlasting."

With these episodes from the Gospel, let us connect the conversion of the apostle, Saint Paul, related in the ninth chapter of the Acts of the Apostles. "But Saul, still breathing threats of slaughter against the disciples of the Lord, went to the high priest and asked him for letters to the synagogues at Damascus, that if he found any men or women belonging to this Way, he

might bring them in bonds to Jerusalem." [10] He obtains the
letters. The young Pharisee, happy and proud of the mission
that has been entrusted to him, leaves for Damascus at the head
of an escort. Of what is he dreaming? Hatred and ambition,
without a doubt.

But now he is thrown to the ground: "Saul, Saul, why dost
thou persecute me?" he hears. And he answers: "Who art thou,
Lord?"—"I am Jesus, whom thou art persecuting. Arise and go
into the city, and it will be told thee what thou must do." [11] Saul
gets up, blind, his garments dusty. And in this unkempt condition, he enters the city, on the arm of one of his companions.
For three days he can not see, he can not eat or drink. Helplessness, solitude, humiliation: this is what Paul finds at
Damascus where he had thought to come, in the brilliant flash
of a mission for the high priest, to bring terror to Christ's
faithful followers whom he so proudly hated.

At the end of three days, Ananias comes to find him in the
house of Judas where he had taken refuge. Ananias lays his
hands on Saul; "and straightway there fell from his eyes something like scales, and he recovered his sight, and arose, and
was baptized. And after taking some food, he regained his
strength." [11]

Thus it was that by the low door of humiliation, Paul, the
great apostle, entered into Christianity and into the light of the
marvelous mystery of which he was to be the preacher and the
minister.

These traits have not just simply an episodic value. They
place us in the presence of a law of the diffusion of the divine
light and mercy, a law which Jesus Himself formulates one
day in a prayer of thanksgiving. It was when the seventy-two
disciples who had been sent to preach, returning with great
joy, said: "Lord, even the devils are subject to us in thy
name." Jesus rejoiced in the Holy Spirit and said: "I praise

[10] Acts 9:1-2.
[11] Acts 9:4-7; 18-19.

thee, Father, Lord of heaven and earth, that thou didst hide these things from the wise and prudent, and didst reveal them to little ones. Yes, Father, for such was thy good pleasure." [12] God gives His treasures to the humble, but hides them from the proud and self-sufficient.

This is the law that guides Jesus as He goes about doing good. There is no sin that He does not meet with, and in circumstances that could have been dangerous for anyone else. He stops at the home of Zachias, the publican, at Jericho. He defends Mary, the sinner; Mary who pours out perfume on His sacred head, anoints His feet and wipes them with her hair. But there is one relationship into which Jesus does not enter and against which he revolts, indignant; He will have no part with the pride of the Pharisees, and He condemns it with strong reproaches.[13]

Jesus Christ continues His action in the Church according to the same law. All the masters of the spiritual life assert this, and most specially those who have experienced the overflowing abundance of His grace. Saint Teresa says:

I do not remember that He has ever granted me any of the outstanding favours of which I shall speak later save when I have been consumed with shame by realizing my own wickedness.[14]

Saint Angela of Foligno writes:

The more the soul is afflicted, stripped, and deeply humiliated, the more it acquires, with purity, an aptitude for the heights. The elevation of which it becomes capable is measured by the depth of the abyss in which it has its roots and foundations.[15]

The same ardent note marks the testimony of Ruysbroeck:

When man, his eyes burnt with love, considers in the depth of his soul the immensity of God . . . then turning his gaze upon himself, counts his crimes against the great and faithful Lord . . . there is no self-scorn profound enough to satisfy him. . . . He falls into a strange

[12] Luke 10:17-21.
[13] Matt. 23:13-28.
[14] *Life*, xxii; Peers, II, 141.
[15] Cf. *Sainte Angèle de Foligno;* French translation by Hello, ch. xix.

astonishment, the astonishment of not being able to despise himself enough. . . . He resigns himself then to the will of God . . . and, in this intimate abnegation, he finds true peace, invincible and perfect, a peace that nothing will trouble. For he has been precipitated into such an abyss that no one will go there to seek him. . . . Yet, it seems to me that to be plunged in humility, is to be plunged in God, for God is the bottom of the abyss, above everything and beneath everything, supreme in height and supreme in depth; that is why humility, like charity, is capable of continually increasing. . . . Humility is so precious that it obtains the things that are too high to be taught; it attains and possesses what words do not attain.[16]

Ruysbroeck remarks also that humility does not necessarily have its source in sin:

Our sins . . . have become for us sources of humility and of love. But it is important to be mindful of a source of humility much higher than this. The Virgin Mary, conceived without sin, has a humility more sublime than the Magdalen's. The latter was pardoned; the former was without spot. But that absolute immunity, more sublime than any pardon, causes a higher thanksgiving to mount from earth to heaven than does the conversion of Mary Magdalen.[17]

Saint Therese of the Child Jesus counts on this attractiveness of humility and of poverty to make the divine mercy descend to her soul. The love of poverty becomes the fundamental quality of her way of spiritual childhood. In a letter to her sister Marie he writes:

O my dearest Sister, please understand your little sister, understand that to love Jesus, to be His victim of love, the weaker one is, without desires or virtues, the more apt one is for the operations of that consuming and transforming Love. The desire to be a victim is enough of itself, but one must consent to stay always poor and without strength, and that's the difficulty, for where are we to find the man truly poor in spirit? He must be sought afar, says the psalmist.[18]

And again to her sister Céline:

[16] Cf. Ruysbroeck, French translation by Hello, Bk. III, "L'Humilité."
[17] Cf. Ruysbroeck, *ibid.*
[18] Letter to Marie, Sept. 17, 1896; *Collected Letters,* p. 289.

The poorer you are, the more Jesus will love you.[19]
There you have Jesus' character: as God He gives, but He requires humbleness of heart.[20]

Saint Therese interpreted in this way her experiences. She felt that it was her littleness that attracted the graces God had bestowed upon her so abundantly. An episode of seemingly small importance at the end of her life was to show this with special clearness. The Saint was in her cell, suffering from fever. A religious who to her represented justice came in with Mother Agnes, who stood for the sweetness of mercy, to ask her to do a difficult piece of painting. Saint Therese of the Child Jesus could not control a slight gesture of impatience. The two religious excused themselves and left, understanding her fatigue. That first involuntary movement, provoked by the fever, was deeply humiliating to the Saint. In the evening she wrote Mother Agnes a letter, saying:

Your little girl has just been shedding more tears; tears of repentance, but even more of gratitude and love. Ah! this evening, I showed my virtue, my TREASURES of *patience!* And I, who am so good at preaching to others!!! I am glad you saw my imperfection. . . . Little Mother, you will realize that this evening the vessel of divine mercy has overflowed for me! Ah! from this moment I realize that all my hopes will indeed be fulfilled . . . the Lord will do marvels for us, infinitely beyond our *immeasurable desires!* [21]

The light that shone out from that humiliation pierced the dark veil that was over the future and disclosed to Saint Therese the extent of the mission that would be hers.

The irresistible attractiveness of humility allows us to establish a certain equivalence between humility and the gift of God to a soul, that is, its perfection. "To know the all-ness of God and the nothing-ness of man," proclaims Saint Angela of Foligno, "that is perfection."

Saint John of the Cross affirms in all his teaching that the

---

[19] Letter to Céline, March 12, 1889; *Autobiography,* p. 268.
[20] Letter to Céline, April 26, 1894. *Collected Letters,* p. 225.
[21] Letter to Mother Agnes of Jesus, May 28, 1897. *Ibid.,* p. 336.

"nothing," a complete realization of poverty, equates with obtaining the "all" which is God.

In naive language, an Arabian Carmelite, Sister Marie of Jesus Crucified, whose soul remained simple and candid in the midst of marvelous experiences and the most extraordinary graces, said:

> Without humility we are blind, in darkness; while with humility, the soul walks in the night as in the day. The proud man is like a grain of wheat thrown into water: it swells up, it gets big. Expose this grain to the sun: it dries out, it is burnt up. The humble man is like a grain buried in the earth: it goes down, it is hidden, it disappears, it dies, but in order to live again.
>
> Imitate the bees—she said—gather everywhere the essence of humility. Honey is sweet; humility has the taste of God; it makes one taste God.[22]

Humility is attractive to God! Everywhere that it is found, there God is. And everywhere that God is here below, He clothes Himself, as it were, with a garment that conceals His Presence from the proud and reveals it to the simple and the little ones. When Jesus came to this world, it was as an infant wrapped in swaddling clothes. That was the sign given to the shepherds: "And this shall be a sign to you," the angel said, "you will find an infant wrapped in swaddling clothes and lying in a manger." [23] The sign of humility always marks the Divine here below.

Any commentary would only dim the light of our Lord's own example and teaching with regard to the necessity of humility. Likewise, there is scarcely need to draw conclusions. When the spiritual person has come to this point where the virtues of themselves cannot operate perfectly in their own domain, and where his soul can make no further progress unless under the impulse of the Holy Spirit, it is clear that he can obtain this help only by humility. He will offer himself to the warmth of the divine light only through humiliations,

[22] Cf. R. P. Buzy, *Vie de Soeur Marie de Jésus-Crucifié.*
[23] Luke 2:12.

counsels Pascal. He will be taken captive and transformed by
God only if he is humble; and the divine action will ordinarily be according to the measure of his humility. *Sapientiam
praestans parvulis:* God gives His wisdom to the little ones.
Humility will become his spiritual means of subsistence. Such
is the law under which every soul lives. It will progress only
by submitting to it. "Height and depth bring forth one another," declares Saint Angela of Foligno. And Saint Teresa:
"In the sight of Infinite Wisdom, believe me, there is more
value in a little study of humility and in a single act of it than
in all the knowledge in the world." [24]

God cannot resist humility. He loves it so much that in
His eyes it can supply for all the rest, because it effectively
wins all the gifts of God.

## B. Degrees and forms of humility

Progress in humility and the development of grace are so
closely related that Saint Benedict, in his "ladder of perfection,"
distinguishes twelve degrees of humility corresponding to
twelve degrees of the spiritual life. However interesting and
justified the distinction may be, we shall not adopt it, because
we find that on the practical plane of the moral life it is very
difficult to distinguish these twelve degrees and the passage
from one to the other.

It seems preferable to distinguish the degrees of humility in
a more general way, according to the light that falls upon it;
and its different forms according to the forms of pride to
which it is opposed.

In explaining why the virtue of humility is so singularly attractive to God, Saint Teresa gives an enlightening definition:

I was wondering once why Our Lord so dearly loved this virtue of
humility; and all of a sudden—without, I believe, my having previously thought of it—the following reason came into my mind: that
it is because God is Sovereign Truth and to be humble is to walk in

[24] *Life,* xv; Peers, I, 92.

truth, for it is absolutely true to say that we have no good thing in ourselves, but only misery and nothingness; and anyone who fails to understand this is walking in falsehood. He who best understands this is most pleasing to Sovereign Truth because he is walking in truth.[25]

As an attitude of truth before God, humility will consequently be in close dependence on the light that illumines it. The venerable Jean de Saint Samson [26] emphasizes this point. Following Saint Bernard, he distinguishes, in the *True Spirit of Carmel,* two kinds of humility: one that he calls clear and reasonable; the other, fervent.

## 1. REASONABLE HUMILITY

Clear and reasonable humility is illumined by the light of reason and is grounded in a work of self-examination and of meditation on supernatural truths and examples from the life of our Lord. The soul, seeing its powerlessness to act rightly, its faults, its sin or again, the abasements and humiliations of Christ, understands the necessity of humiliating itself in order to live according to the truth that its intelligence discovers, and to imitate the divine Model.

## 2. FERVENT HUMILITY OPPOSED TO FORMS OF PRIDE

Fervent humility, "more infused than acquired," says Jean de Saint Samson, is produced in the soul by a ray of divine light which, revealing the transcendence of God, and giving light on the poverty of the soul or a mystery of Christ, thus shows the soul its place in the perspective of the Infinite or in comparison with Christ. Of this, Jean de Saint Samson says:

Reason here can do no more. A man thus rapt in the silence of eternity, outstripping his power of intellect, his intelligence and himself, fails totally to comprehend. He then sees how shortened and limited is all human power for understanding that infinite Immensity.

[25] VI Mansions, x; Peers, II, 323.
[26] Jean de Saint Samson (1571–1638), a lay brother at the Carmel of Dol and of Rennes, a musician and blind, "the brightest torch of the Reform of Touraine" and "a mystic of the highest flight," says Bremond.

Jean de Saint Samson calls reasonable humility "deception and untruth" as compared with fervent humility; he makes use of hyperbole and superlatives to supplement the poverty of the symbolic language that mystics generally employ and which is limited for him because of his physical blindness.

All the saints avow that the distance is vast between fervent humility and reasonable humility. The light that the first produces, because it comes directly from God through the gifts of the Holy Ghost, is incomparably more intense than the light of the second, which proceeds from the human intellect:

> When the Spirit of God is at work, there is no need to go about looking for ways of inducing humility and confusion; for the Lord Himself reveals these to us in a very different manner from any which we can find by means of our puny reflections, which are nothing by comparison with a true humility proceeding from the light given us in this way by the Lord. This produces a confusion which quite overwhelms us. The bestowal upon us of this knowledge by God so that we may learn that we ourselves have nothing good is a well-known experience, and the greater are the favours we receive from Him, the better we learn it.[27]

This intense light not only places in relief one's exterior faults; it casts light on the depths and, in a manner, the very being of the soul, thus disclosing its absolute littleness and poverty before the Infinite. Again, from Saint Teresa:

> It also sees clearly how extremely unworthy it is, for in a room bathed in sunlight not a cobweb can remain hidden. It sees its own wretchedness. So far is vainglory from it that it cannot believe it could ever be guilty of such a thing. For now it sees with its own eyes that of itself it can do little or nothing . . . Then its past life comes up before it and all the truth of God's great mercy is revealed. The understanding has no need to go out hunting; for its food is already prepared.[28]

"I am He who is," God said to Moses. And to Saint Catherine of Siena, our Lord also said: "Do you know, my daughter, who you are and who I am? You are she who is not. I am He who is."

[27] *Life*, xv; Peers, I, 95.
[28] *Ibid.*, xix; 112.

In all cases of fervent humility, the soul is more or less consciously aware of the Being of God who, with His majesty
and power, confronts the soul in darkness, discovering to it
what it really is.

And so that light, like the Word of God, produces what it
expresses. While in the case of reasonable humility, the conviction that is created in the mind still needs an act of the will
to express it in one's attitude and life, the light of fervent
humility is not only overpowering, but also efficacious. It
creates a profoundly intense feeling that pervades one's whole
being, a living experience of its littleness and misery, which
places the soul in the attitude of truth.

Such an experience and realization give value to fervent humility. Often painful at the same time as peaceful, the experience seems to have brought joy to Saint Therese of the Child
Jesus:

O Sun, my only Love, I am happy to feel myself so small, so frail
in Thy sunshine, and I am in peace.[29]
I can always make myself happy, and profit by my imperfections.[30]
I fall into many imperfections, but I rejoice in them . . . It is so
sweet to feel one-self weak and little.[31]

We never tire of listening to such sweet accents of love.
Perhaps there is no other saint in whom we could admire so
peaceful and so joyous a triumph of fervent humility. Moreover, Saint Therese of the Child Jesus considered it the great
grace of her life:

I prefer to own in all simplicity that *"He that is mighty hath done
great things to me"*—and the greatest is that He has shown me my
littleness and how incapable I am of anything good.[32]

Fervent humility was at the root of all her greatness:

Then, as I reflected that I was born for great things, and sought the
means to attain them, it was made known to me interiorly that my

[29] *Autobiography,* xi, 187.
[30] *Ibid.,* viii, 126.
[31] *Novissima Verba,* July 5.
[32] *Autobiography,* ix, 138.

personal glory would never reveal itself before the eyes of men, but that it would consist in becoming a Saint.

This aspiration may very well appear rash, seeing how imperfect I was, and am, even now, after so many years of religious life; yet I still feel the same daring confidence that one day I shall become a great Saint. I am not trusting in my own merits, for I have none; but I trust in Him Who is Virtue and Holiness itself. It is He alone Who, pleased with my feeble efforts, will raise me to Himself, and, by clothing me with His merits, make me a Saint.[33]

The same humility is also at the base of her whole doctrine of spiritual childhood "for the more one is weak, without desires and without virtues, the more one needs that consuming and transforming Love."

Fervent humility, a fruit of the action of the Holy Spirit, is the one that attracts His new outpourings of love. It is the virtue that brings the soul into the fourth Mansions, and makes it progress towards the summits of the spiritual life.

Having made the distinction between reasonable humility and fervent humility according to the nature of the light that produces them, we think it difficult to push the distinction farther by trying to evaluate the intensity of the light that produces each, and the perfection of the interior attitude that it creates; for both escape a precise analysis.

A clearer and more practical way to distinguish them seems to be to point out the diverse goods that serve to feed pride; and consequently, the diverse forms of pride that humility must successively fight. Under that aspect, we can consider humility as opposed to the pride that draws on external goods, to pride of will, pride of intellect, and to spiritual pride. In order to combat these forms of pride, more and more subtle, and more and more dangerous as they are sustained with goods that are more and more precious, humility must itself become finer and deeper. A logical progression in humility is thus established—in reasonable humility as well as in fervent humility.

[33] *Autobiography,* iv, 55.

## 3. PRIDE IN EXTERNAL GOODS

The external goods in which one takes pride are all those that secure honor and consideration for their possessor, and therefore, exterior advantages and qualities; such as beauty, fortune, name, rank, honors. These goods simply constitute a façade—brilliant perhaps—which, as we know, conceals our interior poverty very ineffectually. And yet we like to dwell on them in secret admiration of our own supposed excellence, and we display them to win honor and praises. But the world is not deceived; after satisfying what convention requires, it reserves to itself the right to pass interiorly the severe judgment of justice.

This pride, the most foolish but also the least dangerous because exterior, is ordinarily the first to give way before the light of humility:

> It is weary of the time when it paid heed to niceties concerning its own honour, and of the mistaken belief which it had that what the world calls honour is really so. It now knows that to be a sheer lie and a lie in which we are all living. It realizes that genuine honour is not deceptive, but true; that it values what has worth and despises what has none; for what passes away, and is not pleasing to God, is worth nothing and less than nothing. It laughs at itself and at the time when it set any store by money and coveted it.[34]

Saint Teresa makes a special issue of the point of honor, for she is Castilian and the daughter of knights of the sixteenth century, in the country of the Cid.[35] The question of honor

[34] *Life,* xx; Peers, I, 129.
[35] On the matter of honor, Saint Teresa writes:
> I see some people whose actions are very holy and who do such wonderful things that everyone is astonished at them. God bless me, then! Why are such souls still on earth? How is it that they have not reached the summit of perfection? What is the reason for this? What can it be that is impeding one who is doing so much good for God? Why, simply his punctiliousness about his reputation! And the worst of it is that this sort of person will not realize that he is guilty of such a thing, the reason sometimes being that the devil tells him that punctiliousness is incumbent upon him.
> Let such persons believe me, then: for the love of the Lord let them believe this little ant, for she speaks because it is the Lord's will that she

kept her from certain dangers when she was a young girl, for she would not have wanted to do anything against honor. The concern for honor, so deeply rooted in her, was to be purified only in its time. A feeling of gratitude towards the persons that she saw, kept her attached to those parlor conversations that she did not give up at Father Baltasar's request; only the divine word that she heard in her first rapture, made her renounce them. And was there not also that satisfaction that she found in the company of the best society of Avila and in conversations that she so easily made brilliant and witty, as well as supernatural.

The example of Saint Teresa shows us that an inordinate attachment to external goods, especially where those of the family or relations are concerned, can be so tenacious that it will yield only to the purifications of the sixth Mansions. What the Saint says of the souls immured in the third Mansions, because too reasonably attached to the goods of the earth or concerned about their honor, portrays for us the grave consequences of such deordination.

For this reason, the Saint treats with severity any form of pride or susceptibility:

> You will say that these are little things which have to do with human nature and are not worth troubling about; do not trifle with them, for *in religious houses* they spread like foam on water, and there is no small matter so extremely dangerous as are punctiliousness about honour and sensitiveness to insult.[36]

---

should do so. If they fail to remove this caterpillar, it may not hurt the whole tree, for some of the other virtues will remain, but they will all be worm-eaten. The tree will not be beautiful: it will neither prosper itself nor allow the trees near it to do so, for the fruit of good example which it bears is not at all healthy and will not last for long. I repeat this: however slight may be our concern for our reputation, the result of it will be as bad as when we play a wrong note, or make a mistake in time, in playing the organ—the whole passage will become discordant. Such concern is a thing which harms the soul whenever it occurs; but in the life of prayer it is pestilential (Life, xxxi; Peers, I, 213).

[36] *Way of Perfection,* xii; Peers, II, 52.

A day will come when the soul will enjoy a quiet laugh when it sees "men of prayer making a fuss about niceties concerning their honour"; for it will know very well "that if they subordinated the authority due to their positions to the love of God they would do more good in a day than they are likely to do as it is in ten years." [37] But the soul thus enlightened has already arrived in high regions of the spiritual life; and on its journey, it has met with other forms of pride.

### 4. PRIDE OF WILL

The pride that resides in the will is fed by the goods that the will finds in itself: its independence, its power to command, and its strength of which it has become aware. It is expressed by a refusal to submit to established authority, an exaggerated self-confidence, and a dominating ambition. It is this pride that declares the *Non serviam*, I will not serve, and that disorganizes all society, the family as well as civil society, by destroying the subordination which is the principle of order and of collaboration.

Moreover, it refuses submission to God, or makes this difficult. Or again, believing in the power and efficacy of its own efforts, even in the domain of the supernatural, it does not understand the word of Jesus: "without me, you can do nothing," [38] nor that of Saint Paul: "it is God who of his good pleasure works in you both the will and the performance." [39] Thus pride of will, by refusing to yield to any, is opposed to the reign of God and to the dominion of His grace.

Jesus Christ alone who came to serve and not to be served, who made Himself obedient unto death, even to death on the cross, can teach by His example the nobility and the value of submission. But the abasements of Christ—when it becomes necessary to share in them—seem folly to Christians as long as the light of God has not shone upon their soul.

[37] *Life,* xxi; Peers, I, 134.
[38] John 15:5.
[39] Phil. 2:13.

The earlier stages of contemplative prayer, by revealing obscurely to the soul a transcendent Presence in the sweet surge of quiet or in the helplessness that comes of aridity, attack this pride by captivating the will. By plunging the faculties in the divine darkness and giving them an experimental contact with God, the prayer of union breaks down this pride completely, rendering the will docile to the good pleasure of God. A long and difficult labor of asceticism can supply for that mystical grace and invite the divine rapture which will unite the will with the divine Will.

### 5. PRIDE OF INTELLECT

Pride of will ordinarily springs from pride of intellect. The *Non serviam* of the rebel angels proceeded from a proud complacence in their own light. Fascinated by their personal splendor, those spirits would not turn their gaze to the eternal light of God. Fixed in that attitude because of the simplicity of their nature, they renounced the beatific vision and condemned themselves to eternal privation of God. The sin of the angels was the sin of pride of intellect.

Because of the failures to which human nature is subject, under the law of the passions and of change, this sin in man has some excuse and hope of pardon and repentance. Nevertheless, it is still one of the gravest sins and heavy with consequences, for it is in the highest human faculty and withdraws it from the divine light whose transcendence demands submission.

In establishing the principle of private judgment, the Protestant freethought has exalted pride of mind. By proclaiming the absolute rights of reason, the French Revolution made intellectual pride a social sin. Scientific discovery, seeming to confirm reason's claim to be the supreme arbiter in every domain to the exclusion of God, has made this a quasi-irremissible sin for the minds of the masses of our times.

This social sin, the latest fruits of which are philosophic

agnosticism, political liberalism, and scholastic laicism with which the atmosphere is saturated, has penetrated into the most protected circles; it manifests itself by the habit of bringing everything before the tribunal of one's own judgment and by the difficulty of submitting to the simple testimony of authority. Hence faith becomes more exacting of distinct lights and, less docile, it journeys more slowly in the dark towards its divine object. It is that very pride, the cause of the apostasy of the masses, which refuses access to the Fountain of living waters that could appease so many souls, thirsty for light and for life. It, too, explains why so many beautiful minds, believers, stop short before the divine obscurities into which one can penetrate only by the simple gaze of contemplation.

Pride of intellect finds a remedy, however, in contact with revealed truth and its mysteries, and in meeting with wise men and great minds. Acts of faith and the study of revealed truth provide some purification for it.

But it will be thoroughly purified in its depths only when light itself breaks in upon it, painful at first and dim, until it produces the semi-brightness of dawn. Then, whether the soul has been dazzled by a suspension of its faculties in the lights that come from the Infinite, or whether it has suffered long the obscurity of the divine darkness, it will have understoc that God is inaccessible to the human intellect, that Hi. thoughts and His plans are not our thoughts and plans, and that the highest knowledge that we can have of God is to understand that He is above all our knowledge and intelligence. Respectful and loving before the divine Reality, it no longer dares to set up as an idol the brilliance of reason; it rejoices in knowing nothing, in being capable of nothing, in understanding nothing, in order that trusting in a faith that is now pure and strong, it may penetrate farther into the transluminous darkness of the mysteries that are proposed to it.

In these regions where human knowledge fails, pride of intellect is purified; and then that light floods the soul, which discloses all things in their proper place in the perspective of eternity. For this reason, Teresa wishes that those who have authority over peoples might be given this light:

> Blessed is the soul which the Lord brings to an understanding of the truth! Oh, what a state this would be for kings! . . . What uprightness there would be in their kingdoms! How many evils would be prevented—and might have been prevented already! [40]

These reflections and this wish must assuredly be ours today, when the decadence of Christian civilization, the disorders and struggles that are afflicting the world, take their source from false lights or ideologies constructed by pride of mind.

## 6. SPIRITUAL PRIDE

The Gospel offers us a striking example of spiritual pride, the attitude it begets, and its chastisement, in the parable of the Pharisee and the Publican: [41]

"Two men went up to the temple to pray, the one a Pharisee and the other a publican." As was fitting, the Pharisee went up to the sanctuary. If he had remained at the back, the others would have been astonished, with good reason; for he was a religious man of some importance. He prayed thus: "O God, I thank thee that I am not like the rest of men, robbers, dishonest, adulterers, or even like this publican. I fast twice a week; I pay tithes of all that I possess." Certainly, that is all true; he is boasting of nothing that he does not really do. "But the publican, standing afar off, would not so much as lift up his eyes to heaven, but kept striking his breast, saying, 'O God, be merciful to me the sinner!' " The publican, a veritable and detested thief, puts himself too in the place that belongs to him and confesses the sins he has committed. Both are true; but the Pharisee boasts of his virtue, the publican humbles himself for his sin. God seems to forget both the virtue and the sin. In the first man, He sees only conceit; in the second, only

[40] *Life,* xxi; Peers, I, 131.
[41] Luke 18:9-14.

humility. "I tell you, this man went back to his home justified rather than the other." *Divites dimisit inanes, exaltavit humiles* . . . He hath exalted the humble and sent the rich away empty.

The Pharisee who boasts before God of his spiritual works is later found boasting to Jesus of his faithfulness to the law of Moses and of his descent from Abraham, which makes him one of the chosen people. This proud fidelity that had become crystallized in numerous exterior practices, hinders him from recognizing Him whom the patriarchs and the prophets longed to see and did not see, the promised Messias, the very Word Incarnate who is standing there before him.

A man of spiritual pride boasts not only of his works as if they were uniquely his, but also of his spiritual privileges. To belong to such a state in life, to a religious institute which numbers among its own certain great saints, which possesses a spiritual doctrine, a wide influence, is indeed a privilege that entails responsibility; but it can encourage a spiritual pride that makes one barren and blind in the presence of new manifestations of the divine mercy.

Spiritual gifts too can serve as pasture ground for pride. The graces of prayer enrich the contemplative, leave their profound mark in the soul, give a precious experience, strengthen the will, refine the intellect, increase the power of action, secure to the spiritual person a powerful radiation. These graces are always received with humility and gratitude, dispositions which they in turn deepen. The light that accompanies them disappears; their effects remain in the soul. Then, temptation can come, subtle and unawares. It comes almost necessarily, so tenacious is pride and the devil so wicked. The soul uses these spiritual riches to exalt self and to attract notice, to serve a need for affection or for domination, or simply to make its personal ideas triumph.[42] One's personality, idolatrous of itself,

[42] In a letter addressed to Saint Teresa who had asked him if they had not done well in taking away the charge of master of novices from P. Gabriel Espinel who made his novices practise public mortifications that were a little strange; and also, how to convince the father of his error, P. Báñez, after

is substituted for God; and what it received to be used as an instrument and a means, it uses to impose itself as an end and a god for itself and others.

*Corruptio optimi pessima.* The corruption of the best engenders the worst. We cannot think without shuddering of certain lamentable falls of souls that had been greatly favored by God. Luther would not have formulated his theory of the faith that justifies, if he had not experienced the pacifying floods of divine mercy; and he would not have been able to attack religion, striking it at the point where faith is grafted in intellect, if he had not previously discovered—at least in an incipient purification of faith—the vulnerability of this point of intersection of the natural and the supernatural. And there have been others, before and after Luther, using the privileges of their intimacy with the Master, if not to betray Him like Judas with a kiss, at any rate, to feed their pride and make their own personality triumph.

Is it not because they have turned to their own profit the charisms with which they have been favored, that the Sovereign Judge will pronounce on them this astounding sentence which He Himself foretells:

Many will say to me in that day, "Lord, Lord, did we not prophesy in thy name, and cast out devils in thy name, and work many miracles in thy name?" And then I will declare to them, "I never knew you. Depart from me, you workers of iniquity!" [43]

Woe, then, to spiritual pride that is founded on the gifts of God. The divine jealousy is displayed with the more severity, since the goods that are taken from God by pride are more elevated, more gratuitous, more purely the work of God Himself. Mercy shows itself more jealous than justice. Aggrieved by pride, it shows itself more exacting in the realm of the supernatural favors which the soul enjoys as free gifts, than in

approving and justifying the decision, shrewdly added: "As to convincing the Father, perhaps you would succeed if he were not spiritual."

[43] Matt. 7:22-3.

that of the natural gifts and virtues which the soul can properly claim.

The Pharisee who proudly displays his good works, goes away with empty hands. The same Pharisee, who boasts of the privilege that made him a son of Abraham, is totally blind in the light of the Word. The prophet who took pleasure in his charism goes into eternal fire.

Only the saints, who have seen under the light of God the gravity of such a pride, can explain to us the strictness of God on this point and the severity of His judgments. Let us listen to Saint Therese of the Child Jesus at the end of her life, when she had already arrived at transforming union:

> Dearest Mother, if I were unfaithful, if I committed even the slightest infidelity, I feel that I would pay for it by terrible troubles, and I could not accept death.[44]

Rightly are we surprised at this avowal from the lips of the apostle of trust and of mercy, who had written that the gravest faults could not stop the movement of her filial confidence in God. "Of what infidelity are you talking?" they asked her. And her answer was:

> Of a proud thought, voluntarily entertained; for example this: I have acquired such a virtue, I am certain of being able to practise it; for that would be to rely on my own strength, and when one has come to that point, one is in danger of falling into the abyss. And if I should say: O my God, I love you too much, you know it, to stop in a single thought against faith, my temptations would become so violent that I would certainly succumb to them.[45]

Standing in the light that shines on the highest summits, Saint Therese of the Child Jesus well knew that a sin of spiritual pride could still shake the magnificent edifice of her perfection, and stop the torrent of divine mercy from pouring into her soul, although she had arrived at transforming union!

The response of Saint John of the Cross to Christ who asked what he desired as a reward evinces the interior fears of the

[44] To Mother Agnes, Aug. 7, 1897, *Novissima Verba.*
[45] *Ibid.*

Saint, of the same nature as those of Saint Therese ot the Child Jesus: "No other thing, Lord, than to suffer and be despised." What is there to say except that the Saint, he also having come to transforming union and the full flowering of his graces as mystical doctor, still feared those mists of pride that the devil could cause to arise from the awareness of his state and the fruitfulness of his grace, and which would have veiled the intimacy of his union and stopped him in his progress to the depths of God.

Subtleties these, some will say. Yes, perhaps, for our souls so little spiritual; but realities that are perceived in strong and terrifying relief by the purified gaze of the saints. And so, Saint Angela of Foligno said in her spiritual testament to those who were around her:

> My children be humble; my children be meek. I am not speaking of the exterior act; I am speaking of the depths of the heart. Do not worry yourselves about honors, nor dignities. O my children, be little so that Christ may exalt you in His perfection and in yours. . . . Dignities that puff up the soul are vanities that are accursed. Flee them, for they are dangerous; but listen, listen. They are less dangerous than spiritual vanities. To make a show that one knows how to speak about God, to understand the Scriptures, to accomplish miracles, to make a parade of one's heart lost in the Divine, that is the vanity of vanities; and worldly vanities are, after that supreme vanity, small faults quickly corrected.[46]

The ravages of spiritual pride are truly vast and terrible in the world of souls. If, as a rule, it is only the fall from extraordinary graces that leaves such stricken ruins, nevertheless there are numerous souls too proudly satisfied with themselves, complacent in the favors and results obtained, who have come to a definite stop in the spiritual life and lost all fervor and spiritual energy.

## C. Means for acquiring humility

The grave evils to which pride gives rise, the forms increasingly subtle under which it disguises itself, must arouse in the

[46] *Sainte Angèle de Foligno;* French translation by Hello, p. 341.

spiritual man a salutary fear and dread of it; while the divine riches that humility draws down, make it supremely desirable. But how is humility to be acquired? We can treat only briefly here this practical problem which we have touched upon in many places.

From the First Mansions on, Saint Teresa has stressed the fact that the soul must establish the foundations of humility on a knowledge of self. The examination of conscience furnishes data for that knowledge.

The Saint takes care to warn us from the beginning, however, that the most thorough self-knowledge is acquired not by direct introspection, but by a consideration of the perfection of God. She puts us on our guard against the false humilities kept alive by the devil, which prolong useless reflection on self, produce constraint in action, and finally engender discourage.-ment.[47]

Besides, examination of conscience could result at best in reasonable humility. But it is fervent humility that the soul needs in the stage of the spiritual life at which we have arrived. There are several points we might consider concerning its acquisition.

1. Fervent humility is the *fruit of the light of God* on the soul. Hence it would be vain to hope to acquire it by one's own efforts alone.

Furthermore, pride is a crafty enemy that seems to elude every attack, fleeing always farther into the depths of the soul. It rises up more dangerous from the blows that are dealt it, boasting of the triumphs of the very humility that claimed to have destroyed it.

Nevertheless, although acts of humility have of themselves only a relative efficacy, they are a testimonial of our good will which God accepts and rewards with His efficacious graces. Saint Teresa advises:

[47] Cf. PERSPECTIVES, iii, "Knowledge of Self"; How to acquire it, p. 45.

Ask the superior, as soon as a temptation comes to you, to give you some lowly office to do, or do some such thing, as best you can, on your own initiative, studying as you do it how to bend your will to perform tasks you dislike. The Lord will show you ways of doing so and this will soon rid you of the temptation.[48]

Not rarely, in fact, an abundant flow of graces issues from the actions and attitudes of a humility striving to be sincere, and expressly desiring an increase of divine truth and light.

2. *Prayer* is the means recommended by our Lord for the obtaining of divine favors. "What can we do about it, sisters?" asks Teresa. And she gives the answer: "To me the best thing seems to be what our Master teaches us: to pray, and to beseech the Eternal Father not to allow us to fall into temptation." [49]

A poor man, conscious of his misery, holds out his hand. A proud man who is aware of his pride, must make himself a beggar for the light of truth that brings humility; and his prayer must be the more earnest as his pride is greater, and because humility is the foundation and condition of all spiritual progress. Frequently, Holy Church puts on the lips of her religious the ardent supplication of the *Miserere,* and asks pardon and light for those in sin. The proud man, conscious of his sin that God has cursed, must constantly put himself in the last place among sinners if he would draw towards him a glance from the divine Mercy. As he grows in the habit of humbly begging, he will cause to spring up within him a source of light and of life.[50]

3. If it is necessary to ask for the light of humility, it is no less important to *receive it well.* When the soul, placed under that purifying and humiliating light which discloses to it the evil within, sees "clearly how extremely unworthy it is—for in a room bathed in sunlight not a cobweb can remain hidden;

[48] *Way of Perfection,* xii; Peers, II, 52.
[49] *Ibid.,* xxxviii; 165.
[50] Saint Therese of Lisieux composed a "Prayer to Obtain Humility" (*Autobiography,* p. 317).

[when] it sees its own wretchedness, [and when] so far is vainglory from it that it cannot believe it could ever be guilty of such a thing," [51] it must pour out its gratitude to God for that light and keep with great care the pleasing conviction that it brings. This is a response to prayer.

4. There is another response, less agreeable sometimes, but one which must be accepted with the same gratitude: *humiliation* itself.

Humiliations bring before us our defects, our evil tendencies perhaps already retracted, our failures, or even the errors if not the malevolence of our neighbor. These are so many precious testimonies of God's solicitude which brings into use for the formation of souls, all the resources of His power and His wisdom. How can we judge them otherwise, when we see every great grace spring from humiliation as from its natural soul? To accept them is a duty; to thank God for them indicates that one has understood their value; to ask for them with Saint John of the Cross is to have already advanced far into the depths of divine Wisdom. Saint Therese of the Child Jesus writes:

> We must number ourselves humbly with the imperfect, see ourselves as *little souls* which God must uphold from instant to instant. . . . Yes, it is enough if we humble ourselves and bear our imperfections patiently: that is true sanctity.[52]

"Learn of me for I am meek and humble of heart," Jesus proclaims. Humility and meekness are His characteristic virtues, the personal perfume of His soul, which He leaves wherever He goes and which mark the places where He reigns.

The humility of Christ, fervent humility *par excellence,* proceeds from the light of the Word which dwells in Him and overwhelms Him with its transcendence. For between the divine nature and the human nature of Christ Jesus, united by the bonds of a hypostatic union, there is the distance of the In-

---

[51] *Life,* xix; Peers, I, 112.
[52] To Genevieve, June 7, 1897; *Collected Letters,* p. 342.

finite. This Infinite overpowers the human nature of Christ and plunges it into abysses of adoration and humility where no other could follow Him, for no other has ever contemplated so closely and so exhaustively the Infinite.

But this Infinite is Love that gives itself, oil that is poured out. And so, in crushing the soul, it fills it with fragrance, with peace and joy. Jesus Christ is as meek as He is humble.

Humility and meekness, strength and gentleness, fragrance of Christ [53] and also of fervent humility; here we have the authentic sign of divine touches and a discreet but importunate call to the mercy of God for new visitations.

[53] With a great deal of penetration, the Abbé Huvelin, director of P. Charles de Foucauld, used to say that the whole of Christianity resides in a loving humility.

# CHAPTER V
# Silence

> *The heavenly Father has uttered only one word: it is His Son. He says it eternally and in an eternal silence. It is in the silence of the soul that it makes itself heard.*[1]

The gift of self attracts in return the mercy of God; humility increases the soul's capacity for grace; silence protects the efficacy of God's action in the soul.

In the First Mansions, Saint Teresa stressed the necessity of recollection if we would discover the presence of God in the soul and the treasures He has hidden there. Now in this second phase of the soul's progress, the need for silence becomes imperative. Previously it was sufficient to be recollected from time to time; a recollection that is as frequent and constant as the action of God is now an absolute requirement.

We must, then, speak of silence. The importance and difficulties of the subject could lead us into a long discussion. One must bear in mind, however, that it would be rather illogical to discourse too much about silence. And yet, in order to give the essential and the most practical in this matter, two chapters seem necessary. The first will explain the necessity and the forms of silence; the second will study the relations between silence and solitude.

## A. Necessity of silence

Any task at all that requires a serious application of our faculties, presupposes the recollection and silence that render it

[1] Saint John of the Cross, Maxim 307.

possible. The scientist needs silence to prepare his experiments. The philosopher recollects himself in solitude to put order into his thoughts and penetrate into them.

The silence that the thinker is avid for, that his intellectual energies may not be disturbed in their reflections, is still more necessary for the spiritual man, that he may apply his whole soul to the search of its divine object.

In the Sermon on the Mount, Jesus tells us how we must seek solitude for prayer;

When thou prayest, go into thy room, and closing thy door, pray to thy Father in secret; and thy Father, who sees in secret, will reward thee.[2]

The contemplative prayer proper to the state to which we have come has very particular requirements of silence and solitude. In contemplation, divine wisdom not only enlightens the intellect; it acts on the whole soul. And so it demands of it a complete orientation of its being towards God, a recollection and tranquility of what is deepest within, in order to receive the action of Love's transforming rays.

In a forceful expression which cannot but awaken profound echoes in every contemplative soul, Saint John of the Cross enunciates this divine requirement. He writes:

The heavenly Father has uttered only one word: it is His Son. He says it eternally and in an eternal silence. It is in the silence of the soul that it makes itself heard.[3]

"God sees in secret," our Lord had said. Saint John of the Cross adds: God works His divine operations in silence. Silence is a law of the highest divine operations: the eternal generation of the Word, and the production in time of grace, which is a participation of the Word.

This divine law surprises us. It goes so much against our experience of the natural laws of the world. Here below, any

[2] Matt. 6:6.
[3] Maxim 307.

profound transformation, any great external change produces a certain agitation and noise. The great river, for example, reaches the ocean only by the sounding onward rush of its waters.

In the Holy Trinity, the generation of the Word (splendor of the Father who expresses Himself in that luminous and clear radiance of Himself which is the Son) and the procession of the Holy Spirit (the mutual exchange of the Father and the Son in infinite torrents of Love that constitute the Third Person) take place in the bosom of the Trinity in the silence and peace of the divine immutability in an eternal present. No movement, no change, no slightest stir, signalize to the world or to the finest sensibilities of creatures, this rhythm of the Triune Life whose power and effects are infinite.

In presence of that eternal immobility and silence which conceal the secret of the intimate life of God, the Psalmist cries out: *"Tu autem idem Ipse es"*: [4] But thou, O my God, art always the selfsame, while the world is ceaselessly changing.

We must await the vision face to face in order perfectly to enter into the peace of the divine immutability. Nevertheless, already here below, participation in the divine life through grace brings us under the law of the divine silence. It is in silence, adds Saint John of the Cross, that the divine Word, which in us is grace, makes Himself heard and is received.

Baptism works a marvelous creation in the soul of the child. A new life is given it, a life which will permit it to perform divine acts as a son of God. We hear the words of the priest, "I baptize thee . . ."; we see the water flow over the forehead of the infant; but, of the creation of grace, which requires nothing less than the personal and omnipotent action of God, we have perceived nothing. God has spoken His word in the soul, in silence. And it is in the same silent darkness that the further developments of grace ordinarily take place.

When the darkness gives way to a dawn at the time of cer-

4 Ps. 101:28.

tain divine visits, the soul always has an experience of the divine silence among the riches that it enjoys. This passing of
God is nearly always heralded by passive recollection. It takes
place in silence; and the impression that disappears last is a
delightful peace and silence.

But let us leave to the poetry of Saint John of the Cross the
care of translating these high experiences:

> My Beloved [is for me] the mountains,
> The solitary, wooded valleys,
> The strange islands,
> The sonorous rivers,
> The whisper of the amorous breezes,
>
> The tranquil night,
> At the time of the rising of the dawn,
> The silent music,
> The sounding solitude,
> The supper that recreates and enkindles love.[5]

In the richness and variety of these symbols, what is to be
sought, if not the musical expression of the divine anointing
and the sweet silence into which God has drawn the soul.

God speaks in silence, and silence alone seems able to express Him. For the spiritual person who has known the touch
of God, silence and God seem to be identified. And so, to find
God again, where would he go, if not to the most silent depths
of his soul, into those regions that are so hidden that nothing
can any longer disturb them.

When he has reached there, he preserves with jealous care
the silence that gives him God. He defends it against any agitation, even that of his own powers. With Saint John of the
Cross, he exclaims:

> O nymphs of Judaea
> While mid the flowers and rose-trees
> The amber sheds forth perfume,
> Dwell in the outskirts
> And desire not to touch our thresholds.[6]

[5] *Spiritual Canticle,* st. xiii, xiv; Peers, II, 27.
[6] *Ibid.,* st. xxxi; 29.

The nymphs, which are the restless sense powers, being kept outside in their own domain, the soul now begs God not to let His graces and lights descend upon them, so that His communications may not be contaminated by their sharing in them, nor the interior powers forced to leave this silence:

> Hide thyself, dearest one,
> And look with thy face upon the mountains,
> And desire not to speak.[7]

Thus the movement of the soul to its inmost silent depths, in order jealously to protect the purity of its contact with God, is sketched in these stanzas of the mystical doctor.

An aspiration for silence is found in all the mystics. Could we believe that anyone had experience of intimate commerce with God, who had not at the same time experience of this inner silence? All the spiritual masters insist on its necessity, each one in his own symbolic language.

Saint Teresa distinguishes seven successive Mansions, and it is only in the seventh, the innermost, that profound union takes place. Tauler signalizes a deep volition, more interior than the active faculties. Ruysbroeck and Saint Angela of Foligno speak of height and of depth, of two abysses which mutually engender one another. Saint John of the Cross says that the "deepest center" of the soul, where the joy of the Holy Spirit "gently and lovingly awakens," the limit to which the soul can attain, is God within it.[8]

But in the whole of hagiography can anything be found that describes so well the atmosphere of deep silence in which God speaks to the soul as does the vision of the prophet Elias on Mount Horeb?

Fleeing from the anger of Jezabel, and fed by the bread given him by an angel, the prophet had walked for forty days in the desert and had come to Horeb, the mount of God *par*

[7] *Ibid.*, xxxii; 29.
[8] *Living Flame*, st. i; Peers, III, 25f.

*excellence,* on which Yahweh had manifested Himself several times to Moses. And here:

> The word of the Lord came unto him, . . . and he said to him: Go forth, and stand upon the mount before the Lord. And behold the Lord passeth. And a great and strong wind before the Lord overthrowing the mountains, and breaking the rocks in pieces: the Lord is not in the wind. And after the wind an earthquake: the Lord is not in the earthquake.
> And after the earthquake a fire: the Lord is not in the fire. And after the fire a whistling of a gentle air.
> And when Elias heard it, he covered his face with his mantle, and coming forth stood in the entering in of the cave.[9]

The Sinaitic theophanies to which Moses had been witness, are renewed before Elias on the same mountain: a strong wind that breaks the rocks, a trembling that shakes the earth, a fire that burns the heavens and the soul of the prophet. Elias is not moved by them. God had announced to him that He was going to pass. These turbulent, external visitations do not suffice for his purified soul, eager for a divine manifestation more pure and more profound than that which stirs the senses, with its exterior and sensible forms. The Lord that he longs for and awaits is not in the wind, nor in the earthquake, nor even in the fire which symbolizes so well the God of armies and the grace of the prophet, who rose up like a flame and whose word was burning as a torch.

But now comes the gentle whisper of the breeze. Elias, the prophet, with an external roughness often violent, but with a penetrating and purified gaze of faith in his noble and delicate soul, hides his face under his mantle so as to be recollected. His expectation was not in vain. God has passed, and has manifested Himself in the lofty, pure way that Elias was hoping for. We must hear Saint John of the Cross, specialist in divine things, comment on this awareness of God in order to understand its quality:

> When it is said that God communicates by the ear, that expression describes a very lofty and a very certain fact. Thus, when Saint Paul

[9] III Kings 19:11-15.

wished to describe the loftiness of his revelation, he said not, *Vidit arcana verba,* still less, *Gustavit arcana verba,* but *Audivit arcana verba quae non licet homini loqui.*[10] Which is as though he had said: I heard secret words which it is not lawful for a man to utter. As to this it is thought that he saw God, as did our father Elias, in that whisper. For even faith, as Saint Paul says likewise, comes by bodily hearing, even so that which faith teaches us, which is the substance of understanding, comes by spiritual hearing." [11]

Incomparably above any and all prophetic experience is that of Jesus Christ, in whom human nature was hypostatically united to the divine nature which it enjoyed through the beatific vision. How could He not, then, have felt a constant need of taking refuge in silence which permitted Him to give Himself up exclusively to the rapture of the Word and the sweet floods of divine unction, poured out on Him silently? The retreat for nearly thirty years at Nazareth, the sojourn in the desert for forty days before beginning the public life as if to store up reserves of silence, the frequent return into solitude in the calm of the night in order to renew them—all this is explained much better by that deep need, that weight of God who draws His divine Son into the regions where He lives and gives Himself, than by any need of Christ for light or strength for the accomplishment of His mission.

Thirsty for God because she also had already found Him, Saint Teresa was to the same degree thirsty for silence. The foundation of the Convent of Saint Joseph of Avila, the first of her Reform, sprang from that need. At the Incarnation Convent, the absence of enclosure, the large number of religious, the mitigation of the Rule, had killed the silence that Teresa and Christ needed in order to cultivate their intimacy and to be perfectly united.

Teresa therefore left the Incarnation where she had lived for almost thirty years. Besides, she wanted to recover the primitive ideal of Carmel and the perfect observance of her Rule. Carmel had its origin in the desert and always retains not only a

[10] II Cor. 12:4.
[11] *Spiritual Canticle,* st. xiii, xiv; Peers, II, 83.

nostalgia for it, but a real need of it in order to live and to bloom. Saint Teresa was of the race of those hermits who dwelt on the holy mountain, and for whom Saint Albert, patriarch of Jerusalem, codified the monastic customs into a Rule which insists at length on silence.

In order to revive that primitive ideal, Saint Teresa set out to re-create the desert. She would establish it in the bosom of cities. Such was the principal aim that directed the organization of Saint Joseph's of Avila, the triumph of the practical genius of the Saint and the model for other foundations.

The monastery would be poor—people do not go to see the poor; the enclosure, rigorous. The religious would not work in common; each was to have her own cell. The grounds would be spacious, with little hermitages where one could find, at certain times, more solitude. These convents were to be paradises of divine intimacy where Christ would come to rest a while in silence with His own. On her journeys, the Saint had the same care for silence, so that the atmosphere might remain divine around her and her daughters.

In our twentieth century, the contemplative dreams with a little melancholy of the age when Teresa, traveling through uninhabited rural areas on an ox-cart fixed like a Carmelite cell, still felt the need for her hours of recollection and asked the drivers to respect them. We live in a fever of movement and activity. The evil is not simply in the organization of modern life, in the haste that it imposes on what we do, the rapidity and facility that it affords our changing of place. A more profound evil is in the feverish nervousness of temperaments. People no longer know how to wait and be silent. And yet, they appear to be seeking silence and solitude; they leave familiar circles for new horizons, another atmosphere. Most often, however, this is only so as to divert themselves with fresh impressions.

Whatever changes time may bring, God remains the same, *Tu autem idem Ipse es;* and it is always in silence that He utters His Word and that the soul must receive it. The law of silence is imposed on us as on Teresa. The high-strung excitability of the modern temperament makes it more urgently important, and exacts of us a more resolute effort to respect and submit to it.

## B. Forms of silence

There is an exterior silence of the tongue and of natural activity, and a silence of the interior powers of the soul. Each of these has its own special rules; so much so, that a study of them must be made separately.

### 1. SILENCE OF THE TONGUE

In current parlance, to be silent means not to talk. This indicates the importance of the mortification of the tongue for the practice of silence.

Of the tongue it has been said that there is nothing better and nothing worse. A source of incomparable good, it provokes the gravest evils. The apostle Saint James says this emphatically in his Epistle:

> In many things we all offend. If anyone does not offend in word, he is a perfect man, able also to lead round by a bridle the whole body. For if we put bits into horses' mouths that they may obey us, we control their whole body also. Behold, even the ships, great as they are, and driven by boisterous winds, are steered by a small rudder wherever the touch of the steersman pleases. So the tongue also is a little member, but it boasts mightily. Behold, how small a fire—how great a forest it kindles! And the tongue is a fire. . . . Every kind of beast and bird, and of serpents and the rest, is tamed and has been tamed by mankind; but the tongue no man can tame. . . . With it we bless God the Father; and with it we curse men, who have been made after the likeness of God.[12]

The description is vigorous and complete. To insist on the gravity of the sins of the tongue that he mentions would doubtless be outside our purpose here; for souls of prayer, at the stage to which we have come, have been corrected on this point

[12] Jas. 3:2-9.

or at least sufficiently warned. Yet the teaching on the importance and the difficulties of the mortification of the tongue is of much value and applies directly to our subject.

The spoken word exteriorizes what is most intimate and personal to the soul, its thoughts and sentiments; it communicates them to others. This communication can be a benefit for the one who gives and the one who receives. In the first, the love that gives, opens out beautifully, finds strength and joy. The other is enriched with light and with all that love gives in communicating. These exchanges through the word are at the basis of social life, of all education, of progress in every domain, including the developments of the faith. Faith comes through hearing, remarks the apostle Saint Paul, and how could one believe if there were no preaching?

But excess is injurious. Mortification of the tongue must keep a right measure in these exchanges.

Expression, which exteriorizes, lays bare the depths of the soul. For a moment, the depth disappears; its restful shadows and its silence are dispersed. God, who had sought the deep quiet of the inmost center of the soul for the creative action of His divine life, seems hampered by its exteriorization.

Likewise, the communication from outside which was meant to enrich, often merely disturbs the silence of the soul and the divine work in it by bringing in useless things that are distracting, subjects of temptation, in short, causes of disquiet which increase the difficulties of interior recollection and risk precluding the divine action.

Of the harm done by conversations, the soul is sometimes warned by an uneasiness. Saint Therese of the Child Jesus admits to having been for a long time saddened at having given out the secret of the beauty and the smile of the Virgin whom she had beheld. Who of us has not felt the perfume of a more intimate prayer or of a contact in communion with God disappear in an idle conversation? These particular experiences draw our attention to a loss that is usual in such a case, although it may not be perceived.

And so talkativeness—that tendency to exteriorize all the treasures of the soul by expressing them—is extremely harmful to the spiritual life. Its movement is in reverse direction from that of the soul which becomes increasingly interior in order to be nearer to God. Drawn towards the external by his need to say everything, the talker cannot but be far from God and all profound activity. All his inner life passes through his lips, and flows out in words that bear along with them the fruits of his thought and soul. He thus becomes more and more spiritually impoverished. For the talkative person no longer has time—and soon no taste—to be recollected, to think, nor to live deeply. And by the agitation that he creates around him, he hinders fruitful work and recollection in others. Superficial and vain, the talker is a dangerous person.

We would not call talkativeness, however, the conversations, even though prolonged, that the duties of one's state and a well-regulated charity require. Many authentic contemplatives were persons who mingled in the world or were prolific writers, such as Saint Vincent Ferrer, Saint Bernardine of Siena, Saint Francis de Sales, Saint Teresa herself, and Saint John of the Cross. In these necessary and charitable exteriorizations, the spiritual man finds a means of being united with the will of God; and he is happily surprised, on returning to the depths of his soul, to find the Spirit of God there, waiting to welcome his return.

On the other hand, the dangers of loquacity are not entirely banished from spiritual conversations, from accounts of our intimate life with God. True, it is at times a duty to tell of one's inner dispositions and of graces received; it is ordinarily the only means of submitting them to direction and receiving light and help concerning them. Writing them down in a notebook helps to define them; sometimes, it discloses their riches and makes it possible to draw upon them in less luminous hours.

And yet, the austere Rule of Carmel, following Isaias, without despising these benefits and needs, proclaims: Your strength will be in silence and hope; in silence which keeps intact and pure the energies of the soul and preserves them from dispersion; in hope which tends to God, to find in Him light and support. Long spiritual effusions scatter the lights and forces that have been received and, consequently, are weakening. In much talking, one wastes and squanders; and the soul is drained. In expressing to satiety even to God the ardent sentiments of a fervent Communion, the soul divests itself of its strength for action: all the vigor that was taken in from God is poured out in that savoury flow of words.

Discretion will have to preside also over written accounts (whether for oneself or the director) that they be neither too frequent nor too copious. Do we not find that the analysis and the clearer consciousness that are the fruit of them are often more harmful than useful? They require a return on self, and hence a halt in the march towards God. They incur the danger of supplying food for pride and spiritual gluttony, which beginners hardly escape. It is for each one to decide if these spiritual reports are not above all flattering mirrors in which the soul displays itself with complaisance; and if it would not better use the gifts of God by leaving them behind in the shadow of forgetfulness, while it moves on directly towards God Himself.

*Cultus justitiae silentium est:* silence is both a fruit of sanctity and a requirement for it. And so Saint Teresa many times over warns beginners of the danger in which their desire for the apostolate places them. In order to give without depleting themselves, they must wait till they can ceaselessly renew their energies at the divine Source by habitual union.

"I do not want to be a spiritual prattler," writes Elizabeth Leseur. "I want to keep this great calm of soul . . . give of self only what can be received with profit by others, guard the rest in the deepest corners as the soul guards its treasure, but

with the intention of giving it when the proper time comes."
Saint Teresa and Saint Therese of the Child Jesus pour out all
the treasures of their soul in immortal writings; but, under the
order of superiors and at a moment when the overflowing
plenitude of their love could only be enriched by giving itself
completely.

The asceticism of silence is so important that monastic Rules
have fixed the precise ways to practise it, adapted to each religious Order. From its desert origins, Carmel has kept the
grand silence which extends from Compline to Prime of the
following day, and which makes of the convent a desert during these hours of the night that are most favorable to profound prayer. During the day, a relative silence is kept, which
forbids every idle word.

But silence, in order not to become tense, calls for relaxation. This relaxation, or re-creation, forms a part too of the
asceticism of silence and, according to Saint Teresa, is one of
its most important and most delicate elements. Did not the
Saint say, before the foundation of the first convent of Discalced Carmelites at Duruelo, that she was bringing the young
Father John of the Cross to the foundation of Valladolid, not
to impart to him spiritual knowledge, nor to prove his virtue
which she knew to be heroic, but to show him their type of life
and especially how they took their recreation? Teresian recreations! At times the Saint was seen leading the joyful choir of
her daughters with castanets or a tambourine, or sternly re-
proving the inopportune devotion of someone who preferred
praying to recreating on a feast day! It is true that she was
seen also in ecstasy, dying at not being able to die, one day in
1571 when the young Isabelle of Jesus sang the couplet:

> Oh! to see Thee with my eyes,
> Gentle and good Jesus!
> Oh! to see Thee with my eyes
> And die immediately.

And at times they admired in recreation the charm of Teresita, the niece of Teresa; or they spoke of the unhappiness of the Church of France, ravaged by Protestantism; or of the moral misery of the peoples of the West Indies.

Into these recreations there flashed all the life of the soul of the Saint; all the gifts of her daughters were displayed. Relaxed thus under the divine gaze, those souls resumed the austere yoke of the Rule, rested and recreated; and in the silence of their convent, they found again the sweet company of their Beloved.

### 2. MORTIFICATION OF NATURAL ACTIVITY

Natural activity can, like talkativeness, disturb the silence in which God speaks to the soul. It poses a practical problem as delicate as that of the mortification of the tongue, if not more so. Let us state it as clearly as possible, showing first its *dangers*.

That natural activity can disturb the silence of the soul no one doubts, for experience on this point is painfully instructive. By the orientation it gives the faculties, the fatigue and even the enervation that it brings on, by the cares that accompany it, natural activity dissipates the soul, destroys recollection, multiplies obstacles to the return to prayer, and invades prayer itself, making it very difficult if not impossible.

When this activity overflows into the daily life to the point of leaving no place, or an insufficient minimum place, for prayer and silent turning to God, it becomes activism. Activism takes cover under numerous and often noble excuses: necessities of life, urgent duties of one's state, fear lest a certain milieu win and dissipate souls, joys to be had in generous action which opens up and enlarges one's power, the aridites and apparently useless abjection of prayer, and above all a great pity for souls who surround us and whose extreme material or spiritual misery is a constant appeal to our Christian charity.

Activism presents itself ordinarily as a natural tendency to which one yields. At times it may be an error not only practical, but speculative; one finds it so in many Christians, even the well educated. It becomes then a sort of religious positivism which believes only in the value of human activity for the production of supernatural effects and for building up the mystical body of Christ. It neither understands nor admits that a notable part of the day should be reserved for silent prayer; and especially, that entire lives be vowed exclusively to prayer and sacrifice, to the end that deep sources of life may spring up in the Church.

The heresy of good works, whether it rests on a natural tendency or on a conviction, because it denies in practice by neglecting it, the action of the Holy Spirit in the soul and in the Church, weakens the spiritual life, renders sterile the apostolate even though it be adorned with brilliant external success; and it often leads to lamentable moral and spiritual catastrophes.

On the other hand, do we not often find in the other camp, I mean among the contemplatives, a kind of contempt for action even to the point of scorn for the active life, and a firm conviction that the contemplative life alone is capable of producing high sanctity? This practical error grows out of an exaggerated fear of the dangers of activity, and a certain spiritual gluttony in souls too much attached to the delights of union with God.[13] We must therefore now consider the *necessity* of activity:

[13] Rather frequently we find Saint Teresa concerned to fight against this prejudice or tendency of contemplatives. Here is what she says in the *Book of the Foundations:* "What is the reason of the discontent which we generally experience when for a great part of the day we have not been withdrawn apart and absorbed in God, although we may have been employing ourselves in these other matters? There are two reasons, I think. One, the more important, is a kind of self-love which insinuates itself here, and so subtly that we do not realize that we are more anxious to give pleasure to ourselves than to God. For, of course, when one has begun to taste 'how sweet the Lord is,' one finds more pleasure in allowing the body to rest from its labours and the soul to receive His gifts. . . .

"The second reason which can account for this discontent is, I think, that, as solitude brings with it few opportunities for offending the Lord, the

1. Is it not true that God the Father, whose perfection is set before us as a model,[14] is pure act as well as light and spirit? He contemplates Himself, engenders His divine Son, spirates infinite Love. And these intimate operations of His triune life do not hinder the overflowing of His life into the world, nor the action of His wisdom, "worker of all things" [15] who "reacheth from end to end mightily and ordereth all things sweetly." [16]

2. Charity which is a participation in the life of God is, like God, contemplative and active. Communicative of itself, it manifests itself by prayer and sacrifice; but also, by external activity.

Speaking of a man who would be satisfied to let his faith be only an interior assent of the mind, or a feeling, the apostle Saint James writes:

> What will it profit, my brethren, if a man says he has faith, but does not have works? Can the faith save him? And if a brother or a sister be naked and in want of daily food, and one of you say to them, "Go in peace, be warmed and filled," yet you do not give them what is necessary for the body, what does it profit? So faith too, unless it has works, is dead in itself.[17]

In the evening of this life we shall be judged on love, says Saint John of the Cross. But our Lord states more precisely still, the necessity of that love which is expressed in good works: "Come thou blessed of my Father. I was hungry and you gave me to eat; thirsty, and you gave me to drink . . ."

In the perfect flowering of transforming union, such love is

---

solitary soul seems to be purer . . . This certainly seems to me a more suffi-cient reason . . . than that of obtaining great favours and consolations from God. It is here, my daughters, that love is to be found—not hidden away in corners but in the midst of occasions of sin" (*Foundations*, v; Peers, III, 20, 25).

[14] "You therefore are to be perfect, even as your heavenly Father is per-fect" (Matt. 5:48).

[15] Wis. 7:21.

[16] Wis. 8:1.

[17] Jas. 2:14-17.

drawn irresistibly to the works of the apostolate. Saint Teresa writes of souls at this spiritual height:

What they desire now is not merely not to die but to live for a great many years and to suffer the severest trials, if by so doing they can become the means whereby the Lord is praised, even in the smallest thing.[18]

Thus Saint Therese of the Child Jesus, in Chapter XI of her *Autobiography,* tells of her burning desire to fulfil all vocations, to undergo all torments, and to work to the end of time.

How then can we condemn works that love calls for? Theology, moreover, with Saint Thomas, considers the mixed life in which contemplation overflows in fruitful works, as the most perfect form of life and hence superior, considered in itself, to the purely contemplative life.

3. This is what the catechism also teaches in a very simple form when it says that God created us to know Him, to love Him, and to serve Him; to serve, by the activity of all our powers and faculties.

That God has ordained human activity to enter as a necessary element into the realization of His grandest designs, is one of the most beautiful and astounding truths. The Holy Spirit builds the Church and sanctifies souls with the instrumental co-operation of the apostles and their successors to whom it has been said: "Go, teach all nations, baptizing them in the name of the Father . . ." God gives the increase, but it is Paul who sowed and Apollo who watered. "How are they to believe him whom they have not heard? And how are they to hear, if no one preaches?" [19]

If the priest does not preach, does not consecrate, does not work, souls die of starvation. Where he is absent, faith disappears. Let a parish remain twenty years without a priest, said the Curé of Ars, and its people will be adoring beasts. On the other hand, where the priest is active, zealous, and holy, the Christian life develops and sanctity appears.

[18] VII Mansions, iii; Peers, II, 340.
[19] Rom. 10:14.

Although it is a secondary cause, leaving the primacy to the action of grace, apostolic activity has a tremendous importance in the growth of divine life in souls.

4. Necessary to the life of the Church, activity is also indispensable to the maintenance of good human balance.

*Vita in motu,* it can be said. Life is in movement; it is manifested by movement, and needs movement. Joy, health, balance are found in a moderate activity, proportionate to one's strength. To want to annihilate the natural energies of one's sense powers or higher faculties, reducing them to a state of inaction—even were this for the sake of the superior good of perfect contemplation—would be to expose oneself to physiological disorders and a rupture of human balance. Accumulated energies soon overrun the will, subjecting body and soul to the rebound of violent instincts, with tyrannical force.

5. The contemplative lives ordinarily in community: this imposes on him the duty of taking his share in the tasks of the common life. But even if he should be completely dispensed from charitable services in the society of his brethren, he would still need the diversion that external works secure, for the development of his contemplation.

Saint Teresa avows that at times she felt herself burning with so intense an interior fire, and urged by such an impulse to serve God in something, that certain occupations of charity were a relief to her.[20] It may also happen that the faculties, as it were stupefied and agitated after an unusually strong divine rapture or deep recollection, are incapable of any interior activity, although having the desire for it. To force them into it would be dangerous. Then the diversion afforded by a moderate activity permits them to recover their energies and normal equilibrium; and afterwards to bear, without weakening, new touches of the divine Guest dwelling in the soul.

"Exceptional cases," some will object. Perhaps indeed; but to be pointed out nevertheless, for they concern souls whose

[20] *Life,* xxx.

failure in the contemplative life would be all the more regrettable, in that they are admirably endowed to progress in it and
favored by an intense action of God.

We might mention too in passing, those souls of whom
Saint Teresa speaks in the *Book of the Foundations*. These also
seem to be gifted for contemplation; but they give way under
the slightest divine action. The prolonged prayer which fills
them with joy and sweetness brings them at once to a psychical
swoon most dangerous to their psychological and spiritual
balance. The life of Martha is best for them, not that of Mary,
proclaims Teresa with authority.[21]

We come now to situations that are more frequent—almost
banal, they are so common. In the midst of painful purifications, in those indefinable states in which obscurely and profoundly God's action, and sin, and often pathological tendencies, conflict with one another, the soul of the contemplative
is inclined to reflect on itself. It analyzes its suffering, dwells
on the causes and remedies, and thus increases and prolongs it
uselessly. But if it goes out of itself, especially to do acts of
charity, the soul leaves the field free for God's action, forgets
its trial without diminishing its purifying value, and keeps all
its strength to serve God and to suffer usefully.

Saint Therese of the Child Jesus used to recommend turning to works of charity when it was getting too dark in the
soul. The Carthusian has his workshop in his hermitage, and a
little garden. Among the solitaries of the Thebaïd, manual
work was in great honor; and the Carmelite Rule insists as

---

[21] "I know some, souls of great virtue, who have been in such a state for
seven or eight hours and have believed it all to be rapture; and every virtuous practice affected them in such a way that they immediately relinquished
control of themselves, because they thought that it was not right to resist
the Lord. If they were to go on in that way, and to find no remedy, they
would gradually lose their senses or die" (*Foundations,* vi; Peers, III, 27).

This counterfeiting of high mystical graces, not because of a person's
perversity but rather his psychical weakness, greatly preoccupied Saint Teresa.
She gave the entire Chapter vi of the *Foundations* to describing it and indicating remedies. The chapter is remarkable for the penetration and finesse
of its psychological and psychiatric analyses.

much on work as on silence. Jean de Saint Samson, in his *Véritable Esprit du Carmel* (*True Spirit of Carmel*), makes it a duty of superiors to oblige any religious who persists in staying always in his cell, to go outdoors. This well-known blind brother who added luster to the Carmelite Reform of Touraine seems to have made it his principal aim to annoy the spiritual gluttony of any contemplative, too eager for the tranquility and delights of silence.

These ventures of the contemplative soul sallying forth to exterior activity are often painful. They seem to involve a renunciation of all that contemplation yields of joy, of delights, of grace, or even simply of subtle but deep peace. They impose on the faculties that are purified or in the way of purification, a return to painful occupations, to disquieting contacts with natural realities or with souls whose defects the contemplative cannot fail to see. It is the entirely human that is met with, in all that is irksome to the soul bathed in the light of God, and that threatens to invade it with its impurities. We have only to think on the word of our Lord: "O unbelieving and perverse generation, how long shall I be with you?"; [22] or again, on the anguish of the Curé of Ars and his repeated attempts to flee from his distressing ministry and retire into the solitude of a Trappist monastery. And yet it was necessary that Christ remain with His own to work out the Redemption; and that the holy Curé of Ars consent to lose his peace of soul in order to become a great saint and marvelous converter.

6. How then can we resolve this problem of activity and prayer, of maintaining the silence that is indispensable to contemplation and yet carrying on activity. The religious will usually find in the rule of his order and the will of his superiors the measure to be kept, with all the useful precisions. Outside of the religious life, the solution to this problem is bound up with the other problem of one's vocation and the practical organiza-

[22] Matt. 17:16.

tion of one's life. Supposing for now that all this is settled in the individual case—we shall take it up soon again in speaking of solitude—here are a few directives:

*a.* Give scrupulously to prayer the time prescribed for it by obedience, and guard it jealously against the encroachments of activity. Excessive and disordered would be any solicitude for temporal goods, or even for souls, which claimed regularly that allotted time. Under pretext of charity or of zeal, this might be indicative of a lack of confidence in God who also "watches over Israel" and will fulfil scrupulously His obligations, if we are faithful to ours. "Seek first the kingdom of God and His justice," it is truly written, "and these things shall be given you besides." [23]

*b.* Give to activity, especially to the duties of one's state, all the time and all the energy that perfect accomplishment demands. Even a concern for keeping the presence of God, or reserving for God alone a part of one's strength, would not be sufficient motive for holding back from the task assigned any of the physical or intellectual energies that it requires.

The work that is the will of God permits us to commune with God through our will and charity as efficaciously as prayer itself permits us to grasp God through the intellect and faith. These two communings through faith and through charity complete one another and harmonize to create sanctity.

The problem of vocation being once settled, and consequently of one's duties of state, any discussion on the value in itself of such or such a way of life is useless—on the excellence of the contemplative life or the active. Vocation places each one in the relative order that it commands and which becomes by that fact the better one for those who are called to it. The acts that it imposes are for those who follow it the most sanctifying. The duties of state that it entails are for them the only way to holiness.

[23] Matt. 6:33.

Alas, how many mistakes, how much waste of time and of energy result from false lights on this point, or from errors in perspective. Deceived by personal tastes and attractions, we go about doing supererogatory works of charity, or we save ourselves for supplementary prayers, and thus divert energies that were needed to accomplish some duty of state that was really assigned to us in the providential plan. The supernatural motives that we so readily find to back up such vagaries do not excuse the secret selfishness concealed in them, and do not repair the harm done to the soul and to those it was meant to serve.

*c.* Activity is beneficial to the soul which carries it on in union with the will of God. It becomes harmful if it is feverish.

Who does not know the feverish excitement that grips the faculties sometimes even before they act; but more often, during the course of an action. It withdraws them from the dominion of the will, from the control of reason and the influence of the supernatural motive, gives them up blind and tremulous to the fascin tion of the end to be attained and the work to be done in a set time. The result is disorder in the activity itself and lack of due moderation. Excitement is harmful to the spiritual life, for it cuts the contact between the natural activity of the faculties and the supernatural virtues which ought to direct and form them. The order is turned upside down: it is the work that takes over the direction of the powers.

One can re-establish order and place the activity again under the dependence of the higher faculties of the soul only by calming the feverish agitation that has disturbed and upset everything. Ordinarily, it requires a shock to do this: the shock of a sudden diversion, for instance, or a sharp stopping of the activity. The soul recollects itself, imposes silence and tranquility on its powers, takes them in hand again, finds God once more, and goes back to its task. This will then be better done because done in calm and order. But shocks do not come without a sort of violence; repeated too often, they could break and exhaust one's energies, exasperating them. Renewed with wise discretion, however, they discipline the overflowing waves of natural activity and secure to the soul a certain mastery of itself. Especially, they give testimony to God of the good will of the soul that submits and thus attracts new inflowings of divine grace. They prepare the soul for the complete victory of God over its most rebellious active powers.

*d.* There are two periods in the development of the spiritual life when the problem of uniting activity with contemplation usually becomes more agonizing for the soul, and when illusion on this point is both easier and more dangerous.

The first spiritual experiences of contemplation, which have all the delicate and sweet charms of a lovely dawn, arouse an eagerness for supernatural impressions and an intense need for the repose and silence in which they are produced. This need, which is accompanied by a certain distaste and even at times an inability for either external or intellectual activity, asserts itself with the rigor of an absolute. The soul longs for complete solitude and would like to escape from all troublesome activity. And yet, neither physically nor morally nor spiritually is the soul capable of supporting such isolation and inactivity. To satisfy this desire would be to doom to disorders already mentioned and to loss of balance, faculties that cannot yet bear the constraint of an absolute repose. Attractions created by divine graces already received are ordinarily a call to contemplation and mark an aptitude for it; but they are blind. Only prudent and experienced direction can indicate to each one, according to his temperament and grace, how he is to respond by a wise mixture of passive silence, exterior activity, and intellectual work. Clearly, a soul just taking its first steps in the religious life, whatever may be its desires for absolute silence, needs a prudent diversion of activity in order that it may bear, without weakening, the restraints of the regular and rigid routine that is imposed upon it.

Almost the same problem arises when the soul, already strengthened by numerous works and perhaps with rich supernatural experiences, seems fixed in habitual contemplation. Then, whether this contemplation be painful or delightful, it creates a great need for silence. The soul feels itself capable of braving the rude asceticism of the desert and is hungry for it. Who could stop it? God does—by providential events or through superiors. The riches of that soul are transparent; the spiritual balance that it has attained can be seen. It draws others. Then comes the torture of important works and multiple cares that are put upon it under the form of duties of its state. Which is it to believe: the interior call that rises from its inmost depths, or the exterior call no less explicit? It is beset in two directions and, as it were, scattered. Do its attractions deceive it; or must it blame events and free causes, and defend itself against them?

Both calls come from God. Their opposition is only apparent. In reality, they complete one another, as the soul will come to see. They harmonize, as do the action of motor and brake for the progress and safety of a vehicle. Thus the soul is incited to strive for the perfect life of God. The Holy Spirit urges it to the charity that gives and is given; and at the same time He holds it back lovingly, that it may not spend itself in exterior activity. Now He draws it into the depths of the divine life; and again, He procures diversions of external activity for it, to ensure its balance. The faults that the soul commits in this phase of its spiritual life will be more profitable for it than many a victory carried off in less perilous circumstances. They will increase the humility that attracts God, and the indulgent charity that draws men. It is for these souls that Saint Teresa writes:

We must needs be careful, in doing good works, even those of obedience and charity, not to fail to have frequent inward recourse to our God. And, believe me, it is not length of time spent in prayer that brings a soul benefit: when we spend our time in good works, it is a great help to us and a better and quicker preparation for the enkindling of our love than many hours of meditation. Everything must come from the hand of God. May He be blessed for ever and ever.[24]

### 3. INTERIOR SILENCE

It is in the deep center of the soul, in its most spiritual depth, that God dwells and carries on the mysterious operations of His union with us. What matter, then, the external noise and activity, provided silence reigns in this spiritual domain of our divine Guest. Interior silence is the most important. Exterior silence has value only in the measure that it favors the inner.

But the actual acquirement of interior silence is bristling with difficulties that put contemplative souls to torture. A little gain in that direction is followed by an agonizing loss in another, an almost absolute impossibility of disciplining the faculties that were previously docile to prayer. The soul is worried, is restless. Errors in tactic are frequent; and the more so, because of current prejudices concerning the interior pacification that accompanies spiritual progress.

Saint Teresa often relates in detail her sufferings on this score, saying that these were intensified by her ignorance of certain laws of psychology and of God's action in the soul. In this connection she wrote these words, already quoted several times:

O Lord, do Thou remember how much we have to suffer on this road through lack of knowledge. . . . Hence proceed the afflictions of many people who practise prayer, and their complaints of interior trials . . . so that they become melancholy, and their health declines, and they even abandon prayer altogether.[25]

In order to ward off crises that are so disastrous and afflicting, let us try to clarify the problem of interior silence.

We have distinguished two phases in the development of

[24] *Foundations*, v; Peers, III, 26.
[25] IV Mansions, i; Peers, II, 233-4.

the spiritual life. In the *first phase,* which includes the first three Mansions, God intervenes only with general help; the soul keeps the initiative in prayer and directs the activity of the faculties. In the *second phase,* which begins at the fourth Mansions, God intervenes with that particular help which, progressively, establishes the predominance of the divine activity over the activity of the powers of the soul. Each one of these two phases requires a different asceticism for the practice of interior silence.

1. During the first period the soul can grow in recollection and interior silence by applying the psychological laws that govern the activity of the human faculties. The will can exercise direct control over the imagination and the understanding. It can stop their activity, turn it away from such or such an object, fix it on another of its choice. But this direct control could not be constant. It takes place by successive acts that could not be multiplied to the point of being continuous. Between times, the faculties recover a certain independence of the will. Then they respond to the laws of a succession of images, and are diverted by the impact of external perceptions. Yet the will can bring this activity too under its control indirectly by choosing a setting where the faculties have fewer objects to distract them, and more to lead them back to the thought of God.

In the *Way of Perfection,* Saint Teresa describes quite minutely this delicate asceticism of active recollection. We have previously [26] heard her tell in detail how important it is to clear the "palace of vulgar people and all kinds of junk," [27] to have recourse to Christ, and to "get an image or a picture of this Lord—one that you like," [28] "to have a good book, written in the vernacular," [29] to "use a great deal of skill," [30]

[26] Cf. THE FIRST STAGES, ii, iii, iv, vi.
[27] *Way of Perfection,* xxviii; Peers, II, 118.
[28] *Ibid.,* xxvi; 109.
[29] *Ibid.*
[30] *Ibid.;* 110.

and to put forth persevering efforts until we have acquired an habitual facility for entering into active recollection.

And when we begin to pray we shall realize that the bees are coming to the hive and entering it to make the honey.[31]

2. The second phase requires a notably different method for the practice of silence.

*Description:* God now intervenes with particular help; His supernatural action is in the soul and faculties, but in different degrees and different ways. The divine rapture that captivates by its sweetness, or paralyzes the soul in aridities, is not uniform in its effects. Starting from the depths of the soul, it usually affects the will first, radiates rather often to the intellect, but rarely fetters the memory and the imagination. Complete rapture or suspension of all the faculties is produced only in the graces of mystical union of the fifth Mansions and in the ecstasy of the sixth, and lasts a very short time. On the other hand, the captivation of the will may be prolonged considerably in a sweet prayer of quiet or of passive recollection which also affects the senses.

During the time that the will is thus held captive and is sweetly bound to the divine Reality, the other faculties have no mistress to obey. They go here and there, without guide or law, towards God as towards the most futile things. If the will pursued them to bring them back and control them, it would lose contact with the Supreme Good. It must not.

At times, by a quick touch or by a radiation of grace, some delightful effect of contemplation reaches those volatile faculties. They profit then by the strength they receive, to turn also to the divine Reality with an urgency that runs great risk of disturbing the soul's contemplation and the silence that this requires. If God responds to their desires for Him and lays hold on them anew, there is produced in them that motion to and fro, so often described by Saint Teresa, which can make

[31] *Ibid.*, xxviii; 116.

one think there has been prolonged suspension of the faculties. The divine seizure of these faculties can also be painful and fatiguing. Painful or sweet, it draws them during prayer to a feverish activity; after prayer, it ordinarily awakens in them a need for independence, and frequently brings on a kind of frenzied activity.

It appears, then, that contemplative graces, producing different and sometimes contrary effects in the lower and higher faculties, divide them rather than unite them, establishing zones of profound peace and zones of disordered commotion. Saint John of the Cross speaks of the peaceful depth of the soul and distinguishes it from the turbulent outskirts to which he relegates the discursive reason and sense powers.

Let no one think, moreover, that growth in contemplation will assure a durable and constant tranquility in all the faculties. These are fickle, restless powers and always remain so. Saint Teresa and Saint John of the Cross are still lamenting their deviations when they have arrived at the peace of spiritual marriage. John of the Cross makes us take note, too, that a disquiet can be provoked in these faculties by the action or simply the presence of the devil. Perhaps we ourselves know by experience how sharp is the suffering caused by such a duality and unrest, while the soul is longing for silent peace and the repose of perfect union. But let us listen to Saint Teresa, always so helpful in her descriptions:

At other times I find myself unable to formulate a single definite thought, other than quite a fleeting one, about God, or about anything good, or to engage in prayer, even when I am alone. . . . It is the understanding and the imagination, I think, which are doing me harm here. My will, I believe, is good, and well-disposed to all good things; but this understanding is so depraved that it seems to be nothing but a raving lunatic—nobody can repress it and I have not myself sufficient control of it to keep it quiet for a moment.[32]

Only quite recently it chanced that for a full week I was in such a condition that I seemed to have lost all sense of my debt to God and was unable to recapture it. I could not remember His favours; and

[32] *Life*, xxx; Peers, I, 201.

my soul had become so stupid and so much occupied (I know not
with what, or how; it was not that I had bad thoughts but that I was
incapable of thinking any good ones) that I would laugh at myself
and find it pleasant to realize how low a soul can sink when God is
not forever working within it. . . . The soul collects wood and does
all it can by itself, but finds no way of kindling the fire of the love of
God. It is only by His great mercy that the smoke can be seen,
which shows that the fire is not altogether dead. Then the Lord comes
back and kindles it, for the soul is driving itself crazy with blowing
on the fire and rearranging the wood, yet all its efforts only put out
the fire more and more.[33]

These states of powerlessness and turmoil in the faculties
were particularly distressing to the temperament of Teresa,
so ardent and so well balanced. Such descriptions reappear
under various forms in her writings. There is no use in multiplying quotations. Yet here again is what the Saint says of her
inner state while she was writing the *Interior Castle,* having
already arrived at spiritual marriage:

As I write this, the noises in my head are so loud that I am beginning to wonder what is going on in it. As I said at the outset, they
have been making it almost impossible for me to obey those who
commanded me to write. My head sounds just as if it were full of
brimming rivers, and then as if all the water in those rivers came
suddenly rushing downward; and a host of little birds seem to be
whistling, not in the ears, but in the upper part of the head, where
the higher part of the soul is said to be.[34]

The noise does not grow less as one goes deeper into the
interior Mansions; the descriptions given by Saint John of the
Cross bear out this fact. We cannot say that it increases, but
it is certain that the purified soul is more painfully affected by
it; and also, that the noise is localized in the most exterior
faculties.

*Practical directives.* How is one to react against this disquiet
of the faculties and cultivate interior silence in the second phase
of the spiritual life?

We have heard from Saint Teresa that she laughed at the

[33] *Ibid.,* xxxvii; 264.
[34] IV Mansions, i; Peers, II, 234.

noise and her helplessness: "Sometimes I laugh at myself and realize what a miserable creature I am and then I keep an eye on my understanding and leave it alone to see what it will do." [35] The Saint had rightly understood that it would be vain to fight against superior forces—both that of God which produces such effects in our human faculties unfitted to His action, and that of the devil who tries to take revenge on the sense faculties for the defeats he undergoes in the higher regions of the soul.

1. Direct attack is useless and even harmful; and that, from the beginning of the contemplative states. Saint Teresa affirms this, speaking of the prayer of quiet:

> When the will finds itself in this state of quiet, it must take no more notice of the understanding than it would of a madman, for, if it tries to draw the understanding along with it, it is bound to grow preoccupied and restless, with the result that this state of prayer will be all effort and no gain and the soul will lose what God has been giving it without any effort of its own. . . .
> When one of you finds herself in this sublime state of prayer, which, as I have already said, is most markedly supernatural, and the understanding (or, to put it more clearly, the thought) wanders off after the most ridiculous things in the world, she should laugh at it and treat it as the silly thing it is, and remain in her state of quiet.[36]

The advice of the Saint is very firm; and easily justified. The first duty of the soul is to respect God's action within, and to favor it with the co-operation of a lively faith. If the soul runs after the restless faculties, it leaves its divine Guest and risks losing the graces of contemplation with which He is favoring it. Moreover, we know the psychological law, that the will, by attending to images and sensible realities, is drawn to their level.

2. The duty of the soul, on the contrary, is to flee towards God, betaking itself by a positive movement to the peaceful and dark regions where He is acting; even going beyond those regions to attain to the very Source whence come the sweet in-

[35] *Life,* xxx; Peers, I, 201.
[36] *Way of Perfection,* xxxi; Peers, II, 130, 132.

flowings of divine grace. Acts of faith and of love, a more and more delicate longing which flows back to God, will produce this incessant and peaceful movement, keeping the soul above the noise of the outskirts and itself, in contact with God in the hiding place of the night of faith.

3. But sometimes flight will not be possible, the soul being already caught by the tumult or by an obsession; the faculties, tired out and enervated, falling constantly back on themselves. What can one then do except lament humbly to God, that He may come to deliver the soul and calm it.

Even then, however, experience will reveal means for maintaining a loving patience and avoiding the fatigue that debilitates. Saint Teresa relaxed occasionally, on considering the wanderings of her imagination, to laugh at them. But this particular means might be dangerous for a soul less highly elevated than hers. Saint Therese of the Child Jesus used to recite slowly the "Our Father" and the "Hail Mary." Each one will find the prudent diversion that relaxes without distracting the depth of the soul; to mention for example: a vocal prayer, a physical attitude of restful recollection, reading a passage from Holy Scripture, saying a prayer to the Blessed Virgin, keeping one's gaze fixed on the tabernacle, returning to a thought or a scene from the Gospels, chosen before prayer. Any of these can serve the faculties as a rallying point that will keep them from straying away.

4. These diversions form part of the strategy of indirect control of the faculties. Although it is useless and harmful to combat directly their disturbances, it is still possible to calm them indirectly by taking from the field of their activity whatever can distract and excite them. A safeguard over the senses whose perceptions foster the disquiet is, then, a duty.

The mortification of the senses will be carried on in the direction indicated by the unrest that asserts itself during prayer. This agitation, more clearly than detailed examens, will point out the attachments that are an obstacle to God's action in the soul. Thus it will define the domain in which the asceticism of silence must be practised outside of prayer.

We know that this asceticism will not do away with the trouble; but it will at least strengthen our will to reduce it. It will offer to God the meritorious testimony of our desire for silence and of our faithfulness in seeking Him alone.

5. Disquiet during prayer will also guide the soul in practising the anagogical acts which must complete the guard over the senses. Starting with the principle that the theological virtues are engrafted in the natural faculties—faith, in the intellect; charity, in the will; hope, in the imagination and the memory—Saint John of the Cross teaches us to discipline the natural faculties by exercising the theological virtues that correspond to them. By strengthening the theological virtues, one subjugates and purifies at the same time the faculty whose attachments are preventing God's action in the soul.

Such is the problem of silence, complex and subtle to baffle all analysis. This exposition allows us at least to glimpse how difficult is the art of it, almost disappointing. In trying to make peace reign in regions where God's direct action meets with the influence of the devil, the incapacities of human weakness, and the reactions of our evil tendencies, even the most generous effort could not avoid blunders, faults, frequent suffering, and apparent failure. And so it is indeed by humiliation and patience, more than by the perfection of an art however necessary, that the soul will succeed in attracting the Mercy that purifies, heals, and brings tranquility.

# CHAPTER VI

# Solitude and Contemplation

*I will lead her into the wilderness:
and I will speak to her heart.*[1]

The contemplative who has experienced the inflowings of
the divine sweetness, or the touches of God Himself, derives
from them a taste for silence and an imperious need of solitude. For him, silence and solitude seem to be identified under
the power and attraction that lift up his soul to regions more
exalted.

## I. NECESSITY OF SOLITUDE

We find the prophet of the Old Testament, chosen by God
for his prophetic mission, leaving his family and his tribe, and
fleeing to the desert. Likewise, the intoxication of the first
graces of the religious life and the insufficient silence of his
surroundings impelled John of the Cross to seek a Carthusian
monastery. Our Lord Jesus Christ, whose humanity was hypostatically united to the Word, remained for thirty years in the
unknown solitude of Nazareth; and, on the threshold of His
public life, He withdrew for forty days into the silence of the
desert, to which He frequently returned in the course of His
apostolic life.

Solitude and God's action in the soul mutually call to each
other and seem inseparable. "I will lead her into the wilderness: and I will speak to her heart," [2] says the Lord through
the prophet Osee. Thus in all ages, God has formed in solitary
places the great contemplatives and the instruments of His
great works.

[1] Osee 2:14.
[2] *Ibid.*

Moses, after receiving at the court of the Pharaoh the best education that could be given in his time, is urged by a providential event to go into the desert. There he lives for forty years; there God manifests Himself to him in the burning bush and confers on him his high mission as leader of the Hebrew people. John the Baptist is drawn into the desert by the weight of the singular grace received on the day of the Visitation of Our Lady. Not until the age of thirty does he leave it, filled with the Spirit of God and ready to accomplish his mission as precursor. Saint Paul, after his conversion, retires into Arabia; [3] and, under the direct action of the Holy Spirit, prepares for his special mission in the apostolate. Out of solitude come the great bishops of the first centuries to build our Christian civilization. Later, Saint Ignatius of Loyola receives, during his year of solitude at Manresa, the lights that permit him to write the book of *Spiritual Exercises,* and to organize the Society of Jesus. And the Order of Carmel, which has given the Church her great mystical doctors, had its birth in the desert. There it lives, or at least it returns there incessantly for the atmosphere which can provide for its attractions and the development of its life.

Not only silence, then, but also solitude is necessary, that God may utter His word in the soul, and that the soul may hear Him and receive His transforming action. This is because the desert offers to the contemplative incomparable riches: its bareness, its silence, the reflection of God that it shows forth in its simplicity, and the divine harmonies that it holds in its poverty.

The asceticism that the desert imposes on anyone who gives himself up to it is hard; but it is supremely efficacious because it proceeds by way of absolute detachment. The desert withdraws the senses and passions from manifold satisfactions that stain the soul, and from impressions that blind and enslave. Its austerity impoverishes and detaches. Its silence isolates one

[3] Gal. 1:17.

from the external world, leaving to the soul only the uniformity of the cycles of nature and the regularity of nature's life, and thus obliges it to enter into that interior world that it went to the desert to seek.

But this poverty and silence are not a barren void; they are purity and simplicity. To the soul that has known its tranquility, the desert discloses that reflection of the divine transcendence, that immaterial ray of the divine simplicity which the soul bears in itself, that luminous trace of Him who passed in haste [4] and who remains present in His creatures by His action. The desert is filled with the presence of God; its vastness and its simplicity reveal Him; its silence imparts Him. Those who have studied the history of peoples have rightly noted that the desert is monotheistic, that it stands against a multiplicity of idols. This is an important observation, proving that the desert too yields its soul to those who let themselves be enveloped by it, and are attuned to it—yields the unique and transcendent Being who fills it.

Hence we understand how, in that purifying detachment and transparent simplicity of the desert, the spiritual understanding of the Christian contemplative can be refined and enriched in contact with the presence of God. Faith gives him certitude of this divine Presence, and experience has already rendered it real. He can go even into those regions where the gentle whisper of the Word can be perceived, and the sweet embrace of the Father, in the spiritual atmosphere aflame with the Spirit of Love. Sustained by these riches in order to go farther, the soul progresses in that interior bareness and simplicity of which the desert has yielded the secret, to attain to the very Being and Life of God, by a faith that is increasingly more pure. It is after walking for forty days in the desert, that Elias, on the desolate Mount of Horeb, hears the gentle whisper that reveals the divine Presence.

And so it is normal that the contemplative who has per-

---

[4] *Spiritual Canticle,* st. v; Peers, II, 49.

ceived God in the tranquil night of the inner and outer desert, in the "sublime and delicate anointings and touches of the Holy Spirit" of such "delicate and subtle purity" that they can be easily disturbed and hindered,[5] should yearn not only for recollected cloisters, but for solitary hermitages and the silent bareness of the desert. If he did not have such an attraction, the genuineness of his spiritual experience could well be doubted.

The truths of which we have just spoken cannot be questioned, because they rest on experiences the value of which we cannot deny.

But they raise a very practical problem. Must one dwell in the desert in order to become a contemplative, and to ensure the development of contemplative graces? Or, more precisely: Does contemplation, which has always need of silence, require likewise habitation in the desert?

One element of the answer to that question is furnished us by the testimony, already quoted, of Saint Teresa on the spiritual and contemplative value of activity imposed by obedience:

Believe me, it is not the length of time spent in prayer that brings a soul benefit: when we spend our time in good works, it is a great help to us and a better and quicker preparation for the enkindling of our love than many hours of meditation. Everything must come from the hand of God.[6]

But other motives oblige us to separate the dual problem of solitude and silence.

### 2. IMPOSSIBILITY OR DANGERS

Very numerous are the spiritual persons for whom life in solitude can be only an unrealizable dream. This one is married, has charge of a family; consequently his duties impose on him an absorbing daily task in the midst of the tumult of the world. Another has a vocation to the external apostolate and is

[5] *Living Flame*, st. iii; Peers, III, 81.
[6] *Foundations*, v; Peers, III, 26.

engaged in the multiplicity of good works that his zeal has created, or at least must carry on. There was a time when they might have hesitated between the solitary life and that which is now theirs. But the time is no longer. Moreover, they made their choice, acting in obedience to the light of their vocation. They are taken up with obligations from which they cannot withdraw, and that God requires them to fulfil faithfully.

We must ask, then, if apostolic activity—necessary for the extension of the kingdom of God—and accomplishment of the most sacred duties of family life are incompatible with the demands of contemplation and of a very elevated spiritual life. There are many souls who are thirsty for God and who feel their desires sharpening in the excessive activity to which the most authentic of their duties bind them. Could they be condemned never to arrive at the divine plenitude for which they long, because God has taken them away from the solitude of the desert? We cannot think so; for it is the same Wisdom who imposes on them these external duties and who calls every one to the Source of living water. Divine Wisdom is one and consistent in His calls and requirements. "Spirit of the power of God," strong and sweet, Wisdom makes play of obstacles, to pour out graces into holy souls throughout the ages, and make of them friends of God and prophets.

Besides, life in solitude requires a strength and certain qualities that nature reserves to an elite. On fleeing from the world and one's fellowmen, one does not leave oneself. When set against natural horizons and in a limited field of activity, the self stands out, is often disturbed, and always obtrudes itself on the psychological consciousness. Inactivity enervates; solitude and silence amplify the inner tumults and at the same time refine the powers that perceive them. The movements of the soul and its faculties, its thoughts, images, impressions, sensations, spring up in rapid succession without any external impact to interrupt them or to modify their course. They are inscribed in the soul. They impose themselves with an obsessing and often painful keenness to the point of veiling completely at times the supernatural realities that the soul had hoped to contemplate in itself and in God. The soul, withdrawing to the desert in order to find God, often finds there only itself.

And we must add that the evil spirits, they too, inhabit the desert, take refuge there after their defeats, to find a resting-place.[7] They tempt with special violence those who dwell there, as we know from the gospel account of the temptation of Jesus and from what hagiography tells us of the holy anchorites. We recall too that the evil spirits excel in increasing the confusion created by a restless inactivity to turn it to their advantage, to make their wares attractive and lay their snares. These considerations help us to understand that the desert demands valiant souls and well-balanced temperaments. It is truly the country of the strong.

How many illusions there may be even in the most sincere and ardent desires for the eremitical life! The masters whose experience and function place them at the entrance to the deserts to receive the good-willed, know this well; and, to the supernatural benevolence that they evince, they always add a prudent reserve that the future justifies only too often. Is it not said that the Carthusian monastery eliminates nine out of ten of the postulants that it receives and tries. Among these souls of good will, sincere but insufficiently enlightened, there are certainly some misanthropes, a burden to themselves and others. There are dilettantes seeking novel impressions. There are persons who are restless, or simply lazy and fond of rest. But there are also poor melancholics in search of obscurity and suffering; weaklings, highly sensitive, whom a failure or even the prospect of making an effort has discouraged. And there is also a rather large number of spiritual souls who have had a certain mystical experience, and are eager for quiet and for supernatural impressions, but are too weak nevertheless or too

[7] Luke 11:24.

little purified to undergo stronger ones or to bear with themselves without external diversion.

Each case seems to be a new case on which experience alone can throw light. If wise direction does not take care of them, solitude breaks these souls with an almost brutal force and pitilessly rejects them as physical and moral wrecks. To be true, let us add that it sometimes keeps them, and that these souls, not finding God as had been hoped for them, give the impression that they might better have fulfilled their life elsewhere.

If the solitude of the desert were absolutely necessary for the development of contemplation, we would have to conclude that all those who cannot have access to it, or were not able to stand it, or who support it so poorly, are forever barred from arriving at contemplation, which would then be the rare privilege of a few.

This is a discouraging opinion, and yet rather widespread. Is it not this that has produced the deep cleavage between the contemplative life and the active, to the extent of making us think that these are two decidedly distinct ways, obeying entirely different laws? As a consequence, it presents the contemplative person and the active as two brothers, if not at odds, at least completely unlike; limiting the first to a gaze on the eternal, the second, to temporal occupations; freeing the first from any intervention in the life of his time, and the second from any aspiration for a profound interior life.

Against this strict division, satisfactory only to those logicians who would be more concerned for conceptual clarity than for objective truth, a correct view of the spiritual life protests as do the actual lives of the saints. Already, in speaking of the gifts of the Holy Spirit, we have seen how two saints like Saint Teresa and Saint John Bosco, with an exterior and spiritual life so dissimilar because guided by such different gifts of the Holy Spirit, resemble each other astonishingly in the charisms they enjoy when they reach the summits.

### 3. THE LIFE OF THE PROPHET

But let us return to the problem that we have touched upon
and that we must solve. In what measure does contemplation,
or more generally the profound action of God in the soul, require solitude? In order not to wander off in purely speculative
considerations, let us try to stay close to the real, and look to
concrete cases for the practical solution.

The life of the prophet in Israel seems helpful in this matter,
especially when the principles that guide it are made clear to
us by the use that Carmel makes of them.

Holy Scripture shows us in the development of the life of
the Hebrew people the institution of what has been called
prophetism in Israel. Over the chosen people that He had
brought out from servitude in Egypt and led into the land of
Israel through the ministry of Moses and Josue, God reserved
to Himself absolute authority. He was both the God and the
King of Israel. When His people were unfaithful, He gave
them up to bondage under the neighboring nations, and raised
up judges to deliver them when the chastisement had opened
their eyes to their fault.

One day the Israelites went to find Samuel, their judge, and
asked for a king who would be constantly at their head. The
request displeased God and He said to Samuel: "They have not
rejected thee, but me, that I should not reign over them . . .
yet testify to them, and foretell them the right of the king,
that shall reign over them." [8]

God did not want to sacrifice any of His rights over the people entrusted with the Messianic promises. To keep all His
power over them, He set up a line of prophets, establishing
these as His spokesmen until the Babylonian captivity. Thus
the prophet is a man chosen by God to defend the divine
rights over Israel against the authoritarianism and impiety of
the kings and against the infidelity of the people.

[8] I Kings 8:7-9.

This choice confers on the prophet a permanent mission and an extraordinary power. Certain ones among the writer prophets tell us of their calling. We have for example Jeremias.[9] Isaias too tells how he was called to the mission of prophesying, and how a seraph purified his lips with a burning coal. We are less well informed on the calling of the prophets who did not write, and whom we call prophets of action. Scripture shows us Elias the Thesbite, rising up suddenly "like a flame" and beginning his mission as a prophet.[10]

This vocation is a veritable seizure by God, who separates the prophet from his surroundings, from his family, and leads him into the desert. The prophet, having become in the full sense of the word "a man of God," lives thereafter on the margin of society, isolated by his grace and his appurtenance to God. He has no fixed abode; he goes where the Spirit moves him, remains where it sets him, often wandering through Palestine, for the most part living in solitude. And what does he do? He waits on orders from God, is attentive to His voice; and for that, stays constantly in His holy presence: *Vivit Dominus in cujus conspectu sto!* He is living, the Lord in whose presence I stand! exclaims Elias, the greatest of the prophets of action.

This response that springs from faith and complete surrender to God produces an attitude eminently contemplative. In solitude, marvelous exchanges are established between God and the soul of the prophet. God gives Himself with a generosity that is often increased because of the infidelity of His chosen people; He satisfies in the prophet His need to pour out His love. Sometimes the prophet receives in his soul the grace of all Israel. He surrenders himself with a more and more perfect abandonment; his spiritual gaze, his faith, are purified.

In analyzing in our last chapter the vision on Mount Horeb, we saw the sublime and delicately pure response of the prophet

[9] Jer. 1:5-10.
[10] III Kings, 17; Eccles. 48:1.

Elias when God presented him with exterior supernatural manifestations. It is God alone that he longs for, and he shows himself satisfied only when he has found Him in the whisper of the gentle breeze. One can scarcely guess the work of sanctification and transformation that are effected in this meeting; it would take the penetration and pen of Saint John of the Cross to enter into and describe the intimacies of God with His prophet. "What dost thou here, Elias?" the Lord asks. And the prophet answers: "With zeal have I been zealous for the Lord God of hosts; because the children of Israel have forsaken thy covenant. They have destroyed thy altars; they have slain thy prophets with the sword. And I alone am left; and they seek my life to take it away." [11] The interests of God are the interest of the prophet. The flame of divine justice consumes him, and its fires are almost too burning. God lets the prophet know that there are still in Israel seven thousand men who have not bent the knee before Baal.

The prophet is a great seer of eternal things, and a familiar friend of God. But it is not solely to find in him a faithful friend that God has made the prophet; it is to have in hand a docile instrument of His will. An order from God and the prophet sets out at once to execute his perilous mission—to take a message of chastisement to the king, to assemble the people on Mount Carmel, to immolate the priest of Baal, or to lay the prophetic mantle upon Eliseus.

These missions are difficult; the prophet feels the fatigue of them, sees their dangers, experiences his own weakness. But God shows amazing solicitude for the needs of His envoy. The crows bring him food at Carith. The flour and oil of his hostess, the widow of Sarepta, are miraculously replenished while the famine lasts. An angel twice brings him bread to sustain him during his forty days' journey through the desert! The power of God is in all the deeds and words of the prophet. He prays, and immediately fire from heaven comes

[11] III Kings 19:14.

down upon the sacrifice he has prepared on Carmel. "Elias rose up like a flame," says Ecclesiasticus, "and his word burned like a tourch." The king Ochozias sends a troup of fifty armed men to seize him: the prophet calls down on them too the fire of heaven that consumes them. A second troup meets with the same fate. The third receives pardon because of the humble attitude of its commanding chief.

To draw a practical lesson from these facts, let us abstract them from the terrible and marvelous signs that accompany them, and retain only the harmonious union of contemplation and action that the prophet shows forth in his life. We must note, then, that the harmony of this synthesis does not come from merely a wise balance of external occupations and spiritual exercises, from an equilibrium established by prudence, which would both satisfy the aspirations of the soul for divine intimacy and allow for the needs of the apostolate. Balance and synthesis are realized in the life of the prophet by the very God who has seized him and moves him. The prophet is constantly in search of God, and constantly surrendered to the movements of the Holy Spirit within him and without. He gives himself up, and that is his whole occupation. It is for God to dispose of him, to detain him in solitude or to send him thither and yon. His utter *abandon* will successively bring him into the most secret intimacies of God and urge him on to the most daring exterior enterprises; but it will always bring him back, his deeds accomplished, to God who dwells in the desert. *Vivit Dominus in cujus conspectu sto!* Thus harmony between contemplation and action is realized by divine Wisdom Himself, thanks to His hold on the prophet, and to the prophet's fidelity.

The role of the prophets in Israel ended at the time of the Babylonian captivity. But Elias had formed a school. Disciples had gathered round him. Later, hermits came to establish themselves on Mount Carmel and in the Palestinian solitudes, to live by his spirit and his grace. The Order of Carmel claims this noble lineage.[12] Teresa in her turn leads souls to the summits of transforming union by indicating the laws of divine rapture and of co-operation with God's action. The Mansions of the interior castle are only stages on the way to union. At the summit is realized the harmonious synthesis that we have admired in the prophet: the soul there lives in perfect union with God, and at the same time is devoured with zeal for His glory. Then it is truly a "daughter of Elias" and lives by his spirit.

It is precisely because that spirit of Elias had taken possession of her soul that Saint Teresa was aware, at the time that the Carmelite convents were multiplying, that something essential was lacking to her work. The Carmelites in their cloister could become great contemplatives, could burn with the flame of divine love; but they could not, like the prophet, surrender themselves to God for exterior works. And so she increased her insistence with the superior general of the Carmelites to obtain authorization to found monasteries of contemplative Carmelite friars, devoted also to the ministry of souls. She had not yet founded her second convent of Carmelite nuns of the Reform before that permission was granted.

We do not need to go into the history of those difficult foundations nor the struggle of which they were the occasion. The disputes that arose at the beginning, as well as those that came up later in the very bosom of the Carmelite Reform, interest us only for the practical conclusions that they furnish concerning our subject.

The prophet, like the just man, has no laws other than those of Holy Wisdom, who sustains and inspires him. His state is a state of perfection, the one described in the last Mansions. He is elevated to it by his extraordinary calling. But not all who aspire to the prophetic spirit and want to live by it, can claim a like privilege. They will come to it, but through successive stages, by practising an asceticism, by organizing their life. The prudence that the prophet, entirely submissive as he was

[12] V Mansions, i; Peers, II.

to divine Wisdom, could afford to neglect, resumes its rights and imposes its rules on those who make the spiritual ascent more slowly.

How can one go directly to the summits of the prophetic ideal, live by it in fact—that is, unite contemplation and action—before possessing all that it entails? Here arises the almost eternal conflict between two different tendencies: the contemplative temperament, which is afraid of losing its contemplation; and the active temperament, which finds joy and delight only in action. Both of these tendencies considered in their extreme are doomed to failure: the first, in a spiritual egoism that neglects the gift of self; the second, in a dissipation of energy that destroys contemplation. This conflict occurred in the very bosom of the Teresian Reform. A man of genius, and a great religious—the greatest of the Reform, they say, after Saint Teresa and Saint John of the Cross—Father Thomas of Jesus, gave to this problem a solution, of which the fruitful effects show the excellence. His life and work belong to the general history of the Church.

### 4. THOMAS OF JESUS

Thomas of Jesus (Diaz Sanchez of Avila) was born in Andalusia in 1564, while Teresa was having her first peaceful years at Saint Joseph of Avila. Of remarkable intelligence, at nineteen he had exhausted the various branches of ecclesiastical learning and was studying civil law at Baeza, while John of the Cross was rector of the College of Carmelites. Studying at Salamanca a little later, he had the opportunity—thanks to one of his friends, a relative of Saint Teresa—to read a copy of the works of the Saint. He was captivated by it; and, when his friend entered the Order of Discalced Carmelites, he followed. Professed in 1587, priest in 1589, he was sent to Seville as professor.

Here this contemplative finds himself now dedicated to action. A practical problem presents itself: how to combine contemplation and action in his life as religious and professor. He reflects, he prays, he co-ordinates his ideas and his experiences. He writes a memoir. In this memoir he recommends, at the center of the Teresian Reform of the Discalced Carmelites, the creation of monasteries that would be veritable Carthusian solitudes. In these solitudes, called "holy deserts," austerities would be greater, silence continual. There would be moreover isolated hermitages to which the religious would withdraw during Advent, Lent, or other times. The purpose of this sojourn in the desert is to maintain the contemplative spirit, to preserve the subjects and the Order against the invasion of activity. It is also to prepare the soul for action by submitting it more profoundly to the inflowing of divine grace. The holy desert is to ensure the equilibrium of the mixed life by safeguarding for contemplation the principal directive influence that it must keep. Such is the recommendation of the religious professor.

The memoir is presented to Father Doria, who is frightened by the project: he fears lest the desert empty the monasteries of their best subjects—a rather narrow calculation that we cannot hold too much against him, for two years later he approves the project and allows it to be carried out.

A desert is founded, then, at Bolarca on the banks of the Tagus. But Father Thomas of Jesus, after inaugurating the movement, cannot profit by it; for he is a professor and soon becomes the provincial of Old Castile at thirty-five. He founds another desert at Salamanca and, when his term as provincial is over, he retires there. He stays for seven years as its prior.

These are fruitful years for Thomas of Jesus. He drinks at the Source of living water, and prepares himself to make its refreshing graces spring up from his soul for all who came to him, hungry and thirsty for God. He meditates, he works. But now Pope Paul V, who has heard of him, summons him to Italy to start out on a missionary apostolate. He hesitates. An interior light confirms the call of the head of Christianity. Like

Elias in his cave, living in the presence of God, he has felt the
zeal for God's glory burning within him. Had not Teresa herself felt these ardors after the peaceful years at Saint Joseph of
Avila? The same grace produces the same effects in souls.
Father Thomas of Jesus leaves for Italy and puts himself at
the disposition of the pope.

To respond to the desires of the pope and at the same
time to fulfil a hope dear to Saint Teresa, he proposes to the
holy father to found a third Carmelite Congregation, called "of
Saint Paul," a congregation to be devoted uniquely to the missions. We are now at the beginning of the seventeenth century:
this contemplative is a forerunner in the history of the Church.

Father Peter of the Mother of God, general of the congregation in Italy, who had sustained Father Thomas of Jesus in his
plans, dies in the meantime. His successor has the brief for the
erection of the Congregation of Saint Paul retracted. Then
Thomas of Jesus, in exile from Spain, suspect among his Ital-
ian brothers, falls into disgrace. He profits by this to put in order
and write down his thoughts on the missionary apostolate. The
work that he composes, *De procuranda salute omnium gentium*,
is a veritable summa of the missionary apostolate, and was to
be a long time the classical manual adopted by the Congregation of the Propaganda. Thomas of Jesus recommends especially the creation at Rome of a central organization to support,
direct, and co-ordinate the apostolate throughout the world—
an organization that was in fact set up and became the Congregation of the Propaganda. He treats also of the necessity of
having special seminaries for the missions, for each race.

The pope meanwhile does not forget Thomas of Jesus. By a
happy intervention, he restores him to favor and entrusts him
with the foundations in France and Belgium for which he had
summoned him.

In 1610 Father Thomas of Jesus is in Paris to make the first
moves that were to end the following year in the foundation of
the Carmelite monastery, rue de Vaugirard. When the time

comes for its opening, he is already in Flanders where M. Ana de Jesús had received him with great joy. Superior of the Carmelite nuns and provincial of the friars for twelve years (1611–23), he multiplies monasteries and convents in Brussels, Louvain, Anvers, Cologne, Tournai, Malines, Liège, Valenciennes, on and on. Nor does he ever forget that a holy desert is necessary to the life of his Order; in 1619 he establishes one at Marlagne, near Namur.

In the midst of his foundations and administration, he still finds time to finish his great treatises on the spiritual life: on the *Practice of Living Faith,* on *Prayer,* and on *Divine Contemplation.*

In 1623 he returns to Rome as general definitor. There he has a holy death in 1627.

Father Thomas left an example and a teaching of the highest spiritual interest.

The prophet, as we saw, shows forth the harmonious balance of contemplation and action, effected by God's hold on the soul. By the creation of holy deserts, Thomas of Jesus teaches us how to offer ourselves progressively to that divine captivation and how to cultivate balance in our life, while awaiting God's conquest of it. The *more precise lessons* of his practical teaching, which will serve as conclusions to this study, can be thus stated:

1. Solitude, because of the quality of the silence that it secures, is necessary to the development of supernatural contemplation. It must, then, form part of every contemplative life.

2. It suffices if this solitude be intermittent; but being intermittent it must be all the more profound. And it must be more protected as it is more threatened by invasions of the world.

3. The activities of the apostolate can be united with contemplation thus protected, and sustained with the daily bread of prayer. There results a harmonious balance which purifies both, enriches them, and mutually renders them fruitful.

4. It is the perfect balance of contemplation and action which characterizes the prophet, and makes the perfect apostle.

Such is the teaching of Thomas of Jesus; its import and value for our time seem tremendous.

# CHAPTER VII
# Contemplation

*If God gives a soul such pledges, it is
a sign that He has great things in store
for it.*[1]

The gift of self, humility, silence: these not only surrender
the soul to the direct action of God, but exercise an almost irresistible pressure on the divine liberty, forcing God as it were
to intervene in the spiritual life of the soul through the gifts
of the Holy Spirit.

What is the nature and what are the effects of this intervention, we must ask. And further, how is one so to comply with
the diverse modes of the divine action, as to assure its whole
efficacy. Before taking up this subject, Saint Teresa herself
meditates and prays; for it constitutes the most important part
of her treatises, especially of the *Interior Castle*. She says:

Before I begin to speak of the fourth Mansions, it is most necessary
that I should do what I have already done—namely, commend myself to the Holy Spirit, and beg Him from this point onward to speak
for me, so that you may understand what I shall say about the Mansions still to be treated.[2]

Let us do the same, for we cannot penetrate into these new
regions without a special help from God, as the Saint explains:

For we now begin to touch the supernatural and this is most difficult to explain unless His Majesty takes it in hand, as He did when
I described as much as I understood of the subject, about fourteen
years ago. . . .[3]

The understanding is incapable of describing them in any way accurately without being completely obscure to those devoid of experi-

[1] *Way of Perfection*, xxxi; Peers, II, 133.
[2] IV Mansions, i; Peers, II, 230.
[3] *Ibid.* cf. also *Life*, xi-xxvii.

ence. But any experienced person will understand quite well, especially if his experience has been considerable.[4]

We are entering here into the domain of mystical theology which by definition is a science of hidden mysteries. Teresa modestly expresses regret that she has not as much knowledge as would be needed to throw full light on this subject:

> For many purposes it is necessary to be learned; and it would be very useful to have some learning here, in order to explain what is meant by general and particular help; . . . and learning would also serve to explain many other things about which mistakes may be made.[5]

She does not try, therefore, to give a scientific explanation but limits herself to explaining "the feelings of the soul when it is in this Divine union." [6] The mystical science of John of the Cross comes to her aid, clarifying her own descriptions, astonishingly delicate and precise as these are.

The harmonized teaching of the Reformers of Carmel have provided us the most sure guide in these regions of mystery, and given to mystical theology its most solid principles and firmest bases. And very fortunately; for we are seeing in our day a marked return to these questions. Spiritual snobbishness, some say. It seems not so; at least, not ordinarily. Rather, the current intellectual confusion and uncertainty as to the morrow are creating an intense need of the absolute and the transcendent. Perhaps the masters of Carmel from the height of heaven are witness to the many inquiring and restless minds who are seeking their doctrine, a throng of souls eager for spiritual light and life. With what tenderness these givers of the Divine and the Infinite must stoop down to assuage the anguish and hunger of these souls. May they help us also, that we may not weaken their message!

[4] *Ibid.*
[5] *Life,* xiv; Peers, I, 85.
[6] *Ibid.,* xviii; 106.

## A. Contemplation in general

The intervention of God in the spiritual life will usually first occur in the direct relations of the soul with God; consequently, in prayer. It will transform prayer into contemplation. Hence it is contemplation that offers itself first of all to our study.

### 1. DEFINITIONS

Many definitions have been given of contemplation. The following one is from Richard of Saint Victor:

*"Contemplatio est perspicuus et liber contuitus animi in res perspiciendas.* Contemplation is an attentive synthetic view, penetrating and loving, which attaches the mind to the realities that it is beholding."

Saint Thomas defines it:

*"Simplex intuitus veritatis.* A simple gaze on truth."

The Carmelite theologians of Salamanca, the *Salmanticenses*, commentators of Saint Thomas, added a word to that definition. They say:

*"Simplex intuitus veritatis sub influxu amoris.* A simple gaze on truth, under the influence of love."

These three definitions illumine and complete one another.

That of Saint Thomas, skeleton in appearance, has retained only the essential which, by its very conciseness, it puts in relief. Contemplation is an act of knowledge, a simple act that penetrates the truth, without discourse, in a quasi-intuitive way.

The *Salmanticenses* insisted on underlining the role of love in that knowledge; for love, although not essential to the act itself of contemplation which is a simple gaze on truth, is nevertheless essential to its beginning and its end. It is love that moves the mind to gaze on truth; love simplifies that gaze and fixes it on its object. In supernatural contemplation, it is through love that the soul knows, and not by the clearness of the light. Finally, the fruit of this contemplation is an increase of love. Love is, then, the beginning and the end of contemplation; it fixes and simplifies the soul's gaze; and it is from love that knowledge proceeds in supernatural contemplation. It was right that contemplative Carmelites should add to the definition of Saint Thomas the words *sub influxu amoris*.

The definition of Richard of Saint Victor adds also its light. By stressing that contemplation is a *contuitus* (an attentive synthetic view), it brings out the fact that contemplation is a living synthesis of fragmentary impressions that the soul has acquired ordinarily by successive regards. This global view is only apparently confused. It seems to neglect exterior details; but this is only in order to penetrate into the thing itself with the power of love that fixes the gaze on reality. Richard of Saint Victor points out that the *contuitus* is penetrating, is loving, and that it attaches the mind to reality.

The latter definition, almost descriptive, furnishes an interesting explanation of the genesis and nature of contemplation. We would have some difficulty, however, in finding these elements in supernatural contemplation; and so we shall retain the definition of the *Salmanticenses* as the best because the most complete, and applicable to all the forms.

### 2. ITS FIRST FORMS

Contemplation has various forms and degrees. There is no question of reserving the term "contemplation" to the supernatural or infused contemplation of which Saint Teresa speaks, beginning with the Fourth Mansions. Any act of knowledge and simple gaze on truth under the influence of love is genuine contemplation. Here it will suffice to qualify briefly each one of its forms, drawing on experience.

### a. *Aesthetic*

Suppose we are on a cliff, looking out over the vast swell of the ocean. My view takes in the details: a few fishermen's boats here and there; on the horizon, a ship; the sky's blue that the waves reflect; the slightly moving mass of the waters; the long and far-distant horizon. But now my gaze draws to a focus, details disappear, life emerges from this spectacle, a life that issues from the moving mass and the horizons weighted with the infinite. There is communication and exchange between the ocean and my soul. While an aesthetic emotion satisfies my senses and holds my attention fixed, the tableau is in turn enriched with all the impressions that it suggests, with all the life, all the associations with which my moved soul fills it. There results a synthetic view, neglecting the details in order to penetrate deeper into the living reality that holds me captivated, because I love it. I have had the experience of a real contemplation, enriching my soul with impressions, perhaps unforgettable ones, which may have a profound intellectual and moral influence on my development.

Such a contemplation bears on sensible realities; it is made through the senses and produces an aesthetic emotion. It is a lower form of contemplation; we shall call it aesthetic contemplation.

### b. *Intellectual*

Next is intellectual contemplation—that of the philosopher who, after persevering work, has found the solution to his problem: "Here it is, the idea, the principle which explains everything, in which and by which the somewhat tumultuous world of my thoughts is brought into harmony," he thinks. Or the contemplation of the scientist who, after repeated experiments, has found the law for which he has long been seeking: "Here it is, in precise terms, the law that explains everything."

Principle and law shine out before the intellectual gaze of the philosopher and the scientist—rich and simple, luminous and profound, a living synthesis. They analyze it (the principle, the law), fathom its meaning, marvel at it, love it for all the efforts it represents, for all the light they receive from it, and also for all the promise it has for the future. The philosopher and the scientist take delight in their discovery. An affective joy brings to rest the activity of the intellect, arrests their gaze which is allayed, a time at least, by the indefinable charm and vitality of the new light. Their gaze is synthetic, affective, simple. This is intellectual or philosophic contemplation.

### c. Theological

We now come to a higher level of contemplation. Here the theologian who, with all the vigor of his intellect and tenderness of his love for God and for the men whom he must instruct, studies revealed truths and searches into their formulas. Often he too is enraptured with admiration before the light that shines out from them, the beauties that they reveal; and his spiritual gaze comes to rest, tranquil, full of love, penetrating more deeply into those formulas so divinely filled with light and with life.

One need not be a theologian to experience this theological contemplation, any more than one has to be a qualified artist to feel one's faculties calmed by a profound and living gaze at the grandeur of a majestic spectacle. Thus every Christian whose faith is animated by love can contemplate a dogma of revealed truth or a gospel scene.

We place ourselves in the presence of Jesus in Gethsemane. The night is clear; olive trees with strange shapes throw a gloom over the valley. The garden is darksome; at the entrance is Jesus, His face to the ground. We approach . . . Jesus moans, seems to stir, to pronounce words intermittently. Drops of blood bead His face. All this reveals to us a terrible interior drama, the assaults of sin against the sacred humanity of Christ. Our gaze remains fixed on this agonizing sweat of blood; but it no longer sees the details. It penetrates further into the living reality. It sees the Lamb of God, who takes away the sin of the world, in a more than human agony under its overwhelming weight. Motionless, calm, full of sorrow we look on; and, as we gaze, the light enters deep and living into our inmost soul.

In these attitudes of the theologian or the simple man of faith in the presence of a divine truth or an event in the life of Christ, we recognize the simplified prayer of which we spoke in describing the Third Mansions, and that we defined as a gaze in silence.[7] Without doubt, this prayer of simplicity is true contemplation, a simple gaze on truth under the influence of love.

The contemplation of the theologian and the man of simple faith has aspects in common with philosophical contemplation. It involves the same attitude of the intellect which first takes up some subject, then penetrates it more profoundly, and finally comes to rest in the light of a deeper truth, under the influence of love. Yet we reserve a special name for the contemplation of the Christian as such; we call it theological contemplation because it differs notably from the preceding by reason of its object. While philosophical contemplation bears on a truth discovered by the unaided intellect and therefore a natural truth, theological contemplation has for its object a supernatural truth that faith makes known.

Theological contemplation, which still is human by reason of the faculty that produces it but is already supernatural by its object,[8] brings us next to a consideration of supernatural or infused contemplation.

## B. Supernatural contemplation

### I. WHAT IT IS

Supernatural or infused contemplation is the highest form of contemplation, that form to which the mystics, Saint Teresa

---

[7] Cf. THE FIRST STAGES, x, "Supernatural Wisdom and Christian Perfection," p. 310.

[8] In some cases there is, in this theological contemplation, an action of God through the gifts of the Holy Spirit, which adapting itself to the human mode of acting perfects the activity of the intellect and enlightens it.

and Saint John of the Cross in particular, reserve the name of contemplation. It answers excellently to the definition of contemplation given by the *Salmanticenses:* a simple gaze on truth under the influence of love. The truth to which this contemplation attains is not the revealed truth of faith which theological contemplation seeks to penetrate, but the divine Truth itself.

In order to be put within our reach, supernatural realities are clothed in formulated dogmas which borrow concepts and symbols from the created world. In this way, we try to set forth the infinite perfection of God by attributing to Him all the qualities that we know in creatures, qualities raised to an eminent degree and freed from the creature's imperfections. This is the most perfect expression of the divine transcendence of which the human mind is capable; but it is by way of concepts and analogy.

We must, however, beware of thinking that because it is simply analogical this expression yields only a cold concept or a symbol empty of the riches it is meant to provide. Saint John of the Cross stresses that revealed dogma (or dogmatic formulas adapted to the human intellect) contains under its silvered surfaces the gold of divine Truth itself for those who believe.

Into this divine Truth—life, light, essence of God—faith penetrates, as into its proper object, each time that it posits an act. Faith has for its object, then, mystery; and in this realm it cannot long continue since its activity is ordinarily bound to that of the intellect. The intellect is made for clarity, and how could it rest in mystery's darkness? It returns to the formula of revealed dogma and to reasonings.

But now out of the darkness of the mystery there arises (through the gifts of the Holy Spirit) a confused light, an I-know-not-what, that makes one find peace and sweetness in the mystery, that holds faith there or brings it back, freeing it from the discursive operations of the intellect and causing it to find rest and support in this light beyond all distinct lights.

God has intervened through the gifts of the Holy Spirit, has perfected faith, and produced supernatural contemplation. *Fides illustrata donis:* faith has been enlightened by the gifts, as Father Joseph de Spiritu Sancto says magnificently well.[9]

This infused contemplation is fully supernatural. Its object is the divine Truth itself. It is realized by faith, an infused supernatural virtue; and it is perfected by direct intervention of God through the gifts of the Holy Spirit.

The supernatural organism of infused contemplation is brought into action by love: *sub influxu amoris,* say the *Salmanticenses.* Love is essential to it. Love is at the beginning of the movement of faith towards divine Truth. It is through love that God intervenes to hold faith to its divine object; and it is through the gifts of the Holy Spirit, those "capacities engendered in the soul by the love of charity," that the divine interventions take place. Again, it is in a touch with the Divinity, a union of love, that the act of faith and the divine rapture of the soul terminate.

Finally, it is from the contact of love that contemplative knowledge proceeds. Saint John of the Cross writes:

> These lofty manifestations of knowledge can only come to the soul that attains to union with God, for they are themselves that union; and to receive them is equivalent to a certain contact with the Divinity which the soul experiences, and thus it is God Himself Who is perceived and tasted therein.[10]

Love not only simplifies the gaze of the soul; it engenders knowledge. Being supernatural charity, which brings about connaturality with God, love attains to contact with God; and in this contact it is enriched with the experience of God Himself.

Contemplation is, then, the science of love, the "secret wisdom"—again from Saint John of the Cross—"which, as Saint Thomas says, is communicated and infused into the soul

---

[9] Cf. Gardeil, *La structure de l'âme et l'expérience mystique,* where one can find a detailed explanation of the definition.

[10] *Ascent,* Bk. II, xxvii; Peers, I, 196.

through love." [11] It is a loving attention, calm and peaceful. It proceeds from love, progresses by steps of love, *gressibus amoris,* and reaches its perfection in the perfection of union, realized by love.

## 2. EFFECTS OF SUPERNATURAL CONTEMPLATION

The effects of supernatural contemplation are very deep and extremely varied. They differ for each degree of union and each grace. Saint John of the Cross, with his charismatic grace of mystical inspiration,[12] was pleased to describe, in the *Dark Night of the Soul,* in the *Spiritual Canticle,* and the *Living Flame of Love,*[13] some of the operations of God, the responding vibrations of the soul, and the riches received in this contemplation.

Certain philosophers have applied themselves to showing the value of the knowledge acquired through contemplation. For them, contemplation would be precious especially on account of the intimate vision of being and of the world that it secures.

It is indeed true that contemplation brings precious lights. But these are not the effects that John of the Cross is seeking. From these he is perfectly detached and does not want to rest in them an instant; for he knows that his progress towards God would be that much delayed.

The same fear of a halt on the way urges him repeatedly to put us on guard against all supernatural phenomena that accompany infused contemplation but do not form part of it.

[11] *Dark Night,* xvii; Peers, I, 456. Cf. Saint Thomas, *Sum. Theol.,* II-II, q. 45, a. 2.

[12] Cf. the article *"A propos de l'inspiration mystique de saint Jean de la Croix"* by P. Marie-Eugène de l'E. J. in *Saint Jean de la Croix, docteur de l'Eglise,* editions de l'Abeille, Lyon, 1942.

[13] In the commentary on stanza iii of the *Living Flame,* "In whose splendours," Saint John of the Cross brings out most clearly both the divine communications in contemplation and their effects in the soul.

In this general exposition of contemplation, we can only mention them; a study of the particular effects of contemplation must be made in each one of the stages or mansions.

The Saint has only one desire and asks only one thing of supernatural contemplation: that it may lead him to perfect union, to transforming union by a connaturality of love. That, in fact, is the end to which it is directly ordered; that is its essential effect. Incomparably more penetrating then natural contemplation, which reaches to the inner riches of light and of life in created things; more profound too than theological contemplation which makes its own the mysteries of eternal light contained in revealed truths; supernatural contemplation penetrates even to divine Truth, has contact with God Himself, the uncreated Light, the all-consuming Fire, the limitless Ocean, the Sun with burning rays. It keeps the soul united with Him, and submits it to the enriching and transforming action of the Infinite.

In supernatural contemplation the soul, like a mirror exposed to the rays of the sun, is all aglow with the light of the divine Sun that shines upon souls; like a sponge immersed in the ocean, it is permeated with pure waters from the Fountain of living water; like the log thrown into a fire, it too is transformed into fire by the all-consuming Fire which is God.

These different comparisons, found in the lyricism of Saint John of the Cross and other mystics, are used to express the soul's progress in intimate union and the all-pervasive action of the divine Life, wrought in contemplation. By it the soul is purified, illumined, adorned with light, with beauty, with the riches of God, transformed from brilliance to brilliance unto a likeness of the Word of God. John of the Cross says:

This is an infused and loving knowledge of God, which enlightens the soul and at the same time enkindles it with love, until it is raised up step by step, even unto God its Creator.[14]

This transformation in God is the single end towards which the desires of a truly contemplative soul can tend, a soul committed to the road of "nothing" on its way to the Absolute.

[14] *Dark Night*, xviii; Peers, I, 462.

## 3. THE SIGNS

Among the psychological effects of contemplation, Saint John of the Cross and Saint Teresa have distinguished several that are sufficiently constant and characteristic to be given as signs of supernatural contemplation.[15] Saint John of the Cross has taken care to note them in two different places, in the *Ascent of Mount Carmel* and in the *Book of the Nights*. Saint Teresa too, in the Fourth Mansions, is concerned to point out what characterizes the supernatural intervention of God with particular help.

### a. *Utility of signs*

Supernatural contemplation imposes new duties on the soul. Up to the present, the soul has had to direct and activate itself. Henceforth its first duty is to respect and favor the divine interventions, to show itself docile and silent in submitting its action to God's.

If it did not adopt this attitude of peaceful surrender that God demands of it, the soul would run the risk of wounding the divine Mercy that has bent over it, of stopping the flow of divine communications and consequently of not profiting by the graces that come to it through contemplation.

To return to forms of spiritual activity which are no longer timely when God is acting in the soul, can produce only trou-

[15] One might be surpised that the masters of Carmel, and especially Saint John of the Cross preferred to look for the signs of supernatural contemplation in an analysis of the psychological effects that it produces on the activity of the faculties and in psychological awareness, rather than in an analysis of the contemplative act itself, seeking in it the constitutive elements that we stressed in the definition of contemplation.

An analysis of the interior mechanism, such as we made for philosophical and theological contemplation, is not possible for supernatural contemplation. We are here in the presence of supernatural powers, the virtue of faith and God Himself through the gifts of the Holy Spirit—whose activity escapes any direct perception; the mystery which is the object of faith and into which it penetrates is essentially obscure.

Not being able to analyze directly the supernatural activities which take place in contemplation, the spiritual masters are reduced to discerning the effects and resonances in the psychological domain.

ble, disquiet, and perhaps discouragement if one perseveres in such a refusal of the favors of God.

On the other hand, to abandon too soon the discursive work in prayer because one thinks oneself favored with contemplation, is to lose one's time and incur the danger of establishing oneself in an idle quietude which attains neither to the infused light of God nor to the lights acquired by the work of the faculties. After warning of this danger, Saint John of the Cross invites the soul that is beginning to be favored with contemplation, to resume from time to time the discursive operations of the faculties.

It would be more dangerous still, to take for true contemplation what is only an unhealthy deformation of it; for passivity could then only favor a sad physical and perhaps moral collapse.

As wise and loving directors, Teresa and John of the Cross owed it to us, then, to throw all possible light on these regions of the spiritual life, and thus help us to discern supernatural contemplation.

### b. *Explanation of the signs*

In the *Ascent of Mount Carmel* [16] Saint John of the Cross gives "the signs which the spiritual person will find in himself and whereby he may know at what season it behoves him to leave meditation and reasoning." And in the *Dark Night* [17] he gives "the signs by which it will be known that the spiritual person is walking along the way of this night and purgation of sense." These signs are almost identical, characterizing moreover from the viewpoint of the senses, the same moment of the spiritual life. The Saint expresses them, however, in slightly different terms; and so it is possible to compare them and explain one by the other.

In the *Ascent of Mount Carmel* the Saint writes:

[16] *Ascent*, Bk. II, xiii; Peers, I, 114.
[17] *Dark Night*, lx; Peers, I, 373.

The first sign is his realization that he can no longer meditate or reason with his imagination, neither can take pleasure therein as he was wont to do aforetime; he rather finds aridity in that which aforetime was wont to attract his senses and to bring him sweetness.[18]

In the *Dark Night*, where this sign is given third, Saint John of the Cross says that this inability of the faculties comes from the fact that God is communicating Himself to the purified spirit in which there is no process of reasoning, by an act of simple contemplation in which the senses cannot participate.

The second is a realization that he has no desire to fix his meditation or his sense upon other particular objects, exterior or interior.[19]

The Saint adds the important precision that this distaste does not imply an inactivity or paralysis of the faculties:

I do not mean that the imagination neither comes nor goes (for it is wont to move freely even at times of great recollection), but that the soul has no pleasure in fixing it of set purpose upon other objects.[20]

In the *Dark Night* he makes it explicit that the failure of the soul to find pleasure in anything whatsoever created is a sign that the aridity does not come from recently committed sins and imperfections; for in that case the soul would feel some desire to taste other things than those of God.

In the same treatise the Saint calls attention to a sign which is, it seems, a consequence of this aridity; it is that

ordinarily the memory is centred upon God, with painful care and solicitude, thinking that it is not serving God, but is backsliding, because it finds itself without sweetness in the things of God. And in such a case it is evident that this lack of sweetness and this aridity come not from weakness and lukewarmness; for it is the nature of lukewarmness not to care greatly or to have any inward solicitude for the things of God.[21]

The first two signs, powerlessness of the faculties and lack of taste for any created thing, are negative signs, insufficient in

18 *Ascent,* Bk. II, xiii; Peers, I, 115.
19 *Ibid.;* 116.
20 *Ibid.*
21 *Dark Night,* ix, Peers, I, 374.

themselves. The powerlessness could come from negligence, and in that case the soul would have little desire to get over it. Both together might proceed from "melancholy or from some other kind of humour in the brain or the heart, which habitually produces a certain absorption and suspension of the senses, causing the soul to think not at all, nor to desire or be inclined to think, but rather to remain in that pleasant condition of wonder." [22]

And so, conjointly with the first two signs, there must be found the third which is positive and, according to the Saint, the most important:

The third and surest sign is that the soul takes pleasure in being alone, and waits with loving attentiveness upon God, without making any particular meditation, in inward peace and quietness and rest, and without acts and exercises of the faculties; . . . the soul is alone, with an attentiveness and a knowledge, general and loving, as we said, but without any particular understanding, and adverting not to what it is contemplating. [23]

This positive sign, the most important characteristic, is the only one that Saint Teresa indicates when, in the Fourth Mansions, she takes up the problem of the discernment of supernatural contemplation. [24] Here she shows that the supernatural intervention of God by a particular help is manifested much more clearly in the delight or sweetness of it, than in knowledge. It is the quality of the spiritual delight and the way in which it comes to the soul that make one certain of supernatural contemplation. Her psychological analysis, very simple and penetrating, nicely completes the explanation of the third sign as given by Saint John of the Cross:

These two large basins can be filled with water in different ways: the water in the one comes from a long distance, by means of numerous conduits and through human skill; . . . this corresponds to the

[22] *Ascent*, Bk. II, xiii; Peers, I, 116.
[23] *Ibid.*
[24] Saint Teresa does not give the two negative signs set down by Saint John of the Cross; but in the Fourth Mansions she returns frequently to the disquiet and powerlessness of the faculties.

# CONTEMPLATION

spiritual sweetness which, as I say, is produced by meditation. It reaches us by way of the thoughts; we meditate upon created things and fatigue the understanding. . . .

To the other fountain the water comes direct from its source, which is God, and, when it is His Majesty's will and He is pleased to grant us some supernatural favour, its coming is accompanied by the greatest peace and quietness and sweetness within ourselves . . . this water begins to overflow all the Mansions and faculties, until it reaches the body. It is for that reason that I said it has its source in God and ends in ourselves. . . .

I was thinking just now, as I wrote this, that a verse which I have already quoted, *Dilatasti cor meum,* speaks of the heart's being enlarged. I do not think that this happiness has its source in the heart at all. It arises in a much more interior part, like something of which the springs are very deep. I think this must be the centre of the soul. . . .

Apparently, as this heavenly water begins to flow from this source of which I am speaking—that is, from our very depths—it proceeds to spread within us and cause an interior dilation and produce ineffable blessings, so that the soul itself cannot understand all that it receives there. . . . It is not a thing that we can fancy, nor, however hard we strive, can we acquire it, and from that very fact it is clear that it is a thing made, not of human metal, but of the purest gold of Divine wisdom.[25]

Incomparable psychologist that Saint Teresa is, for whom there are no hidden recesses of the soul, she has discerned that the sweetness springs up from the inmost depths, and that it bears within it the seal of its supernatural origin. Thus, the Joannine and Teresian signs of the supernatural action of God very happily complete one another.

The first two negative signs, inability and aridity, given by John of the Cross, point to the disorder of the senses and intellectual faculties in the presence of the supernatural which transcends them, and the activity of divine Wisdom, for which they are not fitted. The third sign, positive, is drawn from the very experience of love in the regions of the soul which have become capable of receiving it.

The first two signs permit one to discern contemplation either when the soul, in its confusion at the novelty, has not

[25] IV Mansions, ii; Peers, II, 237-8.

become aware of its experience of love; or when that experience is so pure and so simple that it is imperceptible.

The analysis of the third sign by Saint Teresa supplies a criterion for evaluating the nature of the union. To the experienced soul, the nature of the divine touches will be indicated by these mysterious signs given by the Saint, namely, the inner depths at which the contacts take place, and the quality of the sweetness that they bring.

Are these precisions now going to make it always easy to discern supernatural contemplation? We do not nurse any such illusions. In spite of the clearness of the signs, it is difficult to be sure there is infused contemplation in individual cases.

### c. *Complexity of individual cases*

After explaining the third sign, the most important and certain, Saint John of the Cross warns us several times that it is often difficult to discover. He says:

> It is true, however, that, when this condition first begins, this loving knowledge is hardly realized, and that for two reasons. First, this loving knowledge is apt at the beginning to be very subtle and delicate, and almost imperceptible to the senses. Secondly, when the soul has been accustomed to that other exercise of meditation, which is wholly perceptible, it cannot realize, or is hardly conscious of, this other new and imperceptible condition, which is purely spiritual; especially when, not understanding it, the soul allows not itself to rest in it, but strives after the former, which is more readily realized.[26]

He stresses likewise, in the following chapter, that this same knowledge will be imperceptible as long as it continues very pure:

> Here it must be made clear that this general knowledge whereof we are speaking is at times so subtle and delicate, particularly when it is most pure and simple and perfect, most spiritual and most interior that, although the soul be occupied therein, it can neither realize it nor perceive it.[27]

[26] *Ascent*, Bk. II, xiii; Peers, I, 117.
[27] *Ibid.*, xiv; 121.

And to this difficulty is added another which comes from the intermittent nature of contemplation, especially in its early stages. Natural activity of the faculties and contemplation alternate in such a way that it is difficult for the soul to distinguish the latter from distraction or from a momentary drowsiness of the faculties.

Moreover, the very different descriptions of supernatural states belonging to the same stage in the spiritual life, as given by Saint Teresa and Saint John of the Cross—two contemporary saints who compared their experiences—afford us a slight idea of how diverse are souls and their graces, how personal and particular are their responses to God's action in them, and the expression of their interior states. Nothing is so varied as the graces of the saints, the ways by which God leads them, and their experiences of the supernatural. The signs of the divine intervention described by our masters of mystical science are certain and constant; but we will have to know how to discover them under forms and in spiritual climates that differ widely.

The difficulties are singularly increased by pathological tendencies which the purgation of the senses in this period will often bring to an acute state, to the point that they seem to dominate the psychological field and cover all the rest. It is indeed the "sick man under treatment," to use an expression of Saint John of the Cross, that the spiritual director often will have to examine and guide. How can anyone dare to assert that under manifestations that seem quite unhealthy and partially are so, there exists a contemplative action of God? And yet, the progress of a soul is at stake; and if God is truly intervening, prudent submission to His action can alone assure both the spiritual progress of that soul and the purification of the pathological tendency. These observations do not concern, as can be easily seen, exceptional or abnormal cases. They have application to those borderline cases in which the most diverse elements meet, cases that actually are so numerous that one might even call them normal in the world of souls. We can understand that these need an experienced spiritual director to make them take cognizance of the action of God in their souls, and to point the way surely at this important crossroad of the spiritual life.

The suffering and the anguish loom large before the splendid horizons that are opening. Must not the soul, like Christ, suffer before entering into glory? Yet, declares Saint Teresa, speaking of contemplation, "if God gives a soul such pledges, it is a sign that He has great things in store for it." [28]

[28] *Way of Perfection,* xxxi; Peers, II, 133.

# CHAPTER VIII
# Call to the Mystical Life and to Contemplation

*As He said we were all to come . . . I feel sure that none will fail to receive this living water unless they fail to keep to the path.*[1]

After considering the nature and the effects of supernatural contemplation, which transforms the soul from light to light unto the likeness of the Word of God, how could we not desire to be thus seized by God, that He may sanctify us to the full measure and power of the grace to which He has destined each one of us?

But in the face of this legitimate desire, a question comes to mind, a mystery which seems to stop and break our flight of soul. Are we really called to contemplation? Is not this a favor reserved to a privileged few?

Several years ago this problem was very much discussed. To reconsider it thoroughly here would delay us too much. Its practical importance does not allow us, however, to neglect it completely.

We shall therefore propose briefly a twofold answer of right and of fact, which we think ought to safeguard both the truth of the principles and the reality of the facts. A preliminary distinction between contemplation and mystical life will be of help here.

[1] *Way of Perfection.* xlx; Peers, II, 85.

## A. Preliminary question

In ordinary language, if not in the thought of specialists, contemplation and mystical life are taken to mean and to designate one and the same thing. This confusion has given rise to many discussions and numerous errors. Let us begin by making the necessary distinctions.

Mystical life is the spiritual life marked by the habitual intervention of God through the various gifts of the Holy Spirit.

Contemplative life is the life of mental prayer marked by the habitual intervention of God through the particularly contemplative gifts of knowledge, understanding, and wisdom.

Mystical life, then, is a broader term than contemplative life which is only one form of it, but one of the most elevated. An active life, properly speaking, can become mystical by the habitual intervention of God through the gifts concerned with action, gifts of counsel and of fortitude, for example.

Referring to what we said in the chapter on the gifts of the Holy Spirit, we may repeat that the real distinction of the gifts does not reach to the essence of what each one of them transmits; this remains identical under diverse forms.[2] And so, whatever may be the gifts that God uses to intervene in souls, it is to the same holiness and the same participation in His divine life that He leads all, by different ways.

Yet the oneness of sanctity does not take away the distinc-

---

[2] The apostle writes: "Now there are varieties of gifts, but the same Spirit; and there are varieties of ministries, but the same Lord; and there are varieties of workings, but the same God, who works all things in all. Now the manifestation of the Spirit is given to everyone for profit. To one through the Spirit is given the utterance of wisdom; and to another the utterance of knowledge, according to the same Spirit; to another faith, in the same Spirit; to another the gift of healing. . . . But all these things are the work of one and the same Spirit, who divides to everyone according as he will" (I Cor. 12:4-11):

What the apostle says of charisms in the primitive Church is applicable to sanctity and its various forms in all ages. In all, it is constituted by union with the Holy Spirit; and the Holy Spirit who dwells in all the saints, gives to each one a special reflection of His beauty, a particular form of His power. Cf. *supra,* chapter on "The Gifts of the Holy Spirit," p. 338.

tion of the gifts nor of the ways that these govern, namely, that of the contemplative life and that of the mystical life in which it may be that contemplation will not appear.

## B. Question of right

*Are all souls called to the mystical life and to contemplation?*

A distinction has been very well made between a general call and a particular or proximate call.

The question of a general call may be stated thus: Can all souls, theoretically, attain to the mystical life and to contemplation? And, of a particular or proximate call thus: Do all souls have the practical means for attaining it?

### 1. GENERAL CALL

Can all souls, theoretically, attain to the mystical life and to contemplation?

Without hesitating and without distinguishing between mystical life and contemplation, one can give a very firm answer in the affirmative to this question.

The mystical life, in fact, and contemplation, do not require other powers than those that baptism gives to every soul: the infused virtues and the gifts of the Holy Spirit. Every soul possessing the seven gifts received at baptism can be moved by God and brought by Him to the plentitude of the mystical life, including supernatural contemplation.

But, some will object, since the exercise of the gifts, if not their development which is bound to that of the entire supernatural organism, depends on the free intervention of God, it still is necessary that God actually will to elevate the soul to the mystical life and to contemplation. The apostle advises us that God gives His grace to souls only according to the measure that He has chosen for each one.[3] Would it not, then, be rash on our part to determine upon this plentitude of the life of grace as the measure willed by God for all souls?

[3] Rom. 12:3.

This is a serious objection, sometimes overlooked, which brings us face to face with the mystery of the designs of God for each soul. Too easily it is forgotten that truly the divine liberty intervenes as the principal factor in the distribution of grace. Yet we can bring enough light to this mystery to enable us to maintain the affirmative answer to the question as to the general call.

We do know those desires of God which necessarily follow from His nature. God is Love and is therefore the Good, communicative of itself. To give Himself is an essential movement of His nature. He finds incomparable joy and glory in the diffusion of His grace in souls; and most especially, in His perfect reign in each one of them. His free will is captivated by the movement of His love. How could that will resist the call of the gifts of the Holy Spirit in souls that long to be filled with His holy love? Moreover, He Himself it is who makes of grace a seed as it were, capable of growth and development. He is the sower; He has sown the seed in our souls, and has thereby decreed efficaciously that He wants it to spring up, to grow, to ripen, to produce fruits according to all the power that He has given it. We are God's tillage that He waters after the sowing, and protects against outside enemies. Indeed everything that we know of the diffusive power of love in God, and of His sanctifying will, allows us to assert that God does will the perfect development of His grace in us, and that in order to procure it, He uses all the means at His disposal, including interventions through the gifts of the Holy Spirit. The freedom of His mercy is sufficiently safeguarded by the wide diversity of graces in each one, and the varied degrees to which its perfect development will lead.

This is the doctrine on the general call that Saint Teresa proclaims in very clear terms. Speaking not only of the call to the mystical life, but explicitly of the call to contemplation, she says:

Remember, the Lord invites us all; and, since He is Truth Itself, we cannot doubt Him. If His invitation were not a general one, He would not have said: "I will give you to drink." He might have said: "Come all of you, for after all you will lose nothing by coming; and I will give drink to those whom I think fit for it." But, as He said we were all to come, without making this condition, I feel sure that none will fail to receive this living water unless they cannot keep to the path.[4]

At the beginning of the following chapter, the Saint, careful to make these forthright assertions agree with what she had previously said on the different ways of souls according as they are active or contemplative,[5] adds:

In this last chapter I seem to have been contradicting what I had previously said, as, in consoling those who had not reached the contemplative state, I told them that the Lord had different roads by which they might come to Him, just as He also had many mansions. I now repeat this: His Majesty, being Who He is and understanding our weakness, has provided for us. But He did not say: "Some must come by this way and others by that." His mercy is so great that He has forbidden none to strive to come and drink of this fountain of life. . . . It is certain that He will forbid no one to come: indeed, He calls us publicly, and in a loud voice, to do so. Yet, as He is so good, He does not force us to drink.

So take my advice and do not tarry on the way, but strive like strong men until you die in the attempt, for you are here for nothing else than to strive . . . always pursue this determination to die rather than fail to reach the end of the road.[6]

These energetic statements from Teresa must be understood at least for a general call to contemplation.

On his side, John of the Cross writes:

And here it behoves us to note why it is that there are so few that attain to this lofty state. It must be known that this is not because God is pleased that there should be few raised to this high spiritual state—on the contrary, it would please Him if all were so raised.[7]

[4] *Way of Perfection,* xlx; Peers, II, 85.
[5] *Ibid.*
[6] *Ibid.,* xx; 85-6.
[7] *Living Flame,* st. ii; Peers, III, 51.

We think that these quotations from the two masters in mystical science should remove all hesitation as to the general call to the mystical life and to contemplation.

The question as to the proximate call demands more various answers.

## 2. PROXIMATE CALL

Does God call efficaciously all souls to the mystical life and to contemplation, giving them the grace and the means to attain to it?

To give a completely affirmative answer would be equivalent to saying that the development of the supernatural organism which the mystical life requires is a minimum to which every soul must attain if it is faithful to the grace and means put by God at its disposal.

What would we say, then, of souls saved by absolution for the dying, or of infants who die after baptism? And what of many others so apparently disinherited naturally and supernaturally, whose salvation does not seem to be doubtful and yet who have not had the slightest surmise of the mystical life and contemplation. We are presenting cases that seem clear. The mystery that surrounds souls must hide many other similar ones, but less apparent.

These reservations made, of which God alone knows the extent, it seems we have not the right to restrict to a few privileged souls even the proximate call. It is written that divine Wisdom lifts up His voice in the public places to call to His banquet of light and of love all who are humble and little.[8] The Master sends His servants out into the highways and byways to fill the vast room of the divine espousals.[9] Saint Teresa comments on these texts, saying that God calls all to drink at the Fountain of living water.[10]

[8] Prov. 8:4.
[9] Luke 14:15 f.
[10] The Saint is speaking of a call to contemplation and not only to the mystical life.

Why explain this call, made so urgently, in the sense of a general call that would not include a proximate and immediate call to the greater number of souls? Would this not falsify the meaning? We must think that it is the multitude of Christians that God calls, and to whom His sanctifying will gives the practical means for arriving at the mystical life.

We are prone in our thinking to limit the modes of God's action in souls to familiar forms known to us; hence we tend to restrict the number of proximate and efficacious calls. And yet the ways of God are many. There is a different one not only for each great saint, but for each soul, even the most humble. How can we dare to limit them to those only that we know, and assert that there are none beyond our familiar horizons?

Holiness is one, it is true, but its gifts are varied to infinity. All are called to the fullness of divine union and of charity, though the roads that lead to the summit come from starting points far remote from one another. Their windings and their aspects differ widely. Enormously diverse indeed are the virtues and the gifts in the saints.

We must respect the mystery of God's working in souls; in its darkness we cannot see the infinite resources of His sanctifying Wisdom. But we must not deny what the weakness of our gaze cannot discover. Let us believe the urgent call of Wisdom to the mystical life, since Wisdom itself declares it to be so. Let us believe the word of the saints, whose spiritual sense was otherwise refined than ours. And what do they say?

Saint Teresa says that there are many ways to go to God, as there are many mansions in heaven; [11] that certain souls on the way do not have the delights of contemplation as a means to advance, but that the Master will finish by letting them drink at the Fountain of living water if they are faithful. The experience of any spiritual director who has followed the progress of many faithful souls will bear out, we think, this state-

[11] *Way of Perfection,* xvii.

ment of Saint Teresa. And this same experience will further add that most of the time it has noticed in the spiritual life of the faithful an activity of the practical gifts when that of the contemplative gifts has been retarded.

Whatever be the solution given to this problem of the general and the proximate call to contemplation and the mystical life for the generality of souls, all those who have experienced hunger and thirst for God must consider the proximate call as unquestionable for them. The interior echo confirms that call and makes it certain. Let them take, then, as addressed to themselves the exhortation of Saint Teresa to her daughters:

> So take my advice and do not tarry on the way, but strive like strong men until you die in the attempt, for you are here for nothing else than to strive . . . always pursue this determination to die rather than fail to reach the end of the road.[12]

## C. Question of fact

*Are there many souls who attain to the mystical life and to contemplation; and how explain the failure perhaps of the majority?*

The question of the call, even in its proximate aspect, remains a speculative problem. We here take up the facts, not with the curiosity of the mere inquirer, but with concern for gathering any observations that might illumine our progress to God.

Saint Teresa supplies us with a general answer to the first question in the description of the different Mansions. The Teresian Mansions, even those that we qualified as periods of transition, mark not only stages in the ascent; each one of them is also, unfortunately, a landing-place where a large number of souls remain fixed.

Among the seven Mansions only four, the last, concern the mystical life. The first three constitute a phase of the spiritual life characterized by the predominance of the activity of the

[12] *Way of Perfection,* xx; Peers, II, 86.

virtues in their human modes. This division orientates, in a precise way, our search.

### 1. SOULS OUTSIDE THE CASTLE

Even before considering the souls who are in the first Mansions, let us cast a glance at those who are outside the castle because not in possession of grace.

About them, we may ask this question: Can there be an authentic mystical life in non-Christians, or in Christians who are not in the state of grace?

To that question, only a negative answer can be given in principle, for the mystical life requires supernatural charity. But there are a few points to be considered:

1. Outside of, or rather beside the mystical life properly so-called which has the effects of transformation, there are interventions of God, or manifestations of a divine action exterior or interior, which touch the internal or external senses of a pagan soul or of one in the state of mortal sin. God can speak or manifest His power to any intelligent creature whatever, and make known to Him His will; and that, by miraculous or supernatural means.

One may even accept that God might choose a soul deprived of grace as an instrument of His designs, conferring on it a mission or a charismatic power for the benefit of others. But in this case, the divine manifestation touches only the senses and other faculties, and has no sanctifying effect. To refuse this power to God would be to limit His dominion. Holy Scripture furnishes us several examples of divine manifestations of this kind to false prophets, to Balaam for example, who prophesied in the name of God although he was a priest of idols.

But such cases must be very rare. When one is faced with mysterious phenomena of the kind, therefore, one must seek an explanation in natural or preternatural causes before attributing them to a divine intervention.

2. These extraordinary divine manifestations can be destined

in the thought of God to produce in the pagan or a soul in the state of sin a psychological jolt, to change his interior dispositions. Saint Paul is struck down on the road to Damascus, and has a vision. "Who art thou, Lord?" he cries out in his surprise. "I am Jesus, whom thou art persecuting. . . . Arise and go into the city, and it will be told thee what thou must do." [13] His submission obtains for him grace immediately, and surrenders him to the action of the Holy Spirit.

The effect of the miraculous event has been to break and make docile. The will submits, conversion is effected, and the mystical life can begin.

3. In some pagan Mohammedans, and especially in non-Catholic Christians, one might admit that there exists a genuine mystical life with its sanctifying effects. These souls would be only apparently infidel, but would actually be related to the Church by their faith in the Trinity, in a Mediator, by the practice of virtue; and would be truly in the state of grace.[14] These possible cases can be verified only with difficulty.

## 2. SOULS IN THE FIRST THREE MANSIONS

We come now to the souls that are in the first three Mansions, or in the first phase of the spiritual life. To say that there is in them a mystical life would be formally to contradict Saint Teresa who characterizes this phase by the predominance of the activity of the human faculties aided by the grace of God.

The mystical life does not exist ordinarily in these souls; that is a certain fact. But since this phase requires the state of grace, to what extent will direct interventions of God, which we have admitted as possible in certain infidels, be produced in these Christian souls? Here we are obliged to make some distinctions.

1. First, the charismatic interventions of God that we found

[13] Acts 9:5-6.
[14] Cf. *Études Carmélitaines,* the penetrating study of P. Elisée de la Nativité, on the mystical experience of Ibn 'Arabi, Oct. 1931.

in infidels will be met with, and more frequently, in these faithful souls. Yet, even though such interventions were habitual, these souls might never be elevated above the third Mansions, and might even fall into grave sin. In His description of the Last Judgment, our Lord lets us hear the claims of certain wonder-workers who will have prophesied in His name, and whom the Master will declare He does not know.

2. In connection with the intervention of the Holy Spirit in the sanctification of the soul, Saint Thomas asserts that it is not in the power of reason, even enlightened by faith and infused prudence, to know all things; and "consequently, it is unable to avoid folly. . . . God, however, to Whose knowledge and power all things are subject, by His motion safeguards us from all folly, ignorance, dullness of mind and hardness of heart, and the rest. Consequently, the gifts of the Holy Ghost, which make us amenable to His promptings, are said to be given as remedies to these defects." [15]

Also: "By the theological and moral virtues, man is not so perfected in respect of his last end, as not to stand in continual need of being moved by the yet higher promptings of the Holy Ghost." [16]

From this one might conclude that the direct intervention of the Holy Ghost through the gifts is necessary for any supernatural act.[17] At least that such intervention is needed in order to perform the more difficult acts, to avoid certain temptations, and consequently to persevere in the state of grace in all the periods of the spiritual life.

In the souls that are in the first three Mansions, therefore, there will be these interventions of the Holy Spirit. They do not, however, create the mystical life properly so-called; for this requires not only the intervening of God through the gifts, but the predominance of activity through the gifts over the

[15] *Sum. Theol.*, I-II, q. 68, a. 2, ad 3.
[16] I-II, q. 68, a. 2, ad 2.
[17] Cf. Gardeil, the article "Dons du Saint Esprit" in the *Dictionnaire de théologie Catholique*, for the opinions of theologians on this point.

activity of the virtues. Yet they do mark a progress towards more considerable interventions.

3. It will be asked if these more considerable interventions are produced at least from time to time in the first three Mansions. And the answer seems to be that they are.

Nature does not proceed by jumps; likewise divine Wisdom moves all things strongly and sweetly from beginning to end. Wisdom prepares the future and announces it. There is no definite state in which God establishes souls that was not shared in, in some measure, in advance. Before habitually enjoying the vision of the Holy Trinity, Saint Teresa had been many times favored with that vision, and long previously. The prayer of quiet of the fourth Mansions must usually be preceded by passing states of quietude.

Saint Teresa insistently repeats that the spiritual progress of the soul does not resemble the growth of the human body which remains without decreasing from the height acquired. The soul goes up and down. There is nothing more normal than the to and fro movement of a soul established habitually in one Mansion, going back at times, or again rising to higher Mansions.[18]

Experience with souls confirms the fact of this transitory elevation of devout souls to higher Mansions. Independently of those mystical graces, ordinarily elevated ones—graces of conversion, for instance—that mark rather frequently the beginnings of the spiritual life and sometimes make known to the soul the states that it is to realize later, there are others much more frequent, but also of much less note. There is a quiet that takes hold of one sometimes after Holy Communion, for instance; or a supernatural recollection that comes with a simple gaze at the tabernacle, which a great number of devout souls, if not all, experience on different occasions. These supernatural impressions are inscribed in the spiritual life as phenomena of which the soul is hardly aware in the midst of

[18] Cf. PERSPECTIVES, ix, "Spiritual Growth," p. 136.

its daily struggles or aridities whose nature it misunderstands, and on which it dares not build hopes of a higher life. The prudent counsel of a wise director might be the only way to enlighten the soul as to the value of the gift received, and prepare it discreetly for the more elevated and frequent ones that God intends it to have in the future. If no one instructs it on this point, perhaps its whole life will pass in the conviction that mystical graces are strange phenomena reserved to the privileged, about which it need have no concern.

### 3. SOULS IN THE SECOND PHASE

With regard to the second phase (IV-VII Mansions), in which the mystical life opens out, we first must ask:

1. Do many souls attain to it?

We shall try to see what is the mind of Saint Teresa on this.

The Saint tells us that "the Christians are numerous who remain in the outer court of the castle," [19] that is, who are not in the state of grace. Numerous also—is it not the great multitude—are those who inhabit the first Mansions, leading a Christian life which is poorly sustained with a few exterior practices and rarely concerned with interior acts of love or with the thought of God.

In the second and third Mansions are persons solicitous about piety; and according to Saint Teresa [20] they are many, who do not go beyond the third Mansions.

On this point, Saint John of the Cross makes a precise statement:

Not all those who consciously walk in the way of the spirit are brought by God to contemplation, nor even the half of them—why, He best knows.[21]

This half and more are those who remain in the third Mansions and do not know the contemplation proper to the fourth.

[19] I Mansions, i; Peers, II, 203.
[20] *Life*, xi.
[21] *Dark Night*, ix; Peers, I, 378.

It is, then, the large majority of Christians who do not enter into the mystical life.

There remain an elite who arrive in the fourth Mansions; an elite, moreover, taken from all states and ranks of society. And let us not reduce too much the number of Christians who constitute this elite. Saint Teresa says that she knows "many souls who attain thus far." [22] And Saint John of the Cross, speaking of the same period, makes the same encouraging statement.

If we consider the intense hunger and thirst for God today, manifested by greater faithfulness to prayer, a love of silence and retreat, an eagerness for knowledge of the spiritual life, and real fruits of virtue, we may with justice think that what Teresa and John of the Cross said of their time can be applied with no less truth to our own time which is witness to a spiritual renewal, full of hope.

2. But the masters of Carmel add:

And I know, too, that those who go farther, as they ought to do, are so few that I am ashamed to confess it.[23]

Such is the night and purgation of sense in the soul. In those who have afterwards to enter the other and more serious night of the spirit, in order to pass to the Divine union of love of God (for not all, but only the smallest number, pass habitually thereto), it is wont to be accompanied by grave trials.[24]

Very clearly, then, Saint Teresa and Saint John of the Cross distinguish among those who arrive at supernatural contemplation two unequal groups: the first, and the more numerous, which includes those who remain in the fourth Mansions, having an intermittent, imperfect contemplation, and undergoing a purgation of the senses that is slight and prolonged; the second, which includes the rare privileged souls who, by the purification of the spirit, become truly spiritual men. Why these stops and failures in regions that are already so elevated? Lack

[22] *Life*, xv; Peers, I, 90.
[23] *Ibid.*
[24] *Dark Night*, xiv; Peers, II, 395.

of generosity, is the answer of both Teresa and John of the Cross:

O Lord of my soul and my Good! Why, when a soul has resolved to love Thee and by forsaking everything does all in its power towards that end, so that it may the better employ itself in the love of God, hast Thou been pleased that it should not at once have the joy of ascending to the possession of this perfect love? But I am wrong; I should have made my complaint by asking why we ourselves have no desire so to ascend, for it is we alone who are at fault in not at once enjoying so great a dignity. . . . But so niggardly and so slow are we in giving ourselves wholly to God that we do not prepare ourselves as we should to receive that precious thing which it is His Majesty's will that we should enjoy only at a great price.[25]

Saint John of the Cross, in turn, insists:

And here it behoves us to note why it is that there are so few that attain to this lofty state. It must be known that this is not because God is pleased that there should be few raised to this high spiritual state—on the contrary, it would please Him if all were so raised—but rather because He finds few vessels in whom He can perform so high and lofty a work. For, when He proves them in small things and finds them weak and sees that they at once flee from labour, and desire not to submit to the least discomfort or mortification, or to work with solid patience, He finds that they are not strong enough to bear the favour which He was granting them when He began to purge them, and goes no farther with their purification.[26]

He had previously written in the *Ascent of Mount Carmel:*

And when He says "Few there be that find it," the reason of this must be noted, which is that there are few who can enter, and desire to enter, into this complete detachment and emptiness of spirit. For this path ascending the high mountain of perfection leads upward, and is narrow, and therefore requires such travelers as have no burden weighing upon them with respect to lower things, neither aught that embarrass them with respect to higher things.[27]

In the Prologue to the *Ascent*, he says that what decided him to write was:

to relieve the great necessity which is experienced by many souls, who, when they set out upon the road of virtue, and Our Lord desires to

[25] *Life*, xi; Peers, I, 63.
[26] *Living Flame*, st. ii; Peers, III, 51-2.
[27] *Ascent*, Bk. II, vii; Peers, I, 88.

bring them into this dark night that they may pass through it to Divine union, make no progress. At times this is because they have no desire to enter it or to allow themselves to be led into it; at other times, because they understand not themselves and lack competent and alert directors who will guide them to the summit.[28]

Lack of light, lack of generosity especially, it is for these reasons that the steep paths of high sanctity are so little frequented.

These statements from the masters of the spiritual way confirm the complaints of Love who is not enough loved. And yet, He calls us all to the Fountain of the living water of intimate union with Him, and His will is that all should be saints!

[28] *Ascent*, Prologue; Peers, I, 12.

# CHAPTER IX
# Theology and Supernatural Contemplation

*Whoever, therefore, humbles himself as this little child . . .*[1]

The study of contemplation is today in astonishing favor. Its success is not without some dangers. In this loving knowledge which, in the simplicity of its act, offers such varied aspects to the admiration of minds that differ widely, each one is in danger of underscoring heavily the element that attracted him, of interpreting it according to his own mental coloring, and of thus falsifying the notion of supernatural contemplation. This danger has not been completely avoided.

Thus, we have the rather strange but very touching spectacle of those modern thinkers, and not the least among them, who appeal to contemplation to get themselves out of the enclosure in which they have been walled up by their own agnosticism. The salvation of the intellect, to quote one of them, would be assured by the contemplative, who attains to the real beyond conceptual formulas and appearances.

For these philosophers, mystical contemplation is a mode of intuitive knowledge, very elevated indeed and very penetrating, but a mode simply human. One attains to it by a certain asceticism and under certain influences still poorly defined. And so the way is strewn with wrecks. Some religions are favorable to it and recognize the particularly happy successes of Catholicism; but this mode of knowing is independent of the exclu-

[1] Matt. 18:4.

sive rights of any religion. For all the more reason is it independent of assent to any special dogma. Mystical contemplation is only a high and admirable intellectuality.

For other thinkers, informed psychologists and sensitive artists, contemplation would be an emotion more profound than all the others, a vital spirit, pure dynamism whose various forms would be met with in all religions, being independent of religious belief or even practice. Besides, they say, is there not opposition between the cold intellectuality, the dry precision of dogma, and the warm life, the daring liberty of the mystic.

All these thinkers—"good subjects to become our friends," Saint Teresa would have said—drawn towards contemplation and the contemplatives by a desire for light, or by a deep need of their soul, admire profoundly Saint John of the Cross, Saint Teresa of Avila, and Saint Therese of the Child Jesus; but in studying them, they neglect the content of their faith and their submission to the Church. They are hoping to find an empirical method for realizing their desire for contemplation, and they are dreaming of a myst__ism without dogma and a contemplation without theology, for all humanity.

Then there is the error, not so marked but of the same kind, that is found in some Christians, often fervent but ordinarily with little education, who have seized upon the role of love or rather of affectivity in contemplation, and minimize the benefit of the study of dogma in order to attain to it. Sentimental souls these, for whom contemplation means nothing else than long mystical effusions, and who no longer know how to taste divine truth except in the unction of the confidences of a soul favored by God.

On the other hand, we have the intellectual theologian, a respectable and worthy savant, a brilliant and sometimes profound mind, who approaches the study and explanation of contemplation speculatively as a theologian and practically as a preacher and spiritual director. Given to study, he would not err in the speculative explanation of a doctrine for which Saint Teresa and Saint John of the Cross have determined the principal points. He has the very laudable desire of combating sentimental spirituality which is not illumined by the light of dogma. He therefore preaches the necessity for study, and his efforts are directed to that sound popularization of theology that can be so fruitful. But relying on a personal experience acquired in a very limited field, he asserts that theological education is necessary for all high and healthy spirituality. He ordinarily evaluates the latter in terms of the former and judges souls, institutions, and spiritual currents according to the culture that they show, or the form of intellectuality that they assume. And so he manifests, if not scorn, at least disfavor for any spirituality that is not armed with its intellectual discipline, and treats it as sentimental or dangerous. Without suspecting it, and perhaps with the best good faith in the world, he is subjecting supernatural contemplation of which we are here speaking to theology.

Maybe we have set forth these errors too specifically. As a matter of fact they appear generally under the form of tendencies rather than in explicit statements. Yet, they are definite and dangerous enough for us not to neglect them. They oblige us to examine carefully the relations between theology and contemplation; from these considerations we shall deduce several practical corollaries.

Theology and supernatural contemplation have a common object, namely, divine truth. They approach the divine truth with different instruments; consequently, they could not grasp it in the same way. While theology, using reason enlightened by faith, works on dogmatic truth—the perfect expression in human language of divine truth, but an expression that remains analogical—contemplation, through faith perfected in its exercise by the gifts, is borne beyond the covering that the dogmatic formula is, and penetrates to the very reality that is divine Truth.[2]

Thus there are close relations between theology and contemplation, which derive from a community of object; yet they are differentiated by the way in which they grasp it. We can state these relations more precisely for the greater good of both.

### I. CONTEMPLATION IS A TRIBUTARY OF THEOLOGY

First of all it should be stressed that contemplation is a tributary of theology, for it cannot normally attain to divine truth in its essence without passing through assent to the dogmas of revealed truth of which theology furnishes it the formula.

This statement goes farther than what was previously said as to the necessity of the study of dogmatic truth for the development of the life of prayer in general.[3] Here, there is question of supernatural contemplation which certain modern philosophers would like to separate from all dogmatic data.

These thinkers, who recognize so willingly the superiority and marvelous successes of Catholic mysticism, ought not to neglect the testimony of those same great spiritual persons whom they surround with such respectful veneration, all of whom evince by their attitude and their words, complete submission to the dogmatic teaching of the Church.

Saint Teresa affirms so frequently and so energetically her concern for submission to the Church and to her theologians, that it seems useless to cite precise texts. As to Saint Therese of the Child Jesus, she is so careful about orthodoxy that she refuses to read a work whose author is, not a heretic, but simply in revolt against his bishop. There is no doubt in their minds that the search for God requires as an essential condition assent to the revealed truth which the Church teaches.

Revealed truth gives us light for the journey to God. This

---

[2] Cf. chapter vii, "Contemplation," p. 456, for what has been previously said.
[3] Cf. THE FIRST STAGES, v, "Spiritual Reading," p. 214.

truth it is which, at every instant, must enlighten our way and, in the shadows, let us glimpse the end. To refuse to submit one's mind to the formula of dogma that expresses it, is to destroy in oneself faith and charity; it is, in fact, to render impossible supernatural contemplation, of which these two theological virtues are the active instruments. Although it is true that in a few exceptional cases the number of truths that the intellect must accept can be reduced to a minimum, in no case could assent to some dogmatic truths be dispensed with, for such assent is essential to faith.[4]

Let us note, moreover, that the dogmatic formula is not merely an analogical expression of divine truth, that is, a symbol or natural sign of divine truth; it bears within it the divine truth that it expresses. It does not just direct us towards the truth like an arrow pointing out the road; it lets us share in the very truth it conveys.

This is what Saint John of the Cross explains in his commentary on the eleventh stanza of the *Spiritual Canticle:*

> O crystalline fount,
> If on that thy silvered surface
> Thou wouldst of a sudden form the eyes desired
> Which I bear outlined in my inmost parts!

Speaking of the soul's longing for God, the Saint says:

The propositions and articles which faith sets before us she calls a silvered surface. For the understanding of this and of the other lines, it must be noted that faith is compared to silver with respect to the propositions which it teaches us, and the truths and substance which

[4] The refusal to assent to a known revealed truth is always a sin against faith. But we should remark that among dogmatic truths there are only some, the knowledge of which is of necessity as a means; that is, absolutely indispensable for faith and the supernatural life. These are truths concerning the intimate life of God (the Trinity) and the mediation of Christ. Knowledge of the others is of the necessity of precept; that is, it should not be neglected.

An implicit assent to the first will sometimes suffice. Thus could be explained the existence of the supernatural life and of graces genuinely mystical in non-Christians. Cf. the study by Father Eliseus of the Nativity, "Is the Mystical Experience of Ibn 'Arabi Supernatural?" in *Etudes Carmélitaines,* Oct., 1931. Cf. especially the theological conclusions, pp. 162-169.

they contain in themselves are compared to gold; for that same substance which now we believe, clothed and covered with the silver of
faith, we shall behold and enjoy in the life to come, fully revealed and
with the gold of the faith laid bare. . . .

So that faith gives and communicates to us God Himself, but covered with the silver of faith; but it fails not for that reason to give
Him to us in truth, even as one that gives a vessel of silvered gold
gives none the less a golden vessel because it is covered with silver.[5]

The close relation between the formulated dogma and divine
truth could not be more clearly set forth. The formula is not
empty; it clothes the substance of divine truth itself. That the
contemplative penetrates already here below, although in an
imperfect way, the gold of the substance that is Truth, beyond
the silvered surface of its expression, is what Saint John of the
Cross goes on to say in the commentary:

By the eyes are understood, as we said, the Divine truths and rays;
which, as we have likewise said, are set forth to us by faith in its
unformed and hidden articles. . . . And she calls these truths "eyes"
by reason of the greatness of the presence of the Beloved which she
feels, so that it seems to her that she is ever gazing at it.[6]

It is clear that according to the thought of Saint John of
the Cross, one could not separate here below the two elements, that is, the pure gold of truth and its silvered surfaces
which are the dogmatic formulas. In order to find divine truth,
one must have recourse to the formula of dogma that expresses and contains it. Any contrary teaching would not only
run counter to such or such a passage in his writings, but would
render unintelligible the ensemble of his doctrine and his constant personal conduct.

We may say, then, that any attempt to arrive at a mysticism
without dogma is contrary to the doctrine of Saint John of the
Cross and to the very nature of contemplation. Whatever may
be the intuitive power of some minds, there is no empirical
method that could possibly enable them to bridge the gap between natural contemplation and supernatural contemplation.

[5] *Spiritual Canticle,* st. xi; Peers, II, 66.
[6] *Ibid.*

One can attain to resting in the supernatural Transcendent and being transformed by it, only by passing through faith to dogma and by surrendering to the action of the particular help given by God to the soul, through the gifts of the Holy Spirit.[7]

In judging severely the intellectualist attempts at a natural mysticism, we cannot refrain from expressing our sympathy however for those who are thus striving, because of their evident sincerity, the affectionate respect they have for the mystics, and the spiritual breath that they are causing to pass into modern philosophy, as well as the hope that they bring to it.

But let us leave to an eminent thinker the care of explaining in a better-turned language this dependence of contemplation on the dogmas of revealed truth:

The soul of Saint John of the Cross is faithful to the teaching of the Church. In him, the most abyssal experience is in accord with the data of theology, and, although there is here a secret bond, in the eyes of reason, between the truth that is lived within and the truth formulated without and hidden under the letter of the dogma, it is nonetheless the same plenitude of truth to which faith cleaves first, and later lives by penetrating into the dark, into the mystery, into the denseness of light freed of human distinctions and dispersions. Does anyone think that the age-old tradition from which Christian spirituality draws its nourishment is only an outside covering, and that once the soul is divinely transformed, the covering can be thrown away like an empty shell? On the contrary, is it not likely and reasonable to think that this tradition, which was at the origin of spiritual growth, should remain as an indispensable nourishment? Much more; in the doctrine of the Saint, we glimpse a place of connection, where the human and apparent disjunction between the letter and the life of faith is surmounted. For, just as the night of the passive purgations is already surmised in the active night, so mental prayer is already secretly present in meditation; and inversely, when the profound life of the mental prayer of a soul returns to the plane of discursive thought, do we think that mental prayer is abandoned? In this return

[7] With his usual mastery, M. Maritain has made a study of the degree of natural knowledge of God to which the highly developed techniques of India could bring one. Natural mysticism, even when practised by temperaments so well gifted for it and so docile, could not in any single case, without the special help of the gifts of the Holy Spirit, lead to genuine infused supernatural contemplation, such as the masters of Carmel describe it. Cf. J. Maritain: *"L'Expérience mystique naturelle et le vide,"* in *Etudes Carmélitaines,* Oct., 1938.

to meditation, is not thought very often sustained and vivified by an intimate and permanent life of prayer? Theological works, philosophical works even, have been written during a state of mental prayer. When John of the Cross writes commentaries on his poems and restores the science of the spiritual life, the human break between the mystical silence and the reasoned word does not prevent its being still divine grace that is being transmitted. That is why, when John of the Cross expresses himself by drawing on Sacred Scripture and the teaching of the Church, the accent is such that it seems to us impossible to see in this return to distinct representations, a conventional symbolism; but there are strong reasons for seeing in this return to a word that reveals itself as supernatural, the word according to which the soul invaded by God expresses itself in truth.

And there is more. To live the life of Jesus Christ is surely another thing than speaking historically of Christ. To live the life of the Holy Trinity is not the same as to speak of it as a mathematician or even a theologian. But it is a question of living Jesus Christ and the Holy Trinity, that is, question of a superhuman plenitude manifest under the human and precise letter of revealed truth. The second stanza of the *Living Flame* is clarifying in this respect, with the commentary that accompanies it:

> Oh, sweet burn! Oh, delectable wound! . . .
> That savours of eternal life!

And Saint John of the Cross writes: "Although the soul here (referring to the three Divine Persons) names the three things, because of the properties of their effects, it addresses only one of them, saying: 'Thou hast changed death into life.' For they all work in one, and thus the soul attributes the whole of their work to one, and the whole of it to all of them." [8]

### 2. CONTEMPLATION GOES BEYOND THE FORMULAS OF THEOLOGY

Although supernatural contemplation is a tributary of theology, it goes beyond the formulated expression of revealed truth. Saint John of the Cross calls it a "secret ladder." It reaches to Truth itself; and because it goes beyond anything that can be described with analogical similitudes, one can say of it that its proper domain is the dark mystery of divine Truth.

[8] "L'Ame de saint Jean de la Croix," by M. Paliard, professor of philosophy at the Faculty of Aix-en-Provence; conference given on the occasion of the fourth centenary of the birth of Saint John of the Cross, published in *Saint Jean de la Croix et la Pensée Contemporaine,* Editions du Carmel, Le Petit-Castelet, Tarascon-sur-Rhone.

When it manifests itself with all its force, therefore, this mystical knowledge:

has the property of hiding the soul within itself. For, besides perform- ing its ordinary function, it sometimes absorbs the soul and engulfs it in its abyss, in such a way that the soul clearly sees that it has been carried far away from every creature and has become most remote therefrom; so that it considers itself as having been placed in a most profound and vast retreat, to which no human creature can attain, such as an immense desert, which nowhere has any boundary, a desert the more delectable, pleasant and lovely for its secrecy, vastness and solitude, wherein, the more the soul is raised up above all temporal creatures, the more deeply does it find itself hidden.[9]

This experience, a transitory one, indicates the regions to which the soul may be elevated by supernatural contempla- tion. And, continues Saint John of the Cross, this elevation is accompanied by knowledge:

And so greatly does this abyss of wisdom raise up and exalt the soul at this time, making it strike deep into the veins of the science of love. . . .[10]

This secret ladder or contemplation is essentially a "secret wisdom, which, as Saint Thomas says, is communicated and infused into the soul through love." [11] Or again, the Saint will say of contemplation that it is called a ladder because:

it is an infused and loving knowledge of God, which enlightens the soul and at the same time enkindles it with love, until it is raised up step by step, even unto God its Creator.[12]

This science of love, which elevates, enlightens, and en- kindles, does not come by way of the understanding; a simple light, general and spiritual, it proceeds from God into the depths of the soul. God instructs the soul through the sweet anointings of love that He pours out.

In the pure clear water that springs up from the darkness, the soul discovers:

[9] *Dark Night,* xvii; Peers, I, 458.
[10] *Ibid.;* 459.
[11] *Ibid.;* 456.
[12] *Ibid.;* 462.

a wisdom abundant, so full of mysteries that it can be called not only thick, but even curdled, according as David says in these words: *Mons dei, mons pinguis, mons coagulatus.* Which is to say: The mountain of God is a mountain thick and a mountain curdled.[13]

The mysteries of Christ in particular appear to it:

like an abundant mine with many recesses containing treasures, of which, for all that men try to fathom them, the end and bottom is never reached; rather in each recess men continue to find new veins of new riches everywhere, as Saint Paul said of Christ himself in these words: *In quo sunt omnes thesauri sapientiae et scientiae Dei absconditi.* Which signifies: In Christ dwell hidden all the treasures and wisdom of God.[14]

Such are the glorious riches of light that contemplation opens up to the soul, and through it to the Church.

God put into the revelation made to Christ and to the apostles all the truth about Himself that He intended us to have; yet He left to His Church, aided by His Spirit of Truth, the care of exploring this deposit, of making it explicit, of translating into clear and precise formulas the truths contained in it, and of spreading them among the Christian people.

To this work of exegesis, theology brings the power and logic of reason enlightened by faith. Supernatural contemplation further contributes to it, with the great penetration of love. The theologian reasons, deduces, expresses his conclusions in exact formulas; the contemplative gazes on the living depths of Truth. Both are in the service of the same cause. It seems to us, however, that the theologian excels in organizing the positions that are conquered, while the contemplative, more penetrating in his love, often discovers them first, like a daring scout of the advance guard. The history of the definition of dogma throughout the centuries bears this out. It is to the contemplative gaze of Saint Paul that we owe the revelation of the great mystery of Christ whose apostle and minister he calls himself. It is to contemplatives, also, that we owe the exposi-

---

[13] *Spiritual Canticle,* st. xxxv; Peers, II, 166.
[14] *Ibid.,* st. xxxvi; 169.

tion of most of the dogmas, especially those concerned with the privileges of the Blessed Virgin. The contemplative precedes, discovers, and points the way; the theologian follows and establishes the truth.

### 3. CONTEMPLATION SUBMITS ITS LIGHT TO THE CONTROL OF THEOLOGY

It is necessary that theology follow thus in order to verify the affirmations of contemplation, especially those pertaining to dogma. Theology, which represents the teaching power of the Church, is the guardian of the deposit of revealed truth. The contemplative, to whatever sublime heights his contemplation may ascend, must submit his lights to this control.

This is what all the great spiritual persons have done. After stating in the Prologue of the *Spiritual Canticle* that "these stanzas have been composed under the influence of a love which comes from abounding mystical knowledge," Saint John of the Cross nevertheless submits them entirely, together with his commentary on them "to the judgment of Holy Mother Church."[15] Saint Teresa does not dare to trust in her own certitude of the presence of God in her soul and in the lights she received as to the mode of that presence in the graces of union, as long as an enlightened theologian has not confirmed them in the name of the Church.

Any contemplative, however elevated his spiritual life may be, can be mistaken on some point; while the Church is infallible.

What shall we say of the beginner in the spiritual life, or one progressing, whose contemplation is intermittent or imperfect, who can be mistaken as to the nature of his relations with God. In such a soul the light, even authentically supernatural, can be charged with impurities and illusions on passing through faculties that are not yet purified, and that lack besides the natural ability needed to express this experience.

[15] *Ibid.*, Prologue; 24-5.

If, proudly relying on its certitude of the divine communications and on the intoxication they produce, or on the very strength of the light which, illumining one particular point seems to put all the others in shadow, the soul refuses the control of sound theology, there is no error or defection into which it may not fall. Many heresies or unorthodox spiritual movements seem to have issued from authentic mystical experiences; but pride, by refusing to submit them to the teaching authority of the Church, falsified the light, which yet was destined to be inscribed in the synthesis of the dogma and the life of the Church.

### 4. CONTEMPLATION HAS ITS OWN LIVING AND DELIGHTFUL LANGUAGE

Theology then will verify the contemplative lights; but in taking them into the framework of its thought, it will be watchful not to destroy the living spirit that animates them even in their expression. It is in this domain of expression, actually, that the relations between theology and contemplation are most delicate.

The contemplative will translate, in his way, his intimate and personal experience of the mystery of God. If his contemplation is authentic, the light that he brings from that experience is certain. But he has found that light in the sweet inflowing of the spirit of love from which he cannot separate it. These experiences of the Divine have something very powerful at the same time as indeterminate, which is the seal of the Infinite. Because they proceed from the inmost depths of one's being, espouse its forms, and make all the soul's powers vibrate in response, they borrow from what is most profound in one, most strong, most personal, in order to express themselves. Thus the soul's response, as well as the expression of it, will be subject in some measure to the qualities and the defects of the temperament of the mystic.

This expression will not be in the well-defined language of

theological concepts; these would be too precise to translate the riches of the realities glimpsed and the delicate vibrations produced in the whole human being of one who is attuned to them. It will rather seek images, symbols, words with a less defined meaning, as being more all-embracing, not so constrained, and consequently better suited to translate the Infinite. And the mystical experience will enrich this lyricism with the warmth and sweet strength of the impression received.

When the mystical experience is very elevated, when it affects a purified soul and its powers, when it finds faculties refined enough to transmit it to us, it then brings us the harmonious sound of all the human riches of a soul, singing, exultant and vibrant, under the light and the touch of the Infinite. No more powerful nor more delicate lyricism could be found, nor poetry more sublime. Divine by the spirit that animates it, that reigns over it, and by the joy that it gives, this poetry is also as human and as varied as are souls.

Listen to Saint Angela of Foligno, strong, impetuous, using words that spring forth in jets of flame, not being able to contain the tumultuous ardors of her repentance and the excess of love that pierces her soul; Saint Gertrude, gentle and pure, a dove with a clear and affectionate gaze, whose actions and outpourings are regulated by Benedictine peace; Saint Teresa, ardent and luminous, boundless in her desires and discreet in her counsels, sublime and well balanced, a royal soul, maternal and divine, the human genius at its most concrete and most universal. We know also Saint Therese of the Child Jesus, a bird that has only a light, soft down, as she will say, but with the eyes and heart of the eagle and of great souls; and so her voice that seems childlike to us has powerful effects when it sings of the light of the Word and the love of the Holy Spirit. And finally the master, our mystical doctor, Saint John of the Cross who knows all the resonances of divine love and the reflections of its light; with his theological knowledge he explains these in harmonious order, and with the consummate skill of an artist and a poet he pours out words that pulsate with the movement of his love.

Even when it does not occur with that perfection which we find in the giants of sanctity, supernatural contemplation singularly enriches with life and light any person that has experienced it, and communicates to his words a force and a warmth that they radiate with great fruitfulness. It may happen that this expression sacrifices art to concern for souls, precision to life, but, says Saint John of the Cross comparing preaching to a concert:

> Little does it matter that one kind of music should sound better than another if the better kind move me not more than the other to do good works. For, although marvelous things may have been said, they are at once forgotten if they have not fired the will.[16]

Eloquence vivified by true spirituality, although having none of the artifices of "the persuasive words of wisdom" [17] is supremely fruitful, because it is living water that faith has caused to spring up from that fountain of the Spirit that each soul bears within.

We could continue to differentiate contemplation from theology in their expression, and stress the fact that the formulated dogma which is the work of the theologian is a certain and exact statement of divine truth in the language of human thought, while the work of the mystic is an attempt to put into living words the direct experience of that Truth.

But why continue differentiating and opposing, when the most important thing is to unite. It is actually their meeting in a soul that has made the eminent thinkers and great masters of all times. There are the Pauls and the Augustines; the Fathers of the Church, with their moving and profound language, who instituted the Christian order and thought; the saints whom the Spirit of God places at each turn of history

[16] *Ascent*, Bk. III, xlv; Peers, I, 333.
[17] I Cor. 2:4.

to guide the Christian people towards its end, the building up
of the Church.

### 5. THEOLOGY MUST SUSTAIN CONTEMPLATION IN ITS PROGRESS

Theology must render contemplation still another service;
this is, must regulate and sustain it in its progress, which is at
times dangerous and often afflictive.

We are here treating of a very delicate subject, in which
we would not want to stray from the truth ourselves, nor mis-
lead others by improper terms.

The mystical experience affects all the powers of the soul;
yet because it proceeds from love and bears within it a vague
echo of the Infinite, it seems to flee the intellectual framework
of thought, which oppresses it with its precision and bounds.
It moves into the domain of the interior and external senses
where it can display its riches and its life. The result is that
the contemplative, in the beginning, shows a certain diminution and inability in the intellectual life. At the same time,
there is an exaltation in the sense life, enriched by the divine
sweetness that is overflowing into it; and often, even a marked
preference for that sensible spiritual activity at the expense of
intellectual activity. This spiritual beginner no longer wants to
be anything but mystical, and becomes almost anti-intellectual.

The danger can be grave; there is the danger of illuminism,
eager for sensible manifestations of the spiritual, constantly
seeking the light and support of these manifestations in all
stages of the moral and spiritual life. Thus human balance is
jeopardized; for, to keep it requires that intellect be our guide
in all circumstances, and especially in the realm of mystical
joys and lights. Saint John of the Cross professes so much
respect for reason, that he demands that it examine things with
the more care, where extraordinary manifestations are present.[18]

The study of revealed truth will ward off this danger which

[18] *Ascent*, Bk. II, xix; Peers, I, 149.

would gravely compromise the spiritual life, by giving to the intellect the food it needs in order not to weaken, and the means to fulfil its function of control in the moral life.

It happens, too, that the intoxication of the senses, produced by the divine outpourings of love, is followed by very painful reactions. When the delightful impressions are over, the sense powers, and reason itself, are as it were disabled and are restless for that inflowing or rapture under which they could only remain passive, and of which they do not see the cause. We know what was Saint Teresa's anguish after her extraordinary graces. Thus the need for support and control is all the more intense, as the soul now experiences only emptiness, a void that seems the more hollow after the fullness of delight that it has just known. We have the words of the prophet Elias after a day's journey into the desert, when he was fleeing from Jezabel: "It is enough for me," he said. "Lord, take away my soul; for I am no better than my fathers." [19] And this self-loathing came upon him after he had caused the glory of Yahweh to shine forth on Mount Carmel; and after, carried along by the Spirit of God, he had run before the chariot of Achab. "Elias was a man who suffered like us," notes Holy Scripture.

God came to the aid of Elias by sending an angel to bring him a miraculous and fortifying bread. To the contemplative, too, who knows the depths of his misery, there is constantly offered the bread of sacred doctrine. It is on this support of faith, the certitude of truth revealed by God who can neither be deceived nor deceive us, that he finds peace in the bosom of his anguish, light that does not change, and a forgetfulness of graces received that is right.

We can understand now why Saint Teresa, to whom Jesus Himself appeared as a living Book, was so eager to be in touch with theologians. Indeed, she had the immense favor of knowing the greatest of her time: Father Ibáñez, the light of Avila; Father Baron, who enlightens her as to the presence of God

[19] III Kings 19:4.

in her soul; Father Thomas of Medina; the celebrated Father Báñez, her regular consultant, whom she recommends for a Chair at the University of Salamanca; Father García de Toledo, for whom she has a special affection by reason of the magnificent talents and gifts with which God favored him; Father Gracián, her director, and Saint John of the Cross, who is indeed the father of her soul and one of the directors who helped her most.[20] She never tires of testifying to her gratitude to those who were the veritable benefactors of her soul. During the last period of her life, it is especially of great theologians that she asks light for the direction of her soul.[21]

And the daughters of Teresa follow her in this concern for the advice of theologians. The masters of the University of Salamanca have a high esteem for contemplatives of the stature of Ana de Jesús. Among these masters are Curiel, Antolinez, Luis de León, who used to say that Ana de Jesús knew more than he did after all his years of professorship, and Báñez, who after sustaining a thesis in theology, brought his argument to a close by saying: "Finally, even if there were nothing else in favor of this opinion than the certainty that Madre Ana de Jesús shares it, this would be in my eyes a sufficient proof."

Theology and contemplation enjoy mutual esteem and serve one another. Contemplation has a right to the respect of theology, for it grasps their common object in a more perfect way and has more profound effects. Theology makes learned men; contemplation makes saints.

The intellectualist theologians of whom we spoke at the beginning of the chapter seem to lack this respect for supernatural contemplation. True, they are too well instructed not to recognize speculatively its value; but their conviction does not descend to the plane of the practical judgment. If we understand them correctly, we think that this anomaly comes from a

[20] Letter to Ana de Jesús, Avila, end of Dec., 1578.
[21] Cf. THE FIRST STAGES, viii, "Spiritual Direction," p. 273.

confusion in the practical order between theological contemplation and supernatural contemplation.

The theologian, devoted by his vocation to expounding the dogmas of revealed truth, finds in his task an exalted joy, feels his faculties elated by the splendors of truth that is unfolded or elucidated better, lets his intellect rest lovingly at times in the synthetic view of a mystery of our religion. How could it not happen that he would confuse the joys that he experiences in this theological contemplation with those of supernatural contemplation; especially, since in his work he often feels himself helped supernaturally. Besides, his intellect, habituated to clearer lights, endures with difficulty the blurred dazzlement—more painful for him—of supernatural contemplation.

Supernatural contemplation becomes in his thought, because of this personal difficulty in its realization, an extraordinary phenomenon reserved for a few rare privileged souls. He looks to Saint John of the Cross and other mystics for the special lights that they receive from the Infinite; and he does not see that their life of intimacy with God was ordinarily spent in aridities and in the dark night of the mystery of the essential object of faith, to which they have attained.

That the practical errors which flow from this attitude of mind can be very grave where the direction of souls is concerned, one may easily guess.

Theological contemplation and supernatural contemplation do not require the same co-operation on the part of the soul. Intellectual activity is indispensable to the first; the second is sustained above all by peaceful surrender and humility. To impose upon all the intellectual activity that theological contemplation demands would be to cast trouble in a number of souls that have already arrived at supernatural contemplation. It would be to go against their own needs and the will of God for them; it would make them turn back, wresting them from their contemplation, from the tranquility and profit they were finding in the faith. God is truly transforming them; but on condition that they abandon all preoccupation, and calm the activity of their faculties. The intellectualists who make other demands do not understand the teaching of Saint John of the Cross. They are glad to stress in that teaching its intellectual armor in order to have it noted that he belongs to the most sure of the schools of theology; but they neglect the essential points of it, those in which the Saint requires one to go beyond all created things, even the most certain on the intellectual plane, so as to surrender oneself completely to the inflowing of divine light. Why do they not reread the passages in the *Living Flame of Love,* in which the mystical doctor, with so much vehemence, rises up against all those (and the ill-advised director is among them) who trouble the peace of the contemplative soul and hinder it from taking delight in the delicate anointings of the Holy Spirit?

For they are in fact the most secret and delicate anointings of the Holy Spirit. . . . These blessings, with the greatest facility, by even the very slightest of such acts as the soul may desire to make by applying its sense or desire to the attainment of some knowledge or sweetness or pleasure, are disturbed and hindered, which is a grave evil and a great shame and pity.

Ah, how serious is this matter, and what cause it gives for wonder, that the harm done should be imperceptible, and the hindrance which has been interposed almost negligible; and yet that this harm that has been done should be a matter for greater sorrow and regret than the perturbation and ruin of many souls of a more ordinary nature which have not attained to this state of such supreme fineness and delicacy. It is as though a portrait of supreme beauty were touched by the rudest hand, and were daubed with strange and crude colours. This would be a greater and more striking shame than if many more ordinary portraits were besmeared in this way, and it would be a matter of greater grief and pity. For when the work of so delicate a hand has been so roughly treated, who will be able to restore its beauty? . . .

There will come some director who has no knowledge save of hammering souls and pounding them like a blacksmith, and, because his only teaching is of that kind, he will say: "Come now, leave all this, for you are only wasting time and living in idleness. Get to work, meditate and make interior acts, for it is right that you should do these things for yourself and be diligent about them, for these other things are the practices of Illuminists and fools." . . .

Such persons have no understanding of the degrees of prayer or of the ways of the spirit. . . . Say not, again: "Oh, you are making no progress, for you are doing nothing!" For if the understanding of the soul at that time has no more pleasure in objects of the understanding than formerly, it is making progress in walking towards the supernatural. . . . And thus the greater the progress it makes, the farther it must withdraw from itself, walking in faith. . . .

Such persons have no knowledge of what is meant by spirituality, and they offer a great insult and great irreverence to God, by laying their coarse hands where God is working. . . .

But, it may possibly be said, these directors err with good intent, through insufficiency of knowledge. This, however, does not excuse them for the advice which they are rash enough to give without first learning to understand either the way that the soul is taking or its spirit. If they understand not this, they are laying their coarse hands upon things that they understand not, instead of leaving them for those who understand them better, for it is a thing of no small weight, and no slight crime, to cause the soul to lose inestimable blessings by counselling it to go out of its way and to leave it prostrate. And thus one who rashly errs . . . shall not go unpunished, by reason of the harm that he has done. For the business of God has to be undertaken with great circumspection . . . most of all in matters so delicate and sublime as the conduct of these souls, where a man may bring them almost infinite gain if the advice that he gives be good and almost infinite loss if it be mistaken.[22]

The indignant tone of the great mystical doctor tells us the seriousness of the least errors of direction in such matters; and that will serve as our reason for the developments that we are giving to this question.

Many souls would be stopped at the very threshold of the spiritual life by the requirements of advanced study in dogma. The souls are numerous whose occupations do not leave time for study; or who have not sufficient education to apply themselves to such elevated truths with profit. Among them are souls of good will, humble, often heroic in the accomplishment of the duties of their state. Will these never be capable of anything but an inferior and sentimental spirituality? Will they never be contemplatives? Saint Thomas points out two of the beatitudes that are distinctive of contemplatives: *Beati mundo corde* . . . Blessed are the pure of heart, for they shall see

[22] *Living Flame,* st. iii; Peers, III, 81 ff.

God; *Beati pacifici* . . . Blessed are the peacemakers, for they shall be called the children of God. A pure gaze and peace, the fruit of the calming of the passions, these attain to supernatural contemplation. Why add an advanced education in dogma to the requirements of Christ, underlined by the prince of theology?

We note here that, even for minds that are educated and that have the time to perfect their knowledge of theology, excess is to be feared in some cases. The virtue of faith, which supposes some knowledge of revealed truth and is enlightened by its light, is established on submission of the intellect. After having studied, the intellect must still submit itself, in order to assent to the authority of God. Study that would develop the curiosity of the intellect, or its pride, to the point of rendering submission difficult, hesitant, or unstable, would be a hindrance rather than a help to faith.

True, not every profound study of revealed truth will produce such effects. A study that a person makes in order to establish reasonably his faith according to the capacity of his mind and the needs of his education, or to fulfil a duty of his state in life or vocation, will ordinarily be secure against these dangers. But what shall we say of one whose studies in theology are undertaken out of sheer curiosity, or a certain spiritual snobbishness, and pursued in a critical spirit or for purely intellectual enjoyment? His faith, certainly, does not as a rule founder; but supernatural contemplation, that had been envisaged as an end or at least as a goal, is by this way only rarely attained. If the soul of such a one is elevated to it once or twice, the darkness seems so painful and so filled with suffering that it returns to search in the domain of distinct concepts and dogmatic formulas the food that its curious and perhaps self-sufficient mind can no longer do without. Deceived by its intellectual attractions, led astray by the joy found in satisfying them, it will make of its mental prayer, if it remains faithful to this, a kind of study which sometimes will bring it to the-

ological contemplation; but it has forever renounced supernatural contemplation—which it does not moreover understand
or which it judges to be an extraordinary phenomenon. It is
thus deprived of the marvelous work of transformation that
God brings about in souls that are less cultivated perhaps, but
more humble. And God does not will that it should make use
of the authority that its theological learning secures it, to keep
away from His intimacy souls that trust in that authority for
direction.

We have sufficiently explained, we think, why so profound
a cleavage can separate theological study from supernatural
contemplation. May all be so favored as to find a master in
spirituality who, following the Reformer of Carmel, has
enough influence and wisdom to teach them that mental prayer
consists less in thinking than in loving, less in acting than in
surrendering.

There remains for us to point out that sometimes, unfortunately, certain minds fall into doubt as a consequence of
these studies, poorly directed or advanced into regions too
high for their mental strength; doubts that are all the more
painful and tenacious as their faith up to then was more simple
and better settled in their life.

Thus while blessing the modern movements that are working for the popularization of theological and spiritual doctrine,
we think that these must be governed by a wise direction; and
that a work of piety and asceticism must be carried on parallel
with study if souls are truly to find through them the light of
God, and open themselves to His perfect reign of love.

Better than these considerations, examples from among the
saints will show us the line to be followed in these matters.
Saint John of the Cross, the master in supernatural wisdom,
was brilliant in his studies, but "modest" his fellow students
tell us; for throughout all, he was seeking the light of the Infinite. He returned to theological studies in proportion to his
soul's needs. At Baeza, he brought to his monastery the masters

of the university to take part in theological discussions; but at the same time, he blamed that curiosity that inclines one to subtle questions and is not exempt from dangers. He left to the students of Carmel this formula which sums up for them their duty: *Ubi humilitas, ibi Sapientia,* Wisdom is to be found where humility is.

Saint Teresa, who loved knowledge in the learned and wanted solid doctrine for herself and her daughters, lashed amiably at any intellectual pretentions she found among them. The following is a passage from one of her letters to a dearly loved daughter, María de San José, prioress of Seville:

> As I tell you, your letters never tire me: in fact, they cure me of the tiredness caused by other things. I was greatly amused at your writing the date in words. God grant you did not do it to avoid humiliating yourself by writing numerals.
>
> Before I forget: that letter of yours to Father Mariano would have been excellent but for the bit of Latin. God preserve my daughters from parading their Latinity. Don't let it ever happen again and don't allow it in others. I would far rather have them parade their simplicity, which is very proper to saints, than be such rhetoricians.[23]

But there comes a day when she shows herself even more severe. She had received in the parlor an applicant who seemed to meet the conditions for being accepted. The young girl asks a question: "Mother, may I bring my Bible?" In that simple question the holy mother discerns an indication of pride of mind, of intellectual pretentions that would develop: "My daughter, stay at home with your Bible," is her answer. And so it was. The presentiments of Teresa proved correct, moreover; the girl did not stay in another convent where she entered.

Let us end with the account that Brother Reginald has left us of an episode in the life of Saint Thomas Aquinas: One day, the sixth of December, three months before his death, while Saint Thomas was celebrating Holy Mass in the chapel of Saint Nicholas at Naples, a great change came over him.

---

[23] *Letters,* from Toledo, Nov. 19, 1576; Peers, I, 347.

From that moment, he stopped writing and dictating. Was the *Summa*, then, to remain unfinished? To Reginald's complaints, came his master's reply, "I can do no more"; and the other, insisting . . . "Reginald, I can do no more; such things have been revealed to me that all I have written seems to me like straw. Now I await the end of my life, after that of my works."

"Straw!" the teaching of Saint Thomas Aquinas, the prince of theology, when one places it in the presence of the ineffable lights that the Word, the Sun divine, causes to shine silently into the soul that offers itself, pure and peaceful, to the inflowing of its warming rays. That ought to suffice us. And yet we think a comparison between the spiritualities of Saint Therese of the Child Jesus and Sister Elizabeth of the Trinity might still cast a little light on this problem of the relations of theology to supernatural contemplation, and bring to a point the practical conclusions.

### 6. CONTEMPLATION AND SPIRITUALITY

Saint Therese of the Child Jesus and her doctrine of spiritual childhood are universally known. Sister Elizabeth of the Trinity, a Carmelite of Dijon, less known to the majority of Christians, exercises nevertheless in the world of spiritual contemplatives an influence that can be compared to that of the sainted Carmelite of Lisieux.

While still at home, Sister Elizabeth experienced sensibly the presence of the Holy Trinity in her soul. A Dominican, P. Vallée, with the luminous soul of a theologian and contemplative, gives her the explanation of her experiences by expounding for her the dogma of the indwelling of God within us. At the Carmel of Dijon where she entered, Sister Elizabeth lived this dogma and the one that completes it—that the apostle Saint Paul opened up to her in his contemplative Epistles—the mystery of the divine adoption which, through Christ, God extends to all humanity. Having become a victim of praise of the

Holy Trinity and of the diffusion of the divine life in souls, she died after six years of religious life.

Saint Therese of the Child Jesus speaks with confidence and *abandon,* preaches faithfulness in little things, orientates us towards the living Christ in His Crib and His Passion; and all that, with the language and charm of a child. Sister Elizabeth draws us to silent recollection in the splendors of the most sublime mysteries of Christianity and gives the impression of a theologian in the company of Saint Paul or the disciples of Saint Thomas. And so we hear such statements as: The spirituality of Saint Therese of the Child Jesus is a good little spirituality for the use of the multitude and of the simple people; that of Sister Elizabeth is for minds more elevated.

That the spirituality of Sister Elizabeth is a spirituality of dogma cannot be denied; and it must be recognized that this is one of its great merits. But precisions must be made as to the way and the measure in which it is dogmatic.

For Sister Elizabeth, dogma furnished a point of departure or a confirmation of a state already lived, and always serves her as support, in surrendering herself to the inflowings of divine light, or entering into supernatural contemplation and resting in serene tranquility in the darkness which is its fruit. Sister Elizabeth goes beyond all distinct lights, deep into the night: *"Nescivi,"* I know nothing, she will say on returning from her contemplation. This contemplative, of whom some want to make a theologian, is above all a daughter of Saint John of the Cross. Her contemplation is more Dionysian, more in the negative way, than positive, more thick with delightful darkness than clear with light. Most often she lives in an atmosphere without light or breeze, without perfumes or images, and is sustained only by faith and by silence.

Thus Sister Elizabeth feels no need of theological education. P. Vallée gave her everything, she says, the day when he exposed to her the dogma of the divine indwelling. After that, she sees him only rarely. Of Saint Paul she asks the substance of the great mystery, that vaguely outlined and delightful immensity, to lose herself in it joyously without concern for the contours and definitions later fixed by theology.

The mother prioress who was the confidante of Sister Elizabeth the six years that she spent at Carmel, attested that Sister Elizabeth had a rather limited education in dogma and spirituality. She had followed the usual "catechism of perseverance" in her parish, had had in her hands the books that were ordinarily given to novices, nourished herself on the *Spiritual Canticle* of Saint John of the Cross, and the Epistles of Saint Paul—works that she had brought with her to Carmel—had listened with her community to several retreats preached, but had never had any preoccupation with a theological education, properly so-called.

Let theologians learn from Sister Elizabeth to make use of the truths of dogma in order to be recollected in God: they will thus help her to fulfil her mission, which is to attract souls to recollection; and they will then win for her the glory that she longed for, the glory of the praise of God. But that they should appeal to her in order to impose on all spiritual persons a profound and extensive theological education, that seems to us quite contrary to her example and to the exigencies of her spirituality.

In Saint Therese of the Child Jesus, the role of dogmatic truth is less apparent. In her prayers, the little Saint of Lisieux looks at Jesus, seeks "the nature of the good God," recites a vocal prayer in order to relax in her aridities; or again, endures peacefully the disagreeable noise a neighbor is making. But do not be mistaken. Her simplicity is not ignorance; much less, intellectual incapacity. Could it not be rather that she had voluntarily given the primacy to the activity of love in mental prayer?

Saint Therese of the Child Jesus had naturally, a great desire for knowledge, and at one time even wanted to study Hebrew in order to read the Sacred Scriptures in the original texts. But

God Himself, who watched with jealous care over His spouse of election, mortified that desire so she would not fall into the vanity of knowing. She did read, however, some excellent authors: P. Surin, whom she loved, and Saint John of the Cross, who became her master. The Holy Spirit did the rest; and so well that the spiritual doctrine of Saint Therese of the Child Jesus is filled with theological and mystical riches which are the wonder of anyone who is willing to go beyond the veil of simplicity which conceals them. And if we were obliged to compare her on this point with Sister Elizabeth, we would not hesitate to recognize in her thought more originality and perhaps more depth.

But our two Carmelite saints must smile in heaven, hearing us compare them on a plane on which they lingered so little, and to which they never had any pretentions. Neither philosophers nor theologians, they aspired only to know and love God, to become saints. They both succeeded, each one by the way that corresponded with her grace.

Which of the two ways are we to choose in order to become in our turn contemplatives and saints as they were? We do not have the choice. Each one must take the way that grace indicates to him. We shall take, then, not necessarily the one with the highest learning in dogma and spirituality, but the one that will give at the same time the most light on God and on ourselves, that will make us progress in humility; for it is to the humble and the little ones that God gives His Wisdom: Whoever, therefore, humbles himself as this little child, he is the greatest in the kingdom of heaven.[24]

[24] Matt. 18:4.

# CHAPTER X
# Faith and Supernatural Contemplation

*Faith alone is the proximate and pro-
portionate means whereby the soul is
united with God.*[1]

The problems that supernatural contemplation raises seem
to be more and more difficult the more deeply one searches
into it. The overlapping of the human and the divine creates a
complexity that might be taken for confusion. Furthermore,
we are faced with the question of how it is possible to guide
a soul through these pathless regions, where there are only individual ways and particular cases. A great help it would be
to have an over-all view, a synthesis that would permit one
to see the whole extent of the problem, co-ordinate its various
aspects, and thus to situate all the details. Of whom could we
ask this luminous synthesis, if not of Saint John of the Cross?
As mystical doctor, he is qualified to give one. And he has in
fact made such a synthesis, by reducing the whole doctrine of
contemplation to an exposition of the role of faith.

Let us gather his teaching, which promises to be very precious, by studying with him how faith is necessary, what it is,
in what ways it is exercised, what are the characteristics of the
knowledge it secures. Some practical conclusions will readily
spring from such an exposition.

[1] *Ascent,* Bk. II, ix; Peers, I, 98.

## A. The necessity of faith

"Faith alone is the proximate and proportionate means whereby the soul is united with God." [2] This affirmation is not only the subject developed in Chapter VIII of the *Ascent of Mount Carmel;* it is repeated many times elsewhere in various forms. It is a principle on which John of the Cross rests his whole doctrine of contemplation and which regulates its ascetic element. We must stop therefore to explain and prove it.

"Faith alone is the proximate and proportionate means," says the Saint. Other means are not excluded; means perhaps necessary. But there is only one that is immediate and proportionate, to which all the others are subordinated and in which they must converge: namely, faith, the only proximate and proportionate means for union with God.

The union with God of which we are speaking is supernatural union, that which is the fruit of sanctifying grace, a participation in the divine life; the union that introduces us into the intimate life of God as sons of the Father, brothers of Christ, and temples of the Holy Spirit. "That all may be one, even as thou, Father, in me and I in thee; that they also may be one in us," Jesus has said,[3] speaking of the union which constitutes our supernatural vocation.

This union is realized in all souls in the state of grace; it admits of different degrees, determined in each soul by the measure of its grace.

The statement of Saint John of the Cross: "faith alone is the proximate and proportionate means whereby the soul is united with God" amounts to saying that the nonbaptized can come to that union only by faith, since "faith is the beginning of the

---

[2] *Ascent,* Bk. II, ix; Peers, I, 98. The faith of which Saint John of the Cross speaks is a living and active faith; that is, it is animated by charity.

Uninformed, imperfect faith (i.e. without charity), although still a virtue, is an imperfect and dead virtue: "rightly is that faith without works called dead, lazy," says the Council of Trent (cf. Session VI, ch. vii).

[3] John 17:21.

salvation of man, the foundation and the root of all justification." [4] Likewise, the person who is baptized can actualize his
union with God and develop it only through faith.

Faith is the door of entry, necessary for attaining to God.
This is what the apostle clearly asserts: "For he who comes to
God must believe that God exists and is a rewarder to those
who seek him." [5]

These statements from the apostle Saint Paul and from the
Council of Trent would suffice to prove the teaching of Saint
John of the Cross. But the point is too important and too rich
in practical significance, not to explore it more profoundly.
We must answer objections, demonstrate how rigorous and
inescapable are the conclusions, while at the same time vindicating and clarifying this principle.

In order to set off and prove the absolute necessity of faith
for union with God, we shall proceed by elimination, showing
that the powers of knowledge that we possess—senses and intellect—are incapable of bringing us to such union.

The senses—touch, sight, hearing, and the others—have
their domain in the visible world about us, putting us in contact with it. They perceive the accidents, the exterior qualities
of material things, (mass, color, and so on) but they do not
go beyond these. God, however, is pure spirit. There is in Him
neither body nor matter, nor sensible qualities that could make
Him known through sense perception. He entirely eludes the
senses. They could not possibly, then, be a proximate and proportionate means for attaining Him in Himself and uniting us
directly to Him.

It is true that from the perception of the senses, the intellect can abstract universal ideas and, continuing its work on
these, can rise even to God. Thus, from sense knowledge of
movement, life, beauty in the world, we can rise by a reasoning process to knowledge of a God, creator, infinite, and

[4] Council of Trent, VI, viii, n. 801.
[5] Heb. 11:6.

provident. The immensity of the ocean, the magnificance of a panorama, the peace of nature, these recollect the soul, and by their beauty and harmony create in it those deep interior impressions which favor its flight towards the Infinite.

Better still, certain supernatural phenomena can produce on the senses such an impression that the soul, by a spontaneous movement, mounts to God to adore Him and to thank Him. After the miraculous catch of fishes, Peter, who saw the two boats fill up with fish, recognized in this miracle the absolute power of the Master and cast himself at Jesus' feet, trembling with emotion: "Depart from me, O Lord," he said, "for I am a sinful man." [6]

In these different cases, the senses have perceived only sensible phenomena. It is the intellect and the spiritual powers of the soul which, penetrating the sensible data, find God and His grace. A being endowed with no more than sense life, would react only to the sensible as it appears, and would not rise to a knowledge of God.

Sense perceptions are a stage; how useful they are, and even necessary, Saint John of the Cross indicates in the fifth stanza of the *Spiritual Canticle:*

> Scattering a thousand graces,
> He passed through these groves in haste.
> And, looking upon them as he went,
> Left them, by his glance alone, clothed with beauty.[7]

God has passed through sensible nature, as it were, in haste; but that was enough for Him to leave in all things "some vestiges of what He is," "innumerable graces and virtues, making them beauteous with marvelous orderliness." Creatures bear "testimony . . . to the soul concerning the greatness and excellence of God." [8] This testimony is only a trace indicative of God's passing through. To draw spiritual profit from it, one must follow it, but then must go beyond it. To rest in it, or

---

[6] Luke 5:8.
[7] *Spiritual Canticle,* st. v; Peers, II, 48.
[8] *Ibid.;* 48-9.

to settle down to delight in the aesthetic joy that it procures, would be to misunderstand its providential finality; it would be to make an end of what is only a means. God is farther on, beyond all the perceptions of the senses. It belongs to other powers to grasp Him and to establish contact with Him.[9]

Is He, then, within the reach of the intellect? One might think so. God is spirit; and the intellect moves in the world of ideas, as in its domain. The intellect can moreover prove the existence of a self-subsistent and necessary Being, the First Cause. It can discover some perfections of God by attributing to Him the qualities that are in His creatures, and that must be found in Him as in their Cause.

This natural knowledge is assuredly not negligible, and it terminates in a certain union with God by the love that it engenders. It remains, nevertheless, very inferior to that supernatural knowledge that God offers to us of Himself as our last end.

Actually, we are called to know God as He knows Himself and to love Him as He loves Himself; to enter into the intimacy of the three Persons by participating in their operations according to the mode of our created grace. Now, the natural knowledge of God that is acquired by our intellect shows Him to us as the author of the natural order of things, makes known His perfections by the perfections with which He has endowed the works of His hands; but it does not reveal to us the Deity itself, God as God, uniting in Himself in an eminent degree all the perfections of His creatures and living His Triune Life.

[9] Saint John of the Cross does not despise nor flee from sensible nature—any more than does Saint Teresa—to shut himself up in a darkness that would ignore everything outside. He gives it its place in the scale of spiritual values which must lead us to union with God. We know how much the two Reformers of Carmel insisted on having their convents located in places where souls might use the beauties of nature to the advantage of recollection and communion with God. The whole theory of art in Saint John of the Cross flows from the same principle: the artistic realization must be simple, pure, uplifting, and chaste (pure and simple, so as to lead the soul to God without detaining it in aesthetic enjoyment).

We might compare God to a diamond with multiple facets, or to the light of the sun which contains in its whiteness the seven colors of the rainbow—the facets and the colors representing the perfections of God. We can say that the intellect finds and admires successively the facets of the diamond and the diverse colors of the solar spectrum in the reflections that God causes to shine from His works; but that it is not able to take in with a glance, however imperfect, the diamond itself, nor to discover in its simplicity the white light of the sun. It can grasp God only in what appears of Him in His creatures; by studying Him thus in His various reflections, it divides Him in a way to fit the measure of its capacity.

A finite power, the intellect could not, by its own strength, know directly the Infinite, the Deity, and the Life of the Holy Trinity. The intellect knows by abstraction, by seizing the intelligible reality of a being and studying it in the mental word that the mind forms and envelops. How could the human intellect grasp the intelligible reality of the Godhead, abstract it, form a mental word that would express it, and envelop it, when God is infinite and completely overflows it?

This powerlessness of the intellect to know the Deity as it is in itself, and the Triune Life, permits us to conclude that we shall know God in Himself only if He reveals Himself, and at the same time gives us a supernatural power capable of receiving His light. Actually, God has made a revelation of Himself and given us the virtue of faith which is an aptitude for possessing Him in knowledge.

## B. What is faith? [10]

We know the definition of faith that theology and the catechism give: it is a supernatural theological virtue by which

[10] One must not expect to find here a complete and didactic explanation of the Catholic doctrine as to the virtue and the act of faith. We are limiting ourselves to bringing out those truths which clarify the spiritual doctrine of Saint John of the Cross, of which we are here treating.

we believe in God and in the truths that He proposes to us, on the authority of God who reveals them.[11]

The word "virtue," here, signifies not a facility acquired by the repetition of acts, but a power that makes one capable of performing an act; in the present case, "that makes one capable of believing in God."

This virtue is "supernatural." It is given by God; hence it is superaddded to our natural faculties and forms part of the supernatural organism received at baptism.

Faith is a "theological" virtue. It makes us adhere "to God" who is the material object of faith; [12] and, since we believe "on the authority of God who is Truth," God becomes also the motive, the formal object of faith.

In order to treat of faith in its relations with contemplation, and to explain how faith is the only "proximate and proportionate means" whereby we are united with God, let us try to understand the genesis of an act of faith.[13]

Some truth is proposed—let us say, the dogma of the Holy Trinity: one God in three Persons. I find the statement of this truth in a book; or, more ordinarily, I receive it through oral teaching. It is through the *sense of sight or of hearing* that the truth is presented to my intellect. *"Fides ex auditu:* faith then depends on hearing," notes the apostle; and he adds, to emphasize the necessity of this intervention of the activity of the senses: "But how are they to believe him whom they have not heard: And how are they to hear, if no one preaches?" [14]

Having reached the intellect by way of the senses, this truth

[11] The Council of Trent defines it: "A supernatural virtue by which, the grace of God attracting and helping us, we believe as true what God reveals."

[12] Saint Thomas says that faith cannot be "of things seen either by the senses or by the intellect"; and that is why "the Apostle says (Heb. 11:1) that *faith is the evidence of things that appear not"* (*Sum. Theol.,* II-II, q. 1, a. 4, c.).

[13] In the detailed analysis of the genesis of the act of faith, the opinions of theologians differ. It will suffice for our purpose to give the essential steps, generally recognized as such by all.

[14] Rom. 10:14-6.

becomes the object of an intellectual operation. It is not self-evident; neither does it force the assent of the intellect as does a first principle, or the conclusion of a syllogism whose premises were accepted. The intellect must proceed to an inquiry, must look for the signs of its truth. This inquiry bears first of all on the terms that constitute the formulation of the truth: "one God . . . three Persons." These terms are already known, as well as the ideas that they express; but the connection which is affirmed between these terms—connection that constitutes the truth that is proposed—remains a mystery. Nowhere in the domain of its knowledge has the intellect discovered a being in whom "one nature" unites within itself "three persons"; and it does not see how three persons can be so intimately associated in the life and operations of a single nature. Nevertheless, I grant that the enunciation of this truth that is a mystery does not involve any contradiction. The terms "one" and "three" which seem to contradict one another, do not refer to the same thing: one nature and three persons. Hence the truth is credible and I could assent to it if an extrinsic testimony imposed it on me with sufficient authority. Actually, I do accept many facts or truths that I have not verified, on the testimony of someone worthy of credence.

In the present case, who proposes to me this truth? and what is the value of his testimony? It is the priest who speaks in the name of the Church. I can and must, once at least, pursue my inquiry and examine the value of the testimony of the Church. The result is this: The Church, instituted by Jesus Christ, is divine; she has been given the mission of teaching the revealed truth. Moreover, the privilege of infallibility assures the integrity of the deposit of the revelation that has been confided to her. The Church speaks, then, in the name of God, and as God Himself in matters of faith and morals. It is God who speaks through her. God has the right to impose on me truths to be believed. He can neither deceive me nor be deceived. On the other hand, it is entirely normal for my intellect not to be able to comprehend all the divine truths, especially those which concern the intimate life of the Trinity. Hence it is reasonable for me to accept this testimony. In fact I ought to, by reason of the respect and submission demanded by the authority of God and all that comes from Him.

In this inquiry, the intellect has been powerfully sustained by the good dispositions of the will. The inquiry is difficult; besides, its results involve serious risks for the soul. If the testimony is true, it becomes necessary to accept the truth that is proposed, to observe the precepts that are connected with it, even perhaps to change completely one's way of living.

The virtue of faith has already exercised a certain influence on the work of inquiry itself and on the good dispositions that have carried it through. It has enlightened the intellect and fortified the will in this first step:

"The virtue of faith," says Saint Thomas, "gives to the soul an inclination for all that accompanies the act, follows it, or precedes it." [15]

When the inquiry is terminated, the truth, taken in itself, does not appear any more evident than it did before; hence it could not, of itself, compel assent. But the testimony is presented with guarantees of moral certitude. Moreover, the soul possesses enough humility of mind to accept the testimony, and enough affective confidence in the witness to assent to it. The first phase is ended: everything is ready for the act of faith.

The act of faith, according to Saint Thomas, "is an act of the intellect assenting to the Divine truth at the command of the will moved by the grace of God." [16]

This definition shows us that the act of faith is produced conjointly by the intellect which assents in submitting, by the will which commands the assent, and by the theological virtue of faith. The infused virtue of faith enters into this act as the principal cause. It is this that gives it its specific perfection,

---

[15] *In IV Sent.*, III, d. xxiv, q. 1, a. 2, sol. 2.
[16] *Sum. Theol.*, II-II, q. 2, a. 9.

making it supernatural. We are here at the crucial point. Let us try to analyze it without entering into subtleties that are not needed for our subject.

The virtue of faith forms part of the supernatural organism that is given by baptism. While grace is a formal participation —created but real—in the divine nature, faith is a participation in the divine life considered as divine knowledge. It is, says Saint Thomas, "a light divinely infused in the mind of man," "a certain imprint of the First Truth." [17] It is a constant aptitude to know God as He knows Himself, to receive—according to the limited measure of created grace, it is true—but really to receive the light from the dazzling Sun that is God Himself. It is the "sight" of our supernatural life.

The virtue of faith is infused into the intellect in the same way as grace is infused into the essence of the soul. Faith is an operative quality in our faculty of knowing, just as grace is an entitative quality in the essence. The comparison of the cion or shoot grafted into the trunk of another tree might clarify the relation of the supernatural life instilled in the natural life of the soul. The new shoot lives by the life of the trunk whose roots and sap it uses; but while extending the tree, it produces fruits that are specifically its own and not those of the primitive stock. Likewise, the virtue of faith in fused into the intellect uses the data that the latter has abstracted from sense perceptions, but raises its activity to a higher level and extends it into a supernatural domain where it could not of itself penetrate, causing it to produce supernatural fruits or acts which are specifically those of the virtue of faith. Just as the primitive tree is pruned and checked in its growth to receive the new shoot which has its own development and produces fruit, so the intellect humbles itself before the divine mystery, and stops, as it were, its own growth so

[17] "*Lumen quoddam quod est habitus fidei divinitus menti humanae infusum; lumen fidei est quaedam sigillatio primae veritatis*" (*In Boetium de Trinitate*, q. 3, a. 1, sub. 4).

that the faith that it bears may posit its act and yield its supernatural fruit.

A crude comparison, perhaps, but it may help us to see how
the activity of the virtue of faith is bound to that of the intellect and is grafted into it to produce the supernatural act of
faith.[18]

Having set down these principles, let us return to the act
of faith of which we have analyzed all the preliminaries. Henceforth, the soul can make an act of faith, saying: "I believe in
one God in three Persons, because God has revealed it."

This act of assent to the mystery of the Holy Trinity presents itself psychologically perhaps in the field of consciousness
as a simple act of submission of the intellect to the authority
of God, under the movement of the will. The intervention of
the virtue of faith is not, as a rule, grasped psychologically; for
it is a supernatural virtue, experimentally indiscernible in itself. What one can be aware of is the facility that it gives or,
on the contrary, the intensity of the effort that is needed to
posit its act.

[18] These considerations, it seems to us, throw light on the discussion concerning the nature of the supernatural act of faith: "Some," writes Father
Garrigou-Lagrange, "reach the conclusion that our act of faith is a substantially natural act clothed with a supernatural modality: substantially
natural, because it reposes formally on the natural, historical knowledge of
Christ's preaching and of the miracles which confirmed it; clothed with a
supernatural modality, so that it may be useful to salvation. This modality
is often said to resemble a layer of gold applied to copper in order to make
plated metal. We would thus have "plated supernatural" life and not a
new, essentially supernatural life" (Christian Perfection and Contemplation,
p. 63; translated by Sister M. Timothea Doyle, O.P., Herder, St. Louis,
1939).
The essentially supernatural character of the act of faith, taught by Saint
Thomas and his commentators, the Carmelites of Salamanca, and which
seems to us to be guaranteed by the motive of faith (God-Truth) which is
supernatural, as well as by the virtue of faith, which is its principal cause,
is entirely in conformity with the doctrine of Saint John of the Cross and
even demanded by it. How could we explain the purification of faith in the
dark night, and the infused contemplation which is the fruit of it, if the
act of faith is only a natural act of the intellect clothed with a supernatural
modality by faith! On the other hand, everything is clarified if we see in it
an essentially supernatural act produced by the virtue of faith engrafted in
the intellect, whose activity and submission it uses.

But whatever may be the psychological perception or absence of it, when a soul says: "I believe . . . on the authority of God," it has issued a supernatural act; the virtue of faith has entered into action.

It must be noted that the authority of God is now substituted for the motives that made one accept the value of the testimony. The intellect submitted because of the veracity of the Gospels, the miracles of our Lord; now faith leaves buried, in a way, in its foundations those reasonable motives, and posits its act by trusting in the authority of God.

But above all, the act of the virtue of faith, of this supernatural cion grafted into the trunk that is intellect, is a supernatural act that goes far beyond the ordinary and limited field of the activity of the intellect; it attains the First Truth, God Himself, to whom it adheres and makes the intellect adhere, and the whole soul, in an attitude of humble assent. By an act of faith, the soul is borne into "a direct exchange, an intimate union with the interior word of God . . . And as that interior word not only existed at the time of the manifestation of the exterior Word, but subsists, in that it is the eternal word of God, in an eternal present, it lifts up our mind to a participation in His supernatural truth and life and makes it rest there."[19] This contact with the First Truth, the Deity itself, gives to the soul, according to the word of Saint Paul, "the substance of things to be hoped for, the evidence of things that are not seen: *sperandarum substantia rerum, argumentum non apparentium.*"[20] It could be called a veritable "possession of God, obscurely."

These formulas, so full and so luminous, ought to satisfy us; but this truth is at the same time so profound and so consoling that we never tire of searching the masters for some new expression to throw light on a particular aspect of it.

"What takes place in us when we believe," says Msgr. Gay,

[19] Cf. Scheeben. *Dogmatik,* I, 40, n. 681.
[20] Heb. 11:1.

"is a phenomenon of interior and superhuman light." [21] And in his treatise on the Christian Virtues, he explains the contact established by faith:

> As to that which belongs to real perfection, commanded, meritorious, the revealed supernatural—the most delicate senses and the best-trained intellect are utterly incapable of attaining it. Faith alone can give it to us; and not only is faith necessary to make us assent to what is intrinsically revealed, that is, to the divine Reality formulated in human language, but without the grace that initiates it in us, we could not even go as we should to the proofs on which it rests.[22]

Msgr. Gay underlines the role of the virtue of faith in its first phase, when it aids us "to submit to the proofs on which it rests"; but one likes to dwell especially on the happy phrase in which he defines the act of faith as that which makes us "adhere to the inner truth of revelation," that is to say, the divine Reality revealed in human language."

It is to this meeting with the divine Reality that Saint John of the Cross refers, and on it he bases his teaching. We recall the passage from the *Spiritual Canticle* where he points out that faith gives us God Himself—beneath the "silvered surfaces" of its articles there is the "gold of its substance."[23] Because faith attains to God directly it is the proximate and proportionate means for union with Him, the Saint explains in the *Ascent:*

> Such is the likeness between itself and God that there is no other difference, save that which exists between seeing God and believing in Him. For, as God is infinite, so faith sets Him before us as infinite; and as He is Three and One, it sets Him before us as Three and One. . . . And thus, by this means alone, God manifests Himself to the soul in Divine light, which passes all understanding. And therefore, the greater is the faith of the soul, the more completely is it united with God.[24]

---

[21] Conference 17.
[22] *Vie et vertus chrétiennes,* I.
[23] Cf. *supra,* "Theology and Supernatural Contemplation," p. 491.
[24] *Ascent,* Bk. II, ix; Peers, I, 98.

And he illustrates the same thought by referring to the soldiers of Gideon who carried lights in their hands, concealed in pitchers:

If the soul in this life is to attain to union with God, and commune directly with Him, it must unite itself with the darkness . . . that it may have in its hands the light, which is the union of love, though it be in the darkness of faith—so that when the pitchers of this life are broken, which alone have kept from it the light of faith, it may see God face to face in glory.[25]

This identity of the object of faith and of the beatific vision, and this possession of God in a dark manner by faith, have been very aptly described by Msgr. Bertaud, bishop of Tulle. Speaking of the transition from faith to the beatific vision, he writes:

The shadows will fall away; and, without change of object, without new seeking, our gaze will rest upon the Divine Essence. It will be seen that God was the term of our knowledge by faith. That small germ has always contained the Infinite. Some have complained of the lack of beauty and of splendour in the formulas of the faith: have thought them meager and dull. And yet, splendours without limit are contained in them, not straitened, not lessened. The Infinite object is in its integrity in weak syllables. It will shine forth from them one day before our eyes, gloriously bright.[26]

These texts already suggest numerous and interesting conclusions. But let us reserve them for a more complete discussion when we have seen the various modes of exercise of the virtue of faith and the characteristics of the knowledge that it affords us.

## C. Perfect and imperfect modes of the exercise of the virtue of faith

We have already pointed out the two modes of the exercise of the virtue of faith: the first, rational and imperfect, borrows from reason its lights and is regulated by it; the second, wholly

25 *Ibid.;* 100.
26 Cf. Berteaud. *Oeuvres Pastorales,* I, 161-2; quoted in *Dictionnaire de théologie Catholique,* in the article, "Foi," Vol. 6, Pt. 2, 364.

supernatural and perfect, because perfected by the action of God Himself through the gifts of the Holy Spirit.[27] We will follow these two modes in the progressive development of the act of faith, the first phases of which we have previously described.

This act of faith, that the work of the human faculties has prepared and which is the fruit of the virtue of faith, attains the divine Reality contained in revelation. But the activity of the virtue of faith is too closely bound to that of the intellect, for a single act of faith to be able to fix it in its divine object, which is dark to it. The intellect is made for light; and so it could not rest peacefully in darkness. Having gone with faith into darkness, it returns spontaneously to the lights that have served as a basis for the act of faith, and which are given by the formulas of dogma.

It is not, however, in order to doubt or to begin inquiry over again, that the soul returns to the dogmatic truth, but to work with its natural faculties on the divine truth that is proposed to it in human language. Faith invites the intellect to penetrate, to explore that truth, to unfold its meaning with the aid of reasoning and of analogies, to show its agreement and connection with other truths, to draw from it new conclusions.

This is the work of the theologian, eminently useful, which establishes the reasonable bases of faith, makes the avenues that lead to it wider, more accessible, more luminous, displays the riches of revelation by explaining the truth that it contains; and in so doing, elaborates the highest science: theology.

But if it be true that the intellect can do nothing more noble or more useful than to put itself at the service of faith, faith on the other hand can find in the activity of the intellect only a help that is inferior to its own nature and demands. Faith is a supernatural virtue whose object is God, infinite Truth. The intellect is a natural power which can work only on concepts

[27] Cf. THE FIRST STAGES, x, "Supernatural Wisdom and Christian Perfection," p. 310.

that do not go beyond its ken. When applied to revealed truths, the intellect is unable to grasp the proper object of faith, the infinite, divine Reality which lies altogether outside its domain. It can only occupy itself with the analogical concepts in which its divine object is expressed in human language.

It is clear then, that faith will find the intellect to be but an imperfect instrument, with lights and a mode of activity inadequate to it as a supernatural power. This faith, remaining always in the domain of concepts because of its dependence on the activity of the reason, might be called "conceptual faith" or "faith which operates imperfectly."

God alone, through the gifts of the Holy Spirit, can maintain faith on the plane of its divine object, and so ensure its perfect exercise.

The gifts of the Holy Spirit are passive powers produced in the soul by charity. They are, as it were, permanent bases of operation for the Holy Spirit in the soul, the entrance door of the merciful interventions of God. These divine interventions have as their first effect the perfect exercise of the virtues. When faith attains its divine object, God by His gifts lets fall upon the soul outpourings that are delightful and luminous, or simply tranquilizing, which captivate and, at times, paralyze the faculties, giving them a certain attraction for the darkness. These communications hinder faith from having recourse once more to the operations of reason, rather keeping it vigilant with its gaze directed towards the divine Reality, which they reveal to it as a hidden reality—now almost within its grasp, again hardly perceived, but always sovereignly attractive. God has become the light of the soul. Thus, held by its divine object in this obscure and sometimes painful manifestation of itself, faith finds its perfect mode of exercise, that which is appropriate to a theological virtue, having God as object and motive.[28]

[28] Cf. the chapter on "The Gifts of the Holy Spirit," p. 338, for the relations between the virtues and the gifts, especially in the act of living faith.

The faith which, according to Saint John of the Cross, is th
only proximate and proportionate means for union with th
Divine, is *par excellence* this living contemplative faith tha
the gifts of the Holy Spirit have fixed peacefully on its objec
and that draws its sustenance from it. It is this faith that re
quires that we "close the eyes of the understanding to thing
both above and below." [29] This is the faith that effects trans
formation and union, as the prophet Osee declares: *Sponsabc
te mihi in fide,* I will espouse thee to me in faith." [30]

## D. Characteristics of knowledge by faith

In defining faith as "a habit of the soul, certain and obscure," [31] Saint John of the Cross has stressed two qualities of
faith that also mark the contemplation which is its fruit. These
two qualities of obscurity and certitude are of such great practical importance that we have a duty to examine them in the
light of the teaching of the saints.

### I. THE DARKNESS OF FAITH

Saint John of the Cross insists especially on the darkness of
faith as on one of the most important points of his teaching
on contemplation. Faith is an abscure habit, he writes,

because it makes us believe truths revealed by God Himself, which
transcend all natural light, and exceed all human understanding, beyond all proportion. Hence it follows that, for the soul, this excessive
light of faith which is given to it is thick darkness, for it overwhelms
that which is great and does away with that which is little, even as
the light of the sun overwhelms all other lights whatsoever, so that
when it shines and disables our powers of vision they appear not to
be lights at all. So that it blinds it and deprives it of the sight that
has been given to it, inasmuch as its light is great beyond all proportion and surpasses the powers of vision. Even so the light of faith, by
its excessive greatness, oppresses and disables that of the understanding; for the latter, of it own power, extends only to natural knowledge,

[29] *Spiritual Canticle,* st. xi; Peers, II, 66.
[30] Cf. *Dark Night,* Bk. II, ii; Peers, I, 402. "I will betroth thee—that is,
I will unite thee—with Me through faith."
[31] *Ascent,* Bk. II, ii; Peers, I, 70.

although it has a faculty [obediential] for the supernatural, when Our Lord may be pleased to bring it to a supernatural action. . . .

Faith tells us of things which we have never seen or understood, either in themselves, or in aught that resembles them, since they resemble naught at all. And thus we have no light of natural knowledge concerning them, since that which we are told of them has no relation to any sense of ours; we know it by the ear alone, believing that which we are taught, bringing our natural light into subjection and treating it as if it were not.[32]

The darkness comes from the disproportion that exists between our intellect and the object that faith proposes to it. Faith has for its object the things invisible that transcend human reason (the mysteries); hence the apostle says that faith is "the evidence of things that are not seen." [33] The holy doctor of mysticism explains this in a more precise way in the book on the *Dark Night of the Spirit*. He says:

We must here assume a certain doctrine of the philosopher, which says that, the clearer and more manifest are Divine things in themselves, the darker and more hidden are they to the soul naturally; just as, the clearer is the light, the more it blinds and darkens the pupil of the owl, and, the more directly we look at the sun, the greater is the darkness which it causes in our visual faculty, overcoming and overwhelming it through its own weakness. . . . Wherefore David likewise said: that near to God and round about Him are darkness and cloud; [34] not that this is so in fact, but that it is so to our weak understanding, which is blinded and darkened by so vast a light to which it cannot attain. For this cause the same David then explained himself, saying: Through the great splendour of His presence passed clouds—namely, between God and our understanding. And it is for this cause that, when God sends it out from Himself to the soul that is not yet transformed, this illumining ray of His secret wisdom causes thick darkness in the understanding.[35]

[32] *Ibid.;* 70-72.
[33] Heb. 11:1.
[34] Ps. 96:2.
[35] *Dark Night,* Bk. II, v; Peers, I, 406.

These explanations of Saint John of the Cross show us that the cause of the darkness is not the distance between God and faith, between the object and the eye, but is on the contrary the contact between the dazzling divine object and the gaze of the soul.

Ordinarily, this darkness will be the greater for the soul, the nearer it is to God. No human being has sounded the abyss of the Infinite and experienced its obscurity as did the Virgin Mary, whose grace was comparable to no other. Saint John of the Cross writes:

> Now this is a thing that seems incredible, to say that, the brighter and purer is supernatural and Divine light, the more it darkens the soul, and that, the less bright and pure is it, the less dark it is to the soul. Yet this may well be understood if we consider what has been proved above by the dictum of the philosopher—namely, that the brighter and the more manifest in themselves are supernatural things the darker are they to our understanding.[36]

We must not think, however, that faith offers nothing but darkness to the intellect. It presents it with lights of a quality

---

It is in this sense that we must understand John of Saint Thomas, the great theologian of the gifts of the Holy Spirit, who writes: *"Fides attingit Deum secundum quamdam distantiam ab Ipso, quatenus fides est de non visis* (I-II, q.68, disp, 18, a.4, n.14). Faith attains to God, while remaining at a certain distance, in the sense that it attains to Him in darkness." The contact is then real, but the darkness remains and seems to create a distance. When death lets fall the veil, the face to face vision reveals what faith had grasped, but did not see.

John of Saint Thomas, speaking of charity, adds: *"charitas autem attingit Deum immediate in se, intime se uniens ei quod occultatum in fide.* Charity attains to God in Himself, without intermediary, and is united intimately to that which was hidden in Faith." In other words, what faith grasps in darkness, charity makes its own in union. We can then say of faith that it is intentional in the sense that its immediate grasp of its divine object is oriented and ordered to intimate penetration of its object and to a more and more perfect union with Him.

[36] *Dark Night*, Bk. II, viii; Peers, I, 420. Saint Angela of Foligno also has given us something of her experience of this night that is produced by light: "One day . . . I saw God in a thick darkness, and necessarily in darkness because He is too high above the spirit, and everything that can become the object of a thought is without proportion to Him. . . . It is an ineffable delight in the Good that contains all good, and nothing of it can become the object of either a word or a concept. I see nothing. I see All: certitude is drawn from the darkness. The deeper is the darkness, the more the Good exceeds all else; that is the mystery reserved. . . . Be not mistaken. The divine power, wisdom, and will, that I have also marvelously seen, seem less than this. This a whole; the others, one might call parts" (Hello, xxvi, 105-6).

superior to that of all the other sciences. There is more light in a page of catechism than in all the ancient philosophies. In the *Spiritual Canticle,* our mystical doctor calls faith a "crystalline fount" for two reasons, he says. "The first, because it is from Christ, her Spouse, and the second, because it has the properties of crystal in being pure in its truths, and strong, and clear, free from errors and natural forms." [37]

Saint Thomas distinguishes the truths that fall under faith directly and of themselves (*per se directe*); these are the ones that transcend human reason, such as the mystery of the Trinity and the Incarnation. Others fall under faith inasmuch as they are subordinate to those just mentioned (*ordinata ad ista*) and are related to them in one way or another; thus, all the truths that Sacred Scripture contains.[38] The primary object of faith inasmuch as it is transcendent, is essentially obscure; the secondary object, on the other hand, can be grasped by reason and become quite luminous to it. Surrounding the mystery that is dark in itself, then, there is a luminous fringe constituted by truths on which the intellect can act with ease and liberty, although they do fall under faith.

The mystery itself is not completely dark. True, it could not be penetrated in itself. Nevertheless, the Church presents it to us in formulated dogmas adapted to our ways of thinking and of speaking. The formula does not yield up to the intellect the whole secret it contains, but gives an analogical expression of it that the intellect can grasp and on which it can work. Saint John of the Cross, in the same stanza of the *Canticle,* compares these formulas to silvered surfaces under which are hidden the truths themselves and their substance, which are compared to gold.[39] And so the mystery has not only its luminous fringe but also its surface or dogmatic formula which offers its marvelous lights to the intellect.

[37] *Spiritual Canticle,* st. xi; Peers, II, 65.
[38] Cf. *Sum. Theol.,* II-II, q. 8, a. 2.
[39] *Spiritual Canticle,* st. xi; 65 f.

So that faith gives and communicates to us God Himself, but covered with the silver of faith; but it fails not for that reason to give
Him to us in truth, even as one that gives a vessel of silvered gold
gives none the less a golden vessel because it is covered with silver.[40]

The communications which faith makes to the soul transform it in love, giving it a certain likeness of the Beloved as
well as a new light of connaturality. The night is wonderfully
brightened by this light that springs from it. Saint John of the
Cross writes:

And thus faith was foreshadowed by that cloud which divided the
children of Israel and the Egyptians when the former were about to
enter the Red Sea, whereof Scripture says that: *Erat nubes tenebrosa,
et illuminans noctem.*[41] This is to say that that cloud was full of darkness and gave light by night. . . .
So that which is to be inferred from this is that faith, because it is
dark night, gives light to the soul, which is in darkness, that there may
come to be fulfilled that which David likewise said to this purpose, in
these words: *Et nox illuminatio mea in deliciis meis.*[42] Which is as
much as to say: In the delights of my pure contemplation and union
with God, the night of faith shall be my guide.[43]

Shadows and lights of faith seem to dominate in turn according to the successive phases; and this play of light and
darkness is important and notable enough for Saint John of the
Cross to make of it the characteristic sign of the different stages
in the development of the virtue of faith. Thus in its progress
towards perfect contemplation, the soul will first come to the
night sense, "compared to the beginning of night, or the time
when sensible objects are no longer visible, and thus it is not
so far removed from light as is midnight"; [44] next, the night
of the spirit which belongs to the rational part of man and is
"in consequence more interior and more obscure, since it deprives it of the light of reason, or, to speak more clearly, blinds

[40] *Spiritual Canticle,* st. xi; Peers, II, 66.
[41] Exod. 14:20.
[42] Ps. 138:11.
[43] *Ascent,* Bk. II, iii; Peers, I, 72-3.
[44] *Ibid.,* ii; 69.

it"; [45] and finally, the dawn which "is quite close to the light of day, and it, too, therefore, is not so dark as midnight; for it is now close to the enlightenment and illumination of the light of day, which is compared with God." [46]

This dusk and night of the soul are produced by the inflowing of the divine light. The light which is adapted to our faculties as the light of day is to our eyes, fails before the transcendent light of God and of His mystery when faith has penetrated its primary object and is held fixed by the gifts. Before the brilliance of the gold of Truth, the silvered surfaces of dogmatic formulas grow pale. Dusk and night progressively replace the day of reasoned knowledge.

There is not just merely obscurity, however, in that radiance that envelops in darkness the unfitted and sin-stained faculties. The soul is enlightened as to its weaknesses and the true value of things. In the darkness that conceals the Source of the transcendent light that is producing it, a scale of values is established in the perspective of the Infinite.

Moreover, the night purifies the soul and makes it amenable to divine Love. In the measure that it accomplishes its work, night gives way to a rich dawn of light, delightful in its tranquility and peace. But let us not delay now on a subject that we shall have to treat at length.

It will suffice for us here to remark that in faith there is only light; its obscurity is an effect of the transcendence of the light that shines upon the intellect when it searches into God and His mystery. But because Saint John of the Cross, veritable mystic that he was, thirsty for the Infinite, turns his gaze and that of his disciple only to the transcendent light of God, he warns us repeatedly that faith is dark, and that this darkness is the characteristic and certain sign that faith has attained to its true object.

[45] *Ibid.*
[46] *Ibid.*

## 2. CERTITUDE OF FAITH

Faith is "obscure and certain." Certitude is the second characteristic of faith, signalized by Saint John of the Cross.

The certitude of faith may be considered either in the object that faith proposes, or in the subject who makes the act of faith. We can therefore distinguish objective faith and subjective faith.

Certitude as to the object is absolute and superior to any other kind of certitude, by reason of the testimony on which it rests, namely, the testimony of God Himself who is Truth. All other kinds of certitude, even that springing from the evidence of our senses or our intelligence, are bound up with the structure of our human faculties which are subject to error. The truth of faith is independent of all perception and rests on God who can neither be deceived nor deceive us.

Considered in the believer, certitude is nothing else than firmness of assent to the truth proposed. This assent must be complete, without restriction or condition; it admits of no voluntary doubt and requires perfect submission of the intellect.

There are, however, degrees in subjective certitude according to its basis. In the beginning, faith rests indeed on the authority of God, for otherwise it would not be supernatural;[47] but still more on the value of the human testimony and the reasons that make it credible. Progressively, the act of faith frees itself from its natural and reasonable motives, to draw all its strength from the testimony of God. This purification of motive is aided considerably, or even realized, by a growing awareness of the divine Truth. "I see nothing," says Saint Angela of Foligno, "I see All. Certitude is drawn from the darkness." [48]

This higher certitude liberates faith from the reasonable

[47] "*Quia fides habet certitudinem ex lumine infuso divinitus,* Faith has its certitude from the divinely infused light of God" (Cf. Saint Thomas, *In Joannem,* CIV, L.v, n.2).
[48] Cf. Hello, *Sainte Angèle de Foligno,* ch. xxvi.

motives that served as its basis, and directs it towards the darkness that offers it sure and delightful support. "The less I understand, the more I believe and the more I love," Saint Teresa used to say. As to Saint John of the Cross, he has the soul say: "I was in darkness and in surety."

With regard to that faith which suddenly finds its certitude, as well as an unshakable assurance in itself, Jacques Rivière writes:

> Unbelievers notice a sort of violence done to our soul, but they do not discern that this is to fix definitely in it something that passed through it and is in danger of disappearing. They do not see the bird that alighted for a moment; and hence the gesture that we make, in the void it seems, to seize it by the wings, appears absurd to them. . . . But for him who has really felt the bird touch him even slightly, all his logical scruples no longer have any meaning.[49]

If one is not careful, these concise statements could easily lead into error, by creating the impression that one's peace in the assent to truth is the sign that gives the measure of perfection of faith. The serene, blind faith of the untutored would then always be of a quality superior to that of the intellectual in whose mind sincere assent to revealed truth leaves a certain intellectual disquietude and many problems to be resolved. To judge thus would be to forget the demands of the intellect made for light; when faced with the darkness of the mystery that faith presents, it must normally experience a certain uneasiness, if not a disquietude. This dissatisfaction will be all the more marked, as the intelligence is the more developed, more inquiring, or even more restless temperamentally. It will arouse a certain activity of the faculties, a process of investigation, perhaps even a sort of feverish commotion, out of which come formulated objections and unreasonable anxieties. Such is the usual psychological process of the temptation against faith, and the devil will at times be able to increase its violence.

[49] Jacques Rivière. *A la trace de Dieu,* p. 336.

This disturbance is really a temptation. Its development is extrinsic to the certitude itself, which is firmness of assent to revealed truth. The firmness of assent, which flows from the virtue of faith and is imparted by the will, can remain intact in the midst of the turmoil; it may even become stronger and more tenacious because of it. There may be struggle, interior disquiet and tempest, all the more afflictive as faith is more lively and firm; but faith is fortified by it and comes out strengthened and purified.

It may be that the particular mystical experience which paralyzes the faculties and sets them at rest is unable to allay these temptations against faith for two reasons: first because being only intermittent or affecting only certain faculties, it leaves periods of complete freedom to psychological activity; or because, secondly, it throws the soul into a complete darkness which leaves it a prey to temptation.

Temptation against faith is not incompatible, then, with a solidly rooted faith, nor even with an elevated mystical experience. We think it important to underline that it is a trial destined to strengthen a faith that is in its early stages; to purify faith already strong; and even, in the case of souls of a high degree of faith, to supply that redemptive suffering that merits for others light to walk in the way of salvation. A trial that Saint Therese of the Child Jesus suffered comes to our mind; she wrote of it:

During the Paschal days, so full of light, our Lord made me understand that there really are in truth souls bereft of Faith and Hope, who, through abuse of grace, lose these precious treasures, the only source of pure and lasting joy. He allowed my soul to be overwhelmed with darkness, and the thought of Heaven, which had consoled me from my earliest childhood, now became a subject of conflict and torture. This trial did not last merely for days or weeks; I have been suffering for months. . . .

When my heart, weary of the surrounding darkness, tries to find some rest in the thought of a life to come, my anguish increases. It seems to me that out of the darkness I hear the mocking voice of the unbeliever: "You dream of a land of light and fragrance, you dream

that the Creator of these wonders will be yours for ever, you think
one day to escape from these mists where you now languish. Nay, rejoice in death, which will give you, not what you hope for, but a night
darker still, the night of utter nothingness! . . ."

May God forgive me! He knows that I try to live by Faith, though
it does not afford me the least consolation. I have made more acts of
Faith in this last year than during all the rest of my life.

Each time that my enemy would provoke me to combat . . . I turn
my back on the foe, then I hasten to my Saviour, and vow that I am
ready to shed my blood in witness of my belief in Heaven. I tell Him,
if only He will deign to open it to poor unbelievers, I am content to
sacrifice all pleasure in the thought of it as long as I live.[50]

The description given by Saint Therese of the Child Jesus
shows us a temptation coming from darkness and obsession,
whose violence calls forth a more and more firm and tenacious
assent to truth, and discloses the redemptive character of such
a trial. The perfection of the virtue of faith, then, is not measured by the peace that accompanies it. A very strong and pure
faith can know great torments. This is true in all the stages of
the development of the spiritual life. Certitude of faith is
uniquely the firmness of assent to the truth, certain but obscure.
We thought it necessary to emphasize this.

## E. Practical conclusions

The whole practical teaching of the masters of Carmel
springs from the truths here set forth. We shall limit ourselves
to mentioning a few of the most important points.

1. Since faith attains to God and since God, like a consuming fire (*ignis consumens*), is always ready to communicate
Himself, each act of living faith—that is, faith accompanied by
charity—puts him who makes it in contact with that burning
fire, places him under the influence of its light and its flame;
in other words, it procures for the soul an increase of grace,
and hence of participation in the divine nature. Whatever may
be the circumstances that accompany the act of faith—aridities
or enthusiasm, joy or suffering—it attains to the divine Real-

[50] *Autobiography*, ix, 139 f.

ity; and even if I experience nothing of this contact in my faculties, I know that it has existed and has been efficacious. I have drawn from God in the measure of my faith; in a more abundant measure, perhaps, if the divine Mercy has intervened to supply for my deficiencies and to give Himself up in consideration not of my merits but only of my misery.

2. Since faith is the only proximate and proportionate means for attaining to God, any striving for union with God will have recourse to its mediation and activity. Faith alone can lead us to the divine sources of grace. The sacraments themselves, which give grace *ex opere operato,* that is, by their own intrinsic power, normally require faith in the recipient. We must have faith if we would be united to our Lord in the Blessed Eucharist; here even His sacred humanity lies hid. Likewise, the exchange of friendship with God in mental prayer will take place only through faith. Mental prayer, considered from the view of the soul's part in it, is nothing but faith lovingly in quest of God, and may be considered as a succession of acts of faith. Consequently, if, during dryness and powerlessness, the soul perseveringly makes acts of faith and of love, it can be assured that its prayer is good, even if it does not experience the effects of it.

3. Mental prayer, attaining to God only by faith, will take its own perfection from the quality of the faith from which it springs. Hence, we shall find in the development of the life of prayer two phases parallel to the development of the virtue of faith. The first phase, or active prayer, corresponds to that faith which draws light from reason; the second, or passive prayer, is nourished by the living faith that is perfected by the gifts of the Holy Spirit. Conceptual faith, as we have seen, attains to divine Reality, but reverts to the exercise of the faculties to find in them its light and food. The prayer that corresponds to it will truly be a friendy converse with God, but one that is sustained by the activity of the imagination, of the intellect, or of the will. The activity of these faculties is predom-

inant; hence the name of active prayer, the different forms of which we distinguished in the first three Teresian Mansions.

Living or perfect faith on the other hand receives from God Himself, through the gifts of the Holy Spirit, its light and its measure. In the state of prayer animated by it, the soul is drawn towards the divine Reality by the obscure perception of it that it receives through the gifts, and is, as it were, raised above its own natural manner of activity; or at least, it continually tends towards the divine Reality revealing itself. This is called contemplative or passive prayer, because the action of God predominates.

4. Saint John of the Cross gives the signs that permit one to distinguish these two phases of the life of prayer,[51] signs of the greatest importance because of the difference in the conduct that each imposes on the soul.

Since it is true that in active prayer, faith finds its sustenance and its support in the activity of the faculties, the soul has the duty of studying revealed truth, preparing for prayer, and activating the faculties during the prayer, to the extent that such activity is necessary in order to maintain the conversation with God.

In the second phase, that of contemplative prayer, since faith finds its food in God Himself, the duty of the soul is to calm the activity of the natural faculties and, by very simple acts, to sustain the attraction that the divine Reality exercises over it. The operation of the gifts requires that silent peaceful attitude of soul; and the respect due to the divine working, now predominant in the soul, demands a continued orientation towards the Divine.

5. Since prayer finds its supernatural efficacy in the quality of the faith that animates it, and consequently, in the intimacy and frequency of the contacts with God that it secures, contemplative prayer is usually more efficacious than active prayer.

[51] Cf. *supra,* ch. vii, "Contemplation," p. 456.

In the latter, faith is imperfect, having contact with God only intermittently, and closely linked to the natural activity of the faculties; while in the passive, faith—thanks to the gifts of the Holy Spirit which perfect it in its exercise—habitually maintains the soul under the action of God. In active prayer, the soul draws from time to time from the divine fountains; in passive prayer, it remains bathed in the purifying waters and flames of the Holy Spirit where it is transformed from brightness to brightness until it resembles the Divine.

6. One might ask if the desire for a deeper and more rapid transformation of love warrants an effort on the soul's part to rise to passive prayer. It would be sufficient, so it seems, to stop the activity of the faculties after an act of faith, in order to prevent a return to the natural acts and to keep the soul in the obscure reality to which it has just attained. Saint Teresa has treated at quite some length of this attempt, and declares that it proceeds from presumptious pride and that it would be useless.[52]

Supernatural contemplation is a gratuitous gift of divine Mercy. God alone can put in action the gifts of the Holy Spirit which produce it by perfecting the exercise of faith. God bestows it "when He wills and as He wills and having nothing to do either with time or with service. I do not mean that these latter things are unimportant but that often the Lord grants to one person less contemplation in twenty years than to others in one," [53] writes Saint Teresa. And elsewhere she says: "I cannot believe in the efficacy of human activity in matters where His Majesty appears to have set a limit to it and to have been pleased to reserve action to Himself." [54]

Humility alone can claim to draw down these divine gifts, for God resists the proud and gives His grace to the humble. In order to arrive at contemplation, a humble attitude will be

[52] IV Mansions, iii; Peers, II, 241-2.
[53] *Life*, xxxiv; Peers, I, 237.
[54] IV Mansions, iii; 242.

more useful than the most violent efforts. This humility will consist practically in begging "like poor and needy persons coming before a great and rich Emperor," [55] in resorting to the modest forms of active prayer and continuing thus in patient and peaceful labor until God lifts us up to passive prayer:

When thou art invited to a wedding feast, do not recline in the first place . . . but in the last place; that when he who invited thee comes in, he may say to thee: "Friend, go up higher!" Then thou wilt be honored in the presence of all who are at table with thee. For everyone who exalts himself shall be humbled, and he who humbles himself shall be exalted.[56]

The parable of the Gospel can be applied to the letter to the life of prayer: in order to merit to be elevated to contemplation, one must humbly take the last place among the spiritual. And in this last place, it is good to desire higher and quicker means of arriving at perfect union, but always while guarding against any presumptuous effort to procure them on one's own.

7. Contemplation, like the living faith of which it is the fruit, has for its object the Deity itself and can perceive it only as an obscure reality, because of its transcendence. Like faith, it is a knowledge that is certain and obscure. This twofold character of certitude and obscurity, especially the second, will reveal its existence in the soul and be a criterion of its purity. Deep within the multiplicity of impressions, within the interior agitation that rather frequently accompanies supernatural contemplation, the darkness will indicate to the contemplative the regions where living faith is active, which he must protect and where he must take refuge.

Darkness being the revealing sign of the divine Reality, the contemplative, in his contemplation, will have to prefer that darkness to all distinct lights—whether those lights come from the formulas of dogma or even from God Himself—in order that, through it, he may remain in contact with the Divine. He

[55] Ibid.
[56] Luke 14:8-11.

will have to watch, not to allow himself to be drawn away by the disquiet of the lower faculties, not even to put them at peace; nor to let himself be wrapped up by the sweetness that comes from God, nor to follow after the delight of it in the senses. No matter what happens, he must lift up the antenna of his faith above all perceptions and unrest and turn back to the serene and peaceful darkness in which the Infinite is revealing and giving Himself.

Saint John of the Cross tells us how the devil excels in giving knowledge and delights to souls in this state, and deplores the great harm done to the soul that does not understand itself and, taking a mouthful of distinct knowledge and sensible sweetness, prevents itself from feeding wholly upon God when He absorbs it.[57] Likewise, in stanzas xxxi and xxxii of the *Spiritual Canticle,* after asking the lower faculties to remain in their own sphere, the "outskirts," so as not to trouble and distract the hidden inward depth of the soul, he asks God to grant such favors that he may not be able to describe them and the sensual part may have no share in them.[58]

Faith being the only proximate and proportionate means for attaining to God in our progress towards divine union, we must not prefer any natural light to it, nor any supernatural gift however elevated it may be. This utter detachment from all created goods constitutes the whole of contemplative asceticism. Thus faith and hope are purified, and perfect union with God is realized according to the measure of our grace.

8. These developments permit us:

*a.* to estimate at their proper value whatever distinct knowledge or delights we receive in mental prayer. These illumine the way and calm the faculties; they "captivate," to use the expression of Saint Therese of the Child Jesus. They are a precious means for going to God, and the soul must use them with

---

[57] *Living Flame,* st. iii; Peers, III, 92.
[58] *Spiritual Canticle,* st. xxxi-xxxii; Peers, II, 152-8.

gratitude and humility; but attachment to them can change them into dangerous obstacles.

*b.* to state that they are not absolutely necessary for arriving at perfection or even at perfect contemplation. One can conceive of—and actually they exist—contemplative states in which, in the midst of disquiet and trouble in the faculties, there is manifest only that obscure perception of God which is the essential element of contemplation.

*c.* to note that the greatest contemplatives are not necessarily those who receive the most distinct lights as to God; but that, more than all the others, they are aware of the divine transcendence in the transluminous darkness of His mysteries.

*d.* to say that, putting aside the designs of God on such or such a soul and the share in the Passion of His Son that He imposes on it, the state of perfection involves normally a pervasion of that darkness through the whole soul and its faculties which, thereafter purified and made amenable to the Divine, find in it a delightful food. The divine transcendence is better known and hence more obscure than ever, but in that deeper obscurity the soul glimpses the light of dawn. Lights and subtle sweetness, delicate unctions that the senses do not know, that the soul itself seems not to know, so true is it that —with all its strength, with all its being, in peaceful ardors— it is tending towards the divine Reality that is penetrating it and to whom it longs to surrender itself more and more.

Such was the perfect prayer of the most blessed Virgin Mary, all illumined and enflamed as she was with the divine fires; but whose peaceful and ardent faith seemed not to know the riches that she possessed, enabling her to progress always still farther into the luminous night of the Holy Spirit who enfolded her in His Love.